NOTTINGHAM FO

in the 1970's

'A decade of two halves'...

ANDREW S. DOLLOWAY

MMP
Max Media Publishing Ltd.

MMP

Max Media Publishing Ltd.

First published in Great Britain by:
Max Media Publishing Ltd 2017

ISBN 978-0-9954783-4-3

www.maxmediapublishing.com

Max Media Publishing Ltd
49-51 Bancroft Lane, Mansfield, Notts, NG18 5LG
Edited and written by Andrew S Dolloway

Associate design by Simon Meakin at In House Design, Mansfield, Notts.
Printed by Zrinski, Croatia.

INTRODUCTION

This book picks up the story where the last one finished. *(Nottingham Forest in the 1960's, the forgotten decade).* Nottingham Forest were clearly now a team in decline, stuck with a manager and a committee completely out of touch with the realities of the modern game. Relegation might have been avoided for a couple of seasons, but there was an inevitability that it was coming, what else could happen if you sell all your best players?

The story of how this club went from the doldrums of the bottom of Division Two, to the pinnacle of European Champions in such a short space of time is legendary. I was fortunate enough to attend hundreds of games in this decade, from the less than salubrious surroundings of Eastville Stadium, Bristol, to the Olympic Stadium in Munich. I enjoyed great away trips, collecting memories that have lasted a lifetime. The economy might have been bombing, but that just passed me by, I supported the best football team and with the advent of punk rock, enjoyed the best music.

I have tried to capture the excitement of this decade through lots of unseen photographs, memorabilia and the memories of players involved from the era.

The stories from the early years are just as fascinating as the later ones, as far as I am concerned, every player who has worn the Garibaldi, is part of the fabric of Nottingham Forest and the reason we support the club.

I hope you get as much enjoyment out of this book as I did putting it together. COYR.

Andrew S. Dolloway, September 2017

CONTENTS

Welcome to the 1970's, the parties well and truly over. The optimism of the 'Swinging Sixties' had long since vanished, to be replaced by inflation, conflict and trade union disputes. As the value of the pound fell, so did our standing in the world, we were the sick man of Europe, rapidly being left behind in a changing world.

This was the decade that was to give us Glam Rock, Prog Rock, Punk Rock and flying rock, as Britain descended into financial and social chaos but if you were a supporter of Nottingham Forest it would turn out to be the greatest period in your life. It was the decade of two halves, starting badly, getting worse, beige, boring and unadventurous, but ultimately ending in a blaze of unexpected technicoloured glory. December 1969 had seen the Nottingham Forest committee deny the rumours that the club was in financial trouble and needing to sell a player quickly to satisfy the bank.
Whereas in years gone by a committee member would quietly cover a shortfall in the accounts, now the figures were too high. The rumour doing the rounds was that £100,000 was needed within weeks. The club still had some players that were coveted by others.

Brian Clough in particular was a fan of Terry Hennessey and not only had he made a tentative offer, he had also used the media to unsettle the Reds' skipper. When Hennessey was forced to have an appendix operation, it looked to have scuppered any deal, but Terry recovered far quicker than anyone imagined and was back in the team within weeks.

By now Hennessey was fully aware of what was on offer, the football grapevine ensured that, so Forest really had no choice but to sell if they couldn't match his wage demands. Tottenham were thought to be the favourites to land him, although Derby had enquired, even then, there was no appetite to sell your best players to your local rivals. So it was a surprise when Derby clinched the deal for a fee of only £110,000, below what Spurs had original offered and Hennessey's true market value at this time. Brian Clough had been shrewd however, he knew that Hennessey wanted to join Derby and that Forest were desperate for money.

The Hennessey situation was not as cut and dried as it first might appear, the player's form had dipped along with many others over the previous twelve months and the emergence of Liam O'Kane led many fans to call for Terry to be pushed

69-70

NOTTINGHAM FOREST FOOTBALL CLUB

DIVISION ONE 1969 - 70

Back row, left to right: JOHN WINFIELD ALAN HILL BOBBY McKINLAY PETER GRUMMITT BOB CHAPMAN PETER HINDLEY

Middle row, left to right: IAN MOORE TERRY HENNESSEY PAUL RICHARDSON BARRY LYONS DAVE HILLEY HENRY NEWTON

Front row, left to right: JOHN BARNWELL LIAM O'KANE COLIN HALL RONNIE REES

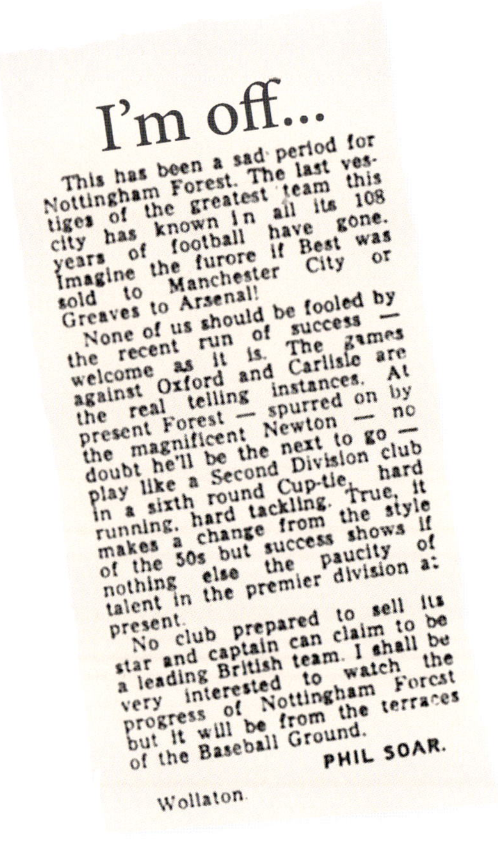
I'm off...

This has been a sad period for Nottingham Forest. The last vestiges of the greatest team this city has known in all its 108 years of football have gone. Imagine the furore if Best was sold to Manchester City or Greaves to Arsenal!

None of us should be fooled by the recent run of success — welcome as it is. The games against Oxford and Carlisle are the real telling instances. At present Forest — spurred on by the magnificent Newton — no doubt he'll be the next to go — play like a Second Division club in a sixth round Cup-tie, hard running, hard tackling. True, it makes a change from the style of the 50s but success shows if nothing else the paucity of talent in the premier division at present.

No club prepared to sell its star and captain can claim to be a leading British team. I shall be very interested to watch the progress of Nottingham Forest, but it will be from the terraces of the Baseball Ground.

PHIL SOAR.

Wollaton.

forward into midfield, so as not to impede the development of the youngster. So Matt Gillies had reluctantly sanctioned the transfer. To many fans it was just another sign that the club was going backwards and they waited to see if and when the fee would be reinvested in new players. Especially coming on the back of another early FA Cup exit to lower league opposition, (this time Carlisle United after a replay). Bill Brindley made a rare first team appearance replacing the injured John Winfield, ending a sequence of 150 consecutive appearances for the Forest left back. There was an interesting letter in the Football Post after Hennessey's transfer from a person that may be familiar to you. Phil Soar, Wollaton, wrote, 'No club prepared to sell it's star and captain can claim to be a leading British team. I shall be very interested to watch the progress of Nottingham Forest, but it will be from the terraces of the Baseball Ground'.

Hennessey's last appearance was away at Crystal Palace, a 1-1 draw. In all he made 183 appearances and scored 6 goals for the Reds. Terry meanwhile was to have a largely unsatisfactory spell at Derby. His career curtailed not only by injury but also by a big fallout with Brian Clough, whom the player blamed for mismanaging his injury problems.

Largely overlooked due to the furore over the Hennessey transfer, there was another break with the past at the club, as legendary keeper Peter Grummitt was allowed to join Sheffield Wednesday for a cut price £30,000. As Peter recalls, "Matt Gillies never fancied me as a keeper, I don't know why, perhaps he thought I was exaggerating my injuries or just plain injury prone. There was one time at Arsenal when he chose to play Alan Hill even when he was injured, instead of me. I didn't want to leave but I wanted to play and the manager made it quite clear that it wouldn't be at Forest. After I left, I played over two hundred more games, I guess that shows I wasn't as injury prone as he thought".

Ironically just four weeks after he left the club, Alan Hill suffered an injury that was to prematurely end his career.
Despite all the negativity, the Reds stretched their unbeaten run to eleven games. During this run, there was also a return to Nottingham for Joe Baker, now with Sunderland and although he was given a rapturous reception by the Trent End, he was in truth a pale imitation of 'King Joe' and he was subbed after only 60 minutes having made little impression. This was also the occasion when his replacement in the number 9 shirt, Alex Ingram, notched his first goal for the club.

During this time there was also a fine 1-0 victory over Liverpool in front of 30,000 fans at the City Ground, Richardson scoring the winner and putting in an excellent performance. The scoreline flattered the visitors who would have been beaten far heavier if the referee hadn't disallowed a couple of goals. In an attempt to keep supporters better informed, it was announced over the tannoy, that Richardson was substituted because he was suffering from a sore throat.

By now the club was comfortably placed in mid table and there was talk of trying to qualify for European competition, but just as quickly the wheels came off, and on a personal note, ended Ian Moore's Mexico World Cup dream. Ian remembers that day, "I had just made my England debut against Holland and performed well I thought. Alf Ramsey had taken me to one

Paul Richardson

Liam O'Kane

"THERE WAS AN ENGLISHMAN, IRISHMAN, SCOTSMAN & A WELSHMAN"...

Dave Hilley

Ronnie Rees

Peter Hindley rises to head the ball towards the Sunderland goal.

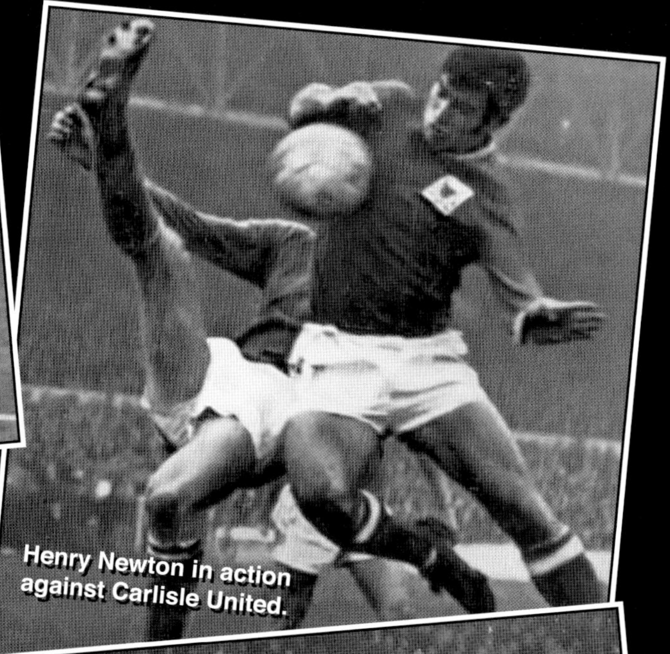
Henry Newton in action against Carlisle United.

EMIGRATING?
RENNIE'S SHIPPING SERVICES
Football Post AND NEWS
Vol. LXI No. 26
NOTTINGHAM SATURDAY JANUARY 31 1970
PAUL'S THE HERO IN FOREST WIN
PAT GIBSON at the City Ground
PAUL RICHARDSON'S first goal of the season

AGAINST THE ODDS!

"It's a goal"...Richardson heads powerfully home against Liverpool.

The Reds go close against Carlisle in the cup!!

RENNIE'S SHIPPING SERVICES
Football Post AND NEWS
Vol. LXI No. 22
NOTTINGHAM SATURDAY JANUARY 3 1970
DEADLOCK...REDS MUST TRY AGAIN
PAT GIBSON at the City Ground
NOTTINGHAM FOREST and Second Division Carlisle United were locked in FA Cup deadlock

side and said I was definitely in his plans. We were due to play Man City at Maine Road, it was a very icy pitch, unplayable really, but in those days games were only called off if it really was desperate. I just went to collect a routine pass when suddenly Arthur Mann slid right through the back of me. It was a naughty challenge but routine for that time. I tried to get up and carry on but it was pretty clear that it wasn't something I could run off. This was in February and I knew I had to be playing before the end of season to prove my fitness if I was to have any chance. I tried desperately to get fit but to no avail, I didn't kick a ball again until the following season. Worse still, I never got near an England squad again after that".

Matt Gillies had now completed more than twelve months in the job. He had done what was asked of him, kept the club up, steadied the team and even balanced the books, but in truth the fans had never taken to him. It didn't help that he was largely thought of as a Leicester man, both as player and manager and also he presented an old fashioned image out of step with present day football.

In Gillies' defence, he could point to the fact that Forest were third bottom when he took over, they were now in eleventh place and over the two seasons had amassed 47 points from 46 games. He also promised new signings were on the way.

Almost inevitably after the injury to Ian Moore, the season began to fizzle out. Without Ian's attacking flair, the team just wasn't the same, they relied on him totally. History showed that Forest amassed twice as many points when Ian was in the team compared to when he wasn't available. Furthermore, a defence that up until then had looked solid, suddenly shipped five goals at Burnley and the bad luck continued when Alan Hill received the arm injury that was to finish his career against Everton. This had been a rough match, that was also to see Alex Ingram sport a bloodstained bandage for much of the second half after a heavy clash of heads. The injury to Hill forced the Reds to use the loan market for the first time, bringing in Dave Hollins from Mansfield Town reserves to cover.

The gentlemanly side of Matt Gillies was illustrated after the next game against Chelsea. The volatile Blues' centre forward Peter Osgood had kicked the ball away after a free kick had been given against him, causing the referee to caution him. Gillies attended a disciplinary hearing the next week to speak on the player's behalf and helped Osgood get off with only a warning.

The letter pages of the Football Post continued to provide controversy and amusement.

AW Dicken (Housemaster) from West Bridgford felt compelled to write, 'Forest fans should take a look at themselves. Homosexuality, violence and a fanatical interest in sport preceded the fall of the Roman Empire, the same ingredients can be seen today, get some perspective'.

March the 14th saw the long awaited rematch with Derby. Forest were weakened by the absence of Alan Hill and Ian Moore. Dave Hollins taking over in goal, showed a nervousness that wasn't expected from a Welsh international, indeed throughout

HECTIC WEEK AT THE CITY GROUND

And Hennessey is set to move

IN THE WEEK that Nottingham Forest collected £30,000 for Peter Grummitt and put themselves in line for upwards of £125,000 for Terry Hennessey, manager Matt Gillies gave an assurance that any money from transfers will be used to obtain new players.

This was his answer to suggestions that the decision to transfer their 27-year-old Welsh international captain had been forced on Forest by financial embarrassment.

Pat Gibson on FOREST

The pressing need for new talent if Forest are to build a side capable of making a realistic challenge to the top clubs next season was one important factor behind a move which was not taken lightly.

Forest only agreed to let Hennessey go after months of consultations between Mr. Gillies and Hennessey, the manager wanting to do the right thing by his club, the player wanting to do the right thing by his family.

The outcome was a statement by Mr. Gillies saying: "I have seen Terry on numerous occasions, and I feel now we have arrived at a stage, where, if we don't allow him to go, he will be compelled to ask for a transfer."

Confirmation

Confirmation that this was indeed a true picture of the situation came from Hennessey himself who said: "I agree entirely with what he has said."

Predictably enough there were plenty of people who chose to ignore the observations and Forest were swiftly lambasted for telling their world-class captain to go. But it wasn't like that at all.

There were a whole number of issues to be considered—like the development of a new centre half in Liam O'Kane the run of nine games without defeat which has given a chance for consolidation and team-building, and the need for more class in midfield and the attack.

And, above all, there were Hennessey's personal wishes. By getting the chance to go now, Hennessey will receive his five per cent of the transfer fee and the opportunity to leave on the friendliest of terms with a club he has clearly served magnificently.

World-class

Since joining Forest in November, 1965, for a then club record fee of over £50,000, Hennessey has played in 185 senior games, maturing into a world-class performer on his switch to a defensive wing half role alongside Bobby McKinlay.

His qualities as a captain were widely praised when he led the Reds to the FA Cup semi-finals and the runners-up spot in Division I in 1967, and were further recognised this season when Wales handed him their captaincy.

His contribution to Nottingham football will not be forgotten — and only time will tell whether it is wise to let him go to Derby, where he will remain constantly in the eye of a critical Trentside public.

In the middle of the Hennessey controversy, another giant of the great Forest side of 1966-7, Peter Grummitt, went quietly off to start a new career with

Styles, Jimmy Robertson and Dave Serella should not have played.

But coach Bert Johnson decided to go on with the fixture and in the circumstances got a wonderful response from his lads.

Leicester must keep going forward

LEICESTER CITY'S advance to the Fifth Round of the FA Cup has caused no astonishment among those who really know them.

Their extra time replay success against Southampton on Wednesday confirmed the long established fact that when the stakes are high enough the team will play the kind of adventurous football that could sweep them back to the First Division.

JOHN WINFIELD
PETER HINDLEY
IAN MOORE
HENRY NEWTON
PETER CORMACK

THE YOUTH TEAM

Back Row *(left to right): Peter Smith, Joe Watson, Steve Baines, Dennis Peacock, Norman Upton, Dave Serella, John Piekalnietis, Paul White, Billy Styles, John Cottam, Alan Buckley, Michael Dilnot.*

Front Row: Duncan McKenzie, Alwyn Carter, Jimmy McCaffrey, John Robertson, Graham Collier, Melvyn Johnson, Maitland Pollack, John Oliver

his nine appearances he never inspired confidence. He appeared on the winning side only once, the last game of the season and conceded twenty two goals.

Terry Hennessey was making a quick return to the City Ground along with other ex Reds Frank Wignall and Alan Hinton for the Rams.
A massive crowd of 42,000 were in attendance and despite the best efforts of the police, there were outbreaks of violence on the terraces. On the pitch, Derby were to get their revenge, although the match was in the balance up until the 87th minute when the Rams' third goal clinched a 3-1 victory. Liam O'Kane hadn't enjoyed the best of starts scoring a fifth minute own goal to send the visitors on their way. Brian Clough didn't endear himself to the locals when he accused the Reds of resorting to, 'strong arm tactics and defensive football'.

Without Ian Moore, Forest clearly lacked a cutting edge and Alex Ingram wasn't supplying the physical presence he had been brought in to provide, giving the team a lightweight look. In his post match interview Gillies told reporters he was looking to make a pre deadline signing, winger John Connolly of St Johnstone was the rumoured target.

Another limp defeat at Hillsborough against Sheffield Wednesday was followed quickly by the heavy Easter programme of 3 games in 4 days beginning with a Good Friday 4-1 thumping at Tottenham.
The next day saw an improvement, Graham Collier returning once again in a 2-2 draw with Newcastle, all the goals coming in a seventeen minute period. The game was played in a downpour, which saw the majority of fans standing on the Bridgford End either move to shelter in the East Stand or huddle underneath the old Shipstones scoreboard.

Matt Gillies alongside new signing, Peter Cormack

The biggest news of the weekend happened off the pitch, Peter Cormack of Hibernian and Scotland was signed for £80,000. Lazily labelled by the press as the 'bad boy' of Scottish football for his frequent scrapes with authority. His latest sending off only a few weeks previously, had persuaded everyone involved, that perhaps it would be best if he continued his career south of the border. Even his own mother was quoted as saying that she wished he would quit football as she was fed up of seeing his name splashed all over the newspapers. Cormack, as he would, denied the accusations, claiming he was a marked man and vowed to clean up his image. Unfortunately the signing wasn't completed before the transfer deadline and he could only play if the opposition agreed.

Cormack was a skilful player, neither a midfielder nor forward, he certainly wouldn't fill the troubled centre forward position, but his slight frame belied a very competitive nature and his peculiar tippy toed way of running, made him further stand out. The Scottish FA then announced that they still intended to pursue charges against him and this resulted in an eight week ban that meant Peter only made one appearance for the Reds that season and also ruled him out of playing for Scotland in the Home International Championships.

Peter was introduced to the crowd before the Bank Holiday Monday game against Manchester United which drew almost 40,000 to the City Ground. This ended in another defeat, 2-1, although Forest were unlucky to have a couple of good penalty shouts turned down.

The Thursday edition of the Evening Post reported that Forest fans had travelled in numbers to the Central League reserve fixture at the Baseball Ground. Unsurprisingly, Derby County and the police were not expecting this and there were recriminations after Reds' supporters had caused extensive damage to toilets and other facilities. This led the Rams' hierarchy to demand that Forest should pay the bill for the repairs.
The league season was drawing to a slow

FOREST

Nottingham Forest wind up the First Division programme at The Hawthorns to give the final 90 minutes of top grade soccer an all Midland flavour.

As is the case with Albion this has, for Forest been a season of disappointments which have offset the high hopes paraded at the start of the campaign, but these have not wiped out the flashes of achievement.

In fact it has been an average season such as hits all clubs at some time or other, when fans prefer to remember the better things rather than the other kind.

Today they come without an old favourite here, I refer to former Birmingham City stalwart **Terry Hennessey** who was snapped up by manager **Brian Clough** for his Derby County squad.

Forest can always be relied upon to add to the atmosphere which surrounds their visits. They play the kind of football which is appreciated here, and are assured of a warm welcome.

Manager **Matt Gillies** guides the destinies of a side which gives 100% in effort every time, and the time must come again when they will reap the full reward.

One of the men who has made a tremendous impression is centre half **Liam O'Kane**, the young Irishman who is emerging as one of the big name centre halves, with, behind him, the redoubtable defensive combination of **Peter Hindley** and **John Winfield.**

The line-up includes men almost as well known to The Hawthorns fans as the Albion players, **Henry Newton, Dave Hilley, Barry Lyons.**

Goalkeeper **Dave Hollins** has taken up where **Peter Grummitt** left off. If it is any news to him **Peter** usually reserved a champagne display for a game here.

Today Forest will be part of of an especially noteworthy event . . . the presentation of the **Evening Mail** 'Midland Footballer of the Year Award' to **John Kaye.**

I am sure that on their behalf I can offer the congratulations of their club to one of the most wholehearted and big hearted players ever to wear the Albion jersey.

But for **Ronnie Rees, Terry's** Welsh international colleague it will mean a reunion with old friends at The Hawthorns.

Whilst Nottingham have to travel some fifty odd miles to reach West Bromwich these meetings come into the category of **derby** clashes, and are therefore invested with more than usual interest and friendly rivalry.

In these days of dwindling First Division representation so far as immediate neighbours of The Hawthorns are concerned, these meetings of Midlands clubs are looked forward to by West Bromwich Albion supporters. The old desire to shout on their side against teams who come into the **old enemy** category adds to the excitement.

Top—Ian Storey-Moore. First England Cap this season, surely more to come?
Alan Hill, transfer success from Rotherham.
Dave Hilley, ex-Magpie now established at the City ground.
Bob Chapman, ex wonder-boy forward, now tough tackling midfield man.
Matt Gillies, has the will-power to overcome the loss of Terry Hennessy to Derby.
John Winfield, ex-striker now stylish full back.

FOREST

BOB BLACKBURN
Birmingham Evening Mail & Sports Argus
Graphics/SPORTSGRAPHIC

IAN'S PLAN TO KEEP FIGHTING FOR FOREST

IAN MOORE, the Nottingham Forest winger who has suffered more injuries at 26 than most players do in a lifetime, hopes to stay clear of trouble this season with a ruse favoured by old-time stars.

Ian will strap his ankles and lower legs with bandages before each game in an attempt to prevent the damage that has interrupted his quest for a regular England place in the last three seasons.

Forest boss Matt Gillies says: "Bandages may not be fashionable, but they should be effective. We all used them in the old days, but they seem to have dropped out of vogue.

"Ian took a bit of persuading because he thought they might affect his game. But once he got used to the extra wadding in pre-season training, he stopped worrying."

Ian realises that he has a lot of time to make up: "I can only do it with an injury-free run, but given luck I'm sure I can make the England squad for Munich in 1974."

So far, Ian's international career has been limited to one appearance in the goalless draw against Holland at Wembley in 1970 — a game in which he so nearly scored the winner, but was ruled off-side.

He earned good reports from the Press — and Sir Alf Ramsey was impressed. But the injury bug struck when a tackle from behind against Manchester City at Maine Road ripped the ligaments in his right ankle.

A season earlier, in 1968-69, Ian had broken his left leg in a game against Leicester City after he had made a devastating start with 18 goals in his first 25 matches.

Yet Ian's courage and resilience was to be tested even more severely when he was injured a third time, playing for the Football League against the Irish League at Carrow Road, Norwich, last season. It was a cruel blow. But he overcame it.

Ian, one of the most lethal wing-raiders in the game, denies that he is injury-prone when he says: "It's just not true. I can take knocks as well as the next man.

"But the point is that my recent injuries were serious enough to cause long lay-offs, although it's something which could happen to anyone.

"I have experienced the rough end of the stick so I'm aware of the trouble that can so easily cut short a player's career, no matter how young or how good he is."

Now Ian Moore is ready for his overdue share of the glory.

FOREST IN ACTION !

Dave Hollins dives bravely at the feet of Witham (Sheffield Wednesday).

Forest go close away at Maine Road Manchester.

Hindley leaps to go close against Manchester United.

Alan Hill foils Joe Royle of Everton.

Forest concede the equaliser to Manchester City.

Hilley scores from close range at home to Newcastle.

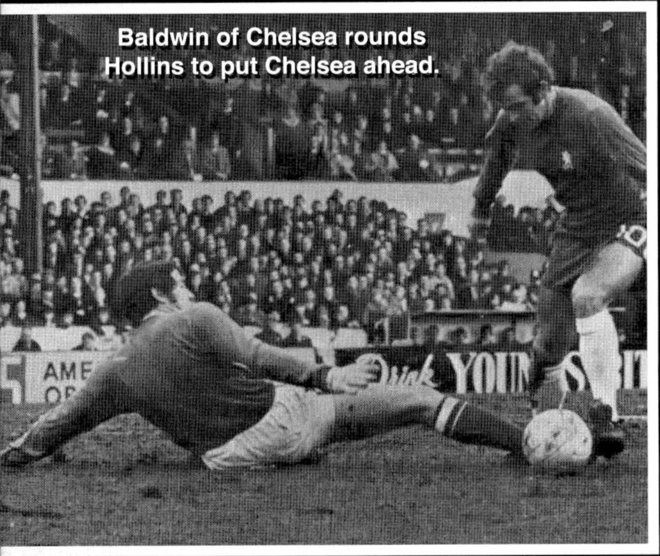

Baldwin of Chelsea rounds Hollins to put Chelsea ahead.

Graham Collier clashes with McFaul of Newcastle.

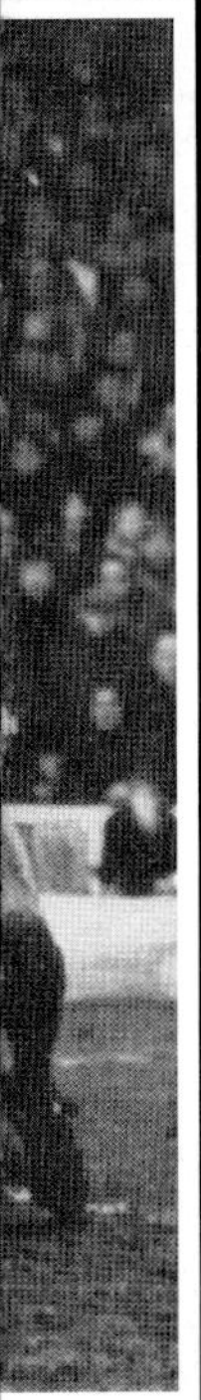

Alex Ingram scores against Derby but the referee disallows it for an infringement.

and excruciating end, Peter Cormack's one and only seasons appearance came at the Hawthorns where the Reds shipped another four goals in a heavy defeat, before a further embarrassing 4-1 home defeat to Coventry three days later. This game saw Henry Newton substituted for the only time in his Forest career, the weight of carrying the team finally caught up with him.

The curtain on the campaign couldn't come down quickly enough for supporters, but at least the team finally gave those long suffering fans something to cheer about, with a 1-0 victory over Ipswich, played out before a season's low crowd of only 10,589 on a Friday evening. Alex Ingram, who could never be faulted for his work rate scored the only goal.

A season that had promised so much at the halfway stage had finished in total anti climax, never in danger of relegation, fifteenth place and thirty eight points, but things had been allowed to drift and only four points from a possible twenty four from the final twelve games, was no way to encourage fans to return to the City Ground next season and although the average gate had increased slightly, this was more due to the fact that the Derby game resulted in a far higher attendance than a run of the mill fixture.

Club Chairman, Jack Levy and Matt Gillies, admire the new Nottingham Forest Rose.

There was of course still the County Cup to sort out, an easy 2-0 victory over Notts that saw a belated debut for Eric Hulme, who had been watching from the sidelines as the more experienced Dave Hollins had endured a torrid end to the season.

There were also a couple of home and away friendlies against ADO of the Hague from Holland, another 4-2 defeat at home, where worryingly the Reds were outclassed by the middle ranking Dutch side. This was a game that saw the last appearance of John Barnwell who came on as a second half substitute. 201 outings with 25 goals doesn't do true justice to the impact John had on the club.

Gradually every player from the successful '67 side was being moved on. The final fixture of the season saw them lose 3-2 to ADO in the away encounter.

In Nottingham, Raleigh workers were out on strike and the jobless figures in the country were the highest since the end of the war. As for the football, Forest's fortunes were falling and the team was lacking in so many areas. The skipper had gone, Ian Moore often targeted by the opposing team's hard men, was worryingly looking more injury prone and the club gave all the impressions that it was falling behind. Football was getting glossier, more personality driven, brash managers such as Brian Clough and Malcolm Allison were now the norm, whilst Matt Gillies who might be well regarded within football was definitely the past.

The question was, would the committee have the nerve to take action and invest the necessary money to strengthen or just hope for the best and inevitably fall back, only time would tell.

'THE LUCK OF THE IRISH RUNS FOR ME'

Says Nottingham Forest's Irish International LIAM O'KANE

IT'S all happening to me— has been ever since Nottingham Forest came over to Ireland and paid Derry City somewhere in the region of £5,000 for me.

When I heard that Forest, an English First Division side, wanted to sign me I just couldn't believe it.

Talk about the luck of the Irish! I must have rubbed shoulders with all the leprechauns in the Emerald Isle.

Just try to imagine how I felt! I hadn't been playing for Derry for very long and, to be honest, hadn't even thought about football as a career.

Full-back Peter Hindley, one of Liam's team-mates in the Forest back four.

Then I heard rumours that Billy Oakes, who scouts for Forest in Northern Ireland, had been along to watch me. Not true, I told myself, he must be looking at someone else in the Derry side . . . or in the opposition.

DEBUT AGAINST LEEDS

But in this case rumour turned out to be fact and Forest made their offer just before Christmas in 1968. And they promised another £5,000 after I had played 20 first-team matches.

The outcome of all this was that a very homesick Irish lad arrived in Nottingham with a suitcase and, of course, a pair of football boots.

At first, I wanted to return home. But gradually I settled down and prepared for at least a couple of seasons in the reserves. My estimate was way out.

Within four months I made my first-team debut — against Leeds United, of all teams. And at Elland Road.

The thrill of making my debut was one I'll never forget. It was a painful experience!

After about half-an-hour, I was taken off on a stretcher with a suspected broken leg. I remember thinking that if the luck of the Irish had been with me when Forest signed me it had now run out on me with a vengeance.

But my luck held . . . examination showed that there was no break, only a damaged nerve.

HOMESICK DEFENDER

I'll say this: before my injury, I began to wish that I was back in Derry. The pace was terrific and the Leeds team were going a bit.

As that was the last match of the season, I didn't get another taste of First Division football until the following term.

My first wearing of the green for Ireland was as a substitute. I came on for the second-half of the match against Scotland at Windsor Park, Belfast earlier this year.

We lost by the only goal, but despite the result I enjoyed the experience. I was chosen for the remaining two games against England and Wales. Again we lost.

Forest midfield man Ronnie Rees scored the winner for Wales and I pulled his leg a bit afterwards for doing a thing like that on a team-mate.

But now we are into a new season. With my usual Irish luck, I hope that I will get through it successfully and help Forest to win something.

It will be a much more pleasant season if I don't meet opponents like Arsenal's John Radford every week.

I know that I haven't been in the game very long, but already I rate him as the best striker I've come up against.

Whenever I mention this, I am asked: "Do you rate Radford higher than Ron Davies of Southampton or Wyn Davies of Newcastle?"

Let me explain . . . I don't have such direct contact with them. This is because at Forest I am the one who does the man-for-man marking and this means I have to try to look after the striker who tries to draw you out of position by moving around. Sammy Chapman takes the other one.

So if we are playing, say, Southampton, I keep an eye on Mike Channon and Sammy marks Ron Davies.

In the Arsenal attack, the man I must look out for is Radford. He doesn't half make me earn my money.

He never stops moving; always on the go. One moment he has gone to the left, the next he is worrying the life out of you on the right.

In my book, Radford is a great player.

But then, the Football League is full of very fine players — and if my Irish luck holds out, perhaps one day I'll achieve my ambition and be as good if not better than the best of them!

FACTS and FIGURES

July 30th 1969, A, v. Maastrich, Loss 0-1, AT 7,000, Hill, Hindley, Winfield, Chapman, Hennessey, Newton, Lyons, Richardson, Hall, Hilley, S-Moore, SUB Grummitt.

Aug 1st 1969, A, v. Rot-Weiss Essen, Loss 0-2, AT 8,000, Hill, Hindley, Winfield, Chapman, Hennessey, Newton, Lyons, Richardson, Hall, Hilley, S-Moore, SUB Barnwell.

Aug 9th 1969, A, v. Ipswich Town, Draw 0-0, AT 19,310, Hill, Hindley, Winfield, Chapman, Hennessey, Newton, Rees, Richardson, Hall, Barnwell, S-Moore.

Aug 12th 1969, H, v. Stoke City, Draw 0-0, AST 22,740, Hill, Hindley, Winfield, Chapman, Hennessey, Newton, Rees, Richardson, Hall, Lyons, S-Moore, SUB O'Kane.

Aug 16th 1969, H, v. Leeds United, Loss 1-4, Scorer Rees, AT 34,290, Hill, Harris, Winfield, Chapman, Hennessey, Newton, Rees, Richardson, Hall, Lyons, S-Moore, SUB McKinlay.

Aug 20th 1960, A, v. Stoke City, Draw 1-1, Scorer Lyons, AT 20,028, Grummitt, Hindley, Winfield, Chapman, Hennessey, Newton, Lyons, Barnwell, Richardson, Hilley, S-Moore.

Aug 23rd 1969, A, v. Arsenal, Loss 1-2, Scorer S-Moore, AT 30,290, Hill, Hindley, Winfield, Chapman, O'Kane, Newton, Lyons, Barnwell, Richardson, Hilley, S-Moore, SUB Hall.

Aug 26th 1969, H, v. West Bromwich Albion, Win 1-0, Scorer S-Moore, AT 22,924, Hill, Hindley, Winfield, Chapman, O'Kane, Newton, Rees, Lyons, Hilley, Barnwell, S-Moore, SUB Hall.

Aug 30th 1969, H, v. West Ham United, Win 1-0, Scorer Hilley, AT 27,097, Hill, Hindley, Winfield, Chapman, Hennessey, Newton, Rees, Lyons, Hilley, Barnwell, S-Moore.

Sept 3rd 1969, A, v. Barrow, Win 2-1, Scorers Barnwell, S-Moore, AT 8,919, Hill, Hindley, Winfield, Chapman, Hennessey, Newton, Rees, Lyons, Hilley, Barnwell, S-Moore, SUB O'Kane.

Sept 6th 1969, A, v. Wolverhampton Wanderers, Draw 3-3, Scorers Newton (2), Rees, AT 33,166, Hill, Hindley, Winfield, Chapman, Hennessey, Newton, Rees, Lyons, Collier, Barnwell, Hilley.

Sept 13th 1969, H, v. Southampton, Win 2-1, Scorers S-Moore (2), AT 23,200, Hill, Hindley, Winfield, Chapman, Hennessey, Newton, Rees, Hilley, Collier, Barnwell, S-Moore, SUB O'Kane.

Sept 16th 1969, A, v. Coventry City, Loss 2-3, Scorers Rees, Collier, AT 26,038, Hill, Hindley, Winfield, Chapman, Hennessey, Newton, Rees, Hilley, Collier, Barnwell, S-Moore, SUB O'Kane.

Sept 20th 1969, A, v. Sunderland, Loss 1-2, Scorer Hilley, AT 16,044, Hill, Hindley, Winfield, Chapman, Hennessey, Newton, Rees, O'Kane, Hilley, McKenzie, S-Moore, SUB Barnwell.

Sept 23rd 1969, H, v. West Ham United, Win 1-0, Scorer Lyons, AT 20,939, Hill, Hindley, Winfield, Chapman, Hennessey, Newton, Rees, Lyons, O'Kane, Barnwell, S-Moore.

Sept 27th 1969, H, v. Crystal Palace, Draw 0-0, AT 23,394, Grummitt, Hindley, Winfield, Chapman, Hennessey, Newton, Rees, Lyons, Hilley, Barnwell, S-Moore, SUB Richardson.

Oct 4th 1969, A, v. Liverpool, Draw 1-1, Scorer Newton, AT 44,859, Hill, Hindley, Winfield, Chapman, Hennessey, Newton, Rees, Lyons, Hilley, Richardson, S-Moore.

Oct 11th 1969, H, v. Manchester City, Draw 2-2, Scorers Lyons, S-Moore, AT 30,037, Hill, Hindley, Winfield, Chapman, Hennessey, Newton, Rees, Lyons, Hilley, Richardson, S-Moore, SUB Barnwell.

Oct 15th 1969, H, v. Oxford United, Loss 0-1, AT 20,734, Hill, Hindley, Winfield, O'Kane, Hennessey, Newton, Rees, Lyons, Hilley, Richardson, S-Moore, SUB Barnwell.

Oct 18th 1969, A, v. Manchester United, Draw 1-1, Scorer S-Moore (PEN), AT 53,702, Hill, Hindley, Winfield, McKinlay, Hennessey, Newton, Rees, Lyons, Hilley, Richardson, S-Moore.

Oct 25th 1969, H, v. Burnley, Draw 1-1, Scorer Lyons, AT 19,771, Hill, Hindley, Winfield, McKinlay, Hennessey, Newton, Rees, Lyons, Hilley, Richardson, S-Moore, SUB Hall.

Oct 29th 1969, A, v. Leeds United, Loss 1-6, Scorer Newton, AT 29,636, Hill, Hindley, Winfield, O'Kane, Hennessey, Newton, Rees, Lyons, Hilley, Barnwell, S-Moore.

Nov 1st 1969, A, v. Everton, Loss 0-1, AT 49,610, Hill, Hindley, Winfield, McKinlay, Hennessey, Newton, Rees, Lyons, Hilley, Richardson, S-Moore, SUB Brindley.

Nov 8th 1969, H, v. Tottenham Hotspur, Draw 2-2, Scorers Rees, S-Moore, AT 24,034, Hill, Hindley, Winfield, McKinlay, Hennessey, Newton, Rees, Lyons, Hall, Richardson, S-Moore.

Nov 15th 1969, A, v. Newcastle United, Loss 1-3, Scorer Hilley, AT 24,207, Hill, Hindley, Winfield, McKinlay, Hennessey, Newton, Rees, Lyons, Hilley, Richardson, S-Moore, SUB Brindley.

Nov 17th 1969, H, v. Rot-Weiss Essen, Win 1-0, Scorer Lyons, AT 4,864, Hill, Hindley, Winfield, Piekalnietis, O'Kane, Newton, McCaffrey, Rees, Hall, Lyons, S-Moore, SUB Brindley, Hilley, Cottam.

Nov 22nd 1969, H, v. Chelsea, Draw 1-1, Scorer Newton, AT 23,808, Hill, Hindley, Winfield, O'Kane, Hennessey, Newton, Rees, Lyons, Hilley, Hall, S-Moore, SUB Brindley.

Nov 29th 1969, A, v. Derby County, Win 2-0, Scorers Lyons, S-Moore, AT 38,225, Hill, Hindley, Winfield, Chapman, Hennessey, Newton, Rees, Lyons, Hilley, Hall, S-Moore.

Dec 6th 1969, H, v. Sheffield Wednesday, Win 2-1, Scorers Rees, Hilley, AT 19,039, Hill, Hindley, Winfield, Chapman, O'Kane, Newton, Rees, Lyons, Hilley, Hall, S-Moore.

Dec 13th 1969, A, v. Southampton, Win 2-1, Scorers Newton, S-Moore, AT 20,153, Hill, Hindley, Winfield, Chapman, O'Kane, Newton, Rees, Lyons, Hilley, Richardson, S-Moore.

Dec 20th 1969, H, v. Wolverhampton Wanderers, Win 4-2, Scorers Hindley, Hilley (2), S-Moore, AT 15,921, Hill, Hindley, Winfield, Chapman, O'Kane, Newton, Rees, Lyons, Hilley, Richardson, S-Moore.

Dec 26th 1969, H, v. Arsenal, Draw 1-1, Scorer Rees, AT 38,915, Hill, Hindley, Winfield, Chapman, O'Kane, Newton, Rees, Hilley, Cottam, Richardson, S-Moore, SUB Piekalnietis.

First Division 1969-70

		Pld	W	D	L	F	A	Pts
1	Everton	42	29	8	5	72	34	66
2	Leeds United	42	21	15	6	84	49	57
3	Chelsea	42	21	13	8	70	50	55
4	Derby County	42	22	9	11	64	37	53
5	Liverpool	42	20	11	11	65	42	51
6	Coventry City	42	19	11	12	58	48	49
7	Newcastle United	42	17	13	12	57	35	47
8	Manchester United	42	14	17	11	66	61	45
9	Stoke City	42	15	15	12	56	52	45
10	Manchester City	42	16	11	15	55	48	43
11	Tottenham Hotspur	42	17	9	16	54	55	43
12	Arsenal	42	12	18	12	51	49	42
13	Wolverhampton Wand.	42	12	16	14	55	57	40
14	Burnley	42	12	15	15	56	61	39
15	FOREST	42	10	18	14	50	71	38
16	West Bromwich Albion	42	14	9	19	58	66	37
17	West Ham United	42	12	12	18	51	60	36
18	Ipswich Town	42	10	11	21	40	63	31
19	Southampton	42	6	17	19	46	67	29
20	Crystal Palace	42	6	15	21	34	68	27
21	Sunderland	42	6	14	22	30	68	26
22	Sheffield Wednesday	42	8	9	25	40	71	25

Dec 27th 1969, A, v. West Ham United, Draw 1-1, Scorer S-Moore, AT 31,829, Hill, Hindley, Winfield, Chapman, O'Kane, Newton, Rees, Lyons, Hilley, Richardson, S-Moore, SUB McCaffrey.

Jan 3rd 1970, FAC, H, v. Carlisle United, Draw 0-0, AT 23,419, Hill, Hindley, Winfield, Chapman, O'Kane, Newton, Rees, Lyons, Hilley, Richardson, S-Moore, SUB McCaffrey.

Jan 6th 1970, FAC, A, v. Carlisle United, Loss 1-2, Scorer McCaffrey, AT 12,840, Hill, Hindley, Brindley, Chapman, O'Kane, Newton, Rees, Lyons, Hilley, Richardson, S-Moore, SUB McCaffrey.

Jan 17th 1970, A, v. Crystal Palace, Draw 1-1, Scorer Chapman, AT 22,531, Hill, Hindley, Winfield, Chapman, Hennessey, Newton, Lyons, Richardson, Ingram, Hilley, S-Moore.

Jan 24th 1970, H, v. Sunderland, Win 2-1, Scorers Ingram, OG, AT 19,544, Hill, Hindley, Winfield, Chapman, O'Kane, Newton, Lyons, Richardson, Ingram, Hilley, S-Moore.

Jan 31st 1970, H, v. Liverpool, Win 1-0, Scorer Richardson, AT 30,838, Hill, Hindley, Winfield, Chapman, O'Kane, Newton, Lyons, Richardson, Ingram, Hilley, S-Moore ,SUB Barnwell.

Feb 7th 1970, A, v. Manchester City, Draw 1-1, Scorer Hilley, AT 21,077, Hill, Hindley, Winfield, Chapman, O'Kane, Newton, Lyons, Richardson, Ingram, Hilley, S-Moore ,SUB Barnwell.

Feb 21st 1970, A, v. Burnley, Loss 0-5, AT 11,185, Hill, Hindley, Bridgett, Chapman, O'Kane, Newton, Lyons, Barnwell, Ingram, Richardson, Hilley, SUB Hall.

Feb 28th 1970, H, v. Everton, Draw 1-1, Scorer Ingram, AT 29,174, Hill, Hindley, Winfield, Chapman, O'Kane, Newton, Hall, Richardson, Ingram, Lyons, Hilley, SUB McCaffrey.

Mar 7th 1970, A, v. Chelsea, Draw 1-1, Scorer McCaffrey, AT 38,280, Hollins, Hindley, Winfield, Chapman, O'Kane, Newton, Hall, Richardson, Ingram, Lyons, Hilley, SUB McCaffrey.

Mar 14th 1970, H, v. Derby County, Loss 1-3, Scorer Newton, AT 42,074, Hollins, Hindley, Winfield, Chapman, O'Kane, Newton, Lyons, Richardson, Ingram, Rees, Hilley, SUB McCaffrey.

Mar 21st 1970, A, v. Sheffield Wednesday, Loss 1-2, Scorer Rees, AT 23,787, Hollins, Hindley, Winfield, Chapman, O'Kane, Newton, McCaffrey, Richardson, Ingram, Lyons, Rees.

Mar 27th 1970, A, v. Tottenham Hotspur, Loss 1-4, Scorer Chapman, AT 36,947, Hollins, Hindley, Winfield, Chapman, O'Kane, Newton, Rees, Richardson, Ingram, Lyons, Hilley.

Mar 28th 1970, H, v. Newcastle United, Draw 2-2, Scorers Lyons, Hilley, AT 21,360, Hollins, Hindley, Winfield, Chapman, O'Kane, Newton, Rees, Lyons, Ingram, Collier, Hilley.

Mar 31st 1970, H, v. Manchester United, Loss 1-2, Scorer Hindley, AT 39,228, Hollins, Hindley, Winfield, Chapman, O'Kane, Newton, Rees, Lyons, Ingram, Collier, Hilley, SUB Richardson.

April 4th 1970, A, v. West Bromwich Albion, Loss 0-4, AT 20,691, Hollins, Hindley, Winfield, Chapman, O'Kane, Newton, Lyons, Richardson, Ingram, Cormack, Hilley.

April 7th 1970, H, v. Coventry City, Loss 1-4, Scorer Rees, AT 15,569, Hollins, Hindley, Winfield, Chapman, O'Kane, Newton, Rees, Richardson, Ingram, Collier, Hilley, SUB McCaffrey.

April 10th 1970, H, v. Ipswich Town, Win 1-0, Scorer Ingram, AT 10,589, Hollins, Hindley, Winfield, Chapman, O'Kane, Richardson, McCaffrey, Lyons, Ingram, Hilley, Rees.

April 14th 1970, H, v. A.D.O.Den Haag, F, Loss 2-4, Scorers Hilley (2), AT 4,702, Hulme, Hindley, Winfield, Chapman, O'Kane, Richardson, McCaffrey, Lyons, Ingram, Hilley, Rees, SUB Barnwell.

April 28th 1970, CC, H, v. Notts County, Win 2-0, Scorers Lyons, Ingram, AT 10,233, Hulme, Hindley, Winfield, Chapman, O'Kane, Richardson, McCaffrey, Lyons, Ingram, Hilley, Rees.

Players Only, left to right :-

Back Row: Henry Newton, John Winfield, Alan Hill, Bob McKinlay, Peter Grummitt, Bob Chapman, Peter Hindley

Middle Row: Ian Moore, Terry Hennessey, Colin Hall, Barry Lyons, Dave Hilley

Front Row: John Barnwell, Ronnie Rees

In between football seasons, Britain had seen a change of government, as the Conservatives defied all predictions and returned with a thirty seat majority. Industrial relations were now so bad it was easier to list who wasn't on strike or demanding more money, rather than those working normally. Inflation was high and calls for wage increases of over 30% were routine. Disputes with the power companies and everyday services such as the Royal Mail and bin collections were directly affecting everyone and the situation only looked as if it would get worse.

It was against this background that football as usual, seemed to be oblivious to the real world as transfer fees spiralled, even average Division One players were now changing hands for over £50,000.

So what could the Forest committee do? There were calls for the club to modernize, become a limited company, the same as every other club and look for wealthy investors. However the traditionalists within the club wanted things to remain the same, they were proud of the club's unique status within football.

Of course after two months off and with the sun shining, Forest along with every other club in the country returned to training full of optimism. With Ian Moore now fully fit and expected to link up with new signing Peter Cormack, there were grounds for thinking that the football might be more exciting and adventurous, but with Cormack untested in English football and Moore seeming to be more prone to injury than ever, there were still lingering doubts.

The goalkeeping problem was addressed by signing Jim Barron from Oxford United for a fee of £30,000. However, Jim wasn't young and hadn't established himself at either Wolves or Chelsea in the top flight previously. In fact he had been forced to drop down a division to get a regular starting position at the Manor Ground. Although a good shot stopper, there were concerns about Barron's ability to deal with crosses as he wasn't the biggest of keepers.

With the signing of Jim Barron, Matt Gillies declared that this was his team and he could now be finally judged on how it performed.

Nottinghamshire Police meanwhile announced that they were introducing new measures at the City Ground to combat the increasing number of incidents, these included dogs and the use of plain clothes officers on the terraces to identify troublemakers. At this time there were

70-71

NOTTINGHAM FOREST FOOTBALL CLUB

DIVISION ONE 1970 - 71

Back row, left to right:

PETER HINDLEY LIAM O'KANE BOB CHAPMAN JIM BARRON TOMMY CAVANAGH (Trainer) ERIC HULME ALAN HILL RAY BRIDGETT JOHN WINFIELD

Front row, left to right:

JOHN COTTAM BARRY LYONS PAUL RICHARDSON HENRY NEWTON DAVE HILLEY RONNIE REES IAN MOORE

WHAT THE PAPERS SAY...

EVENING POST AND NEWS
NOTTINGHAM, THURSDAY, AUGUST 13, 1970
PRICE 6d.

TRENT BUSMEN TO STRIKE ON SATURDAY

By Post and News reporter

TRENT buses will be off the road on Saturday. More than 500 busmen voted today to go ahead with their plans for a series of one-day strikes which will cripple services in Nottinghamshire, Leicestershire and Derbyshire.

The decision was made at a mass meeting lasting more than two hours at the Nottingham headquarters of the Transport and General Workers' Union today.

The strike will be extended over August Bank Holiday to include Sunday and Monday.

"The crews are adamant in their decision which was made by an overwhelming majority," said Mr. Ken Bullivant, the busmen's branch chairman, after the meeting.

Busmen arriving at the Mansfield Road headquarters of the Transport and General Workers' Union for today's meeting.

DISPUTE

EVENING POST AND NEWS
NOTTINGHAM, MONDAY, DECEMBER 7, 1970
PRICE 6d.

THE BIG BLACKOUT

COUNTRY FACES CHAOS AS POWER MEN GO SLOW

Wilford Power Station, Nottingham.

CRISIS POINT...

WHAT IT'S ALL ABOUT

By Post and News reporters

Glimmer of hope

Skinheads scourge of the soccer terraces

SEASON GETS A VIOLENT START

VIOLENCE marked the start of the soccer season on Saturday. Skinheads, spoiling for trouble on and off the terraces, gave the police their biggest headache.

No arrests

Gillies wants more 'savvy' from team

A BIT more football "savvy"—or, if you like, good old-fashioned commonsense — is needed by Nottingham Forest players, declared manager Matt Gillies this week.

David Stapleton on FOREST

Relaxing

Best start

Clampdown on soccer louts 'long overdue'

ACTION being taken by the Home Secretary Mr. Reginald Maudling, in his efforts to stamp out soccer hooliganism is long overdue, Notts County chairman, Mr. Jack Dunnett, said today.

EVENING POST AND NEWS
NOTTINGHAM, FRIDAY, APRIL 10, 1970
PRICE 6d.

BEATLES BREAK UP: PAUL CONFIRMS 'I'M QUITTING'

END OF LENNON-McCARTNEY SONG HIT PARTNERSHIP

PAUL McCARTNEY confirmed today that he has broken with the Beatles — but said he "did not know" if the split was temporary or permanent.

Paul McCartney

TEMPORARY

EMIGRATING? RENNIE'S SHIPPING SERVICES

Football Post AND NEWS

Vol. LXII No. 1 NOTTINGHAM, SATURDAY, AUGUST 15, 1970

CHEERS! WINNING START FOR REDS

PAT GIBSON at the City Ground

PETER CORMACK, of Scotland, and Ian Moore, of England, launched a new goal-scoring partnership on Trentside this afternoon, grabbing one each in the first half-hour to give Nottingham Forest a tonic start against Coventry. Cormack flashed the ball home in the 16th minute from a Barry Lyons' free kick.

And the match passed off almost without incident until shortly before the end when trouble broke out among the crowd in the East stand, where most of the Coventry supporters were. Police moved in to keep order.

Then Moore dived to head the second in the 30th minute following a wonderful burst by Forest's third international forward Ronnie Rees.

Liam O'Kane recovered from a thigh strain in time to take his place in the Reds' line-up.

Attendance: 25,137

Alex Ingram (left), the Nottingham Forest centre forward, watches the ball shoot past Bill Glazier, the Coventry City goalkeeper, as Peter Cormack puts the Reds one up at the City Ground, this afternoon.

no fences or segregation at the City Ground and it was common to see groups of fans charging around and unsettling regular supporters. Unlike today, away fans had to organize themselves quickly into a group to avoid being picked off or try and mingle in with home fans. Even when Derby or Man Utd visited, there were no special arrangements and this made Nottingham a hostile environment for away supporters.

The club announced that due to rising prices, there would be an across the board rise of 1/- on admission prices (decimalisation was still being phased in) and also that the team would be entering the new Texaco Cup competition, contested by a variety of mid ranking English and Scottish teams. Anything to bring in more revenue.

Pre-season results were encouraging, unbeaten on a short tour of Sweden with Cormack and Moore immediately among the goals, before a 1-0 win over Hamburg back at the City Ground. Peter Cormack making an immediate impression with the winner. Alex Ingram after an intensive training programme was given another chance to show that he could adjust to the demands of the English game.

The opening day of the season, Saturday 15th August was an absolute scorcher, with Coventry City providing the opposition. A strike by Nottingham Bus Corporation was expected to keep the attendance down, but many fans formed groups and made their way on foot and in the end it was a healthy 25,000 that turned up. Some City fans had arrived early and attempted to take up a position in the Trent End, this lead to fighting as they were removed and chased onto the East Stand terraces where sporadic skirmishes continued throughout the afternoon. It was reported that an ammonia gun was fired at supporters but this was denied by club officials.

Laurie Coppersmith

On the pitch, things couldn't have gone much better, goals from Barry Lyons and Ian Moore plus a good team performance all round, meant optimism remained high. The early fixtures looked kind to the Reds, the first seven games were all against teams not expected to challenge for honours.

For many years, Reds' supporters had complained about a lack of PR or fan involvement from the club. So in an attempt to rectify this, the club announced a new service asking fans to write in and request a record or perhaps a message to be played out over the tannoy system as part of the pre match entertainment. To this end, Forest engaged the services of top DJ Laurie Coppersmith to bring his professional expertise to the position. Unfortunately he was forced to apologise a few weeks later when he had to admit he had forgotten to bring along his tape recorder cable, and was unable to present his normal show.

Just four days after the Coventry game, the Reds were given a great opportunity to build on the opening day victory, when they had another home game against West Brom. Things looked to be going according to plan when Forest raced into a 3-1 lead with only three minutes left, after another great performance and goals from Rees, Cormack and Lyons. Unfortunately Rees and Cormack both received minor knocks but had to stay on because Chapman had already gone off, replaced by Richardson. Albion took full advantage of the situation, scoring two late goals to grab a scarcely deserved point. The Evening Post reported that, 'Classy Cormack inspires Forest'. Sammy Chapman and Liam O'Kane were now seen as the regular centre back partnership. Sammy seemed to have finally won the fans over, he was often underrated, usually because of a lack of concentration or the uncanny ability to find trouble. He was well regarded by his team mates, but at a cost as Henry Newton explains, "Sammy was a good player, hard as nails, but he lacked pace, though he could read the game well. The trouble was that he was always being fined or suspended. In those days the club didn't pay your wages if you were out suspended, so it was up to the other players to chip in to cover them. It was so bad, I had to put him on my tax form as a claimable allowance".

The unbeaten start continued with creditable away draws at Ipswich and Newcastle, before another Midland's derby with Wolves and a 4-1 victory, the biggest since December against the same opposition. The newspaper headlines were predictable, 'Forest maul the Wolves', but it was another dominant performance, even coming from a goal down after Barron had been beaten by a long range effort. It was particularly pleasing that there had already been six different goalscorers, perhaps the other players would now share some of the burden usually placed on the shoulders of Ian Moore.

Inexplicably though, the goals dried up, seven league games followed without anyone hitting the back of the net, although this run was punctuated by progress in the League Cup against Huddersfield and Texaco Cup action against Airdrie.

Rumours began to circulate that Henry Newton was unsettled, although the club denied it. Henry gives his side of the story. "I was concerned about the direction the club was going, but in those days as a player, you were expected to keep quiet and just get on with your job. I only wanted some assurances that the club was still ambitious. My own form was suffering and after getting close to an England cap, I seemed further away than ever. I really expected and wanted to see out my whole career at Forest, they were my club, I didn't want to leave".

OUR CAMERA CAPTU

Ronnie Rees fires home against West Brom.

Peter Cormack is denied against Leeds United.

NOTTINGHAM FOREST

V

AIRDRIE FC

JIM BARRON

PETER HINDLEY

RES ALL THE ACTION

Cormack again is foiled by the men from Yorkshire.

Hindley equalises from a corner against Wolves.

IAN MOORE

HENRY NEWTON

2—Football Post & News, Saturday, October 17, 1970

Big club page

PUBLIC OUTCRY FOLLOWS SALE OF CAPTAIN

NOTTINGHAM FOREST this week gambled with the club's future and left themselves wide open to the public outcry which followed the sale of Henry Newton to Everton.

That is my verdict on a week when the inevitable drifted into reality. The fans feel frustrated, I'm sure, because they cannot understand fully the reasons behind the Newton affair.

Perhaps, more important, they cannot see a plan behind some of the Reds' policies.

Surely soccer success depends on the number of key men you have to lift the skill and potential of the side. Newton I would have regarded as a greater "untouchable" than Terry Hennessey on the City Ground scene.

Now they have both gone. The situation is even more serious now because although they have got Tommy Jackson in exchange the Reds have not really groomed an understudy in the way that O'Kane was ready to slip into Hennessey's shirt eight months ago.

Heartbreaking

Perhaps even more heartbreaking is the fact that I don't think that Newton really wanted to go. At 26, naturally, he had to think of the future. But as a local product, he had deep roots and business interests in the area, and was approaching the time when he would have been rewarded for 10 years' service with the club.

Throughout the summer of discontent, following the nagging doubts whether he might have clinched the plane to Mexico if he had been with another club, the pressure and strain began to build up — on the club and the player himself.

Just when Henry was getting over the disappointment of Mexico, came a series of unsettling "leaks" to certain national newspapers from mysterious sources.

If the public want the truth on this matter, they should realise the damage done by such factors.

Throughout the summer and this season Mr. Gillies talked and talked to Newton. I know many fans must be wondering if pressure was put on the manager by the committee to sell to get cash for further buys. But I think this allegation can be dismissed.

In the end I think Mr. Gillies came to the conclusion that he could not keep an unhappy player.

Burden

The burden of responsibility and a depressing run of results certainly told on Newton's performances.

But surely a player is assessed over several years, not just a spell when he is struggling in a limited side! In Newton, Forest have lost a man who could inspire by his own example.

Forest must now mount an urgent mission to invest the cash recouped on the sale to get an established top bracket midfield man to help the club back on the rails.

Only a player in the Howard Kendall class will be good enough.

Men who have been linked with Forest so far have been St. Johnstone's John Connolly and Jim Henry, of Dundee United.

But I doubt if anyone will pin down Mr. Gillies to reveal his hand until the signing has been made.

Task

Let us hope that 23-year-old reserve Tommy Jackson, who was kept in the wings at Goodison by Everton's wealth of midfield talent, can rise to the man-size task that now confronts him at the City Ground.

He must slot in quickly, because Sammy Chapman now faces the threat of a further spell of suspension.

David Lowe on FOREST

After Newton search still continues

WHEN ANY top class player of the calibre of England prospect Henry Newton becomes available, you can rest assured that Derby County will be in with a bid to sign him.

This was how the Rams' assistant manager, Mr. Peter Taylor summed up the speculation which arose this week when it was known the Nottingham Forest captain was seeking a move.

"Let there be no mistake about it. We are always looking for good players, and Newton is only one of those we have been interested in.

"We have cash available to buy a player if we consider him good enough for our team, but there is no priority for any specific position.

"For instance, if a better centre half than Roy McFarland became available we would sign him if possible, but then this applies to both Brian Clough and myself. If the Derby board had the chance to get better men for the job, they would replace us," added Mr. Taylor.

No secret

There was no secret about Derby's interest in Newton. They watched the negotiations carefully hoping that Newton's connections in Nottingham might sway him in their favour but it was Everton who secured his services in the end.

Now that the chances of signing Newton have gone, Derby must continue to look elsewhere for players to strengthen their first team squad. The Rams have already used more players in the first team this season than last ...

Mike Beesley at DERBY

... dawning when Mr. Clough has a full strength squad to choose from for the first time this season.

Derby's 1-1 draw at Everton was encouraging for few clubs take points away from Goodison Park. The Rams' defence looked much sounder with the return of McFarland, and John McGovern took his equaliser well.

It was Kevin Hector who made the scoring chance with a fine header, but the inside forward's luck is out at the moment for he is doing everything except score. With John O'Hare showing some of his old form, it should not be long before Derby add to their goal tally.

APPEARANCES

Green, Robson, Carlin, O'Hare, Hector, Hinton 14 each, Mackay 13, Webster 12, McFarland, McGovern 10 each, Durban 9, Hodes, Wignall 4 each, Gemmill 3, Richardson 2, Hennessey, Walker, Daniel 1 each.

GOALSCORERS

O'Hare, Hinton (3 pens.), McGovern 5 each, Hector, Durban 3 each, Wignall, Mackay, own goal 1 each.

●Farewell to Henry. – Here is Newton leading out Forest for the last time at the City Ground against Blackpool.

One point from six a promotion jolt

ONE POINT from the last three matches, which ...

However as the team's form declined, fans were as usual quick to voice their opinions on what was wrong and who was to blame. Alex Ingram typically bore the brunt of their frustration as he was clearly out of his depth and unable to deal with the physicality of uncompromising English defenders. This period in football was brutal, any offence could seemingly be committed without even a caution.

Fans also pointed out that since the glut of players progressing through the ranks in the early sixties, no player since Sammy Chapman in 1963 had left any lasting impression and the club were back to spreading the available money thinly, rather than investing in top talent. Could the departure of club stalwarts such as Tommy Graham and Jack Burkitt from the coaching staff be a reason? Were the youngsters not being nurtured in the Forest way? Gillies tried to address this problem by appointing Bert Johnson to oversee youth development and finding coaching roles for Bob McKinlay and Alan Hill.

Forest had been drawn against part timers Airdrie in the Texaco Cup. The first leg at home was an exciting 2-2 draw and the crowd of over 11,000 wasn't too bad. However there was embarrassment in the return leg, as the Reds crashed out after another 2-2 draw, going down 5-4 on penalties, the first competitive penalty shoot out that the club had been involved in.

Forest by now were slipping down the table as the fixtures became increasingly harder, defeats to Man City and Liverpool, a stale home draw with Leeds, only memorable because the referee had to stop the game and make a loudspeaker plea for the phantom whistler in the crowd to please stop, or he would abandon the game. This poor run culminated in a four goal thrashing at Highbury.

The atmosphere and morale within the club was declining, illustrated by an incident that followed League Cup elimination at Birmingham City, when a few of the players were humiliated by some Forest committee members in the Birmingham boardroom whilst just trying to grab a quick drink before boarding the coach home.

October 10th 1970 and what appeared to be a run of the mill home fixture with struggling Blackpool. A dark overcast day attended by fewer than 17,000 fans. However, this game with hindsight proved to be one of the most pivotal days in the history of the club. Firstly it was Henry Newton's last game in the garibaldi, but more significantly in the 86th minute John Robertson came on as a substitute for Paul Richardson and the first steps on what would turn out to be an illustrious career were taken. John already had a high reputation within the club, it was felt that it was only a matter of time before he claimed a first team place, but would it be right to throw him into a relegation battle? Gillies thought not, as his only other competitive senior appearance of the season was a week later, when he started away at Huddersfield.

Given Matt Gillies' liking for a Scottish player and the fact that he gave him his debut, many people think that John Robertson was discovered during his time at the club, so perhaps the 'Gillies' period wasn't all bad. Sorry to disappoint you, Bill Anderson, during one of his periods in temporary charge had been the man to sign the greatest Nottingham Forest player.

The end of Henry Newton's Forest career came quickly when the club announced that they were willing to listen to offers and a variety of clubs lined up to sign him. Front of the queue was Brian Clough, a long time admirer, but after pinching Terry Hennessey from them, there was no enthusiasm at Forest to let Derby take another star. Everton emerged as favourites and agreed terms. Henry was recommended to make the move by Frank Wignall, who said they were a great club.

Henry gives his version. "I would have preferred to go to Derby, not only were they a team on the up, but I also wouldn't have had to uproot the family. Looking back now, I really should have raised more questions with Everton manager Harry

Tommy Jackson

Catterick about where he was going to play me. They already had Ball, Harvey and Kendall in midfield and another Newton, Keith at left back, so I seemed a little unnecessary. I also had the beginnings of the hip injury that was to finish my career, so I had to manage that as well.

Looking back I just cannot believe that in the space of twelve months, Forest had dismantled the best half back line that they had ever had, whoever thought that was a good idea needed their head looking at".

David Lowe, by now covering the club for the Football Post, argued that the committee had gambled with the club's future and Penpad of Bramcote asked, 'what qualifies those on the committee to run the club?'

Moore... Moore... Moore...

Netherlands

Newcastle United

Burnley

Southampton

Derby County

Peter Cormack narrowly powers a shot wide of the Chelsea goal.

Forest force the pace against Manchester United.

Spotlight on Forest

Sammy Chapman gleefully lashes home against Derby County.

Chapman & Winfield try to close down George Best.

Hindley soars, but Jennings saves for Spurs.

JOHN WINFIELD & BOB CHAPMAN in action against Chelsea

tougher in home matches

● Peter Cormack, Nottingham Forest's Scottish international forward has shouldered a heavy burden this season in fine style.

TRANSFER MOVE SILENCE AT THE CITY GROUND

NOTTINGHAM FOREST seem to be sizing up the situation carefully and cautiously before investing that six-figure cheque from the Henry Newton sale in the transfer market.

Meanwhile, manager Matt Gillies is maintaining a discreet silence about the list of players being checked by the club.

Perhaps some fans feel this approach leaves them out in the cold. But I believe there are several reasons for the hush-hush policy.

Perhaps Mr. Gillies feels he has reached a stage where his arguments can only be proved on the field. In other words, he would sooner set about clinching a deal than talking about his plans and predictions for the vital times ahead.

Secondly, he refuses to name names because he thinks this would be reflecting adversely on players currently filling the respective positions.

Thirdly, there is unquestionable concern of a leak ruining delicate negotiations and perhaps encouraging an auction for a player, inflating prices which favour the wealthier Division I giants.

NO LACK OF INTEREST . . .

Hateley negotiations

Ian Moore was dismayed at what was happening, "As the better players were sold, it obviously made me question my own position. With all due respect to those players brought in, they weren't as good as those leaving, so we were getting weaker. I could see that I really was the only saleable asset left, when would they try and cash in on me? I owed the club loyalty, particularly because they had stood by me when I was injured, but I knew my career was in danger of fizzling out".

As well as the large fee from Everton, Forest would also get Irish International midfielder Tommy Jackson in return. Tommy was a tough tackling type of player and the fact that he hadn't manage to get a regular starting position for Everton was no disgrace, but he clearly was not in the same class as Newton.

George Best as part of his after dinner speaking routine, used to tell the story of a trip abroad with Northern Ireland, when George allowed Tommy to watch from inside a wardrobe whilst he 'entertained' a young lady in his room.

With the team getting weaker, it is only right to examine the role of Matt Gillies in all this uncertainty, surely no manager would want to lose players of the calibre of Hennessey and Newton? Unlike when Billy Walker had been manager, the committee now held all the power and it was clear that the committee had got cold feet about money, transfers and investment. Having had their fingers burnt with Jim Baxter, it wasn't going to happen again and they had already missed the opportunity to redevelop the ground after playing success and the Main Stand fire. So when the bank had begun intimating that they wanted the club to reduce its debt exposure they acted. The members of the committee weren't fools, they were experienced and successful men in their own fields, but whereas in the old days they could afford to quietly cover expenses from their own pockets, the amounts involved in football were now too high to do this.

Nottingham was a successful city, but the 'closed shop' set up at the club, precluded bringing in outsiders with wealth, to help. At Derby, millionaire businessman Sam Longson was bankrolling Brian Clough's spending, but in return, he would inevitably want all the power and as later happened at the Baseball Ground, there could be a clash of egos between the football talent and the money men.

Henry Newton offers his perspective on Matt Gillies, "He should never have been given the job, not because he was a bad manager or person, but his own ill health, (stress brought on by the decline at Leicester) his long association with his previous club and his unwillingness to embrace the changes in football meant he was spectacularly unsuited for the position. Not only that, it was clear that the 'fire' in him had gone out".

Back in the 1970's, English football was dominated by Scots, managers, coaches and players were involved in every successful team and Gillies used this as his own blueprint for change. Every other week the Football Post reported that he

Nottingham, with the Victoria Centre under construction

THE GIRL BEHIND THE MAN

HAZEL NEWTON

ONE of the reasons for a loss of form this season was an injury to Henry Newton which kept him out of the team for some time. But Henry's wife, Hazel, 27, did not mind. It meant a pleasant change for her. She had her busy husband at home a lot more than she would have expected normally

CAROL MOORE

THE GIRL BEHIND THE MAN

THERE'S more to being a footballer's wife than sitting in the stand, glowing with pride at his achievements. When a star is hurt he needs comforting. That's the job of Carol Moore right now. Nottingham Forest's

THE GIRL BEHIND THE MAN!

MARION CORMACK

MARION CORMACK, wife of Nottingham Forest and Scotland striker Peter (inset), is a keen Soccer fan. She rarely misses a home match. Her hobbies are swimming, dancing, driving and playing records

Action from the Reds' encounter at the Hawthorns against West Brom.

Keeper Jim Barron holds up the post, during the FA Cup tie against Luton Town .

Neil Martin pounces to slot home the winner against Burnley!

REDS FI

Ian Moore tucks home the penalty in the Fourth Round tie against Orient...

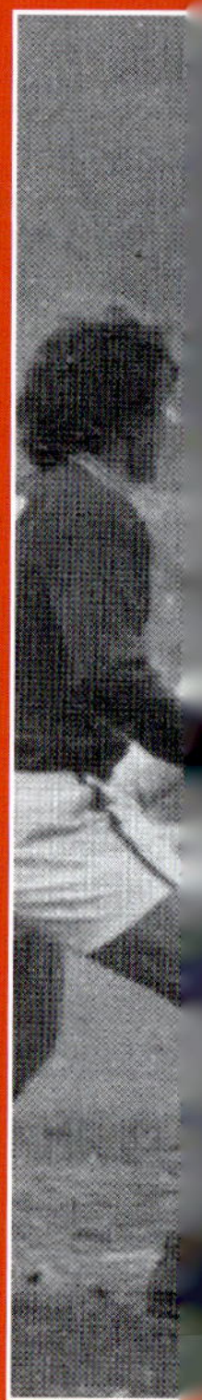

Ian Moore slots home from close range past Newcastle keeper Iam McFaul.

GHT BACK!

Jimmy McIntosh opens his Forest scoring account as he chests the ball home against Luton Town!

Jim Barron, spectacularly tips over the bar from a long range effort at Highbury.

Liam O'Kane (Nottingham Forest)
Tussles with John O'Hare of Derby County...

Doug Fraser
(Nottingham Forest)

N.F. F.C.

Alan Hill

Peter Cormack
(Nottingham Forest)

John Winfield
(Nottingham Forest)

Jimmy McIntosh

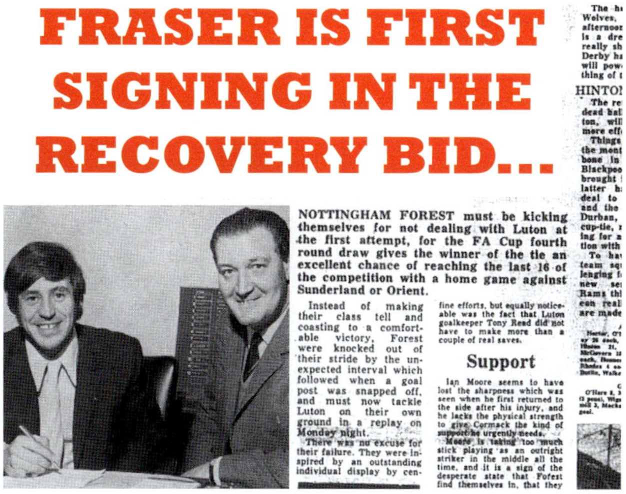

FRASER IS FIRST SIGNING IN THE RECOVERY BID...

NOTTINGHAM FOREST must be kicking themselves for not dealing with Luton at the first attempt, for the FA Cup fourth round draw gives the winner of the tie an excellent chance of reaching the last 16 of the competition with a home game against Sunderland or Orient.

Instead of making their class tell and coasting to a comfortable victory, Forest were knocked out of their stride by the unexpected interval which followed when a goal post was snapped off, and must now tackle Luton on their own ground in a replay on Monday night.

There was no excuse for their failure. They were inspired by an outstanding individual display by cen-

fine efforts, but equally noticeable was the fact that Luton goalkeeper Tony Read did not have to make more than a couple of real saves.

Support

Ian Moore seems to have lost the sharpness which was seen when he first returned to the side after his injury, and he lacks the physical strength to give Cormack the kind of support he urgently needs.

Moore is taking too much stick playing as an outright striker in the middle all the time, and it is a sign of the desperate state that Forest find themselves in, that they

Matt Gillies watches as Doug Fraser signs for the Reds

was off north of the border scouting for players, hoping to pick up a gem. There was no disputing that bargains could still be picked up, but as with Alex Ingram and many others, the number of Scottish players who failed to make the transition was high.

As we will see, practically every new signing Forest were going to make now would be Scottish, with the results clear to see. Jimmy McIntosh, a young winger from Montrose joined almost unnoticed, at the same time as Newton was leaving and made his debut only three weeks later, but the club were really crying out for a centre forward to take the pressure off Cormack and Moore.

Life after Henry began with a 2-0 defeat at Coventry, Tommy Jackson only lasting forty six minutes before going off injured. Off the pitch, Coventry City were still considered a progressive club, their football programme was of the 'magazine' type with articles on items other than football and they offered supporters pre match entertainment and the chance to watch the game from 'luxury' boxes after enjoying fine dining in the 'Sky Blue' restaurant.

Ian Moore was now injured once more, this time playing for the Football League team in a friendly against the Irish League at Carrow Road. Inevitably the goals dried up and in the ten games he missed, only one win was secured. So it must be time for the annual 'why don't we try Peter Hindley up front' letter in the Post, this time Newark Red was the one making the suggestion. Meanwhile Matt Gillies told supporters he wouldn't be rushed into 'splashing the cash' in search of goals.

Graham Collier was given yet another chance to make an impression, five consecutive games, his longest run in the first team, but he didn't impress and failed to score. Alex Ingram was now completely out of the picture, so even Cormack was pushed into playing centre forward, but to no avail. To keep shuffling the pack was pointless, the manager had to buy. The team was playing well and creating chances but without a goalscorer they were always going to struggle. The home game against Spurs aptly illustrated this. Forest dominated for long periods but fell to a 1-0 defeat after conceding to a rare Tottenham attack.

The worry for supporters was that Ian Moore could be sold. Leicester supporters who had turned against Gillies when he was their manager, pinpointed their club's decline to when Gillies sold Gordon Banks and Derek Dougan in 1967. Was history repeating itself?

Jimmy McIntosh who had only signed from Montrose three weeks previously was rushed into the first team along with John Cottam for their debuts at Everton, another 1-0 defeat. McIntosh was in the long line of tricky Scottish wingers who

flattered to deceive. Capable of going past a man, there was usually little in the way of end product and his lightweight frame meant that he could be intimidated out of a game.

To compound matters, Jim Barron was not playing well, it seemed that at least one goal per game could be put down to an error by the keeper, a thirty yarder against Wolves and a weak shot that went between his legs at Anfield were the lowlights.

There was unrest off the pitch, as it seemed revolution was in the air. Vice President Jim Branford was trying to get enough signatures to challenge the authority of the committee with a vote of no confidence, but the committee sensing trouble, attempted to head this off by agreeing to an informal meeting to discuss the fans' grievances. This proved effective, buying them time and eventually apathy set in and the hoped for demonstrations never took place.

November also saw the sacking of assistant secretary Dennis Marshall. Whether this was seen as some sort of cost saving exercise we don't know, but it didn't reflect well on the club and didn't go down well with supporters. Dennis was liked by everyone and he loved the club. Billy Walker once said of him. "Despite war injuries finishing his career as a player, I was determined to

MORE GOALS FOR

1 Neil Martin (red shirt) flicks on the ball across the goal...

2 ...it comes to me - I'm on the extreme left of the picture. Brian Labone has me covered, so I slip the ball to Peter Cormack...

4 ...Peter aims for the far post, but his shot is parried by stand-in keeper Dai Davies...

5 ...he could only push it out to me, and, really miss from such a close range as

IAN MOORE

March was a good month for Ian Moore. The Nottingham Forest winger scored four league goals, and our photographer was at the City Ground to capture the one he notched against Everton. Here, in his own words, Ian recalls the magic moment.

3 ...that's Peter in the number 10 shirt. He makes space for himself and prepares to shoot. The Everton defence is completely split and a goal looks on the cards...

vell, I can't
slide the ball in

6 ...it may not be the greatest of goals, but they all count, don't they? I turn to the lad and give the familiar soccer success sign

Ian Moore
Neil Martin
Peter Cormack

FOCUS ON

PETER CORMACK

Nottingham Forest

Now that Peter Cormack's ambition of playing in the Football League has been realised, he can concentrate on his next: to help Forest and Scotland win major honours. Forest are in a period of re-building, and Peter is a vital part of their plans. Scotland, too, are searching for the winning combination . . . and we have a feeling that Peter can help out on both accounts.

FULL NAME: Peter Barr Cormack
BIRTHPLACE: Edinburgh
BIRTHDATE: July 17th, 1946
HEIGHT: 5 ft. 10 in.
WEIGHT: 10 st. 7 lb.
PREVIOUS CLUBS: Hibernian
MARRIED: Yes
CHILDREN: None
CAR: Ford Capri
FAVOURITE PLAYER: Pele
FAVOURITE OTHER TEAM: Leeds United
MOST DIFFICULT OPPONENT: Tom Smith of Liverpool
MOST MEMORABLE MATCH: West Germany v Scotland, a World Cup eliminator this year
BIGGEST THRILL: Scoring the first goal for Hibs. against Real Madrid, a match which we won 2-0. I was only 17 at the time.
BIGGEST DISAPPOINTMENT: Being beaten 6-2 by Celtic in 1968-69 League Cup Final
BEST COUNTRY VISITED: America
FAVOURITE FOOD: Prawn cocktail, steak and chips
MISCELLANEOUS LIKES: Scoring goals, golfing, driving, watching a good thriller on T.V.
MISCELLANEOUS DISLIKES: Being out of the game through injury, gardening
FAVOURITE T.V. SHOWS: Up Pompeii, Star Trek
FAVOURITE SINGERS: Bandwagon, The Supremes
FAVOURITE ACTORS: Burt Lancaster, Natalie Wood, Richard Burton, Raquel Welch
BEST FRIEND: James McLauchlan Jnr.
BIGGEST INFLUENCE ON CAREER: James McLauchlan Sen. formerly of Tynecastle Boys Club
BIGGEST DRAG IN SOCCER: Being knocked out of major competitions
INTERNATIONAL HONOURS: 4 full caps, 8 Under-23 Caps
PERSONAL AMBITION: To have my own business
PROFESSIONAL AMBITION: To play for Scotland in the next World Cup
IF YOU WEREN'T A FOOTBALLER, WHAT DO YOU THINK YOU'D BE? An artist drawing cartoons
WHAT PERSON IN THE WORLD WOULD YOU MOST LIKE TO MEET? Frank Sinatra

Football Post AND NEWS

VAUXHALL CLIFTON

EMIGRATING? RENNIE'S SHIPPING SERVICES

NOTTINGHAM SATURDAY JANUARY 2 1971

PRICE SIXPENCE

RESULTS AND TABLES

FA CUP THIRD ROUND

MAC MAGIC! REDS FACE A REPLAY

MIKE BEESLEY at the City Ground

ATTENDANCE: 23,230

Division III

Division IV

Forest game

find him a job, as his heart and soul were in Forest".

As points became more precious, so Forest were accused of resorting to rough play. Dennis Law said that he didn't recognize this Forest team anymore and they were also booed off the pitch at Burnley, when Sammy Chapman was booked for the fourth time in only four months, after an incident that saw Eric Probert mysteriously left lying face down in the mud.

The club's lack of goal threat was illustrated by the number of drawn games, 24 out of the previous 57 fixtures. Imagine what the league position might have been if a number of these had been converted into victories.

Due to crowd disturbances at previous games, it was decided that the November meeting with Derby at the City Ground would be all ticket. This resulted in an attendance of only 30,000. Derby themselves were in the middle of a poor run of form, they hadn't progressed after a successful first season back in the top division, but they were still too strong for the Reds, winning 4-2 despite falling behind. Clough again questioned Forest's physical approach. Sammy Chapman and Ian Moore scored the Reds' goals, although if the usually reliable Moore had netted from the penalty spot, things could have been different.

After a sixth successive defeat, 4-1 at Southampton, the Reds slipped to third bottom with only Blackpool and Burnley beneath them. Outside of the football bubble, things weren't much better as the Power workers went on strike and threatened to turn the lights out. Only two days later the Dockers and Postal workers followed and an unhappy Christmas looked in store.

Power cuts for the country were to be implemented on a rota basis, this meant that the home game against Chelsea kicked off at 2.15 pm in order to finish before darkness set in. Sammy was booked once more but the club appealed, citing in his defence, that he was suffering from concussion, so he didn't know what he was doing. The Chelsea game also saw the Trent End hound off young Paul Richardson with chants of, 'Get off and stay off', the atmosphere was getting toxic.

The final game of the year came a week later, a home defeat to Ipswich played out in front of only 14,000 fans. This game saw the first real, concerted chants of, 'Gillies out' and 'Committee out'. There had been calls before, but now it seemed as if the whole crowd wanted him gone. Sections of the Trent End even relocated to a position in front of the Director's Box (where Matt Gillies watched the game from) to make their feelings known. In truth once more the team had played well and created a hatful of chances, hitting the bar three times, but luck just wasn't going their way. The team had now also completed a full calendar year without an away win and in truth were grateful that there were several teams that were worse than them. With the game at West Ham scheduled for Boxing Day failing a pitch inspection, the Reds ended the year third from bottom, only two points clear of the relegation zone.

Before returning to league action, the New Year began with a home FA Cup tie against Luton Town. Given the Reds' poor recent record against Division Two opposition and their current form, this had all the makings of another upset. The game turned out to be an uninspiring 1-1 draw, memorable only for the ten minute delay whilst the goalposts were repaired, after Peter Hindley had pulled them down falling into his own net whilst making a clearance at the Bridgford End After waiting a year for an away victory, two came along at once, league success at West Brom was immediately followed up by another away victory, 4-3 at Luton in the cup replay, impressive because Ian Moore was missing through injury. Cormack, Collier, Lyons and Rees with the goals, whilst Luton's three goals were scored by young centre forward Macolm Macdonald, surely the type of signing the Reds should be looking at.

The victory at the Hawthorns had been preceded by the signing of Doug Fraser from Albion, although he hadn't been allowed to play against his former team. Fraser was a tough combative player, comfortable either in defence or midfield. He was also Albion's former skipper, although he had recently lost his place in the team and nearing thirty, his best days were behind him.

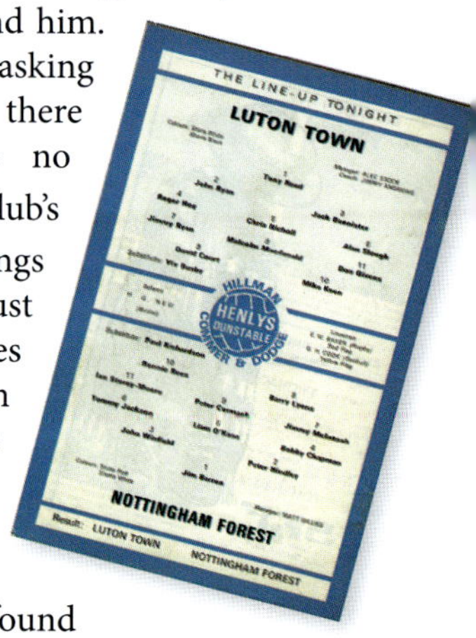

£40,000 was the asking price, clearly there seemed to be no strategy in the club's transfer dealings whatsoever, just more examples of short term reactive thinking. However, in the relegation fight the club found itself in, he was the sort of good honest pro you needed. It really doesn't need to be said, but he was Scottish.

Fraser made his debut in a 2-1 home victory over Newcastle, the returning Moore scoring twice.

Meanwhile Forest had decided to cut

their losses and allow Alex Ingram to return to Ayr United, a loss of £20,000 on the deal. Gillies was sanguine about the affair, claiming that Ingram had filled a necessary gap and a manager cannot be right all of the time.

Sammy Chapman had by now accumulated six bookings and was summoned to Lancaster Gate for a disciplinary hearing. Surprisingly he was only given a six week ban, suspended on the condition that his behaviour improved.

Peter Cormack who had travelled south with a reputation for poor behaviour had been as good as his word and 'cleaned up his act', he had neither been sent off or cautioned since joining and had now been recalled to the Scottish national team.

The reward for beating Luton was another home tie against lower league opposition in Leyton Orient, but yet again the Reds were lucky to escape with a draw. Ian Moore shooting home from the penalty spot, putting the Reds ahead before they were pegged back before half time and if the referee hadn't ruled out an Orient goal, they could have gone out.

The replay was due to take place only two days later at Brisbane Road. Due to poor weather it should never have started, incessant rain meant the ball could hardly move, or as Liam O'Kane put it, "When we came out to kick off, we half expected to see a family of ducks swimming around". The farce was ended at half time with no score and the re-arranged game was scheduled for the following Thursday. This time the Reds made no mistake, a professional 1-0 victory set up a fifth round encounter at Spurs. Graham Collier scored the winner and he also was on target in the next game against Southampton, although he was substituted in both games.

Another helpful bit of advice was offered by MJ Buxton from Breaston who wondered, 'In view of Alan Hill's size, 6'2" and his inability to play in goal because of an arm injury, could he not be retrained as a centre forward?'

The National Postal Strike meant that the club asked fans to visit the ground to collect their tickets for the cup game in London. In the end a sizeable away following were left disappointed, after a listless performance resulted in a 2-1 defeat at Tottenham. Although totally outplayed for the first sixty minutes, the Reds were only two down, before rallying late on and missing out on an undeserved equalizer when they were denied a goal by a great Pat Jennings save.

Matt Gillies declared that Forest could now concentrate on their primary objective of staying up and he set the team a points target of twenty eight, to be achieved by Easter.

After a 2-0 defeat to Chelsea, Gillies finally decided to act, splashing out £65,000 on Coventry's 30 year old Scottish centre forward Neil Martin. Although he had already scored thirteen goals this season, how could the manager and the club justify this sort of outlay on a player that age. To many fans this was harking back to the bad old days of the early 1960's, when a succession of cheap players filled the squad up, players such as Len Juliens, decent enough professionals, but an indication of where the club saw itself in the pecking order of 'top flight' clubs. Even if Martin could shoot the goals to keep the Reds up, he could hardly be described as one for the future. Compare this with Derby's signing of Colin Todd for £170,000 the same week.

Neil Martin made his home debut against Burnley, providing the knock down for Ian Moore to fire home the winner in front of the watching Sir Alf Ramsey. An unsavoury incident occurred when a couple of fans dashed onto the pitch to confront referee Charles Nicholls after he turned down a penalty appeal when Cormack was brought down. In truth the club's hope for survival rested purely on the fitness of Moore, the team on average, picked up twice as many points when he was playing. Two successive defeats, the second a calamitous 3-1 loss to relegation rivals Huddersfield plunged everyone back into despair. After an early first goal for Neil Martin, the Reds appeared to be coasting to victory, but the defence just collapsed. So how can you explain that four days later, they could go to White Hart Lane and pull off a great win? Chapman in particular was singled out for praise as he marked Spurs' dangerman Martin Chivers out of the game, keeping a clean sheet in the process.

The inconsistency of the team was the main concern amongst fans. One week it was if they didn't realise they were in a relegation dogfight, whilst the next they were playing as if their lives depended on it. Ian Moore explains, "The manager appeared to be laid back, he thought we had the ability to play well, but there was no pressure on some players to perform. The defence virtually picked itself as there was no competition for places, the youngsters either weren't good enough or ready to play. Whereas in the past, Tommy Cavanagh could have been relied upon to hand out a few hard home truths, he was being sidelined by the manager and it was not in Bob McKinlay's nature to be loud and demonstrative, even if it was necessary. So at times the team just drifted".

Top flight status was virtually assured after a run of three consecutive victories, including one at the Baseball Ground. Beginning with a 3-2 victory over Everton, a couple

EMIGRATING? RENNIE'S SHIPPING SERVICES

Football Post

Vol. LXII No. 23

NOTTINGHAM SATURDAY JANUARY 23 1971

PRICE SIXPENCE

FOREST FACE MONDAY REPLAY

MIKE BEESLEY at the City Ground

ORIENT shook Nottingham Forest back on their heels with a brilliant breakaway goal two minutes before half-time in their FA Cup fourth round tie at the City Ground this afternoon. Veteran winger Mark Lazarus set up a perfect centre for inside forward Barry Dyson to score with a flying header.

ATTENDANCE: 25,349

RESULTS AND TABLES

FA CUP 4th Round

Shaky Rams given the old one-two as…

RICHARDSON FIRES FOREST FURIES

DERBY COUNTY ……… 1 NOTTM. FOREST … 2

NOTTINGHAM FOREST threw down the gauntlet to neighbouring rivals Derby County at the Baseball Ground last night and went on to score two goals for the first time in an away League match this season and take the spoils earned by a stubborn and uncompromising defensive display, writes MIKE BEESLEY.

It was sweet revenge for Forest, and what was more important virtually assured them of Division 1 football next season. They are now 12 points clear of Blackpool, eight in front of Burnley and move clear of both West Ham and Ipswich.

This third win on the trot also means Forest are within striking distance of the four clubs grouped just one point above them— including Derby — and they now have a chance of finishing far higher in the table than anyone dared hope a fortnight ago.

It was Paul Richardson, a player often unfairly criticised by the Reds supporters, who sparked off this satisfying win over the Rams, which restored the balance of results between the two clubs.

Limped off

Forest had been hard pressed in the opening minutes of the game, and when Richardson limped off with an ankle injury things looked a bit black for the Reds.

Fortunately the knock was not serious and a minute later Richardson was back on the field and shortly after shot Forest into the lead when Barry Lyons found him unmarked on the penalty spot. This was Richardson's first goal of the season.

Derby forced a succession of corners without finding the equaliser, and gradually the Reds began to exert a stranglehold on the Rams attack, which reduced it to a frustrated and ineffective weapon.

There was a touch of arrogance about the way Forest deliberately yielded the midfield to Derby in the second half. The Reds were content to let Derby come at them, and pump the ball away whenever the Rams …

The Forest defence attempts to clear a Derby County attack at the Baseball Ground last night. Players from left to right are: Richardson, Wignall, Chapman and Hindley.

… delicate chip accros the Derby goal, and there was Ian Moore to head his 20th goal of the season.

It was ironic that Derby should finally find the back of the net in the dying seconds of the game. Kevin Hector put in a hopeful shot, which was deflected off Chapman's leg and Jim Barron's shoulder just inside the post.

Full praise

While the Forest defence earned the honours, full praise also to Cormack, Moore and Neil Martin for their non-stop running, and to the equally important grafting of Richardson, Barry Lyons and Doug Fraser in midfield.

It was far from a classic win, but Forest have played a lot better football in several away matches this season and gained nothing for their efforts, so the end certainly justified the means.

Derby looked a pale shadow of their old selves and apart from Colin Todd and John O'Hare none of their players seemed to have much appetite for the job in hand.

They have now taken just one … from their last five games … Clough must …

The Reds' defence stands firm against a Derby onslaught.

Relief for Jim Barron as the ball narrowly goes over the cross bar.

REDS SCORE ONE BUT IT'S EASY

MIKE BEESLEY at the City Ground

NOTTINGHAM FOREST set up a non-stop barrage and peppered the West Ham United goal with shots from all angles this afternoon, but it took a solo effort by Ian Moore to give them the lead after 44 minutes.

ATTENDANCE: 23,032

Ian Moore rounds the keeper to score the winner against the Hammers.

The Nottingham Forest Youth Team, accompanied by Ken Smales arrive for their tour of Zambia.

Back Row (left to right) : P. Wells, B. Johnson, M. Woods, K. Brown, L. Young, D. Hunter, S. Baines, A. Hill, G. Dulson. Front Row: R. Ford, J. Limb, L. Hines, J. Oliver, J. McCann.

from Cormack and one from Moore in front of the Match of the Day cameras, though they were aided by Everton fielding a weakened side in preparation for an FA Cup tie. Peter Cormack's second, was the club's landmark 4,000th goal in league football.

This was followed up the following Saturday with an even more emphatic 3-1 win against Crystal Palace and a hat trick for Ian Moore, who on a personal note registered his 100th goal for the club in front of a disappointing crowd of only 16,000. The game that everyone was waiting for came just four days later and the chance for revenge against Derby at the Baseball Ground. The game had originally been scheduled for January but had been called off due to a water logged pitch. This was not an unusual occurrence at this time, because Derby were widely considered to have the worst pitch in football. Derby themselves were not having a good season, in fact they were only five points ahead of Forest. Home attendances for Forest might be declining, but it was another big following that went down the A52 to see the Reds fully deserved 2-1 win. Goals from Richardson and Moore allied to an outstanding defensive performance grabbed the points. Even Brian Clough couldn't find fault with this one. Matt Gillies pronounced that, "People are now beginning to glimpse the real Forest". Unfortunately another Forest must have turned up for the game at Molineux the following Saturday, as they were crushed 4-0 by Wolves.

Not everyone was impressed by the turn around in form. Frank Parkin from Beeston wrote, 'Compare what football supporters thought about Nottingham Forest in the 1950's, a sporting football side, to what they say now , a dull, physical and unimaginative outfit'.

Liam O'Kane recalls his early days playing alongside Sammy Chapman, "When I came into the team, I suppose you could say I was quite naïve, obviously the standard was far higher than in Ireland, but also this was playing for your living and as a professional sometimes you had to do what was necessary. Players on both sides knew this, so there were no hard feelings. Playing alongside Sammy opened my eyes, he was a hard man. I remember when we used to warm up and Sammy would be staring down the opposition forwards and suddenly he would shout out for all to hear, "Oi Liam, the stupid b*****d hasn't got his pads on, I'm going to enjoy it today", and you just knew what Sammy was going to do. In those days it was accepted that the referees always seemed to let you off with an early foul".

The topsy turvy nature of the season continued over Easter. On Good Friday, the Reds travelled to Maine Road to take on Manchester City. Many supporters had been calling for Duncan McKenzie to be given his chance, especially in light of the goalscoring troubles. Duncan was a maverick, a term often overused but apt for this player. He had a fine range of skills and bags of confidence but somehow he couldn't seem to use them for the team, frustrating colleagues as much as opponents by holding on to the ball, always wanting to beat another man. This day, on his first start of the season, he showed what he could do, scoring two goals in a 3-1 victory and impressing everyone.

Therefore it was a surprise to some when he was left out of the next day's home fixture with West Ham, the previously injured Cormack regaining his spot. A fine solo effort for Moore being the only goal as mid table security beckoned.

The next game against Arsenal showed that the fans were still there if you could give them a team worth watching. A warm Tuesday evening drew over 40,000 to the City Ground, (though many experienced supporters thought the crowd closer to 45,000, higher than the official figure). It was the highest attendance of the season and also better than anything Derby had managed all year. It was a pity that they met an Arsenal team at the height of their powers and on the way to a league and cup double, as they ran out 3-0 winners. Half time music included, 'It's Impossible' by Perry Como, was Laurie the DJ having a laugh?

Survival for the season was finally assured after a 3-2 victory away at Blackpool,

The contestants parade in front of the Main Stand for the half-time 'Hot Pants' competition held during the Alan Hill testimonial match.

Back L - R : Cavanagh, Cormack, Moore, Richardson, Martin, Chapman, Barron, O'Kane, Winfield. Front : Lyons, Rees, McKenzie, Hindley, Fraser, Jackson, Robertson.

Moore scoring an 82nd minute winner. This meant that since the New Year the team had played 17 games, winning 11, losing 6 and drawing none, for a haul of 22 points from a possible 34. This was top six form if it could be maintained over a full season. After an injury to Neil Martin, Duncan McKenzie was handed the number nine shirt for the last four games of the season and although he didn't score, he was gaining valuable experience. His team mates however looked like they had downed tools and coasted to the season's end, failing to score or pick up any points from the three remaining fixtures.

The season finished with a County Cup Final against Mansfield. This not only ended in a 1-0 defeat, but it also saw Peter Hindley sent off after a wrestling match with the Stags' defender Stuart Boam when trying to retrieve the ball. As with Ken Wagstaffe in the 1960's, Forest once more missed out on talent right under their noses as uncompromising centre half Boam joined Middlesbrough and enjoyed a fine career.

Alan Hill had now been told to retire on medical grounds and had taken up a position on the coaching staff. The club had also granted him use of the City Ground for a testimonial game against Notts County. Alan was a popular figure and despite only being with the club for eighteen months, a fine crowd of over 15,000 turned up to pay their respects. They were also treated to a half time 'Hot Pants' competition. Five players, the whole defence of Barron, Hindley, Winfield, Chapman and O'Kane played in every game, league, cups and friendlies. That they should have all avoided injury, or in Sammy's case suspension was amazing, but was this also a sign that there was no competition for places? All of them at various times had suffered from lack of form, reserves John Cottam and Dave Serella were making progress, but were they good enough or ready to be promoted to the first team?

The club had spent money, but had it spent wisely? Was there a plan or were they just reacting to events. They couldn't keep relying on end of season rallies to climb the table, one of these times their luck might run out. History showed what happened to clubs that sold their best players and spent season after season near the bottom of the table. Supporters just had to wait and see.

HINDLEY & WINFIELD

Is there a better pair of full-backs in England?

WHO ARE the most consistently dependable full-backs in English soccer? Think of Cooper, Reaney, Newton, McNab, and all the other internationals — and you wouldn't be far out. But then perhaps have another think!

How about a couple who can boast only a single Under-23 cap between them — and still be the unsung defensive heroes of the First Division?

The club pair who, regularly playing alongside each other, have chalked-up more than 500 first-team appearances — and, each at only 27, should have several years of football left in them.

Full-back John Winfield started his career with Forest as an inside-forward in 1959.

Their names? Loyal one-club men Peter Hindley and John Winfield. Their side — Nottingham Forest. Their stock-in-trade — sheer hard graft and utter reliability.

Both were Forest's own local junior discoveries. Winfield signed as an inside-forward in May, 1959; Hindley as a centre-forward in June, 1961.

Winfield made his League debut — and scored — early in 1962, though Hindley had to wait another twelve months.

But neither could command a regular first-team spot until the inspirational double-transformation to full-back was made, and the great partnership begun.

So far Hindley has just edged in front — with 283 League appearances for Forest to Winfield's 272 — and both men played in all their club's 42 League games last season.

Since their coming together, of course, the former role of full-backs — as such — has tended tactically to become merged amongst a general "back four". But, after so long, up Nottingham way the inseparable names of Hindley and Winfield are as closely linked in partnership as Marks and Spencer or Morecambe and Wise.

They may now be in the "back four" — but they're still the "big two"!

Undoubtedly their most successful season in partnership — at least as far as the record-books go — was that of 1966-67, when their powerful rearguard actions played a vital part in taking Forest within a throw-in's range of the coveted "double".

In that memorable campaign in which Forest finished as First Division runners-up and F.A. Cup Semi-Finalists — Hindley was an ever-present, while minor injuries cost Winfield a mere couple of games.

The likes of Terry Hennessey, Henry Newton, Joe Baker — now all gone — and Ian Moore may have caught more attention from the headline-writers. But they owed much of their assurance to the stability of Hindley and Winfield behind them.

Both arrived at Forest long before present manager Matt Gillies, who's the first to appreciate the defensive wealth he inherited.

"Because they're so solid and dependable, rather than showy," says Gillies, "they've never received the recognition nationally that they've deserved. They're the 'quiet' type of player, while others — perhaps more brilliant on occasions, but never so reliable over a period — catch the eye more.

"But they're the 'unflappables' every manager likes to have on his books, knowing they'll be the equal of any emergency."

How has the game — and their own role in particular — changed since their fine Forest partnership began?

Considerably, they find, When they kicked-off, their basic job as full-backs was to take care of opposing wingers.

"We'd look a right pair now," jokes Winfield, "spending 90 minutes ferretting around for opponents who don't seem to exist any more!"

But both are far happier in their present less-restrictive defensive roles. Winfield, in particular, has a special partiality for a crafty overlap, and each scores an occasional goal.

"We were never allowed that kind of freedom in the 'bad old days'," they say.

"Bad old days?" Yes, certainly, both are quite convinced that the game is far more interesting, as well as immeasurably more skilful, now.

Now club skipper, Peter Hindley has played over 250 times for Forest.

FACTS and FIGURES

Jul 24th 1970, A, F, v. Halmia, Win 3-0, Scorers Cormack, Newton, Rees, AT 4,712, Barron, Hindley, Winfield, Chapman, O'Kane, Newton, Lyons, Cormack, Ingram, Rees, S-Moore, SUB Richardson.

Jul 26th 1970, A, F, v. Landskrona, Win 4-2, Scorers Hilley, S-Moore (3), AT 2,000, Barron, Hindley, Winfield, Chapman, O'Kane, Newton, Lyons, Cormack, Hilley, Rees, S-Moore, SUBS Richardson, Brindley.

Jul 28th 1970, A, F, v. Jonkoeping Soedra, Win 1-0, Scorer Cormack, AT 2,000, Barron, Hindley, Winfield, Chapman, O'Kane, Newton, Hilley, Cormack, Ingram, Rees, S-Moore, SUB Lyons.

Aug 7th 1970, H, F, v. Hamburg SV, Win 1-0, Scorer Cormack, AT 11,185, Barron, Hindley, Winfield, Chapman, O'Kane, Newton, Lyons, Rees, Ingram, Cormack, Hilley.

Aug 15th 1970, H, v. Coventry City, Win 2-0, Scorers Lyons, S-Moore, AT 25,137, Barron, Hindley, Winfield, Chapman, O'Kane, Newton, Lyons, Rees, Ingram, Cormack, S-Moore, SUB Hilley

Aug 18th 1970, H, v. West Bromwich Albion, Draw 3-3, Scorers Rees, Cormack, Lyons, AT 24,423, Barron, Hindley, Winfield, Chapman, O'Kane, Newton, Lyons, Rees, Ingram, Cormack, S-Moore, SUB Richardson.

Aug 22nd 1970, A, v. Ipswich Town, Draw 0-0, AT 19,150, Barron, Hindley, Winfield, Chapman, O'Kane, Newton, Lyons, Rees, Ingram, Cormack, S-Moore, SUB Hilley.

Aug 26th 1970, A, v. Newcastle United, Draw 1-1, Scorer S-Moore, AT 35,132, Barron, Hindley, Winfield, Chapman, O'Kane, Newton, Lyons, Rees, Ingram, Cormack, S-Moore.

Aug 29th 1970, H, v. Wolverhampton Wanderers, Win 4-1, Scorers Hindley, S-Moore (Pen), Rees, Newton, AT 24,343, Barron, Hindley, Winfield, Chapman, O'Kane, Newton, Lyons, Rees, Ingram,Cormack, S-Moore, SUB Hilley.

Sept 2nd 1970, A, v. Stoke City, Draw 0-0, AT 13,951, Barron, Hindley, Winfield, Chapman, O'Kane, Newton, Lyons, Rees, Ingram,Cormack, S-Moore, SUB Richardson. Sept 5th 1970, A, v. Crystal Palace, Loss 0-2, AT 26,510, Barron, Hindley, Winfield, Chapman, O'Kane, Newton, Lyons, Rees, Ingram, Cormack, S-Moore.

Sept 9th 1970, LC, A, v. Huddersfield Town, Draw 0-0, AT 18,165, Barron, Hindley, Winfield, Chapman, O'Kane, Newton, Lyons, Rees, Ingram,Cormack, S-Moore, SUB McKenzie

Sept 12th 1970, H, v. Manchester City, Loss 0-1, AT 28,896, Barron, Hindley, Winfield, Chapman, O'Kane, Newton, Lyons, Rees, Ingram, Cormack, S-Moore, SUB McKenzie

Sept 14th 1970, TC, H, v. Airdrie, Draw 2-2, Scorers Cormack, S-Moore, AT 11,491,Barron, Hindley, Winfield, Chapman, O'Kane, Newton, Lyons, Rees, Hilley, Cormack, S-Moore.

Sept 19th 1970, A, v. Liverpool, Loss 0-3, AT 40,676, Barron, Hindley, Winfield, Chapman, O'Kane, Newton, Lyons, Rees, Hilley, Cormack, S-Moore, SUB Richardson.

Sept 21st 1970, LC, H, v. Huddersfield Town, Win 2-0, Scorers Cormack, S-Moore, AT 15,818, Barron, Hindley, Winfield, Chapman, O'Kane, Newton, Lyons, Rees, Hilley, Cormack, S-Moore.

Sept 26th 1970, H, v. Leeds United, Draw 0-0, AT 31,475, Barron, Hindley, Winfield, Chapman, O'Kane, Newton, Lyons, Rees, Ingram, Cormack, Hilley, SUB McKenzie.

Sept 28th 1970, TC, A, v. Airdrie, Draw 2-2, Scorers Hilley, Cormack, AT 13,177, Barron, Hindley, Winfield, Chapman, O'Kane, Newton, Lyons, Rees, Ingram, Cormack, Hilley, SUB McKenzie

Oct 3rd 1970, A, v. Arsenal, Loss 0-4, AT 32,073, Barron, Hindley, Winfield, Chapman, O'Kane, Newton, Lyons, Collier, Ingram, Cormack, Rees, SUB McKenzie.

Oct 6th 1970, LC, A, v. Birmingham City, Loss 1-2, Scorer Hockey (O.G), AT 23,015, Barron, Hindley, Winfield, Chapman, O'Kane, Newton, Lyons, Richardson, Ingram, Cormack, Rees.

Oct 10th 1970, H, v. Blackpool, Win 3-1, Scorers Cormack, Lyons, Rees, AT 16,618, Barron, Hindley, Winfield, Chapman, O'Kane, Newton, Lyons, Richardson, Ingram, Cormack, Rees, SUB Robertson.

Oct 17th 1970, A, v. Coventry City, Loss 0-2, AT 25,418, Barron, Hindley, Winfield, Chapman, O'Kane, Jackson, Lyons, Richardson, Ingram, Cormack, Rees, SUB Collier.

Oct 24th 1970, A, v. Huddersfield Town, Draw 0-0, AT 17,121 Barron, Hindley, Winfield, Chapman, O'Kane, Robertson, Lyons, Richardson, Collier, Cormack, Rees.

Oct 31st 1970**, H, v. Tottenham Hotspur,** Loss 0-1, AT 25,301, Barron, Hindley, Winfield, Chapman, O'Kane, Jackson, Lyons, Richardson, Collier, Cormack, Rees.

Nov 7th 1970, A, v. Everton, Loss 0-1, AT 39,255, Barron, Hindley, Winfield, Chapman, O'Kane, Jackson, McIntosh, Richardson, Collier, Cormack, Rees, SUB Cottam.

Nov 14th 1970, H, v. Manchester United, Loss 1-2, Scorer Cormack, AT 36,373, Barron, Hindley, Winfield, Chapman, O'Kane, Jackson, Lyons, Richardson, Collier, Cormack, Rees.

Nov 21st 1970, A, v. Burnley, Loss 1-2, Scorer S-Moore, AT 13,013, Barron, Hindley, Winfield, Chapman, O'Kane, Jackson, Rees, Richardson, Collier, Cormack, S-Moore, SUB Lyons.

Nov 28th 1970, H, v. Derby County, Loss 2-4, Scorers Chapman, S-Moore, AT 30,539, Barron, Hindley, Winfield, Chapman, O'Kane, Jackson, Lyons, Richardson, Cormack, Rees, S-Moore.

Dec 5th 1970, A, v. Southampton, Loss 1-4, Scorer Cormack, AT 19,016, Barron, Hindley, Winfield, Chapman, O'Kane, Jackson, Lyons, Richardson, Cormack, Rees, S-Moore, SUB McIntosh.

Dec 12th 1970, H, v. Chelsea, Draw 1-1, Scorer S-Moore, AT 20,060, Barron, Hindley, Winfield, Chapman, O'Kane, Jackson, Lyons, Richardson, Cormack, Rees, S-Moore, SUB Cottam.

Dec 19th 1970, H, v. Ipswich Town, Loss 0-1, AT 14,085, Barron, Hindley, Winfield, Chapman, O'Kane, Jackson, McIntosh, Lyons, Cormack, Rees, S-Moore.

Jan 2nd 1971, FAC, H, Luton Town, Draw 1-1, Scorer McIntosh, AT 23,230, Barron, Hindley, Winfield, Chapman, O'Kane, Jackson, McIntosh, Lyons, Cormack, Richardson, S-Moore, SUB Rees.

First Division 1970-71

		Pld	W	D	L	F	A	Pts
1	Arsenal	42	29	7	6	71	29	65
2	Leeds United	42	27	10	5	72	30	64
3	Tottenham Hotspur	42	19	14	9	54	33	52
4	Wolverhampton Wand.	42	22	8	12	64	54	52
5	Liverpool	42	17	17	8	42	24	51
6	Chelsea	42	18	15	9	52	42	51
7	Southampton	42	17	12	13	56	44	46
8	Manchester United	42	16	11	15	65	66	43
9	Derby County	42	16	10	16	56	54	42
10	Coventry City	42	16	10	16	37	38	42
11	Manchester City	42	12	17	13	47	42	41
12	Newcastle United	42	14	13	15	44	46	41
13	Stoke City	42	12	13	17	44	48	37
14	Everton	42	12	13	17	54	60	37
15	Huddersfield Town	42	11	14	17	40	49	36
16	FOREST	42	14	8	20	42	61	36
17	West Bromwich Albion	42	10	15	17	58	75	35
18	Crystal Palace	42	12	11	19	39	57	35
19	Ipswich Town	42	12	10	20	42	48	34
20	West Ham United	42	10	14	18	47	60	34
21	Burnley	42	7	13	22	29	63	27
22	Blackpool	42	4	15	23	34	66	23

Jan 9th 1971, A, v. West Bromwich Albion, Win 1-0, Scorer: S-Moore, AT 20,015, Barron, Hindley, Winfield, Chapman, O'Kane, Jackson, Lyons, Richardson, Cormack, Rees, S-Moore.

Jan 11th 1971, FAC, A, v. Luton Town, Win 4-3, Scorers Cormack, Collier, Lyons, Rees, AT 23,483, Barron, Hindley, Winfield, Chapman, O'Kane, Jackson, McIntosh, Lyons, Cormack, Richardson, Rees, SUB Collier.

Jan 16th 1971, H, v. Newcastle United, Win 2-1, Scorer: S-Moore (2), AT 21,798, Barron, Hindley, Winfield, Chapman, O'Kane, Jackson, Lyons, Fraser, Cormack, Rees, S-Moore.

Jan 23rd 1971, FAC, H, Orient, Draw 1-1, Scorer S-Moore (Pen), AT 25,349, Barron, Hindley, Winfield, Chapman, O'Kane, Jackson, Lyons, Fraser, Cormack, Rees, S-Moore, SUB Collier

Jan 25th 1971, A, v. Orient, Abandoned, 0-0, AT 19,791, Barron, Hindley, Winfield, Chapman, O'Kane, Jackson, Lyons, Fraser, Collier, Cormack, S-Moore.

Feb 1st 1971, FAC, A, Orient, Win 1-0, Scorer Collier, AT 18,530, Barron, Hindley, Winfield, Chapman, O'Kane, Jackson, Lyons, Fraser, Collier, Cormack, S-Moore, SUB Rees

Feb 6th 1971, H, v. Southampton, Win 2-0, Scorers Collier, S-Moore, AT 18,009, Barron, Hindley, Winfield, Chapman, O'Kane, Jackson, Lyons, Fraser, Collier, Cormack, S-Moore, SUB Rees

Feb 13th 1971, FAC, A, v. Tottenham Hotspur, Loss 1-2, Scorer S-Moore (Pen), AT 46,336, Barron, Hindley, Winfield, Chapman, O'Kane, Jackson, Lyons, Fraser, Collier, Cormack, S-Moore, SUB Rees.

Feb 17th 1971, A, Chelsea, Loss 0-2, AT 19,339, Barron, Hindley, Winfield, Chapman, O'Kane, Jackson, Rees, Fraser, Cormack, Richardson, S-Moore, SUB Collier.

Feb 20th 1971, H, v. Burnley, Win 1-0, Scorer S-Moore, AT 20,873, Barron, Hindley, Winfield, Chapman, O'Kane, Jackson, Lyons, Fraser, Martin, Cormack, S-Moore, SUB Richardson.

Feb 24th 1971, A, v. West Ham United, Loss 0-2, AT 35,601, Barron, Hindley, Winfield, Chapman, O'Kane, Jackson, Lyons, Fraser, Martin, Cormack, S-Moore.

Mar 6th 1971, H, v. Huddersfield Town, Loss 1-3, Scorer Martin, AT 15,798, Barron, Hindley, Winfield, Chapman, O'Kane, Jackson, Lyons, Fraser, Martin, Cormack, S-Moore.

Mar 10th 1971, A, v. Tottenham Hotspur, Win 1-0, Scorer Cormack, AT 21,697, Barron, Hindley, Winfield, Chapman, O'Kane, Fraser, Lyons, Richardson, Martin, Cormack, Rees.

Mar 13th 1971, A, v. Manchester United, Loss 0-2, AT 39,339, Barron, Hindley, Winfield, Chapman, O'Kane, Fraser, Lyons, Richardson, Martin, Cormack, S-Moore, SUB Rees.

Mar 20th 1971, H, v. Everton, Win 3-2, Scorers Cormack (2), S-Moore, AT 21,643, Barron, Hindley, Winfield, Chapman, O'Kane, Fraser, Lyons, Richardson, Martin, Cormack, S-Moore, SUB Rees.

Mar 27th 1971, H, v. Crystal Palace, Win 3-1, Scorer S-Moore (3) (1Pen), AT 16,507, Barron, Hindley, Winfield, Chapman, O'Kane, Fraser, Lyons, Richardson, Martin, Cormack, S-Moore.

Mar 31st 1971, A, v. Derby County, Win 2-1, Scorers Richardson, S-Moore, AT 34,857, Barron, Hindley, Winfield, Chapman, O'Kane, Fraser, Lyons, Richardson, Martin, Cormack, S-Moore, SUB Rees.

Apr 3rd 1971, A, v. Wolverhampton Wanderers, Loss 0-4, AT 20,531, Barron, Hindley, Winfield, Chapman, O'Kane, Fraser, Lyons, Richardson, Martin, Cormack, S-Moore, SUB Rees.

Apr 9th 1971, A, v. Manchester City, Win 3-1, Scorers McKenzie (2), Jackson, AT 33,772, Barron, Hindley, Winfield, Chapman, O'Kane, Fraser, Jackson, Richardson, Martin, McKenzie, S-Moore.

Apr 10th 1971, H, v. West Ham United, Win 1-0, Scorer S-Moore, AT 23,032, Barron, Hindley, Winfield, Chapman, O'Kane, Fraser, Jackson, Richardson, Martin, Cormack, S-Moore, SUB Rees.

Apr 13th 1971, H, v. Arsenal, Loss 0-3, AT 40,692, Barron, Hindley, Winfield, Chapman, O'Kane, Fraser, Lyons, Richardson, Martin, Cormack, S-Moore, SUB Rees.

Apr 17th 1971, A, v. Blackpool, Win 3-2, Scorers Cormack, Hindley, S-Moore, AT 10,028, Barron, Hindley, Winfield, Chapman, O'Kane, Fraser, Jackson, Richardson, McKenzie, Cormack, S-Moore, SUB Rees.

Apr 24th 1971, H, v. Liverpool, Loss 0-1, AT 20,678, Barron, Hindley, Winfield, Chapman, O'Kane, Fraser, Jackson, Richardson, McKenzie, Cormack, S-Moore, SUB Rees.

Apr 27th 1971, H, v. Stoke City, Draw 0-0, AT 13,502, Barron, Hindley, Winfield, Chapman, O'Kane, Fraser, Jackson, Richardson, McKenzie, Cormack, S-Moore, SUB Rees.

May 1st 1971, A, v. Leeds United, Loss 0-2, AT 43,083, Barron, Hindley, Winfield, Chapman, O'Kane, Fraser, Jackson, Richardson, McKenzie, Cormack, S-Moore, SUB Rees.

May 4th 1971, H, CC, v. Mansfield Town, Loss 0-1, AT 9,022, Barron, Hindley, Winfield, Chapman, O'Kane, Fraser, Jackson, Richardson, McKenzie, Cormack, Rees, SUB Robertson.

Back Row: Tommy Cavanagh,Paul Richardson, Ian Moore, Jim Barron, Eric Hulme, Bob Chapman, Peter Hindley, John Winfield, Bob Davies
Front Row: Barry Lyons, Peter Cormack, Alex Ingram, Henry Newton, Liam O'Kane, Dave Hilley, Ronnie Rees

The squad reported back for pre season training with no new additions and worryingly no sign of any either. The club reported a deficit on the balance sheet of £192,000, this perhaps explained why. The money received from transfer fees had largely been spent and the club was making further provision for another fall in gate revenues.

Trainer Tommy Cavanagh was suddenly sacked without explanation, although he had been sidelined for months, (not good enough for Forest, he was later to turn up at Old Trafford). Bob McKinlay was now officially appointed first team trainer to replace him and the role of youth development officer was created for Alan Hill.

Although Ian Moore was offered and signed an unheard of four year contract, he says he was uneasy about the situation. "I was happy when the club showed how much they valued me with the contract offer, but it was clear that without new additions, we were only in for another season of struggle. Appointing Bob McKinlay as trainer might have seemed a good idea but in truth he didn't have the hardness or experience for the job. As a player he was exactly the same, quiet on the pitch, not a shouter or motivator and when he had been captain that responsibility had affected his game". At the League AGM Forest had raised the idea of Sunday football to halt the decline in attendances, it was thought that there was not a great deal of support for this proposal, but in the end the motion was only defeated by 25 to 23 votes. There was also concern at the growth of defensive football, the number of goals scored per game had dropped to their lowest level since the change to the offside law back in the 1920's and the First Division was the worst of all. Violent behaviour on the pitch was growing as financial rewards were increasing and it was announced that referees would be clamping down on the 'hard men'. Sammy Chapman particularly would have to watch his step, he already had a suspended ban hanging over him.

As in previous years, the club visited Germany for a couple of friendly matches. The one against Kaiserslautern was particularly memorable for Ian Moore as he was sent off for retaliation for the first and only time in his career, he had finally cracked after being roughed up all game.

Pre-season concluded with an entertaining 3-2 home win against Hannover 96, a couple of goals for Moore showed his fitness for the new season in the early evening Saturday fixture, timed not to

71-72

NOTTINGHAM FOREST FOOTBALL CLUB

DIVISION ONE 1971 - 72

Back row, left to right: MARTIN O'NEILL NEIL MARTIN ERIC HULME JIM BARRON JOHN COTTAM PAUL RICHARDSON IAN MOORE

Front row, left to right: JIMMY McINTOSH DUNCAN McKENZIE BARRY LYONS BOB CHAPMAN TOMMY JACKSON PETER HINDLEY TOMMY GEMMELL

MOORE SENT OFF— REDS LOSE

KAISERSLAUTERN .... 1 NOTTINGHAM FOREST 0

IAN MOORE was sent off as Nottingham Forest crashed to a 1-0 defeat against FC Kaiserslautern in West Germany last night. Moore received his marching orders after 30 minutes following a foul on one of the German players.

But even without Moore, Forest were able to hold their own and were unlucky to lose this friendly match.

... only goal came in the 28th ... when Hosic beat Barron, ... yed an outstanding game, ... direct free-kick.

Apart from Barron, there were outstanding performances from Bobby Chapman in defence and Peter Cormack in attack.

Deflected

Forest were quickly into the attack when the match started and it was against the run of play that the Germans took the lead when Hosic's shot was deflected off a defender in Forest's defensive wall.

Two minutes later, Moore was ordered off for a foul on Kaiserslautern defender Reinders.

Undaunted by Moore's exit, Forest kept up the pressure and it was only stout defence by the Germans which prevented an equaliser.

Poor finishing also played its part in Forest's downfall as the forwards failed to take a number of chances.

Kaiserslautern looked dangerous in their occasional breaks up-field but, apart from the solitary goal, were easily held by the Forest defence.

Kaiserslautern: Elting; Reinders, Schwager, Diehl, Rehhagel, Bitz, Friedrich, Hosic, Pirrung, Seel (Vogt), Ackermann.

Forest: Barron; Hindley, Winfield, Chapman, O'Kane, Fraser, Rees, Richardson (Jackson), Martin, Cormack, Moore.

TERRY HENNESSEY—his form was the highlight.

IAN MOORE — ordered off after a foul.

JIM BARRON — pla... outstanding gam...

Mansley on

Record en...

By NICK JORDAN

THE Notts. Junior Open Summer Lawn Tennis Tournament, which starts next Monday on The Park grass courts, has attracted a record entry of 160 youngsters from all over the Midlands.

And facing all the headaches of guiding this biggest ever entry through a total of 15 events, is Notts. youngest-ever tournament referee, 20-year-old Mike Elvin.

clash with the Charity Shield game a few hours earlier.

The Match of the Day cameras were present at Anfield to capture the opening day fixture against Liverpool and the first steps to stardom of Kevin Keegan, as Forest were humbled 3-1. Keegan who turned out to be a bargain £35,000 signing from Scunthorpe, had been on Forest's radar, but they had not considered him good enough. The line-up was the regular team from the previous season. Ian Moore had the honour of scoring the first goal of the campaign from the penalty spot. The defeat would have been far heavier but for an outstanding display from Jim Barron as Keegan and Toshack caused havoc.

The usual early season rush of fixtures meant that on Wednesday the Reds made the short trip to Leicester, newly promoted back to the top flight. Despite having by far the majority of the possession, they lost 2-1, Cormack with the goal, but it was a ridiculous own goal from Liam O'Kane that put City ahead. There was also the unusual sight of Matt Gillies watching the action from the touchline, rather than from his usual spot in the Director's Box. The manager had now bowed to supporters' calls and given Duncan McKenzie the opportunity to show what he could do with an extended run in the first team. This was going to give added flair, but would replacing the more hard working and pragmatic Paul Richardson weaken the team defensively? Early signs were promising as Duncan looked as if he was trying harder to be more of a team player.

Forest were to pick up their first win of the season in the next game against West Ham United, another penalty from Ian Moore, although they were grateful to Jim Barron once again for a string of fine saves to clinch the points. A crowd of only 17,000 showed what fans thought of the season's prospects.

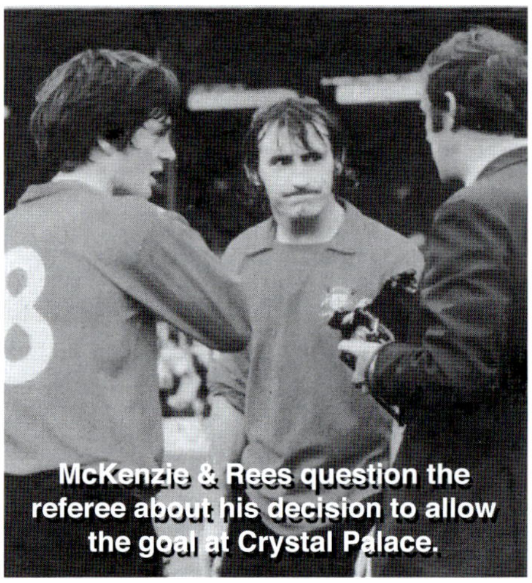

McKenzie & Rees question the referee about his decision to allow the goal at Crystal Palace.

The next fixture then presented them with a fine opportunity to build on that result, when they entertained Southampton a few days later at the City Ground. The Saints were another team forecast to struggle, but a 3-2 home defeat was to be a foretaste of what was to come, regularly scoring but defensive frailties would continually cost them dear. In fact Forest were two up against Southampton and battering them, but contrived to concede three goals all on the counter attack as they chased more goals. With the experience within the team, this was inexcusable.

A turgid 1-1 draw at Selhurst Park against likely relegation rivals Crystal Palace remains in the memory for only one reason. In the first half, the referee had awarded the home side a goal even though to everyone else in the ground the shot had clearly hit the side netting. The referee had overruled Forest's protests and it was not until Palace midfielder Steve Kember sportingly told the referee what had happened that he finally disallowed the goal.

Another draw at home to Stoke was followed by yet another 3-2 home defeat, when Sheffield United visited the City Ground. Again on the balance of play it was not deserved, the Blades scoring two goals in a minute during the second half as the home team laid siege. Newly promoted United were top of the League at this point in an unbeaten start to the season. Ian Moore had thrilled the crowd with a fine individual effort, firing home the opening goal after a mazy dribble from the right wing. Ian had switched wings in search of more action. Though he wore the number 11 shirt, there was far more to Ian's game than mere winger. He was a fine header of the ball with ability to shoot with both feet. Throughout his career he often played down the middle, the best

INTRODUCING...

Began his professional career with Aberdeen before being transferred to West Bromwich Albion in 1963. Joined Forest early this year, making 23 appearances.

Birthplace : **Busby, Lanarkshire.**
Birthdate : **8th December, 1941.**
Height : **5ft. 9ins.**
Weight : **11st. 12 lbs.**
Married : **Yes.**
Children : **Two daughters.**
Car : **Jaguar 3·4.**
Favourite player : **Willie Fernie.**
Favourite other team : **Aberdeen.**
Most difficult opponent : **Ian Moore.**
Biggest thrill : **Winning F.A. Cup.**
Favourite food : **Steak.**
I like : **People.**
I dislike : **Cruelty.**
Honours : **Two international caps.**
Personal ambition : **To be a millionaire.**
Professional ambition : **To win the league with Forest.**
Favourite singers : **Brooke Benton and Ray Charles.**
Hobbies : **Golf and Swimming.**
Best away ground : **St. James' Park.**
Worst away ground : **Turf Moor.**
Soccer dislike : **Being on the losing side.**
Best goal I've seen : **Norman Davidson's for Aberdeen against Hearts at Tynecastle (fantastic flying header from 20 yards).**

DOUG FRASER

One of the most outstanding Scottish players of the past decade with his former club, Glasgow Celtic, and with the national side for whom he has played in many international matches.

With Celtic he appeared in two European Cup Finals, once on the winning side—in 1966/67 when they defeated Inter Milan 2-1 in Lisbon—and on the losing end when three seasons later, 1969/70, they lost 2-1 (after extra time) to Feyenoord in Milan.

On both occasions he scored a goal and although he usually wears a "number three" shirt, he is equally at home in the middle defensive positions.

Birthplace : **Motherwell.**
Birthday : **16th October.**
Height : **6ft. 1inch.**
Weight : **12st. 12lbs.**
Married : **Yes (to Anne).**
Children : **One girl (Karen).**
Car : **Cortina 2000 GT.**
Favourite player : **Jimmy Johnstone**
Favourite other team : **Brazil.**
Most difficult opponent : **George Best.**
Biggest thrill : **European Cup win.**
Favourite food : **Italian.**
I like : **The Trent End.**
I dislike : **Female drivers.**
Honours : **18 full caps, eight League caps.**
Personal ambition : **To have my own business.**
Professional ambition : **To do well with Forest.**
Favourite singer : **Frank Sinatra.**
Hobbies : **Golf, shooting, fishing.**
Best away ground : **Ibrox Stadium.**
Worst away ground : **Benfica's.**
Soccer dislike : **Defeats.**
Best goal I've seen : **Ian Moore's (v. Arsenal, on Boxing Day).**

TOMMY GEMMELL

When Henry Newton joined Everton in October, 1970 Tommy was part of the player-plus-cash exchange transfer. Has now made 40 appearances for Forest.

Birthplace : **Belfast.**
Birthday : **3rd November.**
Height : **5ft. 7ins.**
Weight : **11st. 0lbs.**
Married : **Yes (to Viv.).**
Children : **A boy—Barry.**
Favourite player : **Doug. Fraser.**
Favourite other team : **Manchester United.**
Most difficult opponent : **Doug. Fraser.**
Biggest thrill : **Beating Leeds United in the F.A. Cup Semi-Final whilst with Everton in 1968.**
Favourite food : **Paella.**
I like : **Playing records.**
I dislike : **Smoking.**
Honours : **League Division One Championship Medal. Northern Ireland international.**
Personal ambition : **To win the pools**
Professional ambition : **To do well.**
Favourite singers : **Simon and Garfunkel.**
Best away ground : **Old Trafford.**
Worst away ground : **Turf Moor.**
Soccer likes : **Winning.**
Soccer dislikes : **Losing.**
Best goal I've seen : **Ian Moore's against Arsenal this season.**

TOMMY JACKSON

Had spells with Alloa, Queen of the South, and Hibernian before coming South to join Sunderland. Was transferred to Coventry City prior to joining Forest.

Birthplace : **Tranent, East Lothian.**
Birthday : **20th October.**
Height : **5ft. 10½ins.**
Weight : **11st. 10lbs.**
Married : **Yes.**
Children : **Three sons.**
Car : **Triumph 2000.**
Favourite player : **The late John White (Tottenham Hotspur).**
Favourite other team : **Rangers.**
Most difficult opponent : **Every centre-half.**
Biggest thrill : **Playing first time for Scotland.**
Favourite food : **Steak.**
I like : **Well-mannered Children.**
I dislike : **Gardening.**
Honours : **Three caps (two league, one Under-23).**
Personal ambition : **A happy family life.**
Professional ambition : **To play in the F.A. Cup Final.**
Favourite singer : **Tom Jones.**
Hobbies : **Cars and reading.**
Best away ground : **Upton Park.**
Worst away ground : **Turf Moor.**
Soccer dislike : **Defensive tactics.**
Best goal I've seen : **Geoff. Hurst's third in the final of the World Cup.**

NEIL MARTIN

Peter Cormack against Liverpool.

Duncan McKenzie unfortunately blocks an Ian Moore effort against Sheffield United...

Jim Barron keeps out a close range effort from John Toshack at Anfield.

Neil Martin glances the ball past Eric Martin in the Southampton goal.

EARLY SEASON ACTION!

Ian Moore in action against Stoke City.

Sammy Chapman with Martin Chivers (Spurs).

Neil Martin hurdles the German keeper in pre-season action.

Cormack is denied by Gordon Banks and a resolute Stoke defence.

Duncan McKenzie pounces to put the Reds one up against Chelsea in the League Cup.

MAC THE KNIFE

McKenzie thought he'd scored again but Webb clears off the line to deny him.

CORMACK FAITH IN FOREST FUTURE

by Robert Holmes

APART from the irrepressible Ian Moore, the one man in the Nottingham Forest team who can inspire them to escape from the relegation zone is ebullient Scottish international Peter Cormack.

Signed from Hibernian in March 1970 for £85,000, Peter has become one of the Football League's top Anglos. And he has proved beyond all doubt that top Scottish talent has the skill and flair to survive in the world's toughest League.

Unfortunately for Forest, their 25-year-old inside-forward star was out of action for seven weeks early in the season with torn ligaments and is only now beginning to produce his best form.

Says Peter: "Being out was a terrible blow. Having worked hard in the close season to get really fit I found I had it all to do again when the injury cleared up.

"But everything is fine now and I'm pleased with the way I'm playing, although I would like to get a few more goals."

Cormack scored more than 100 goals in an eight-year career with Hibs, but he readily admits goals are not that easy to come by in the First Division.

"It's a lot harder to get goals now," says Peter. "But I find I've managed to adapt myself to the First Division fairly well.

"It's faster down here, more competitive and more professional, but the players are no better as far as natural ability is concerned."

Tense

Peter admits that he sometimes misses Scotland—"I feel homesick now and then"—but there is one aspect of his past he is glad is over. While he was with Hibs he earned a reputation as a troublemaker on the pitch and suffered several lengthy suspensions.

"It was just frustration," explains Peter. "I was on the transfer list for two years. It seemed as though nobody would come for me or when they did something always seemed to go wrong. I suppose I was tense and let it run riot on the pitch.

"Now I'm at Forest everything is fine. I'm really happy here."

Peter's ambition is to win a trophy at the City Ground, but his immediate aim is to save the club from relegation. "I think we can escape," he predicts. "We've just started to hit form and that draw at Manchester City was a big boost to our morale.

"The basic problem earlier in the season was the centre of the defence. We've been scoring enough goals but we've been letting too many in.

"But Peter Hindley has been switched to centre-half and is doing well. And the signing of Tommy Gemmell has helped to bolster the back four as well.

PETER HINDLEY . . . Switched to centre-half

"Now this has been sorted out I see no reason why we should not stay up."

Cormack is equally as confident about the prospects of his other team—Scotland.

In recent seasons Peter has almost been an automatic choice for the Scotland squad. And the arrival of new manager Tommy Docherty has made no difference to his status.

He came on as substitute in Scotland's last international against Holland when he was still trying to regain his true form after that lengthy lay-off.

Beginning

Although Scotland lost 2-1, Peter sees a new era beginning for Docherty's men.

He says: "With a man as enthusiastic and talented as Docherty in charge, Scotland must now really come to the forefront of international football."

If Peter Cormack can help to save Forest and play a part in bringing much-needed glory to the Scottish team, he is assured of a brilliant future. His glowing talent deserves no less.

VAUXHALL CLIFTON

Football Post

NOTTINGHAM, SATURDAY, OCTOBER 30, 1971

Vol. LXIII. No. 12

FOREST PAY FOR PENALTY MISS

MIKE BEESLEY at the City Ground

YOUTH had its fling at the City Ground this afternoon and provided a crowd of over 37,000 with a feast of soccer excitement, but it was the experienced Derby County winger Alan Hinton who provided the only difference between the sides when he slotted in a penalty kick after 59 minutes.

ATTENDANCE: 37,170

Liam O'Kane, the Nottingham Forest back, falls after clearing the ball from the Derby County left winger Alan Hinton (right) at the City Ground this afternoon.

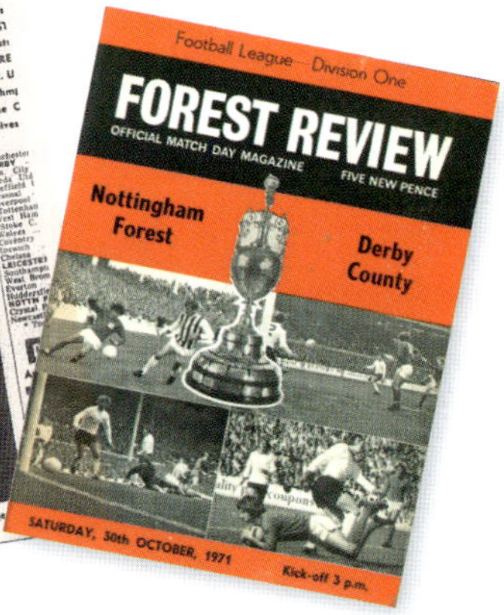

example of this being the 1967 FA Cup game against Everton when he moved inside to replace the injured Joe Baker. Ian cannot understand forwards who complain about 'lack of service'. "If the ball wasn't coming to me I went looking for it", he recounts, "as a forward, I felt it was my responsibility to make something happen. So by moving around, it presented problems for defenders marking me. I hate it when I see a forward, hands on hips, waiting for service on a plate".

Whilst talking to the press afterwards, Gillies said, "All we needed was a little luck". Although writers to the Football Post thought a couple of new defenders might be more useful.

After another draw away at Coventry, this officially became the club's worst start to a season for eleven years, plus there was also real concern about stay away fans, as the home average attendance had dropped by another 4,000. This was creating a vicious circle, a decline in revenue meaning that it was more likely that any remaining assets such as Ian Moore might have to be sold. The situation was not helped by the renaissance over the Trent at Notts County, even though they were playing in a lower league they were seen as a team on the up.

Nottingham as a football city is unique, in that there is not the fierce rivalry between its two clubs, often found in other cities. Throughout both clubs' existence there has been a history of fans following and attending both grounds and there has rarely been crowd trouble when the two sides have met. The various swings in fortunes have often meant that at a particular time in history, either club could claim to be the bigger and it was not until Forest's extended run of success from the late '70s that this cycle was finally broken.

Forest continued to have no trouble finding the back of the net, there were two goals in each of the next two games but only one point to show for it. Firstly a 2-2 draw at home to Manchester City, Moore and McKenzie for the Reds and then a 4-2 loss after leading at Wolves. Forest again were well on top with Ian Moore causing havoc and looking likely winners until a suicidal back pass from Chapman allowed McCalliog to nip in and give the home team the lead, with only thirteen minutes to go.

Alan Buckley

A 2-1 defeat to a poor Huddersfield outfit and with only 15,000 in attendance at such a vital match, should have set the alarm bells ringing, as Forest finally dropped into the bottom two. There were calls for the club to wheel and deal, the defence in particular needed to be shaken up but to the outside it seemed as if the club didn't recognise the mess they were in. Whilst the following week there were the usual letters advising the manager what team to pick, there was also one from Tunbridge Wells Red, 'I am pleased that there was no sign of the usual filthy language, apart from a song telling the Huddersfield supporters where they could stick their Yorkshire pudding'. M Smith of Nottingham wrote, 'The youngsters have to be given their chance, it is bad play that sees them concede so many goals, Gillies seems to have an excuse for every goal conceded'.

It was hoped that the League Cup might offer some respite from league woes. However following a 5-1 victory over Aldershot, they were drawn at home to Chelsea and despite a goal and a good showing from Duncan McKenzie, they were held to a draw and eliminated after a replay. The home game saw the last appearance for Ronnie Rees who left, with Swansea paying a club record fee of £26,000 for the player. Rees who had started the season in the first team had recently found himself out of favour, though it was still a surprise that he dropped three divisions.

Despite the number of goals conceded, the manager continued to have faith in the regular back four; Hindley, Winfield, O'Kane and Chapman. In fact they remained unchanged for 77 competitive games dating back to the 21st February 1970, before an injury to John Winfield ended the sequence. The resulting reshuffle saw Fraser dropping back to full back from midfield.

Although the ability and attitude of those players seemed all right, it is clear that without competition, performance levels are bound to drop. Even the most diehard supporters couldn't say there weren't periods when they should have been left out. Ever since Bob McKinlay was allowed to retire without being properly replaced, the central defensive position had suffered. Who was in charge of scouting at the club? Other top flight teams were raiding the lower divisions, Liverpool had taken Larry Lloyd from Bristol Rovers and West Ham bought Tommy Taylor from Leyton Orient to name but two.

The sequence of 3-2 defeats unbelievably continued in the next game as the Reds went down at home to Liverpool, with only 20,000 turning up for what was usually one of the season's most attractive fixtures. There were two superb goals from Ian Moore, one a twenty yarder and the other a lob from the tightest of angles. This was also probably the first game

The ball rebounds off Tommy Jackson past the Everton keeper to give Forest victory.

Francis Lee beats Jim Barron to put City ahead.

KEEPERS UNDER *STRESS*

Action from our game against Sheffield United.

Ian Moore fails to beat Rams' keeper Boulton from the spot.

Ian Moore narrowly fails to complete his hat-trick as his cross shot just misses the Liverpool goal.

FORES

PAUL RICHARDSON

LIAM O'KANE

PETER CORMACK

T ACES

IAN MOORE

NEIL MARTIN

BOB CHAPMAN

THE CLUB COMMITTEE
Back Row (left to right)-Mr. F. Chambers, Mr. H. Levey (Chairman). Mr. N. W. Crammond, Mr. B. J. Appleby, Seated-Mr. A. E. Chambers, Mr. A. Wood (Vice Chairman), Mr. J. H. Wilmer, Mr. H. W. Alcock, Mr. J. Glenn.

where there had been a mass exodus from the Trent End to the East Stand terraces and there was fighting as both sets of fans clashed before the game. The heavy handed policing in the Trent End was considered to be spoiling the fun and with the continuing decline in entertainment on the pitch, there was an increase in violence off it.

Supporters had been calling for the youngsters to be given a chance. Duncan McKenzie's run in the team returned six goals, but his form along with the teams was beginning to tail off as confidence fell after regular defeats. Gillies used the away fixture with Spurs, to introduce diminutive striker Alan Buckley for his debut, alongside other youngsters, Eric Hulme and John Robertson.

Kirkby in Ashfield born Buckley, had been a regular scorer for the reserves and youth team, but his lack of inches, he stood at only 5'6", raised concerns about his chances of competing in an increasingly physical sport. It turned out to be the most humiliating game of the season with Spurs beating Forest 6-1. The defeat in front of the TV cameras meant the club were now rock bottom and running out of excuses.

One person not to blame for this mess was keeper Jim Barron who had rediscovered his form. "I had a rocky patch the previous season, but now I thought I was in the form of my life. I thought we had a good team but things just wouldn't go right for us and after a couple of unlucky defeats at the beginning of the season the confidence just seemed to go".

That same day, a young Irishman was making his club debut in a reserve fixture against Leeds. Martin O'Neill had been signed from Irish club Distillery for £15,000, famously interrupting a law degree to pursue a career in football. He was not expected to press immediately for a first team place, but such was his progress and the team's form, he found himself in the first team only three weeks later. The player was spotted by Gillies playing for Northern Ireland when he had gone to watch Liam O'Kane. O'Neill had been expected to sign for Hull, but when Forest came in for him, he preferred the chance to play for a Division One team.

The humiliation at White Hart Lane finally persuaded Matt Gillies that he needed to re-organise the defence. For the next game away at Huddersfield, O'Kane was moved to right back and partnered with Doug Fraser, whilst Peter Hindley was moved alongside Chapman in the heart of the defence. Hindley had originally been a centre forward when beginning his career at the club in the early '60s, before moving back to centre half for a time, he had been used particularly in this position by Andy Beattie who played him as a third back wearing the number nine shirt in a tactical innovation. It was as a right back that he had made his name, but now the manager was hoping his more robust approach compared to Liam O'Kane could change the team's fortunes. The manager was immediately rewarded when a much improved defensive display allowed Forest to return from West Yorkshire with both points and a 1-0 victory courtesy of a Barry Lyons' goal.

Two defeats quickly followed though, the first a painful loss to title chasing rivals Derby, 2-0, after Ian Moore had a tame penalty saved by Colin Boulton and also saw a shot rebound off the post after a fine dribble. Derby were handed their lead when Chapman punched off the line and Hinton scored from the spot, this time the attendance was a healthy 37,000. The other defeat was away to Chelsea, again 2-0, where the team played well, controlling the game for long periods without scoring. It was becoming a recurring theme, play well, often score goals and still lose.

After scoring against Notts County in the Jack Wheeler testimonial game, Martin O'Neill's competitive debut came on the following Saturday at home to West Brom. The week's football news had been dominated by the on off transfer of Albion's Asa Hartford to Leeds United. The deal was finally called off, after a medical examination had discovered that the player was suffering from what was described as a 'hole in the heart'. Asa had previously shown no symptoms and was to continue enjoying a full career in football with no ill effects, even spending a short time with Forest in 1980.

The Trent End didn't cover themselves in glory that day, when Asa failed to return their sporting pre match applause, they burst into a rendition of: "There's a hole in your heart dear Asa, dear Asa."

On the pitch however it was a different matter as O'Neill inspired Forest to a crushing 4-1 victory, coming on as a substitute and scoring the second goal, a fifteen yard drive into the roof of the net. At this point the club had an almost identical record as the previous season, but they had scored twice as many goals, it was clear where the problems still lay. Despite the referee's clampdown, Sammy Chapman had somehow avoided trouble, that was until the end of November and the home encounter with Leeds. Although they had a reputation with most teams, their encounters with Forest always seemed particularly spicy. Sammy who was already under the threat of a six week suspension found himself embroiled in a battle with Mick Jones, the Leeds' centre forward. Things came to a head three minutes before half time, when the linesman brought the referee's attention to Jones lying face down in the penalty area with nobody near him. How many times had this scenario occurred over the years? The referee, without actually seeing the incident, decided to send Sammy off. The pair had history, three years before, the referee Syd Kayley had sent off the same player in similar circumstances during

Liam O'Kane was no stranger to injury

Vol. LXIII. No. 18

NOTTINGHAM, SATURDAY, DECEMBER 11, 1971

PRICE 3p

FOREST WIN BUT IT'S SO COSTLY!

MIKE BEESLEY at the City Ground

TOMMY JACKSON made a memorable return to the Nottingham Forest team after a two-month absence when he scored against his former club Everton this afternoon.

A bad-tempered match throughout, the game was marred midway through the second half when Forest full-back Liam O'Kane was carried off on a stretcher with a suspected broken leg after a tackle by Everton defender John Hurst.

Henry Newton, the former Forest captain, put the ball into the net but Everton's hopes for an equaliser were dashed when he was given offside.

ATTENDANCE: 18,639

Tommy Jackson, the former Everton player and new Nottingham Forest's outside right (left), crosses the ball as Henry Newton, of Everton, former Nottingham Forest captain, charges in at the City Ground, this afternoon.

a League Cup tie away at Barrow. With ten men Forest stood no chance, but they weren't helped by two awful O'Kane errors that gifted United their goals.

Martin O'Neill continued to make a good impression. After the Reds tamely fell behind 3-0 at Old Trafford, he scored with a twenty yard shot after coming on as a substitute, but despite Cormack adding another, the 3-2 reverse plunged Forest back to the bottom of the table. As Martin himself says, "I thought this game was all too easy".

There was another bad tempered affair with Everton during the last home game before Christmas. Liam O'Kane suffered a broken leg in a challenge with John Hurst. Remembering the incident Liam is philosophical, "It was a rough old game, challenges going in, especially with Tommy Jackson and Henry Newton up against their old sides. I just remember it being a fifty fifty ball and I came off worse. The referee gave him a severe lecture but didn't even book him. Up until then, I had hardly missed a game, after that it seemed to be one injury after another". Hurst later committed another bad foul on Cormack, again escaping a booking, whilst the Forest player was not so lucky, after he retaliated.

The game was won in bizarre circumstances as Henry Newton, whilst attempting to clear the ball, only succeeded in whacking it against the backside of Tommy Jackson and from there it rebounded past the helpless Everton keeper Gordon West and into the net.

With the loss of O'Kane, Gillies was forced to look for a replacement. He seemed to have come up with a coup when it was announced that Celtic and Scotland full back Tommy Gemmell was to join for what was considered a bargain £40,000 fee. Best remembered for his goal in the 1967 European Cup Final, he had recently fallen out of favour at Parkhead and at only twenty seven was looking to restart his career. Fans were a little perturbed after his first interview, when he was asked whether he had offers to join bigger clubs than Forest, he said yes but he wasn't ambitious and Forest had agreed to pay him the money that he had asked for.

Tommy made his debut against Arsenal on Boxing Day, who also paraded a new signing in Alan Ball, (complete with white boots) a £200,000 capture from Everton, but the game is best remembered by the 42,000 crowd present, for one of the finest goals ever scored at the City Ground.

Martin O'Neill

Ian Moore by his own high standards was not having the best of seasons, the burden of expectation was weighing heavily on his shoulders and in truth it just wasn't fun anymore. He was beginning to regret signing the new contract, although there were rumours that he was a target for one of the big clubs. However, on this day in front of a big crowd, the magic returned. Picking the ball up close to his own penalty area he then set off on a 74 yard run. (Luckily there was a film crew present to record the moment, so we can work out an exact measurement). He went scorching past the Arsenal defenders, until he found himself with only keeper Bob Wilson to beat. Ian then coolly slotted home, for what Ian himself describes as the best goal he ever scored. It was an effort fit to win any match, but Arsenal were a top side and the Reds had to settle for a draw.

Despite this positive result against the reigning champions and a creditable away draw at Maine Road against Manchester City on the first day of 1972, the League positioned worsened throughout January and February with an appalling run of results. Although it might have passed for bad luck, the similarity of defeats surely indicated that something was amiss.

Take the game against Crystal Palace for instance. The Reds attacked virtually non stop, but fell once more to a sucker punch as the visitors broke away for Willie Wallace to score with a diving header on the stroke of half time. Gillies once more bemoaning the team's luck. There was plenty of effort, but it was really only down to fine margins and the team lacked real quality in important positions. The fans would point out that quality had been sold and not been replaced. Ian Moore had played down the middle for this game but he was not as effective as when he was given licence to cut in from the wing.

Rumours about Ian Moore leaving were getting louder. Ian says, "I knew that the club had been approached and also a

Can you name these?...

Turn to page 266 for the answers

CITY GR

From the auth

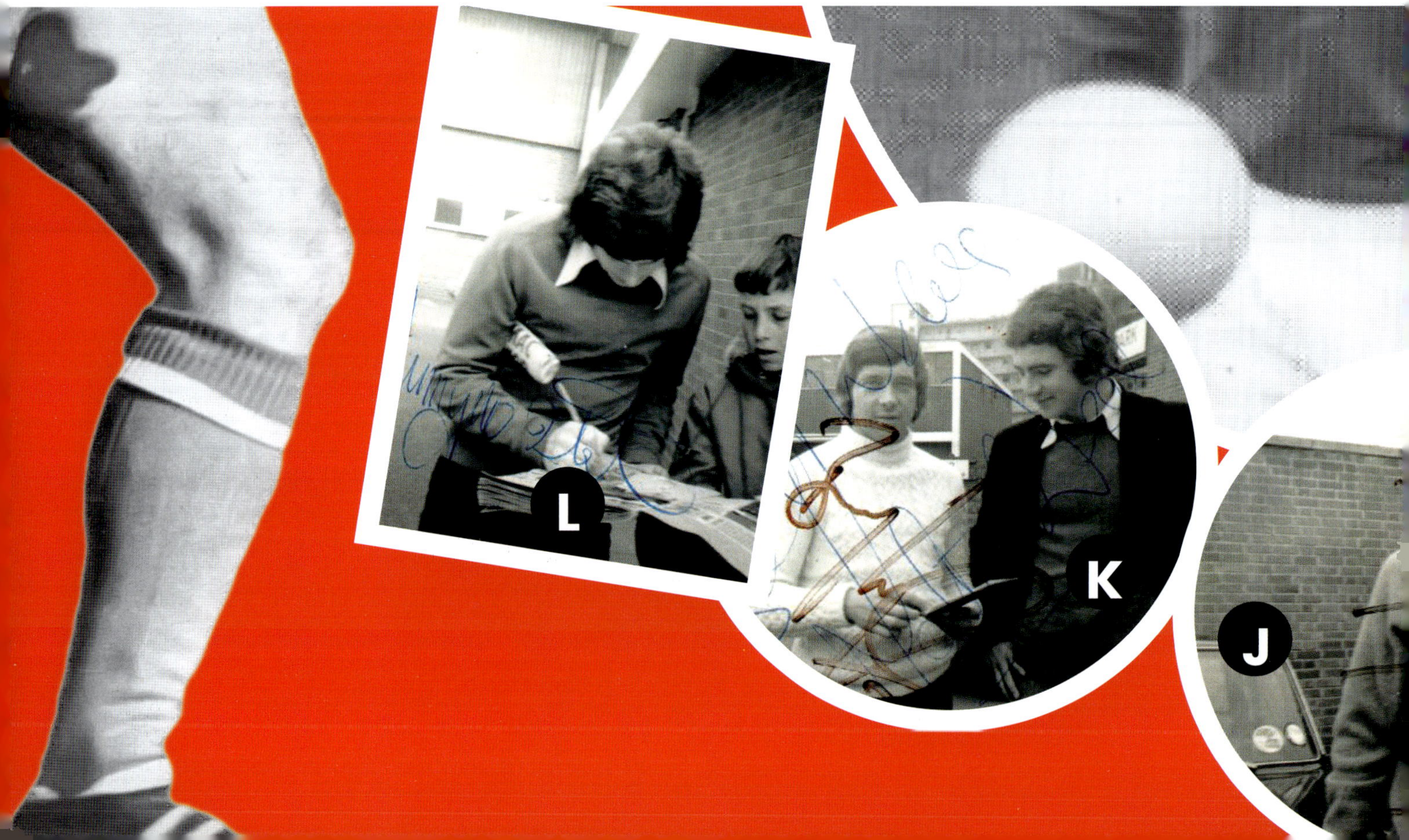

OUND STARS

or's own photograph album

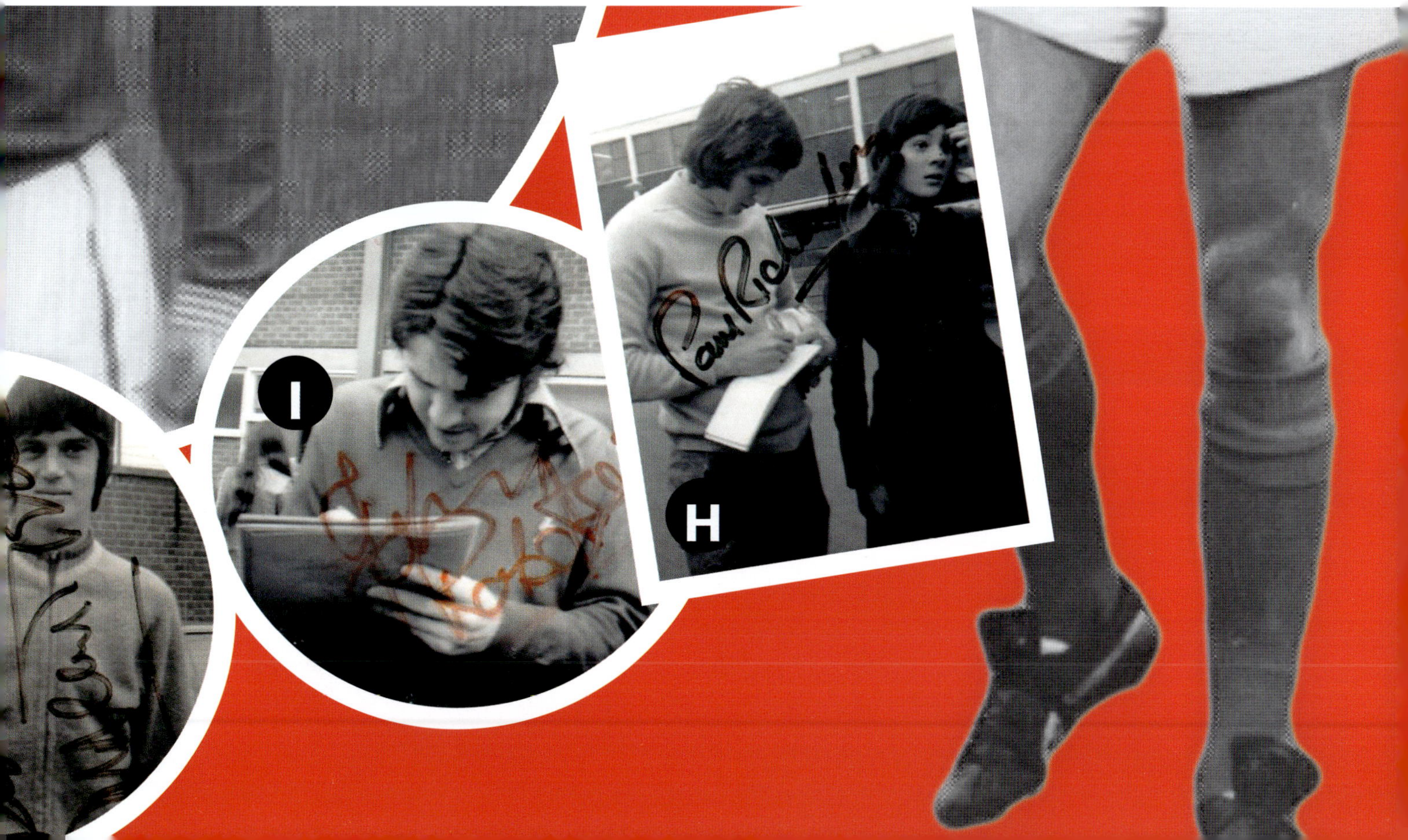

MOORE ON THE MARK

TUESDAY, DECEMBER 28, 1971

Great solo effort has crowd roaring

NOTTINGHAM FOREST .... 1 ARSENAL 1

IAN MOORE has scored some great goals in his colourful reign as top marksman for Nottingham Forest, but the one which earned the Reds a point against Arsenal at the City Ground yesterday, must surely rate as the best of his career.

by Mike Beesley

Picking up a headed clearance from Forest's new full back Tommy Gemmell after 15 minutes, Moore raced downfield to catch the Arsenal defence stretched and out of position. He dribbled past Pat Rice and weaved away from Frank McLintock before shooting low and wide of the advancing Bob Wilson.

...was a magnificent solo ...nd deserved the thunde... ...olade of the 42,750 ...nd also prompted ...hat Forest might ...win over their old

But the champions kept their heads and proceeded to play some vintage football which repeatedly reduced the Forest defence to panic measures, and it was no real surprise when they equalised after 38 minutes. George Armstrong broke clear on the right and although his low cross was a bad one, Paul Richardson mis-timed his chance to clear the ball and it went to George Graham, who picked his spot and curled a perfectly judged chip into the top corner of the net.

Chance missed

Alan Ball, who had a relatively quiet debut for Arsenal after his £220,000 signing from Everton, and Eddie Kelly scraped the crossbar with a first time effort from 20 yards.

Wilson also had to make several first class saves in the entertaining first half to keep out shots by Moore and Cormack but the Arsenal defence always looked safer than their Forest counterparts.

Referee George Hartley had been pretty hard on Forest in the first half, but it was Kelly who was the first player to go into his notebook after 52 minutes when he brought down Cormack as he was going clear.

A minute later Barron had to come out bravely to the edge of his penalty area to block a shot by Radford after a slack back header by Chapman.

Moore was only inches wide...

Blues are lucky

CHESTERFIELD 2
YORK CITY 1

CHESTERFIELD, who had fallen out of their challenging position in Division III, got back on the rails at the expense of lowly York City at Saltergate yesterday.

The Blues, whose previous three League games had ended in defeat, were given a tough passage by York.

Chesterfield took the lead with a fine goal from Kevin Randall after 29 minutes but York equalised in the 40th minute with Chesterfield's defence caught out of position.

Don Burluraux headed in a cross from Dick Hewitt and for a long time it seemed, with the game locked in midfield, that Chesterfield would be able to get no better than one point.

Then Randall, who had combined periods of lethargy with bursts of effective action, got through York's defence, only to be hacked down ... John Mackin... At...

Ian Moore, Nottingham Forest winger scores a brilliant goal — one of the best seen at the City Ground for many a season — against Arsenal at the City Ground yesterday.

Magpies ...

Debutants Tommy Gemmell & Alan Ball square up for the Boxing Day encounter.

Jim Barron saves from John Radford the Gunners' centre forward.

Cormack ends up in a heap against Newcastle.

Wallace scores a break away goal for Crystal Palace.

Hooligans taint club's good name

Mike Beesley on FOREST

NOTTINGHAM FOREST'S attendances are currently 1,000 down on last season's average gates, but chairman Jack Levey would gladly see this figure reduced a bit more if it meant the hooligans who seem intent on dragging the club's name through the mud stayed away from future games at the City Ground.

Incidents such as the stabbing of a Leeds United supporter last Saturday, reflect badly on Forest even though the trouble occurred after the end of the game and over half a mile away from their ground.

This was the second time this season a Reds' so-called supporter has been involved in a knifing incident and the increase in violence of this kind both before, during and after matches is a constant source of worry for the club.

Vicious

"I would like to welcome as many people as possible to the City Ground, but I would have no hesitation in saying hooligans who come to our matches just looking for trouble are not welcome and we would rather they stayed away.

"These kind of vicious young people only drive away other soccer fans who are not prepared to risk getting involved with them and this is a situation we would like to prevent.

"Unfortunately, even with the closest co-operation of the police, it is very difficult to keep out the troublemakers and we can only appeal to all those youngsters at the Trent End who give the team such loyal support, to avoid damaging the reputation of the club," said Mr. Levey.

Forest are far from alone in this difficult problem, but wouldn't it be a pleasant change if the Trent End lads decided to do something themselves about restoring the Reds' image, by proving they can show their loyalty without the attendant distasteful side-effects.

Linesman's view

Sammy Chapman's sending off in the Leeds match last Saturday is still very much a question of what one linesman believes he saw.

The referee, 20 of the players and, I venture to suggest, 99 per cent. of the crowd have been unable to throw much light on incident between Mick Jones and Chapman, which led to the Reds' defender getting his marching orders.

Naturally the club are very determined to do everything possible in their power to ensure Chapman's side of the story is fairly put at his appearance before the FA Disciplinary Committee.

Yet it could easily become a straight question of the linesman's word against Chapman's and this could leave Sammy out on a limb with the six-week suspended sentence already hanging over his head.

As one of the majority who did not see what happened, it would be wrong to comment on the incident, but I felt sorry for Chapman who has made a really conscious effort this season to stay clear of the trouble which has dogged his career.

Coincidence

PROGRESS

couple of people had a word in my ear, but I wasn't going to ask outright for a transfer. The rules back then said if you asked for a move, you forfeited your right to a cut of the transfer fee, so you had to wait for the club to make the first move".

As the club's position worsened so did the behaviour of the fans. Violence erupted in thecup game away at Millwall where the club suffered yet another humiliating defeat, this time 3-1 and the following game against Leicester City, another humbling 2-1 home defeat. Moore opened the scoring and the Reds held on to this early lead until the 85th minute, despite being under seige for the majority of the second half. Worse followed as Leicester grabbed a last minute winner when Hindley deflected the ball into his own net.

Violence reached a peak in a day of trouble at home to Tottenham. The Evening Post reported that Forest fans had gone on the rampage, attacking Spurs' fans and coaches in the Cattle Market car park, there were also several stabbings. Inside the ground there were further demonstrations against the board and manager in front of the Main Stand.

Inexplicably, not taking any notice of supporter's feelings, Chairman Jack Levy told the press that he had to persuade Matt Gillies not to resign after the Leicester defeat, the committee were so out of touch with the fan base. As supporters, we are all too quick to call for the manager's head, but Gillies should by now have been sacked. The responsibility was his, he had voiced no concerns publicly about the sale of the team's best players, he had then scouted for their replacements with an over emphasis on Scotland and after all, he had clearly stated that this was his team and he could be judged on how it performed.

Ian Moore told the Football Post that he had patched up his differences with the club after a clear the air meeting, but he was worried that his image as a good club man might have been harmed. Whilst it was also reported that bizarrely, some members of the committee were more concerned about the length of his hair and the damage it might do to the club's reputation.

The players had been taken to Bournemouth for a few days to take in the sea air before the Tottenham home game, this was a typical Forest ruse from years gone by, they had to try something to get a change. They were not joined by John Winfield who explains why. "I had lost my place to Tommy Gemmell and the manager told me I wasn't going to be part of his plans. Burnley came in with an offer for me and we agreed terms and I was to wait for the paperwork to be completed. I thought it was a done deal and began saying my goodbyes, but the phone never rang and then I picked up the papers and saw that they had signed Keith Newton from Everton and nothing ever was said. I just went back to training at Forest. I always had an up and down relationship with the fans, eventually I thought I had won them over, but during that relegation season there was a lot of blame thrown around".

Due to an injury to Gemmell, John was brought back for the away defeat to Derby, as the Reds were totally outclassed, although he did leave his mark on Kevin Hector as a brutal challenge provoked a free for all amongst the players. John Cottam was also drafted in as the Reds strung five across the back, but to no avail. This game turned out be the last time that Ian Moore pulled on the red shirt of Nottingham Forest, finally calling time on his career at the City Ground, his transfer virtually ensured that the club's stay in the top flight was over.

The transfer or non transfer of Ian Moore to Derby has gone down in folklore, so I think that there is only one person who can absolutely give the definitive story. So it's over to Ian himself, "The club had finally given the go ahead for my transfer and Liverpool, Everton, Arsenal, Man Utd and of course Derby came in for me. It eventually narrowed down to a race between Man Utd and Derby with United the favourites. I went off to Old Trafford to discuss terms, which were quickly agreed, but word came through that the two clubs couldn't agree a fee, so the deal was off. Brian Clough got wind of this and he immediately arranged a meeting at the Walton Hotel on the Friday. Matt Gillies and Ken Smales went down with me but they disappeared sharpish before Cloughie appeared. You must appreciate I had never before negotiated a deal like this, I was on my own. Brian Clough swaggered in, everything was going to be great, just sign this contract and we will fill the details in later.

He then said he was off to the City Ground to get Ken Smales to complete the paperwork, whilst I should remain where I was until he returned. Unknown to me, Forest had now got cold feet about the deal, as fans had got wind of where I was going and they refused to complete the deal. When Brian returned he acted as if everything had gone through and he took me away to the Railway Hotel in Derby where his team often stayed before games. He was attempting to cocoon me away and force Forest's hand. The next day, all the papers were full of deal off stories, but again Brian assured me everything was okay and I would be presented to the crowd as a Derby player that afternoon.

Now I know I can be accused of naivety, rightly so, but who was I to believe? Looking back now it is embarrassing to look at those pictures. After the game I was again taken back to the Railway Hotel to spend the night, before the next day, everybody realized the game was up and I went back home to Bingham. On Monday I received a call from Matt Busby saying Forest and United had now agreed a fee and we should get together to conclude a deal, which we did". It was not an incident that reflected well on all parties. Forest reported Brian Clough to the league and he was fined and warned over his future behaviour, whilst Forest in turn received a cheque for £180,000 rather than the £200,000 they had agreed with Derby. As

"I FELT LIKE I'D BEEN HUNG OUT TO DRY"

IAN MOORE

CLEMENT PIANOS
NOW IN STOCK
BALDWIN UPRIGHT
AMERICA
ZIMMERMANN GERMAN
FIRST NEW PIANOS IN THE MIDLANDS
19-23 DERBY ROAD, NOTTINGHAM

EVENING POST

No. 29,164 — NOTTINGHAM, SATURDAY, MARCH 4, 1972 — PRICE 3p

MANSFIELD SUTTON Edition

INDUSTRIAL OVERALL SERVICE by DAYBROOK Cleaners & Launderers

Clough lashes out after transfer shock

IAN MOORE . . . "I've signed for Derby."

BRIAN CLOUGH . . . "Staggered and dist

SIX DIE IN CAR PLUNGE

Heath warns on prices

MOORE'S MOVE TO DERBY: IT'S OFF SAY FOREST

By Post Reporters

IAN MOORE'S £200,000-plus transfer to Derby County is OFF, decided the Nottingham Forest committee after an emergency meeting today. Their decision followed 12 hours of mystery after Moore had been reported as signing for the Rams.

Forest secretary Ken Smales emerged from the committee meeting and issued the following statement: "Nottingham Forest have not assented to the transfer of Ian Moore to Derby County and the whole situation with regard to the transfer is still under discussion."

Agreement

No reason was given for the club's decision and Mr Smales, Forest manager Matt Gillies and members of the committee refused to comment further.

'Staggered'

17 die in plane crash

Lord Westwood

LEAGUE COULD STEP IN

Pits expect full output

Everton, Manchester Utd. lead cha

MOORE GOES WITHIN A WEEK SAYS GILLIES

Ian Moore

Matt Gillies

By MIKE BEESLEY

IAN MOORE will be transferred by Nottingham Forest before next Thursday's deadline, and Everton and Manchester United are the two clubs most strongly fancied to pay out a record £250,000 fee for his signature.

FRANK O'FARRELL—manager of Manchester United.

WAITING

Robinson preferred by Notts.

Tough cl to Nott and

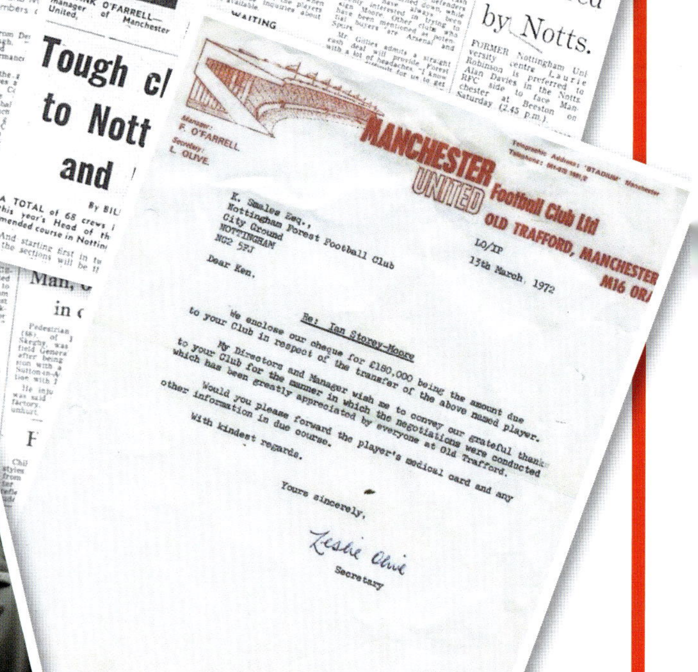

MANCHESTER UNITED Football Club Ltd
OLD TRAFFORD, MANCHESTER M16 ORA

Manager: F. O'FARRELL
Secretary: L. OLIVE

K. Smales Esq.,
Nottingham Forest Football Club
City Ground
NOTTINGHAM
NG2 5FJ

LO/IP
13th March, 1972

Dear Ken,

Re: Ian Storey-Moore

We enclose our cheque for £180,000 being the amount due to your Club in respect of the transfer of the above named player.

My Directors and Manager wish me to convey our grateful thanks to your Club for the manner in which the negotiations were conducted which has been greatly appreciated by everyone at Old Trafford.

Would you please forward the player's medical card and any other information in due course.

With kindest regards.

Yours sincerely,

Leslie Olive

Secretary

CLUB'S BEST ERA IN 107 YEARS IS ENDED

AFTER SEVERAL weeks of speculation and four days of farcical negotiation, Ian Moore finally packed his boots and left the City Ground this week, leaving behind the memory of many wonderful goals and the hollow feeling that this was the end of Nottingham Forest's fight to escape relegation.

Although statistically Forest can still claw their way to safety, most of their supporters will consider Moore's transfer to Manchester United for £200,000 as the end of the best era in the club's 107-year history.

Although the way in which the Moore transaction was carried out left a lot to be desired, the truth of the muddle between Forest and Derby County remains shrouded in

Barron puts up shutters

REDS BOW OUT WITH A POINT

EVERTON .... 1 NOTTINGHAM FOREST 1

NOTTINGHAM FOREST, already doomed to Division II next season ended their sad season on a commendable note by collecting a hard-earned point at Goodison Park last night.

For this they had to thank a gallant defensive stand.

Sparkling start for Tingay

Blues book place with the elite

JIM BARRON . . . standing ovation.

for the relationship between Ian Moore and Brian Clough, let Ian finish the story, "He never forgave me, he blamed me for not standing my ground, whereas he basically hung me out to dry, he thought he could get away with any old stunt. If he ever had to acknowledge me, it used to include a word beginning with B and ending in D".

By selling Ian Moore the club had virtually resigned itself to relegation. During the negotiations with Manchester United they had tried to persuade one of their players to move the other way, but nothing came of that and when you look at the paucity of their squad you were only likely to get a lightweight anyway, so transfer deadline day passed with no additions. What Forest had was what they had to go with.

Bad luck continued to dog the Reds. In the away encounter at West Brom, Barry Lyons recalls the referee telling the players he was going to abandon the match, but after Albion scored just before half time, he reneged on that and the second half was completed in farcical conditions.

Life after Moore began with a 2-0 home defeat to Ipswich in front of only 9,000 fans. The mood wasn't helped when the stadium announcer informed everyone that Ian had scored during the first half on his debut. In another terrible statistic, the only Forest player apart from Ian Moore to have scored in 1972 was Paul Richardson.

Ronnie Rees who had left Forest to return to Wales with Swansea was quoted in an article saying that, "Forest was like a holiday camp and that there was no discipline"', a far cry from the sergeant major days of Tommy Cavanagh.

Suddenly out of the blue came a ray of hope with two wins in three games. The first against a good Chelsea side and included two goals from Tommy Gemmell, one of them a thirty yard special. Plus there was an emphatic 4-0 win against Coventry, who were down there with Forest at the bottom. Gemmell, McKenzie and Richardson with two goals were the scorers. They couldn't possibly pull it off again could they?

Only four points from safety with seven games still to play. It was not unexpected when they crashed back down to earth with a 6-1 drubbing against Leeds and a 3-0 reverse against Arsenal, but with other clubs around stuttering as well, they were still in the same position after these games. The Reds' position was made more unbearable by the news that Derby went top on the same day as the Arsenal game. The team by now had a more youthful look about it, as injuries took their toll. Dave Serella came in for his debut against Arsenal and alongside John Cottam they were the central defensive partnership that would finish the season. The experiment of playing Hindley at centre half hadn't worked and he returned to the full back position.

John Robertson, Alan Buckley and Jimmy McIntosh were given extended runs as belatedly Gillies threw the youngsters in, as really he had nothing to lose. Unbelievably another two successive victories, Newcastle 1-0, scorer Peter Cormack and Stoke 2-0 scorers Gemmell once more and McIntosh, lifted the team off the bottom and within two points of safety with two more home games to follow. The Stoke victory was particularly fortuitous as the home team rested virtually their whole team to prepare for an FA Cup semi-final replay, but who cared.

Next up were Manchester United at the City Ground and the quick return of Ian Moore. There was a fear that Ian might return and score the goal that might relegate Forest. Ian himself didn't want to think about that. He knew he had to be professional but it would have broke his heart had it happened. As it turned out Ian had a poor game and the match fizzled out in a goalless draw. Jimmy McIntosh was the Reds' best player on the day, his darting runs providing some hope. The draw kept Forest in with a slim chance of survival, a fine crowd of 35,000 had given the team great encouragement, but they now needed to win the last two games.

Wolves provided the penultimate opposition. They were in the EUFA Cup Final, so it was hoped that they might have one eye on this competition, but the pressure of the occasion was too much for Forest as they slipped to a 3-1 defeat. Jim Barron having his worst game of the season and was at fault for two of the goals. So the fifteen year spell in the top flight was over. After flirting with relegation for several years the trapdoor had swung open and they had fallen through it. The final Division One fixture was away at Everton, Peter Cormack finishing his Forest career with a goal.

If fans thought it couldn't get worse, just wait. There was one final humiliation to come, a 3-0 hammering by Notts County in the County Cup that finally brought the curtain down on a terrible season.

Despite all the warnings, the club had been allowed to drift downwards, lacking leadership and direction. In truth the team had played better this season than in previous years, seven times they had scored two goals but failed to win. If they had just beaten Crystal Palace in the unlucky January defeat they would have stayed up on goal difference, but they had conceded 81 goals and Matt Gillies had not tried to address the problem until the season was almost halfway through. If the club had identified and brought in a quality defender they might have survived, particularly as they had scored goals. Martin O'Neill personally took relegation hard. Even as one of the younger players who had been at the club for a short time he couldn't understand how it had come to this, after all, they weren't bad players. Now was the time to regroup, could the team make an immediate return? Or would they fall even further, a fate that had befell teams such as Aston Villa and Sheffield Wednesday over recent years.

Most pertinently, would Matt Gillies be the man entrusted with making it happen?

FACTS and FIGURES

Aug 3rd 1971, F, A. v. Kaiserslautern, Loss 0-1, AT 8,000, Barron, Hindley, Winfield, Chapman, O'Kane, Fraser, Rees, Richardson, Martin, Cormack, S-Moore, SUB Jackson.

Aug 5th 1971, F, A, v. Hannover '96, Win 2-1, Scorers Richardson, Martin, AT 8,000, Barron, Hindley, Barron, Hindley, Winfield, Chapman, O'Kane, Fraser, Rees, Richardson, Martin, Cormack, S-Moore, SUB Jackson, McKenzie.

Aug 7th 1971, F, H, v. Hannover '96, Win 3-2, Scorers Martin (2), S-Moore, AT 6,829, Barron, Hindley, Winfield, Chapman, O'Kane, Fraser, Rees, Richardson, Martin, Cormack, S-Moore, SUB Jackson.

Aug 14th 1971, A, v. Liverpool, Loss 1-3, Scorer S-Moore (Pen), AT 51, 427, Barron, Hindley, Winfield, Chapman, O'Kane, Fraser, Rees, Richardson, Martin, Cormack, S-Moore.

Aug 18th 1971, A, v. Leicester City, Loss 1-2, Scorer Cormack, AT 32,079, Barron, Hindley, Winfield, Chapman, O'Kane, Fraser, Rees, McKenzie, Martin, Cormack, S-Moore, SUB Jackson.

Aug 21st 1971, H, v. West Ham United, Win 1-0, Scorer S-Moore (Pen), AT 17,185, Barron, Hindley, Winfield, Chapman, O'Kane, Fraser, Rees, McKenzie, Martin, Cormack, S-Moore.

Aug 24th 1971, H, v. Southampton, Loss 2-3, Scorers Martin, S-Moore, AT 14,350, Barron, Hindley, Winfield, Chapman, O'Kane, Fraser, Rees, McKenzie, Martin, Cormack, S-Moore, SUB Jackson.

Aug 28th 1971, A, v. Crystal Palace, Draw 1-1, Scorer McKenzie, AT 17,699, Barron, Hindley, Winfield, Chapman, O'Kane, Fraser, Rees, McKenzie, Martin, Cormack, S-Moore.

Aug 31st 1971, H, v. Stoke City, Draw 0-0, AT 19,017, Barron, Hindley, Winfield, Chapman, O'Kane, Fraser, Rees, McKenzie, Cormack, Jackson, S-Moore.

Sept 4th 1971, H, v. Sheffield United, Loss 2-3, Scorers S-Moore, Martin, AT 27,041, Barron, Hindley, Winfield, Chapman, O'Kane, Fraser, Rees, McKenzie, Martin, Cormack, S-Moore, SUB Jackson

Sept 7th 1971, LC, H, v. Aldershot, Win 5-1, Scorers McKenzie (2), Martin, Fraser, Cormack, AT 8,380, Barron, Hindley, Winfield, Chapman, O'Kane, Fraser, Jackson, McKenzie, Martin, Cormack, S-Moore, SUB McCaffrey.

Sept 11th 1971, A, v. Coventry City, Draw 1-1, Scorer Cormack, AT 20,380, Barron, Hindley, Winfield, Chapman, O'Kane, Fraser, Jackson, McKenzie, Martin, Cormack, S-Moore, SUB Richardson.

Sept 18th 1971, H, v. Manchester City, Draw 2-2, Scorers McKenzie, S-Moore (Pen), AT 21,488, Barron, Hindley, Winfield, Chapman, O'Kane, Fraser, Jackson, McKenzie, Martin, Cormack, S-Moore.

Sept 25th 1971, A, v. Wolverhampton Wanderers, Loss 2-4, Scorers S-Moore (Pen), Martin, AT 20,631, Barron, Hindley, Winfield, Chapman, O'Kane, Fraser, Jackson, McKenzie, Martin, Cormack, S-Moore, SUB Lyons.

Oct 2nd 1971, H, v. Huddersfield Town, Loss 1-2, Scorer McKenzie, AT 15,693, Barron, Hindley, Winfield, Chapman, O'Kane, Fraser, Lyons, McKenzie, Martin, Jackson, S-Moore, SUB Richardson.

Oct 6th 1971, LC, H, v. Chelsea, Draw 1-1, Scorer McKenzie, AT 16,811, Barron, Hindley, Winfield, Chapman, O'Kane, Fraser, Lyons, McKenzie, Martin, Jackson, S-Moore, SUB Rees

Oct 9th 1971, A, v. Ipswich Town, Draw 1-1, Scorer S-Moore, AT 16,285, Barron, Hindley, Winfield, Chapman, O'Kane, Richardson, Lyons, McKenzie, Martin, Jackson, S-Moore.

Oct 11th 1971, LC, A, v. Chelsea, Loss 1-2, Scorer S-Moore, AT 24,817, Hulme, Hindley, Winfield, Chapman, O'Kane, Richardson, Lyons, McKenzie, Martin, Jackson, S-Moore, SUB White.

Oct 16th 1971, H, v. Liverpool, Loss 2-3, Scorer S-Moore (2), AT 20,945, Hulme, Hindley, Winfield, Chapman, O'Kane, Richardson, Lyons, McKenzie, Martin, Jackson, S-Moore, SUB Robertson.

Oct 23rd 1971, A, v. Tottenham Hotspur, Loss 1-6, Scorer Richardson, AT 35,846, Hulme, Hindley, Fraser, Chapman, O'Kane, Richardson, Lyons, McKenzie, Martin, Robertson, S-Moore, SUB Buckley.

Oct 26th 1971, A, v. Huddersfield Town, Win 1-0, Scorer Lyons, AT 9,459, Hulme, O'Kane, Fraser, Chapman, Hindley, Richardson, Lyons, McKenzie, Buckley, Robertson, S-Moore.

Oct 30th 1971, H, v. Derby County, Loss 0-2, AT 37,170, Hulme, O'Kane, Fraser, Chapman, Hindley, Richardson, Lyons, McKenzie, Buckley, Robertson, S-Moore.

Nov 6th 1971, A, v. Chelsea, Loss 0-2, AT 25,812, Hulme, O'Kane, Fraser, Chapman, Hindley, Richardson, Lyons, McKenzie, Buckley, Robertson, S-Moore, SUB McIntosh.

Nov 13th 1971, H, v. West Bromwich Albion, Win 4-1, Scorers Richardson, O'Neill, McKenzie, S-Moore, AT 20,024, Barron, O'Kane, Fraser, Chapman, Hindley, Richardson, Lyons, McKenzie, Cormack, Robertson, S-Moore, SUB O'Neill.

Nov 20th 1971, A, v. Newcastle United, Loss 1-2, Scorer Cormack, AT 24,583, Barron, O'Kane, Fraser, Chapman, Hindley, Richardson, Lyons, McKenzie, Cormack, O'Neill, S-Moore, SUB Martin.

Nov 27th 1971, H, v. Leeds United, Loss 0-2, AT 29,463, Barron, O'Kane, Fraser, Chapman, Hindley, Richardson, Lyons, Robertson, Cormack, O'Neill, S-Moore, SUB Martin.

Dec 4th 1971, A, v. Manchester United, Loss 2-3, Scorers Cormack, O'Neill, AT 45,048, Barron, O'Kane, Fraser, Chapman, Hindley, Richardson, Lyons, Robertson, Martin, Cormack, S-Moore, SUB O'Neill.

Dec 11th 1971, H, v. Everton, Win 1-0, Scorer Jackson, AT 18,639, Barron, O'Kane, Fraser, Chapman, Hindley, Richardson, Jackson, O'Neill, Martin, Cormack, S-Moore, SUB McKenzie.

Dec 18th 1971, A, v. Sheffield United, Loss 1-2, Scorer Martin, AT 27,663, Barron, Fraser, Winfield, Chapman, Cottam, Richardson, Jackson, O'Neill, Martin, Cormack, S-Moore.

Dec 27th 1971, H, v. Arsenal, Draw 1-1, Scorer S-Moore, AT 42,750, Barron, Fraser, Gemmell, Chapman, Hindley, Richardson, Jackson, O'Neill, Martin, Cormack, S-Moore,

First Division 1971-72

		Pld	W	D	L	F	A	Pts
1	Derby County	42	24	10	8	69	33	58
2	Leeds United	42	24	9	9	73	31	57
3	Liverpool	42	24	9	9	64	30	57
4	Manchester City	42	23	11	8	77	45	57
5	Arsenal	42	22	8	12	58	40	52
6	Tottenham Hotspur	42	19	13	10	63	42	51
7	Chelsea	42	18	12	12	58	49	48
8	Manchester United	42	19	10	13	69	61	48
9	Wolverhampton Wand.	42	18	11	13	65	57	47
10	Sheffield United	42	17	12	13	61	60	46
11	Newcastle United	42	15	11	16	49	52	41
12	Leicester City	42	13	13	16	41	46	39
13	Ipswich Town	42	11	16	15	39	53	38
14	West Ham United	42	12	12	18	47	51	36
15	Everton	42	9	18	15	37	48	36
16	West Bromwich Albion	42	12	11	19	42	54	35
17	Stoke City	42	10	15	17	39	56	35
18	Coventry City	42	9	15	18	44	67	33
19	Southampton	42	12	7	23	52	80	31
20	Crystal Palace	42	8	13	21	39	65	29
21	FOREST	42	8	9	25	47	81	25
22	Huddersfield Town	42	6	13	23	27	59	25

Jan 1st 1972, A, v. Manchester City, Draw 2-2, Scorers Richardson, Martin, AT 38,777, Barron, Fraser, Gemmell, Chapman, Hindley, Richardson, Lyons, Jackson, Martin, Cormack, S-Moore.

Jan 8th 1972, H, v. Crystal Palace, Loss 0-1, AT 19,033, Barron, Fraser, Gemmell, Chapman, Hindley, Richardson, Lyons, Jackson, Martin, McKenzie, S-Moore, SUB O'Neill.

Jan 15th 1972, FAC, A, v. Millwall, Loss 1-3, Scorer Richardson, AT 17,940, Barron, Fraser, Gemmell, Chapman, Hindley, Cottam, McIntosh, Lyons, Cormack, Richardson, S-Moore.

Jan 22nd 1972, H, v. Leicester City, Loss 1-2, Scorer S-Moore, AT 27,250, Barron, Fraser, Gemmell, Chapman, Hindley, Cottam, McIntosh, Robertson, Cormack, Richardson, S-Moore.

Jan 29th 1972, A, v. Southampton, Loss 1-4, Scorer S-Moore, AT 17,043, Barron, Fraser, Gemmell, Chapman, Hindley, Cottam, McIntosh, Robertson, Cormack, Richardson, S-Moore, SUB McKenzie.

Feb 12th 1972, H, v. Tottenham Hotspur, Loss 0-1, AT 20,209, Barron, Fraser, Gemmell, Chapman, Hindley, Cottam, McIntosh, Lyons, Cormack, Richardson, S-Moore, SUB O'Neill.

Feb 19th 1972, A, v. Derby County, Loss 0-4, AT 31,801, Barron, Gemmell, Winfield, Chapman, Hindley, Cottam, Lyons, O'Neill, Cormack, Richardson, S-Moore.

Mar 4th 1972, A, v. West Bromwich Albion, Loss 0-1, AT 16,702, Barron, Hindley, Gemmell, Chapman, Cottam, Fraser, Lyons, O'Neill, Cormack, Richardson, McKenzie.

Mar 11th 1972, H, v. Ipswich Town, Loss 0-2, AT 9,872, Barron, Gemmell, Winfield, Chapman, Cottam, Fraser, Lyons, O'Neill, Cormack, Richardson, McKenzie, SUB McIntosh.

Mar 14th 1962, H, v. Chelsea, Win 2-1, Scorer Gemmell (2)(1Pen), AT 13,349, Barron, Hindley, Gemmell, Chapman, Cottam, Fraser, Lyons, O'Neill, Buckley, Richardson, McKenzie.

Mar 18th 1972, A, v. West Ham United, Loss 2-4, Scorer McKenzie (2), AT 20,960, Barron, Hindley, Gemmell, Chapman, Cottam, Fraser, Lyons, O'Neill, Buckley, Richardson, McKenzie, SUB McIntosh.

Mar 25th 1972, H, v. Coventry City, Win 4-0, Scorers Gemmell, McKenzie, Richardson (2), AT 12,205, Barron, Hindley, Gemmell, Serella, Cottam, Robertson, McIntosh, Cormack, Buckley, Richardson, McKenzie.

Mar 27th 1972, A, v. Leeds United, Loss 1-6, Scorer Cormack, AT 40,866, Barron, Hindley, Gemmell, Serella, Cottam, Robertson, McIntosh, Cormack, Buckley, Richardson, McKenzie.

Apr 1st 1972, A, v. Arsenal, Loss 0-3, AT 33,895, Barron, Hindley, Gemmell, Serella, Cottam, Robertson, McIntosh, Cormack, Buckley, Richardson, McKenzie, SUB O'Neill.

Apr 8th 1972, H, v. Newcastle United, Win 1-0, Scorer Cormack, AT 12,470, Barron, Hindley, Gemmell, Serella, Cottam, Fraser, McIntosh, Cormack, Buckley, Richardson, McKenzie.

Apr 10th 1972, A, v. Stoke City, Win 2-0, Scorers Gemmell, McIntosh, AT 13,907, Barron, Hindley, Gemmell, Serella, Cottam, Fraser, McIntosh, Cormack, Martin, Richardson, McKenzie.

Apr 22nd 1972, H, v. Manchester United, Draw 0-0, AT 35,063, Barron, Hindley, Gemmell, Serella, Cottam, Fraser, McIntosh, Cormack, Martin, Richardson, McKenzie.

Apr 25th 1972, H, v. Wolverhampton Wanderers, Loss 1-3, Scorer Gemmell, AT 16,889, Barron, Hindley, Gemmell, Serella, Cottam, Fraser, McIntosh, Cormack, Martin, Richardson, McKenzie..

May 2nd 1972, A, v. Everton, Draw 1-1, Scorer Cormack, AT 21,513, Barron, Hindley, Winfield, Serella, Cottam, Fraser, McIntosh, Cormack, Martin, Richardson, McKenzie, SUB O'Neill.

May 10th 1972, CC, A, v. Notts County, Loss 0-3, AT 11,273, Barron, Hindley, Gemmell, Serella, Cottam, Fraser, McIntosh, Cormack, Martin, Richardson, O'Neill, SUB McKenzie.

Back Row: John Winfield, Paul Richardson, Neil Martin, John Cottam, Liam O'Kane, Duncan McKenzie
Middle Row: John Robertson, Bob Chapman, Eric Hulme, Jim Barron, Peter Hindley, Jimmy McIntosh
Front Row: Ronnie Rees, Ian Moore, Doug Fraser, Tommy Jackson, Barry Lyons, Peter Cormack

Of course relegation hit Nottingham Forest hard. Billy Walker had spent many years reshaping the club until they had finally achieved promotion in 1957. Money was always tight, but with prudent management the club were always able put out a competitive team, sticking closely to the Nottingham Forest philosophy of playing the right way. There was even an FA Cup victory to savour.

A change of emphasis in the early 1960's to develop home grown talent, had seen many fine youngsters, such as Ian Moore and Henry Newton reach the first team and along with a better quality of signing, real progress was made in ensuring that Forest were seen as an established Division One Club. This culminated in the fantastic 1966/67 season, when they attained their highest ever league position and reached thecup semi final. Crowds were regularly over 40,000, the coffers were full and there were plans to build a super stadium on the banks of the River Trent and compete with the best.
So where did it all go wrong? The rot set in almost as soon as the final whistle blew in 1967. By adopting a penny pinching attitude with players' wages and bonuses, what should have been a great time was sullied as half the team refused the terms offered and the morale was punctured.
The team should have been strengthened, the money was there, but in fact by the time the new season kicked off the squad was weaker, with a couple of fringe players leaving, to be followed by Alan Hinton. Whereas the team had been lucky with injuries, now several players were missing, in particular John Barnwell and there were doubts about Joe Baker's fitness after a long lay-off.

History would show the absolute turning point was the signing of Jim Baxter from Sunderland for the club's first £100,000 purchase. Chairman Tony Wood had let the glamour go to his head and boasted in print and person that Forest would sign the first top class player available. Instead of listening to manager Johnny Carey, they purchased Jim Baxter after seeing him on one of his few good games, as Sunderland beat the Reds. Within eighteen months he was released on a free transfer, Carey was sacked as the scapegoat and the committee from that day on, acted like rabbits caught in the headlights as they began selling off the club's best players whilst reverting back to the old philosophy of journeyman signings. The decline may have taken a few years but it was inexorable and came as a shock to no-one in football, except

72-73

NOTTINGHAM FOREST FOOTBALL CLUB

DIVISION TWO 1972 - 73

Back row, left to right: DAVE SERELLA JOHN COTTAM DUNCAN McKENZIE ERIC HULME JIM BARRON JOHN ROBERTSON ALAN BUCKLEY TOMMY JACKSON

Middle row, left to right: BARRY LYONS MARTIN O'NEILL TOMMY GEMMELL NEIL MARTIN PAUL RICHARDSON BOB CHAPMAN JOHN WINFIELD

Front row, left to right: DOUG FRASER LIAM O'KANE PETER HINDLEY JIMMY McINTOSH GEORGE LYALL

Bob McKinlay puts the players through their paces, pre-season at Wollaton Park.

Forest fans make their feelings known, as Matt Gillies sits impassively in the Main Stand.

have been appar...

It seems that everyone at the club still regards last season's fiasco as something which just happened, and as something no-one could really help or do anything to avoid, but this is just refusing to acknowledge the unpleasant truth.

The quicker the Forest committee, management and players accept their joint responsibility for the failings which ended the Reds' 15-year lease on Division I football, the sooner they might start again to work out a way of putting things right.

Spend now — it's urgent Forest

By Mike Beesley

POOR FORM

The only positive things to emerge from last Saturday's game were on the debit side. While the lack of height and experience up front was fairly predictable, the poor form shown by the midfield trio of George Lyall, Paul Richardson and John Robertson was not so obvious and far more disconcerting.

Lyall started well enough in his League debut for the Reds but never showed the flair he had displayed against Kaiserslautern, while Richardson was well below his best form.

With Peter Hindley unfit, Doug Fraser switched to full back, and there is no doubt Forest missed the Scot's drive and ability to win the ball in midfield for Robertson only hovered on the fringes of the match.

Manager Matt Gillies is ... finishing power up front, and although he praised Martin O'Neill for his non-stop effort, it must be stressed the full potential of the young Irishman will not be realised until he has adequate support alongside him.

FRESH IDEAS

Without under-estimating the problems involved, Mr. Gillies must surely spend some of the transfer money Forest have accumulated over the past six months, and use it to bring fresh ideas and ...

It was disturbing to see how the Reds' drive faded after the interval and long before the end they looked a jaded outfit, allowing a far from inspired Portsmouth side to come right into the game and even threaten to snatch a winning goal.

It must not be forgotten also that Portsmouth would have ... Piper had slotted in his first half penalty kick instead of slicing it wide, so everything taken into account it was not a very satisfactory start for Forest.

ILLUSION

With the reserve team going down 2-0 at Blackpool, and the youth team losing by a single goal in their first Midland Intermediate League Cup game, it was an inauspicious beginning to the season all round.

If Forest were suffering from the illusion that Division II football would be easy they can have no such thoughts left now, and they will do well to remember that Portsmouth have been freely tipped for relegation this season.

Portsmouth had little to offer except resolute defence, but this was more than enough to stifle the uninspired Reds attacks, and augured badly for the games ahead against promotion geared teams like Millwall, Aston Villa and Middlesbrough.

Forest never played as ... they really knew what ... expected from them, and ... was this lack of method ...

obviously enthusiastic, but Forest, who already had a decent stadium opposed the idea. Pre-season consisted of some hard running around Wollaton Park followed by a couple of games, the first a 2-0 victory away at Watford before taking on Kaiserslautern from Germany at the City Ground. Due to the lack of signings the team had a familiar look about it.

As the new season's fixtures were released, the reality of the club's situation sank in, an opening day fixture against Portsmouth, followed by Oxford, Carlisle and Brighton hardly set the pulses racing.

Tommy Gemmell had been handed the captain's role after Peter Hindley declined it and immediately launched into a, "We can get promotion", rallying speech. In truth his performances hadn't lived up to the expectations generated by signing an ex Celtic European Cup Winner, although he was a very popular figure with his team mates. As usual, the opening day's fixture took place on a baking hot August day. It was easier than normal to get autographs as the Pompey players strolled down to the ground after lunching at the Bridgford Hotel, that was situated where the council offices until recently were, just fifty yards from the ground.

A crowd of only 13,000 greeted the two teams, with very few supporters making the trip up from the south coast. Small away followings were to be a feature of this season. Portsmouth an average Division Two outfit would give fans a chance to gauge the quality of opposition Forest would be coming up against. Bearing in mind the poor record that Forest had had against similar opposition in cup competitions, it was hoped that they could quickly come to terms with the division. The club thought that if they could get off to a good start, attendances might hold up, but with the lack of new players the signs weren't good.

Dave Serella kept his place, first alongside Chapman before resuming his partnership with John Cottam. John Robertson started in central midfield wearing the number six shirt alongside George Lyall, Paul Richardson and Martin O'Neill. Whilst the only goal threat seemed to come from Duncan McKenzie, who had been handed the number nine shirt as Neil Martin was still out of favour. The game turned out to be a boring 0-0 draw, Forest quickly running out of ideas, it could have been worse, Norman Piper missed a first half penalty for Portsmouth. On a more mundane note, the Football Post broke

the Forest Committee, when relegation finally came. It was made far worse because of the sharp contrast with what was happening just fifteen miles down the A52. A young charismatic manager and a little investment saw Derby change from a backward outfit, to League Champions in only five years.

It didn't look as if there was any hope of a quick return. Peter Cormack, the absolutely last valuable playing asset was sold to Liverpool for £110,000, meaning that the fans could clearly see that with the unspent Moore money, there should be over £300,000 in the kitty that could be invested. So they waited, surely there had to be some transfer activity, something to stir the interest of supporters, but it was not until late summer and the signing of George Lyall from Preston for a fee of £40,000, that there was any movement in.

George was well regarded in the game, a real bundle of energy and Forest hoped he would emulate the success of Archie Gemmill, who Derby had signed from the same team, but he was to be the only signing and unlikely to make a big difference on his own.

George remembers the transfer. "I didn't want to move to be honest, I was settled in Preston with a new family, but the chairman came and insisted, he said that the club was desperate for money and it would be doing him a favour if I went. When I arrived for training in Nottingham, they seemed a decent bunch of lads, but it was noticeable that the atmosphere was very down and there were cliques within the dressing room".

Jim Wilmer had now taken on the role of chairman and his first task was to inform the Forest fans that there was another price increase for admission. Coming on the back of relegation this didn't go down well, but it wasn't the club's fault, the Football League had imposed a minimum entrance price of 40p at every club.

The club unveiled their new kit for the season, the first change in six years. The new design would be all red, with a collar and a v-neck rib insert, the badge would be embroidered directly onto the shirt and not on a patch.

Also at the League's AGM there was a resolution to extend the half time break to fifteen minutes, but this failed to get the required number of votes, whilst a change to the disciplinary system was passed. From now on, under the new regulations, each various offence that warranted a booking or sending off, would be given a points value according to its severity under a totting up system. Once a player had reached twelve points, it meant an immediate two game ban. This replaced the unfair old system based on weeks, which meant that sometimes a two week ban could mean missing four games but might also mean missing none if a club did not have a fixture or a game was postponed.

George Lyall

Nottingham Council announced it was setting up a task force to investigate the potential for a super stadium to be built in Colwick, for use by both senior clubs. Notts County chairman, Jack Dunnett was

The Reds go close early in the first half against Portsmouh.

FOOTBALL POST

STALEMATE FOR REDS'

John Galley prods home the first goal against Fulham.

Paul Richardson goes close with this effort.

Martin O'Neill opens the scoring at home to Cardiff.

Galley wins this headed dual with the Oxford defence.

JIMMY McINTOSH

'FOREST ARE TOO GOOD FOR THE "SECOND"'

by the club's new skipper TOMMY GEMMELL

SOMETHING stirs down in the Forest. That may sound a bit corny, but I mean it. Ever since we knew that relegation was a certainty, there has been a quiet mood of determination to get back upstairs.

And, with the usual luck which every team needs, I think Nottingham Forest have a fine chance of making a quick return to the First Division. The sooner the better, for a team with Forest's ground facilities has no right to be in the Second Division.

After the disappointment of being relegated last season, the confidence has increased and the feeling at the City Ground is that the team can bounce straight back.

Why not? There is a fair amount of talent in the side and the players will have the advantage of having recently played in a higher grade.

There are few among us who didn't feel disappointed at Ian Moore being sold to Manchester United. Still, transfers are very much a part of football and have to be accepted.

After all, we bought midfield man George Lyall from Preston during the close season and no doubt there are a good number of North End fans who didn't agree with that deal. For their benefit, let me say that George has settled in well.

Goals — or rather lack of them — are our problem. We just cannot seem to score. As a full-back, this may give the impression that I am blaming our forwards. Nothing of the sort!

New Forest skipper Tommy Gemmell (above). The experience of Neil Martin (left) helps the team's young front-runners.

The boys up front have worked really hard at training and in practice matches. They get the ball in the net all right in training sessions, but just cannot produce the same results on match days. And, let's face it, if you don't score, you don't win.

One of these days, however, our boys up front are going to click. Then, watch them score! There are three young players up front, Martin O'Neill, Duncan McKenzie and Jimmy McIntosh, plus the experienced Neil Martin. The snag, I believe, is that when Neil is out they miss his know-how. But they are gaining it for themselves, all the time.

My job as skipper is to try to keep them going, to drive some, coax others. It is the first time that I have been a regular captain and I must say that I was surprised when Manager Matt Gillies offered me the job.

A CHALLENGE

After all, I only joined the club from Celtic in December of last year. I thought someone like Neil Martin, who had a spell as skipper of Coventry, would have been given the job.

During my time with Celtic, the captain was always Billy McNeill. He is still doing a splendid job, so it is obvious that if I hadn't been transferred I would not have become a skipper.

But with Peter Hindley asking to be relieved of the task, I have been given my chance to lead the lads. It's a challenge that I gratefully accept.

But I did captain Celtic once. That was on the black Saturday of the Ibrox disaster when 66 people died as they tried to leave the ground.

That's not a day I wish to remember. My captaincy of Forest will have a much happier ending!

Players and staff at the club's Christmas Party.

TOMMY GEMMELL

THE REDS

GEORGE LYALL

The question is who will follow Gillies?

MATT GILLIES' decision to resign his position as manager of Nottingham Forest could hardly be described as unexpected but it still leaves the intriguing question of who will accept the challenge to try and restore the Reds' image to its former standing in the League?

Rumours are certain to fly around thick and fast until the club's new manager is appointed, and both famous and unknown names are likely to be linked with the job. One can only hope the new man is announced without too much delay.

Mr. Gillies' departure from the City Ground will hardly have come as a surprise to anyone who

wage bill by selling those players who do not fit into his future plans for the club.

It will take time, and the club's impatient supporters must be made to realise this. Anyone who thinks Forest's trouble will miraculously disappear overnight upon the appointment of a new manager is bound to be disappointed.

But the traditions of the club are strong and given the strongest possible backing from the committee in cash and encouragement, it can be done.

The members and supporters also have a very big part to play in helping the new man reshape a Forest team for the future, with the single aim of bringing Division I football back to Nottingham.

Encouraging

By Mike Beesley

● JIM BARRON has proved a sound and reliable last line of defence for Forest this season, and he was particularly pleased to prevent John Galley scoring last Saturday, for the Bristol City striker was Jim's best man when they were both at Wolves.

with tradition and changed its paper colour from pink to white. After a second goalless draw at Hull, Mike Beesley the Reds' correspondent, writing in the Football Post said the club must, 'Spend now, it's urgent. The sooner the committee, the management and the players accept joint responsibility for what's happening, the quicker they might work out how to put it right'. The first win of the season came at home to Oxford United in front of the ATV cameras and before less than 10,000 spectators. The sight of wide open terraces and a barely populated Trent End provided graphic evidence of how far the club had fallen in such a short space of time. George Lyall had the honour of scoring the first goal of the season, quickly followed by a second from Martin O'Neill in a 2-1 victory after Forest had fallen behind to a thirteenth minute goal from Oxford. As Ken Smales put it, "We knew some fans would drift away from the club, but it looks as if they have positively sprinted".

When they followed this first victory up four days later, with a 1-0 win against Brighton, another goal for Martin O'Neill and a rare away victory 2-0 at Carlisle, a brace for McKenzie, you might have been fooled into thinking that the relegation blues had been banished. However, the season was to rapidly deteriorate and the second place achieved in September was to be as good as it got. In fact the match report for the Brighton game claimed that, 'the visitors queued up to miss chances and the pathetic efforts of Forest were laughable at times'. No sugar coating from the local press on this occasion.

Aston Villa, newly promoted from the Third Division, were to at least give a veneer of the big time when they came to the City Ground as the opponents in the first round of the League Cup. A respectable crowd of over 17,000, including a large Brummie contingent created a decent atmosphere and they were to go home happy after a 1-0 win. There was trouble in the East Stand, where the police tried to maintain order by stretching a rope down the terraces to keep fighting fans apart.

The team lost their second game in succession, again by 1-0 at home to Luton, in what was a disjointed, lacklustre performance that again had the fans grumbling. Jimmy McIntosh was singled out for jeers and would lose his place after failing to build on some positive performances from the previous season. This match saw the Trent End divided into four sections after the installation of metal railings. However, it was too late, supporters had already moved over to the East Stand terraces where there was nothing to stop them roaming around.

Martin O'Neill comments on what the atmosphere was like at the ground during this period, "The criticism of the manager and the players affected us all, it seemed at times as if the fans weren't watching what was happening on the pitch, but just venting their anger on everything. Things could have been so much better if they had got behind us".

The manager had by now decided to replace Sammy Chapman with John Cottam, Sammy was on the transfer list and refusing to come off it. This decline in results coincided with the pairing of Cottam with Dave Serella in central defence. They were both steady players, but as it turned out, neither was up to Division Two standard if you wanted to be challenging for promotion. If either of them had been paired with a more experienced player, their development might have been different, but expecting a couple of young lads with so little experience to come in and turn around the team's defensive failings was unfair. Altogether, although they played over two hundred games between them for Forest, this was more a reflection on the standard of the club's playing staff at this time. Cottam was a local lad, strong in the air and although he was loaned out three times, he kept bouncing back into the team. Serella was a more wirey player, sporting a fashionable '70s style moustache, he was often too brave for his own good, regularly leaving the field with blood pouring from another facial injury The start to the season might have been poor, but the team certainly didn't deserve an attendance of only 6,414 for the game with Cardiff City. However, those hardy souls who had come out on a windy rain swept evening at least had the satisfaction of seeing the team beat Cardiff 2-1. O'Neill and Richardson scoring the goals. The fans had turned their back on the team, half an hour before kick off at 7.00pm, there were only 300 people in the whole ground. At this rate, the club was heading for financial disaster as well. The club had money but seemed scared to spend it.

Ken Smales the club secretary had taken it upon himself to write a column in the official programme in an attempt to give some insight into what was

...OOTBALL POST

...LXIV. No. 13. NOTTINGHAM, SATURDAY, NOVEMBER 4, 1972. Price 3p

MACKAY...

Forest's new manager is featured on Page Three and in Editor's View (Page Five).

OTHER MAIN FEATURES

Big Club Comment ..2-3 Talking Soccer 6
Letters ....4-5 Amateurs 17-18-19
Sportrait ....6 Notts. Report 20

REDS WIN IT FOR MAC

MIKE BEESLEY at the City Ground

...NGHAM FOREST produced their best...

Richardson and Fraser to send Robertson clear on the right and from his centre Martin headed wide of the post.

Forest were unlucky not to take the lead after 15 minutes when Fraser found Martin on the left. The centre forward slipped the ball inside to O'Neill who turned quickly and hammered in a fierce shot which beat King but struck Cripps in the stomach a yard from the line.

Hindley managed to hook his shot away.

Forest continued to show plenty of enterprise in their attacks, but the Millwall defence refused to be drawn out which forced the Reds to resort to long range shots which were usually off target.

When Buckley was fouled near the left hand corner flag, Gemmell took the free kick and found Hindley on the far post but the full back's header went high over the bar.

Forest kept plugging away...

John Robertson congratulates Alan Buckley on his goal against Millwall.

Action from the home game against Millwall.

Chapman watches as Lawson in the Huddersfield goal, claims the ball.

Action from the Blackpool game.

JOHN GALLEY Nottingham Forest

happening at the club. Unfortunately Ken couldn't help himself and at times his acerbic comments went too far. For example, he declared that he couldn't take those seriously who were afraid to put their name to a letter that they might have written, instead choosing to hide behind a pen name.

Dave Mackay and his back room staff Bert Johnson, Colin Murphy, Des Anderson and Alan Hill

The writing was on the wall for Matt Gillies after a run of five games without victory, including a heavy 4-1 loss away at Sunderland. He finally put the fans out of their misery when he resigned after a draw at Bristol City but in reality it showed the weakness of the committee when they didn't pull the trigger themselves. Bill Anderson was once more put in charge whilst a replacement was sought. Club Chairman Jim Willmer unbelievably still didn't understand the anger and took the opportunity to attack supporters, "I personally feel that the crowd have been cruel to Mr Gillies. They have not achieved much except to make the players nervous wrecks in their home games".

The change had an immediate positive effect, with a fighting 2-2 draw with Swindon that saw John Robertson net his first senior goal, followed by a win at Sheffield Wednesday. Anderson had immediately recalled the out of favour striker Neil Martin and Sammy Chapman, as he set about restoring confidence. Neil Martin repaying that faith as he scored the winner at Hillsborough

Before a new manager was appointed, there was sad news to report, as reserve players, Tommy (Chalkie) White and Steve Baines were involved in a car crash, in which Tommy tragically lost an eye. At the age of only twenty, after only one first team outing as a substitute at Chelsea, he was forced to retire.

There were great discussions about the type of manager the Reds should be looking for, the general consensus being that a 'Clough' type of tracksuit manager was needed, although as Forever a Red put it, 'It seems as if the committee want to manage the team themselves'.

Red Letter from Calverton offered his suggestion, 'Why not try Peter Taylor, he's a Nottingham lad, perhaps he might like a little of the limelight for himself'. So it was a positive surprise when it was announced that the club had immediately identified Dave Mackay the Swindon Town manager as the person they wanted to replace Gillies. Although inexperienced as a manager, he seemed to have all the qualities needed to be a success and he jumped at the chance to make a quick return to the East Midlands. Despite his association with Derby, reaction to his appointment was positive, but to be fair anybody would have been seen as an improvement. Dave was highly competitive and many players remember well, the tough five-a-side games played behind the East Stand with the manager joining in. Mackay was announced as the new manager shortly before the home game with Millwall, although he watched from the Main Stand as the Reds produced a good performance to win 3-2, Alan Buckley scoring his first senior goal.

Tommy (Chalkie White)

Dave Mackay quickly showed he meant business, his first act was to sack Bob McKinlay, Frank Knight and Alan Hill and replace them with Des Anderson and Colin Murphy. He then spoke to each player individually to lay down what he expected from them and ensure that everyone had a clean slate with him. Jim Barron has this to say about the appointment, "Dave had a terrific enthusiasm and it rubbed off on the players, our appetite returned. To be honest it was a lack of enthusiasm that got us relegated in the first place. Although we had started the season reasonably well, we had been lucky, but it was different under Dave, we were playing better but just couldn't get the rub of the green".

Despite a loss at Cardiff in his first game, the manager showed that he had a different philosophy to the previous incumbent, when he substituted Serella for George Lyall as they chased the game. However, after another loss to Preston, the extent of the job in hand became all too apparent.

Meanwhile the match day programme reported that local lad Viv Anderson was signing as an apprentice and that Trent Buses were going to stop running trips to Forest away games after continuing vandalism.

Dave Mackay's first victory came against Orient, two goals for George Lyall in a 2-1 win, as the manager tried to maintain a more positive approach with Martin and McKenzie playing up front. The crowd figure again slipping below 8,000.

As Mackay continued the evaluation of his playing squad, he was not impressed by the contribution made by Tommy Gemmell, who as one of the most experienced and higher paid players, had been expected to lead the club's promotion push. Gemmell had incurred the manager's wrath after an ill timed back pass that had gifted Burnley a win. Mackay wasted no time, taking the captaincy from him and replacing him in the team by John Winfield. Gemmell was to only make a couple more appearances before he was released to Dundee on a free transfer a couple of months later.

John Robertson however, was singled out for praise, as he now looked like he was growing into the role of a professional footballer, his dribble and cross for George Lyall's first goal against Orient was

AROUND AND ABOUT

NEW SOCCER COURSE

A six week course at the City Ground was well attended as supporters were given the opportunity to see what goes on behind the scenes at Nottingham Forest.

"We Love You, Shankly"!

For recent filming of an episode of 'This is Your Life' the club was pleased to host a group of celebrity Liverpool fans as they got together, to sing a song in praise of Bill Shankly. Amongst those attending were Ken Dodd, Members of the Scaffold & Boxer Alan Rudkin. Mervyn the Groundsman was shocked to find the piano still in the middle of the pitch the next day.

FOREST'S NEW KIT

No, Paul Richardson has not been loaned to the American Soccer League! He is seen in the photograph above modelling a strip designed by David Wharin, 3rd year graphic design student at Trent Polytechnic.

The project was set by Peter Marriot, part-time lecturer on the graphic course, and the photograph was taken by David Young, 1st year photographer.

It is certainly modern in outlook and could be the sign of things to come. Your observations would be appreciated.

THE CLUB DARTS CHAMPIONSHIP

Duncan McKenzie, the reigning champion

Can You Design a New Forest Badge!

The present Forest crest was introduced in 1957 when Billy Walker, the Manager at the time decided on a new badge to replace the one then in use. Due to copyright issues the club needs to change design once more and you can help.

FILLING A STAR'S ROLE

O'Neill goes looking for more work at Forest

MARTIN O'NEILL, a 20-year-old lad from Northern Ireland, was the player who landed the job of filling the shirt vacated in the Nottingham Forest side by £200,000 star Ian Moore.

And although the prospect might have seemed daunting to many, young O'Neill got stuck in early this season and started scoring goals. His early-season form, in fact, brought him three goals in the first eight matches and a whole host of near-misses.

He was top of the Forest goal-scoring charts and played a big part in helping last season's relegation no-hopers to a reasonable start in the Second Division.

O'Neill was almost completely unknown until Moore left for Manchester United near the end of last season. But he got in for a few matches at the end of the season — when Forest were virtually doomed.

Says O'Neill: "It wasn't easy playing in a side which had no sort of confidence. But we got off to a fairly good start this season and there has been more confidence in the side.

"I scored three early goals, but it should have been many more. I remember one save, in particular, which denied me a goal—the one by Bryan King in our match at Millwall.

"I hit it like a rocket from about five yards and I thought it was a 'cert.' But King knocked it away for a corner, even though the force of the shot knocked him off his feet.

"We feel that if we can win most of our home games we could be in with a great chance of promotion. For we fancy our chances of pulling off some good results away from home."

Commenting on the effect the continual criticism of the team and manager Matt Gillies has had on the side, he added: "I am certain that if the fans got behind us, we'd do much better.

"But the fans never seem to be paying attention to the game when they come to the ground—and it does affect our game if we know nobody is paying attention.

"The boss has had lots of criticism, but as far as I'm concerned, he has played a big part in helping me develop my game. He has coached me, helped me gain more know-how and given me numerous ideas and tips—I couldn't have asked for more."

O'Neill, whom Forest captured from Northern Ireland side Distillery, says the hardest part of football in England for him has been fitting into a team.

"I always used to play with the ball when it came to me, but I never seemed to get involved in the match if I didn't get the ball. Now, I look for the ball, look for work and am more aware of team-mates around me. And I'm trying to do more work off the ball, too.

"I think I benefit from the presence of my parents in Nottingham. They have moved over here so I have always got someone to go home to. I think it's probably an advantage, especially when you have come a long way from your original home to play football."

Both O'Neill and Nottingham Forest may have a long way to go yet before they both reach their targets—First Division football again at the City Ground, Nottingham. But the fact that Forest appear to have put last season's troubles behind them and are now playing several very promising youngsters and looking to the future, is a sign of better times for the club.

MARTIN O'NEILL . . . he pays tribute to Matt Gillies

Mackay's plan will come off says Barron

by David Wright

IT WAS enough to make the Sheriff turn over in his grave. The Forest of Nottingham was in danger of rotting away into a state of oblivion. What was needed was a rescue act in the Robin Hood tradition.

Then, last November, Dave Mackay came on the scene. He took them by the scruff of their neck and gave Nottingham Forest a healthy shake-up.

The First Division in three years. That, said Mackay, is his target, and already the once-mighty Forest are beginning to blossom on the Soccer tree. Their F.A. Cup Third Round achievement in twice holding First Division West Bromwich gave them a further boost.

And it's Mackay, with his heart of oak, who's putting this new life into Forest. His unbounding enthusiasm has spread like wildfire through the club.

"Dave's got terrific enthusiasm and it's rubbed off on the players," says goalkeeper Jim Barron. "The players' appetite for the game has returned.

"This is one of the reasons why we got relegated last season. Our enthusiasm seemed to go. But since the new boss came our appetite has returned and the players' attitude has changed completely. We now look forward to Saturdays."

The 6 ft. Georgie previously played for Wolves and Chelsea and is still ambitious to return to the First Division. With Forest? "Yes, why not?" he asks.

"The boss says he gives himself three years to get back in the First Division and I go along with that. We're struggling a bit this season, but I'm sure we'll be stronger next season and be in with a much better chance of getting promotion."

Adds Barron: "We've got some players with a lot of ability, but perhaps they've lacked enthusiasm. But this is what Dave Mackay's now instilling in the team.

"The whole side is definitely playing better these days. Yet early in the season we played six or seven games without losing one, though to be honest we were lucky at times.

"Lately, we've been playing better football without getting the results.

"The game at Oxford apart, we've been playing some fair stuff. We had a good win at Sheffield Wednesday and drew at Aston Villa, though we should have beaten them because we were two-up.

"Our 4-0 win over Blackpool was another good win. We could also have got a draw at Burnley instead of losing by the only goal.

"There was no difference between Burnley and us, but a silly mistake by our defence let them in to score. We played well that day in every aspect of the game."

Barron rates the Turf Moor kids as a sound bet for promotion. "They look certainties to go up," says Jim, "but I wouldn't say Burnley are the best team we've met this season.

"The best I would say are Queen's Park Rangers. We weren't playing particularly well when we met them, but they really did impress me."

A recent arrival at Forest is John Galley, a £33,000 signing from Bristol City. There was no chance of Galley being among strangers, for Barron is one of his closest friends.

"I've known John for a long time," says Barron. "He was the best man at my wedding nine years ago, when we were both at Wolves, and we go on holiday together.

"But I was still a bit surprised by John coming to Forest. I didn't know he was joining until the day before he signed."

NEIL
MARTIN
Nottingham Forest

Dave Mackay and John Robertson look on as the referee decides that no play is possible.

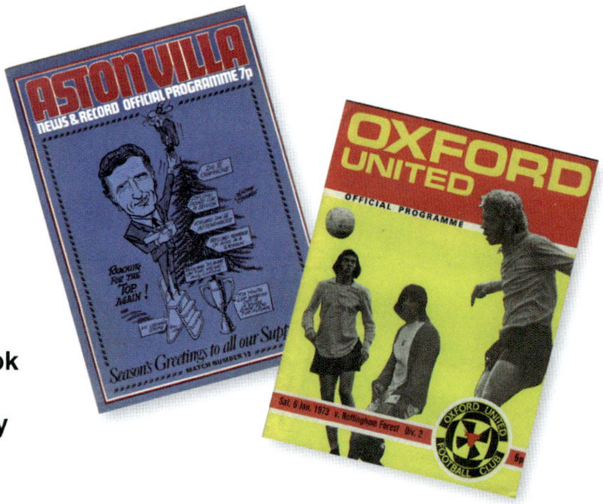

described as pure soccer brilliance by the boss. Writing in the Football Post once more, Mike Beesley told everyone, that promotion was impossible this season and that avoiding relegation was the priority. Whether he was addressing supporters or the club hierarchy itself was not clear.

Harry Richards in his weekly column as Editor, warned those Forest fans still calling for the committee to resign, to be careful what you wish for. Although he disagreed with many of the things that they had done, if they were to leave, the club could be left in a vulnerable position he said, especially as at this moment, there would not be a long queue of businessmen looking to replace them.

The manager waited until the twelfth of December before making his first signing. John Galley was his choice, joining from Bristol City for a fee of £30,000. He had a fine scoring record with Bristol, 90 goals in only 198 games. John was a solid if unspectacular striker, he knew the division and looked a good choice to partner Neil Martin up front. He had been a team mate of Jim Barron at Wolves, where he was also the keeper's Best Man.

Galley recounts those early days, "When I joined Forest it was late on in my career, but I knew I was joining a big club and hoped I would get success. When I arrived though, it was obvious that a lot of people hadn't come to terms with the fact that the club had been relegated and were in Division Two. Initially I played up front with Neil Martin, but eventually it was with Duncan McKenzie, he was a great player but often difficult to play with as you never knew what he was going to do". Galley provided an immediate return on the investment, scoring on his debut at Fulham, but the Reds still fell to a 3-1 defeat.

As Christmas drew near, it was announced that Tony Wood was to leave the club and take up the position of chairman at Arsenal. At one stage he had been instrumental in trying to modernise the club, but as his business interests changed, it meant that he was away from Nottingham for longer periods and felt he couldn't dedicate the time needed. Some people thought it might have been better if he had stayed around to help clear up the mess he had created, but he was off.

Word came out from the club that Geoffrey McPherson had been instrumental in the management changes, as he was to be in the coming years, playing a significant role in the club's history. For younger and newer members of the committee, it was always an uphill struggle to effect any change. At least 1972 ended on a positive note, as the club first battered Blackpool 4-0, with four different scorers in what was the team's biggest victory of the campaign and followed this up with a creditable 2-2 draw at Villa Park. Mackay missed both games with influenza, in fact Forest tried to get the Villa game called off because many of the squad were also suffering. John Galley scored in both games to bring his scoring record to three in three for the Reds, whilst Neil Martin added a couple himself. With a combined age of sixty, could this pair fire Forest up the table?

Before the postponed game with Hull, the club announced the sad news that Frank Chambers had passed away. Frank had served the club with distinction for over thirty years in a variety of roles including chairman, this was another break with the past, Frank had been a Red through and through. Dave Mackay had high hopes for a cup run, not only as a morale booster, but hopefully to provide the cash needed to further strengthen the squad. They were not given an easy draw though, picked out of the hat to visit Division One West Brom. However, they were not without a chance, as they were a poor outfit, struggling badly and would eventually be relegated.
Before that encounter took place, the Reds were in league action, an away defeat at Oxford, that was so bad in the eyes of Red Reg that he felt compelled to write, 'This game was a disgrace to football, the strong arm stuff started by Forest, I want no part of it'. The report of the game includes running feuds between the players, made worse by a weak referee unable to maintain order.
John Winfield for the second game in succession was to score an own goal as the Reds were held 1-1 at the West Brom cup tie, in a game they deserved to win. John Galley continued his impressive start with another goal in a match that was to be the first of four attempts between the two teams to find a winner. The replay on the following Tuesday, played before a season's high crowd of 19,000, ended when it was abandoned after eighty one minutes with the score at 1-1. Thick fog meant it became impossible to carry on and for at least fifteen minutes the fans at either end had to rely on crowd noise to work out what was happening. The fog unusually had rolled in from the Bridgford End, a sight that no fan could ever remember happening before, fog had previously caused problems but used to come from the riverside. Barry Lyons making a rare start, scored the Reds' goal.

With a home victory over Carlisle in between, the teams tried again on the following Monday but no goals even after extra time meant that another replay was needed. This was arranged to be held at neutral Filbert Street, Leicester, where this time Albion made no mistake running out comfortable 3-1 winners, Galley scoring for the Reds.

There was exciting news in late January, when Forest announced a competition to design a new club badge. They had

Barry Lyons fires home against West Brom.

Neil Martiin is foiled by the Albion keeper.

FOOTBALL POST

MONEY!

Read what Jimmy Bloomfield has to say about it on Page 6.

OTHER MAIN FEATURES

FOG FOILS FOREST!!

Neil Martin heads powerfully home against Carlisle.

John Galley powers home a header against Sheffield Wednesday.

Duncan McKenzie in action against Burnley.

Miah Dennehy

Dave Serella

Steve Baines

used the present badge, based on the Nottingham City coat of arms since the early 1950's, but because there was a conflict of interests and copyright issues the club decided that they needed to create a new identity, hopefully to coincide with a change in the club's fortunes. To this end they invited supporters or designers to submit ideas, one of which would be chosen. Paul Richardson meanwhile was getting frustrated by his lack of first-team opportunities, the manager was not to pick him again this season after dropping him after the Fulham defeat in December, so he joined Chapman, Martin, Lyons, Jackson and Winfield on the transfer list.

Although progress was apparently being made off the pitch, the hoped for revival hadn't taken place. It was against this background that Dave Mackay was criticized for his apparent aloofness, after he travelled on his own to the game at Luton. He had arrived in his Mercedes and then watched the game from the Director's Box rather than the touchline. The manager declined the chance to put his side of the story.

Alan Hill was now back at the club and he was asked about the goalkeeping situation, "There were four good keepers", he said, "Jim Barron, Dennis Peacock, Peter Wells and John Middleton, the last two were good enough to go on and play for England", he claimed.

Duncan McKenzie's form had dropped off alarmingly. Moved from centre forward to wide player, he struggled to make an impact. It was decided that a loan spell away might rejuvenate him, so he made the short trip to Mansfield. He was to be so popular at Field Mill, scoring seven goals in six games, that he still gets voted onto the Stags supporters' all-time favourite players lists.

The role of Reds' correspondent for the Evening and Football Post had been passed around the office for several years, but it was now set to be taken over by someone who was to become synonymous with the Nottingham Forest success story. John Lawson had been in journalism up north, but he really wanted to be a sports reporter, so when he was offered the position he couldn't wait to get started. It was a role he was to occupy for the next seven years and even after an industrial dispute meant that he left the paper, his association continued with the club under many guises for the next thirty years.

One of the things that gives John the most pleasure, is recalling the small help he might have given John Robertson to advance his career. John Robertson was to have no bigger supporter than John Lawson, as he immediately recognized the talent and was always pushing his case, even when the evidence didn't seem to support this. In Lawson's first column he said that, 'he has a huge part to play in the club's revival' and always continued to talk the player up.

Dave Mackay quickly realised that the team lacked leadership and when he heard through the soccer grapevine that Frank McLintock of Arsenal might be available, he was straight in. Frank was definitely the sort of character that was needed. Mackay hoped that he might have the same impact he himself had had, when he had moved to Derby. The player himself though, was reluctant to drop down a division and due to his business interests in London chose to join QPR. Mackay did manage to pull off a signing, when Miah Dennehy joined for £20,000 from Cork. Miah was considered a good prospect and Forest had to hold off competition for his signature from several other clubs. Miah was a right winger, a slight figure, the type that the club seemed to specialize in signing. He had pace and a few tricks but in his time at the City Ground, little knowledge of how to best use his talent for the team.

Liam O'Kane's long awaited comeback was getting closer, he had been in full training for a while and turning out for the reserves, but it looked as if he hadn't got over the mental side of his injury as he wasn't competing as hard as he used to. He was eventually eased in at right back, making a few appearances before a few minor niggles caused him to miss the rest of the season.

The manager was using this period of the season to experiment with his line ups, trying to find a blend that might work. The undoubted high spots were the two consecutive 3-0 victories in March against Sheffield Wednesday and Burnley.

Duncan McKenzie returned from his loan spell at Mansfield, restored to the side and given the freedom to express himself. Duncan talks about this period. "I had gone to Mansfield and during training had discussed with the manager Danny Williams about where and how I was to play. He decided to give me a free role and it worked. After scoring a hat trick, Dave Mackay recalled me and said that he was going to build the team around me, as you can imagine I thought that was great".

He might not have scored in the first game against Wednesday, but Duncan tormented the Owls' defence creating the space for O'Neill, Galley and John Cottam to score the goals. The best performance of the season came the following week when champions elect Burnley visited on Grand National Day, this was the race when Red Rum won the first of his titles.

Forest were to make a rare appearance on national television, as the game was featured on Match of the Day. The audience were treated to the sight of McKenzie showing everyone that he was capable of dribbles, feints and also a goal, O'Neill and Lyons scoring the others. 'Scintillating Forest' was the headline. How could the team possibly follow this result with four consecutive losses? Defeats away at Orient, Preston and Blackpool plus home disappointment 3-1 against Middlesbrough, a game that also saw O'Kane hobble off and Chapman receive an injury that meant he was a virtual passenger for the second half.

Luckily enough points had been secured to ensure that there was no prospect of relegation, this at least provided the manager with further scope to carry on experimenting. Steve Baines came in for his debut at Preston alongside Miah Dennehy. Steve was another centre half in the mould of John Cottam, he only made two appearances for the club before making a good career for himself in the lower leagues. He gained fame when he retired from the game, took up refereeing and became one of the few ex pros to make it to the League list.

Front to back: **Trevor Moden, Tony Woodcock & Lee Young**

management were divided. Many fans thought that there was little difference in the quality of the football, whilst others were prepared to give the manager more time and hoped that the youngsters might provide a brighter future. John Lawson thought that there were definite signs of improvement, although he urged Mackay to wield the axe and clear out the deadwood to make way for new additions. There was also a nice article in the Football Post about a young forward called Bert Bowery who was knocking them in for Mapperley Methodists.

The season wound down with a 1-0 home win against Sunderland, Neil Martin the scorer, followed by an away draw at already relegated Brighton, where Dennis Peacock made his debut in goal, replacing Jim Barron, robbing him of the chance of the first ever present season of his career. The team showed seven changes from the lineup that had begun the season against Portsmouth. Miah Dennehy performed well, scoring his first senior goal for the club. The County Cup provided some light relief as the trophy was regained with two 1-0 victories over Notts and Mansfield, before the team jetted off to Portugal to compete in a prestigious end of season tournament with Benfica and Porto. Quite why Forest were invited is not clear.

The game against Benfica was to have a significant impact on the career of John Robertson. Robbo was determined to enjoy the occasion, this was a chance to show everyone the skills he possessed. Unfortunately Benfica and Portugal skipper Mario Coluna took umbrage at some of the youngster's tricks and a fierce challenge left Robertson lying in agony with a cartilage injury. This was such a serious injury that he not only missed the start of the next season but due to complications didn't return to first team action until February. The psychological impact was to affect his game and development over the next couple of years, forcing a change in his own style of play. Forest lost this game 3-0 before losing to hosts Porto, a 1-1 draw followed by a losing 5-4 penalty shoot out.

Hang out with the 'In crowd', at the Sportsmen's Social Club

Forest had found that life in a lower league was not much easier than the First Division. After flattering to deceive early on, the hoped for promotion push never materialized, although at least they hadn't suffered the same fate as Huddersfield who had come down with them. Huddersfield ended up suffering a second successive relegation along with Brighton. Forest eventually finished in fourteenth position, scoring 47 goals and conceding 52.

The only bright spots were the dismissal of Matt Gillies and the experience gained by youngsters John Robertson and Martin O'Neill, plus it looked as if a role within the team had finally been found for Duncan McKenzie. George Lyall had failed to settle and although John Galley had contributed some goals his impact had not been massive.

In reality, unless Dave Mackay could work a miracle, prospects didn't look much brighter for next season.

FACTS and FIGURES

July 31st 1972, F, A, v. Watford, Win 2-1, Scorers Martin, Buckley, AT 3,280, Hulme, Hindley, Gemmell, Cottam, Serella, Fraser, McIntosh, Lyall, Martin, Richardson, O'Neill, SUBS Peacock, Buckley.

Aug 7th 1972, F, H, v. Kaiserslautern, Draw 2-2, Scorers Lyall, McKenzie, AT 4,881, Barron, Hindley, Gemmell, Serella, Chapman, Fraser, McIntosh, Lyall, Martin, Richardson, McKenzie, SUBS Robertson, O'Neill.

Aug 12th 1972, H, v. Portsmouth, Draw 0-0, AT 13,175, Barron, Fraser, Gemmell, Serella, Chapman, Robertson, McIntosh, Lyall, McKenzie, Richardson, O'Neill.

Aug 19th 1972, A, v. Hull City, Draw 0-0 , AT 11,189, Barron, Hindley, Gemmell, Serella, Chapman, Fraser, McIntosh, Lyall, McKenzie, Richardson, O'Neill.

Aug 26th 1972, H, v. Oxford United, Win 2-1, Scorers Lyall, O'Neill, AT 9,591, Barron, Hindley, Gemmell, Serella, Chapman, Fraser, McIntosh, Lyall, McKenzie, Richardson, O'Neill, SUB Buckley.

Aug 29th 1972, H, v. Brighton & Hove Albion, Win 1-0, Scorer O'Neill, AT 10,659, Barron, Hindley, Gemmell, Serella, Chapman, Fraser, McIntosh, Lyall, McKenzie, Richardson, O'Neill.

Sept 2nd 1972, A, v. Carlisle United, Win 2-1, Scorer McKenzie (2), AT 7,624, Barron, Hindley, Gemmell, Serella, Cottam, Fraser, McIntosh, Lyall, McKenzie, Richardson, O'Neill.

Sept 5th 1972, LC, H, v. Aston Villa, Loss 0-1, AT 17,665, Barron, Hindley, Gemmell, Serella, Cottam, Fraser, McIntosh, Lyall, McKenzie, Lyons, O'Neill, SUB Buckley.
Sept 9th 1972, H, v. Luton Town, Loss 0-1, AT 9,495, Barron, Hindley, Gemmell, Serella, Cottam, Fraser, McIntosh, Lyall, McKenzie, Robertson, O'Neill.

Sept 16th 1972, A, v. Queens Park Rangers, Loss 0-3, AT 12,528, Barron, Hindley, Gemmell, Serella, Cottam, Fraser, Lyons, Lyall, McKenzie, Richardson, O'Neill, SUB Robertson.

Sept 19th 1972, H, v. Cardiff City, Win 2-1, Scorers O'Neill, Richardson, AT 6,414, Barron, Hindley, Gemmell, Serella, Cottam, Fraser, Lyons, Lyall, McKenzie, Richardson, O'Neill.

Sept 23rd 1972, H, v. Aston Villa, Draw 1-1, Scorer Fraser, AT 18,082, Barron, Hindley, Gemmell, Serella, Cottam, Fraser, McIntosh, Lyall, McKenzie, Richardson, O'Neill, SUB Chapman.

Sept 25th 1972, A, v. Millwall, Loss 1-2, Scorer Lyall, AT 9,071, Barron, Hindley, Gemmell, Serella, Cottam, Fraser, McIntosh, Lyall, McKenzie, Richardson, O'Neill, SUB Chapman.

Sept 30th 1972, A, v. Sunderland, Loss 1-4, Scorer Richardson, AT 14,155, Barron, Hindley, Gemmell, Serella, Cottam, Fraser, Lyall, Chapman, McKenzie, Richardson, O'Neill, SUB Robertson.

Oct 7th 1972, H, v. Huddersfield Town, Draw 1-1, Scorer Chapman, AT 7,931, Barron, Hindley, Gemmell, Serella, Cottam, Fraser, Lyall, Robertson, Chapman, Richardson, Buckley SUB O'Neill.

Oct 14th 1972, A, v. Bristol City, Draw 1-1, Scorer Fraser, AT 13,861, Barron, Hindley, Gemmell, Serella, Cottam, Fraser, Lyall, Robertson, Chapman, Richardson, Buckley.

Oct 21st 1972, H, v. Swindon Town, Draw 2-2, Scorers Robertson, O'Neill, AT 8,683, Barron, Hindley, Gemmell, Serella, Cottam, Fraser, Lyall, Robertson, Chapman, Richardson, Buckley, SUB O'Neill.

Oct 28th 1972, A, v, Sheffield Wednesday, Win 2-1, Scorers Martin, Richardson, AT 21,807, Barron, Hindley, Gemmell, Serella, Chapman, Fraser, Lyons, Robertson, Martin, Richardson, Buckley, SUB O'Neill.

Nov 4th 1972, H, v. Millwall, Win 3-2, Scorers Buckley, Gemmell, Robertson, AT 11,165, Barron, Hindley, Gemmell, Serella, Chapman, Fraser, O'Neill, Robertson, Martin, Richardson, Buckley, SUB Lyall.

Nov 11th 1972, A, v. Cardiff City, Loss 1-2, Scorer Martin, AT 12,765, Barron, Hindley, Gemmell, Serella, Chapman, Fraser, O'Neill, Robertson, Martin, Richardson, Buckley, SUB Lyall.

Nov 18th 1972, H, v. Preston North End, Loss 0-1, AT 10,832, Barron, Hindley, Gemmell, Serella, Chapman, Fraser, O'Neill, Robertson, Martin, Richardson, Buckley, SUB McKenzie.

Nov 25th 1972, A, v. Burnley, Loss 0-1, AT 12,095, Barron, Hindley, Gemmell, Serella, Chapman, Fraser, O'Neill, Lyall, Martin, Robertson, McKenzie, SUB Richardson.

Dec 2nd 1972, H, v. Orient, Win 2-1, Scorer Lyall (2), AT 7,959, Barron, Hindley, Winfield, Chapman, Serella, Richardson, O'Neill, Lyall, Martin, Robertson, McKenzie.

Dec 9th 1972, A, v. Middlesbrough, Draw 0-0, AT 10,326, Barron, Hindley, Winfield, Chapman, Serella, Richardson, O'Neill, Lyall, Lyons, Robertson, McKenzie, SUB McIntosh

Dec 16th 1972, A, v. Fulham, Loss 1-3, Scorer Galley, AT 8,255, Barron, Hindley, Winfield, Chapman, Serella, Richardson, O'Neill, Galley, Martin,Robertson, McKenzie, SUB Lyall.

Dec 23rd 1972, H, v. Blackpool, Win 4-0, Scorers Martin, Fraser, McKenzie, Galley, AT 10,078, Barron, Hindley, Winfield, Chapman, Serella, Fraser, O'Neill, Robertson, Martin, Galley, McKenzie.

Dec 26th 1972, A, v. Aston Villa, Draw 2-2, Scorers Martin, Galley, AT 37,000, Barron, Gemmell, Winfield, Hindley, Cottam, Fraser, McIntosh, Robertson, Martin, Galley, McKenzie.

Jan 6th 1973, A, v. Oxford University, Loss 0-1, AT 9,056, Barron, Gemmell, Winfield, Chapman, Hindley, Fraser, O'Neill, Robertson, Martin, Galley, McKenzie.

Jan 13th 1973, FAC, A, v. West Bromwich Albion, Draw 1-1, Scorer Galley, AT 15,795 Barron, Hindley, Winfield, Chapman, Serella, Fraser, McIntosh, Robertson, Martin, Galley, Lyons.

Jan 16th 1973, FAC, H, v. West Bromwich Albion, Draw 1-1, Abandoned, Scorer Lyons, AT 19,168, Barron, Hindley, Winfield, Chapman, Serella, Fraser, McIntosh, Robertson, Martin, Galley, Lyons, SUB O'Neill.

Jan 20th 1973, H, v. Carlisle United, Win 2-1, Scorers Martin, Robertson(Pen), AT 6,866, Barron, Hindley, Winfield, Chapman, Serella, Fraser, McIntosh, Robertson, Martin, Galley, O'Neil, SUB Lyall.

Second Division 1972-73

		Pld	W	D	L	F	A	Pts
1	Burnley	42	24	14	4	72	35	62
2	Queens Park Rangers	42	24	13	5	81	37	61
3	Aston Villa	42	18	14	10	51	47	50
4	Middlesbrough	42	17	13	12	46	43	47
5	Bristol City	42	17	12	13	63	51	46
6	Sunderland	42	17	12	13	59	49	46
7	Blackpool	42	18	10	14	56	51	46
8	Oxford United	42	19	7	16	52	43	45
9	Fulham	42	16	12	14	58	49	44
10	Sheffield Wednesday	42	17	10	15	59	55	44
11	Millwall	42	16	10	16	55	47	42
12	Luton Town	42	15	11	16	44	53	41
13	Hull City	42	14	12	16	64	59	40
14	FOREST	42	14	12	16	47	52	40
15	Orient	42	12	12	18	49	53	36
16	Swindon Town	42	10	16	16	46	60	36
17	Portsmouth	42	12	11	19	42	59	35
18	Carlisle United	42	11	12	19	50	52	34
19	Preston North End	42	11	12	19	37	64	34
20	Cardiff City	42	11	11	20	43	58	33
21	Huddersfield Town	42	8	17	17	36	56	33
22	Brighton & Hove Albion	42	8	13	21	46	83	29

Jan 22nd 1973, FAC, H, v. West Bromwich Albion, Draw 0-0, AT 17,069, Barron, Hindley, Winfield, Chapman, Serella, Fraser, McIntosh, Robertson, Martin, Galley, O'Neill, SUB Lyall.

Jan 27th 1973, A, v. Luton Town, Loss 0-1, AT 10,083, Barron, Hindley, Winfield, Chapman, Serella, Fraser, McIntosh, Robertson, Martin, Galley, O'Neill, SUB Lyall.

Jan 29th 1973, FAC, N, Filbert Street, v. West Bromwich Albion, Loss 1-3, Scorer Galley, AT 13,201, Barron, Hindley, Winfield, Chapman, Serella, Fraser, McIntosh, Robertson, Martin, Galley, O'Neill, SUB Lyall.

Feb 10th 1973, H, v. Queens Park Rangers, Draw 0-0, AT 11,617, Barron, Hindley, Winfield, Chapman, Serella, Fraser, McIntosh, Lyall, Martin, Galley, O'Neill, SUB Jackson.

Feb 17th 1973, A, v. Portsmouth, Loss 0-2, AT 11,151, Barron, Hindley, Winfield, Chapman, Serella, Fraser, McIntosh, Robertson, Martin, Galley, Lyall.

Feb, 24th 1973, H, v. Fulham, Win 2-1, Scorers Galley, McIntosh, AT 8.810, Barron, Hindley, Winfield, Chapman, Serella, Fraser, McIntosh, Robertson, Martin, Galley, Lyall.

Mar 3rd 1973, A, v. Huddersfield Town, Draw 1-1, Scorer Hindley, AT 7,473, Barron, Hindley, Winfield, Chapman, Serella, Fraser, McIntosh, Robertson, Martin, Galley, Lyall.

Mar 10th 1973, H, v. Bristol City, Win 1-0, Scorer Galley, AT 8,680, Barron, Hindley, Winfield, Chapman, Serella, Fraser, McIntosh, Robertson, O'Neill, Galley, Lyall.

Mar 13th 1973, H, v. Hull City, Loss 1-2, Scorer Robertson (Pen), AT 7,711, Barron, O'Kane, Winfield, Chapman, Serella, Fraser, McIntosh, Robertson, Martin, Galley, Lyall, SUB O'Neill.

Mar 17th 1973, A, v. Swindon Town, Draw 0-0, AT 10,066, Barron, O'Kane, Winfield, Chapman, Cottam, Jackson, McIntosh, O'Neill, McKenzie, Galley, Lyons.

Mar 24th 1973, H, v. Sheffield Wednesday, Win 3-0, Scorers Galley, O'Neill, Cottam, AT 10,488, Barron, O'Kane, Winfield, Chapman, Cottam, Jackson, McIntosh, O'Neill, McKenzie, Galley, Lyons, SUB Robertson.

Mar 31st 1973, H, v, Burnley, Win 3-0, Scorers McKenzie, O'Neill, Lyons, AT 12,552, Barron, O'Kane, Winfield, Chapman, Cottam, Jackson, McIntosh, McKenzie, O'Neill, Galley, Lyons.

Apr 7th 1973, A, v. Orient, Loss 0-3, AT 6,373, Barron, O'Kane, Winfield, Chapman, Cottam, Jackson, McIntosh, Robertson, McKenzie, Galley, Lyons.

Apr 14th 1973, H, v. Middlesbrough, Loss 1-3, Scorer McKenzie, AT 9,258, Barron, O'Kane, Winfield, Chapman, Cottam, Jackson, McIntosh, O'Neill, McKenzie, Galley, Lyons, SUB Robertson.

Apr 21st 1973, A, v. Preston North End, Loss 1-2, Scorer Hindley, AT 7,701, Barron, Hindley, Winfield, Baines, Cottam, Robertson, Lyall, McKenzie, Galley, O'Neill, Dennehy.

Apr 23rd 1973, A, v. Blackpool, Loss 0-2, AT 8,322, Barron, Hindley, Winfield, Baines, Serella, Robertson, McIntosh, Lyons, McKenzie, Jackson, O'Neill.

Apr 24th 1973, H, v. Sunderland, Win 1-0, Scorer Martin, AT 10,306, Barron, Hindley, Winfield, Cottam, Serella, Robertson, Lyall, O'Neill, Martin, McKenzie, Dennehy.

Apr 28th 1973, A, v. Brighton & Hove Albion, Draw 2-2, Scorers Dennehy, McKenzie, AT 9,709, Peacock, Hindley, Winfield, Cottam, Serella, Robertson, Lyall, Chapman, Martin, McKenzie, Dennehy.

May 2th 1973, CC, A, v. Notts County, Win 1-0, Scorer Dennehy, AT 11,118, Barron, Hindley, Winfield, Chapman, Cottam, Robertson, McKenzie, Lyall, Martin, O'Neill, Dennehy.

May 5th 1973, CC, A, v. Mansfield Town, Win 1-0, Scorer Galley, AT 8,409, Barron, Hindley, Winfield, Chapman, Cottam, Robertson, Lyall, Lyons, Martin, McKenzie, Dennehy, SUB Galley.

June 20th 1973, F, N, v. Benfica, Loss 0-3, AT 5,500, Peacock, Hindley, Winfield, Chapman, Cottam, Jackson, Robertson, Martin, Dennehy, O'Neill, McKenzie, SUB Serella.

June 23rd 1973, F, N, v. Porto, Draw 1-1, Scorer McKenzie, AT 20,000, Peacock, Serella, Winfield, Chapman, Cottam, Jackson, Lyons, Martin, Dennehy, O'Neill, McKenzie, SUB McIntosh.

Back Row: Dave Serella, John Cottam, Duncan McKenzie, Eric Hulme, Jim Barron, John Robertson, Alan Buckley, Tommy Jackson
Middle Row: Barry Lyons, Martin O'Neill, Tommy Gemmell, Neil Martin, Paul Richardson, Bob Chapman, John Winfield
Front Row: Doug Fraser, Liam O'Kane, Peter Hindley, Jimmy McIntosh, George Lyall

The country was still wracked with economic and social problems. Rampant inflation, industrial unrest and the threat of terrorist bombings from the IRA contributed to a feeling of unease. Whilst David Bowie and 'Glam Rock' lent the period a superficial veneer of colour, the reality was more beige. As Britain, nicknamed 'the sick man of Europe' lurched towards terminal decline, violence on the picket lines and the terraces were mere symptoms of a wider malaise. Football, once the escape from reality for the working man, now often became a pastime to be avoided.

Locally with the promotion of Notts County, the first competitive Nottingham derby since 1957 would take place. No longer could the Reds take for granted their position as top team in the city.

The most significant change at the City Ground came off the pitch, when the new club badge was unveiled. The winning design came from David Lewis, a designer/lecturer at Trent Polytechnic. The tree was taken as the most appropriate symbol of the club and the water because of the proximity of the River Trent. The badge was very much in keeping with other new designs of the period, the stylised ram at Derby and the owl at Sheffield Wednesday were other examples. There were obviously those that didn't like the new badge, but generally the new design was well received and quickly became adopted and recognized throughout the wider football community.

Someone at the club also decided to change the colour of the team's socks from red to black with a red turnover. These had been used with the away kit of white shirts black shorts, but why they were used with the home strip, we will never know.

There was little transfer activity to report. Doug Fraser was released to Walsall for a small fee, whilst the only signing was Steve Peplow on a free transfer from the manager's old club Swindon. Dave Mackay had money to spend, he tried to sign Rod Thomas and Geoff Merrick, but couldn't persuade either the player or the club to do business.

In general club matters, Paul White who had not been successful as a player with the club, was appointed assistant secretary to Ken Smales. The club also decided to reward its older fans and introduced an OAP turnstile, with a 25 pence entrance price. Duncan McKenzie unveiled another of his skills, this time hurling a golf ball the length of the pitch. Along with jumping

73-74

NOTTINGHAM FOREST FOOTBALL CLUB

DIVISION TWO 1973 - 74

Back row, left to right:

JOHN COTTAM MARTIN O'NEILL NEIL MARTIN DAVE SERELLA JIM BARRON PETER HINDLEY LIAM O'KANE JOHN GALLEY JOHN WINFIELD

Front row, left to right:

MIAH DENNEHY BARRY LYONS JIMMY McINTOSH GEORGE LYALL TOMMY JACKSON DUNCAN McKENZIE JOHN ROBERTSON BOB CHAPMAN

Bill Anderson

Liam O'Kane

John Cottam

Jim Barron

George Lyall

Dennis Peacock

George Lyall and Tommy Jackson prepare to take a free kick against Aston Villa.

Tommy Jackson fires in after an indirect free kick was touched to him, only eight yards out from the Luton goal.

McKenzie heads home the equaliser against Aston Villa.

McKenzie adds his second in the 3-0 win against Millwall.

POST

Nottm. Forest ...4	Luton Town 0
Crystal Palace ...1	Notts. County 4
Derby County ...1	Chelsea 0
Peterborough 2	Mansfield Town .1

Vol. LXV. No. 1 NOTTINGHAM, SATURDAY, AUGUST 25, 1973. Price 3p

BOMB SCARE CLEARS LORD'S

A major bomb alert stopped the third Test between England and the West Indies at Lord's today.

The full house crowd of 28,000 was asked to leave the ground by main exits leaving cars and luncheon baskets behind.

The players — England were batting at the time — sat in the middle of the pitch surrounded by police.

The drama started at 2.40 as Bob Willis was walking in to bat with England 208 for eight.

Giving the warning over the loudspeakers, Billy Griffith, secretary of the MCC, said: "I am sorry to have to tell you that we have received a bomb warning.

"I must ask you therefore to leave by the main exit taking your personal belongings with you, including luncheon baskets, and quietly and slowly move out of the ground by the main exits as soon as possible. I ask that nobody will take a car out of the ground."

Ten minutes later, with crowds still milling about, another announcement came requesting people to leave.

"It is in your own interest to leave, particularly those in the stands and at the Nursery end. This is a police warning."

By 3.15 p.m. after play had been suspended for more than half an hour, the crowd had visibly thinned, although some 3,000 were still out in the middle of the pitch. Some were chanting "We want cricket."

Some spectators were content to bask in the warm sunshine.

There was an indication that play could resume soon when officials asked stewards to take up their positions and also for spectators still on the pitch to clear the field of play.

Spectators were allowed back into Lord's after about an hour.

JACKSON INSPIRES GOAL HUNGRY REDS

JOHN LAWSON at the City Ground

NOTTINGHAM FOREST gave their 1973/4 campaign a rousing send-off with a confidence-boosting win over a strong Luton Town side here this afternoon.

Attendance 10,793

Tommy Jackson scored twice in the first half — one from the ...

programme only 11 minutes old.

The goal certainly triggered more positive action

cars, Duncan was also a good all round sportsman, excelling at golf, darts and snooker. Lots of club trivia, but all the fans really wanted were new faces on the pitch.

Hope for the future came with the performances of the youngsters in a competition taking place in Germany, where not only did they win it, but Viv Anderson was named player of the tournament. Under Mackay, the team embarked on an extensive series of pre-season matches, starting in Wales before moving on to Ireland, ending with a couple of local games back in England. George Lyall remembers that, "Pre-season was really hard, but the manager was of the opinion that playing matches was the best way to full fitness".

It seemed as if the manager was vindicated, when the players hit the ground running and demolished Luton Town 4-0 in the season's opener at the City Ground. Tommy Jackson who had replaced the injured John Robertson, chipped in with two, one of them from only six yards out, his shot somehow finding its way through the entire Luton team on the goal line after an indirect free kick was touched to him. McKenzie and Martin completed the scoring. The manager preferred Cottam and Serella as his defensive partnership, whilst O'Kane kept out Peter Hindley at right back.

Another promising performance in the second game, but no points, after Lyall made a bad mistake at Oxford. This was followed by another home win over Sheffield Wednesday, 2-1 and a couple of goals for McKenzie. John Galley was a surprise choice in midfield, as Mackay shuffled the pack.

The away form, as usual at Forest, was causing concern. Another calendar year gone by without a win. Two different approaches were taken in the next couple of fixtures to remedy this. Firstly at Hull, the manager packed the midfield, even bringing back Hindley into the team to break up play. The result was a not unexpected 0-0 draw. For the next game away at West Brom he reverted to his more preferred attacking style, which resulted in a 3-3 draw, this after going two goals behind and then being 3-2 up, before having to settle for a point. Two more for McKenzie, was he finally to become the star his talent always promised?

Forest's reward for this promising start was fourth place and this was further consolidated after another two McKenzie goals were enough to defeat Swindon, in what was considered by the manager to be the worst display of the season. They could even have gone second three days later as they entertained a poor Preston side managed by Bobby Charlton, but could only draw 1-1 and with frustrations rising Neil Martin was sent off for dissent in the 87th minute.

Forest had three players in the Northern Ireland squad for the World Cup qualifier against Bulgaria that was played at Hillsborough, Sheffield. Due to the troubles in Ireland, countries were refusing to travel there, so they were forced to play on main land Britain.

Dave Mackay was not satisfied despite the team's good start to the season, he told the press he had instructed all the coaches at the club to analyse the club's playing system to see where improvements could be made.

Although the fans were pleased, there was still concern about the prospects for young players at the club. This came to the fore, after Alan Buckley was sold to Walsall after starting only five games for the first team. Alan went on to score over two hundred League goals during his career.

'Do the Reds hold young players back?' wrote M Smith, Wollaton.

The club was again linked with Swindon's left back Rod Thomas. John Winfield remembers the on-going banter, "I always sat at the front of the bus and some of the lads thought it was funny to keep shouting out Rod Thomas, as if he was sat at the back with them. I told them he would cost the club a lot of money and wouldn't improve the team a jot". Another link with the past was broken when Barry Lyons, who had not regained his best form, joined York City, initially on loan before making the move permanent.

A couple of goalless away games followed. A loss to Bolton, after another terrible back pass led to a goal, this time Paul Richardson was the culprit, before the team returned to winning ways with another convincing 3-0 defeat of Millwall and the now regular brace from McKenzie. Eamon Dunphy wrote about this encounter in his best-selling book, Only A Game, 'The lads have got the needle with them, they were doing nothing until Frankie (Saul) got sent off and then suddenly they are buzzing around taking the mickey. They had looked a load of bottlers, we'll stuff them on Wednesday'. He was referring to the fact that the two clubs had been drawn to play each other in the League Cup. As it turned out, he was right, but not until a replay, after the first game at the Den had ended 0-0, Millwall winning 3-1 at the City Ground.

After the promising start to the season, results and performances had begun to slip and worse still, Dave Mackay was about to resign as manager and join Derby County. Over in Derby, Brian Clough's relationship with Rams' chairman Sam Longson had been deteriorating rapidly. Initially the two had been close, but as Clough's media appearances grew and he became an ever more controversial figure, the chairman felt he had to rein him in and told Clough that he had to get club permission before doing any activity that might reflect badly in any way on the club or its image. Of course Clough reacted badly to this, he thought that Longson was jealous and wasn't slow in reminding him that neither the club or the chairman were anything until he had arrived. Things came to a head during a heated boardroom meeting that ended with Clough and Taylor both offering their resignations, never thinking they would be accepted, but they were.

Despite player and fan protests, the Derby chairman stuck to his guns and cast around for a manager big enough to

IAN BOWYER Nottingham Forest

Bowyer's move to the north was success road

by CHRIS COLES

IAN BOWYER, the Nottingham Forest winger has rediscovered his appetite for competitive football since moving northwards from London.

Bowyer, a recruit who emerged under the guidance of Joe Mercer when he was in charge at Manchester City, found himself out in the cold at both City and Orient, the London club he joined from Manchester.

Bowyer's problems at Orient arose mainly due to his inability to settle in London.

He and his family missed the northern way of life and both he and Orient manager George Petchey soon realised a move would be in the player's interests.

Bowyer took a large step of the way back home with a move to Orient's Second Division colleagues, Nottingham Forest. And now, although the man who signed him—Dave Mackay—has since departed, Bowyer has improved immensely in the last few months and has played a leading part in Forest's bid to sneak a promotion place.

Born at Ellesmere Port, Bowyer scored just over 20 goals in around 100 appearances for Orient. But he never really found his best form with the East London club who were persuaded to pay out £30,000 for his signature.

Now, however, Bowyer admits he has settled much better in Nottingham. He's just recently moved into a house there with his family, and says: "I have found the move northwards much to my liking. I found it hard to settle in London because I simply wasn't used to that life. I had never lived there before and I certainly missed Manchester.

"That sort of thing obviously affects a footballer's performance on the field. If he's not settled, things seem much more difficult.

"I feel I've fitted in nicely to the team play at Forest. I like their style and I'm happy with the way things are going."

Ironically, both Orient and Nottingham Forest are strong candidates to win one of the promotion places at the end of this season. For Orient, it has been a happier story than last season when they were almost relegated to the Third Division and Bowyer admits: "We struggled a lot last season. But I always knew there were some really great players at Orient."

When Orient went to Forest for a vital promotion match at the end of February, it was the Nottingham side who came out on top 2-1. Forest had played another London side a few days before that — Millwall — and Bowyer didn't score in either game.

But, particularly against Millwall at the Den, Bowyer proved his worth—and showed how much his game has progressed.

So now, Bowyer looks ahead—possibly to the First Division. "I'd love to get back there—particularly to play against City at Maine Road," he says. "And I think we'd do well if we got there."

Certainly, the presence of Bowyer's front-running colleague — Duncan McKenzie — makes Forest look an infinitely bigger threat to any side. McKenzie's goal-scoring talents this season have put him in the £200,000 class and his goals . . . and Bowyer's improved form . . . will play a big part in any Forest promotion plans.

IAN BOWYER (left) moves in to challenge Millwall goalkeeper Bryan King

JOHN
GALLEY

GEORGE
LYALL

Ian Bowyer, Nottingham Forest's new striker from Orient, has created a favourable impression in the two games for his new club. This goal at Blackpool was worth a point.

Loss of Mackay a savage blow to Forest

THE LOSS of Dave Mackay and Des Anderson to Derby County is a savage blow to Nottingham Forest's bid to bring First Division football back to the City Ground.

But the departure of the managerial pair only serves to illustrate how difficult a job faces the Forest committee.

They believed that in Mackay they had appointed the man who within two or three seasons would see the Reds back to the top flight.

They have found out the hard way that getting their man is only half the battle. Keeping him is the more worrying factor.

Inevitable

... has developed at the City Ground were not enough to influence giving serious consideration to staying with Forest.

What Forest have got to do now is capitalise on the ambition and enthusiasm that rubbed off from Mackay and Anderson and hope the new manager will provide other qualities to add to them.

Without doubt, Forest have made progress in the ...

By John Lawson

... they respected him for it and responded accordingly.

But what the players' reaction will be now is anyone's guess. They have got used to his ways, style and theories and now they have to start all over again, adapting to a new manager's technique.

Policies

It won't be easy for them because the incoming manager is sure to have hard-line policies of his own.

Under Mackay, Forest have become — not without cost — one of the most attacking-minded sides in the Second Division. Who's to say that's the method ...

... season disruption they wanted.

For this reason alone, I'm pleased the Forest committee have not acted hastily in appointing a new manager for the sake of filling the position as quickly as possible.

Getting the wrong man could have the same affect as wasting the money they still have available for new players. I'd much prefer them to take their time, consider all implications before naming their choice.

Spare a thought this weekend for Forest's £40,000 striker Ian Bowyer.

Two and a half years ago Jimmy Bloomfield bought him for Orient from Manchester City ...

Allan Brown faces quick testing

... before entertainment. "I beleive in playing to a team's strengths and that all depends on the nucleus of your side."

Tightening

Whether he decides Forest have the right blend for flowing, imaginative football, home and away, remains to be seen.

But he has intimated there could be a tightening ...

... that surrounded the resignation of Hill cannot hide the fact that he has been doing a fine job behind the scenes.

The contacts he has built up in youth and schools football were all to Forest's good in the years ahead. Now Derby County will reap the benefit.

Mackay, Anderson, Murphy, Hill ... only Bill Anderson and Bert Johnson remain.

fill the boots of Brian Clough. He settled on Dave Mackay, a former fan's favourite. Forest realized they couldn't stand in his way and after Mackay was offered the job, they agreed to release him, but they were to receive no compensation, because the manager was not under contract.

Just as it seemed that the Reds had turned their fortunes around, they were now forced to look for not only a new manager, but also a whole new backroom staff, as they too, all followed Mackay to Derby.

The image that Dave Mackay projected, perhaps did not live up to the reality as George Lyall explains, "From the outside he gives the impression of being a hard man, he certainly was on the pitch, but as a manager he was quieter, more considered, sometimes I think he let players get away with things he shouldn't have. Perhaps handing out a few more bollockings was in order, but the players certainly didn't think the season would collapse after he left. Dave loved playing in the five-a-side games and even then you could see what a quality player he must have been".

Duncan McKenzie recalls the effect he had on him,"I was loaned out to Mansfield by Dave, but after he had heard a few good reports about where and how I was playing, he came to see for himself. I then returned to the Forest team and my role had changed. Dave loved a bit of showboating, he'd tell me to trick my way past opponents and wanted me to turn it on for both the team and fans. Dave Mackay was the key manager in getting me to reach my potential as a footballer. All the lads respected Dave and he inspired them". In light of this, it is surprising that Super Red of Heanor thought, 'In fifty years, I have never seen a side so lacking in skill'.

When appraising Dave Mackay's time with the Reds, we can see that he had stopped the rot, but we will never know if he would have brought success to the club, after all he wasn't around long enough to implement the changes he would have liked. That aside, his parting gift was a good one, when he signed Ian Bowyer from Orient for a fee of only £40,000, a transfer that was to have a profound impact on the fortunes of Nottingham Forest over the next thirteen years.

Dave Mackay welcomes new signing Ian Bowyer

Ian gives us the background to this transfer, "I had joined Orient from Man City, dropping down a division, but I was having such a rough time there, I would have gone anywhere. Although I had played quite regularly and scored goals, the crowd never took to me, so it was a relief to get away. Orient was a world away from what I was used to with regard to facilities and living in London was certainly different. I was a country boy at heart, even though we had good accommodation in Muswell Hill. I enjoyed my time there, but when I heard that Forest were interested in me, it was always a move I was going to make. Although they were below us in the table, I just felt that the prospects were greater. It was disappointing that Dave left shortly after I arrived, but I had enough confidence in my ability to think that I would be okay whoever was appointed manager".

Ian Bowyer only played two times under Mackay, the first was a scoring debut at Blackpool, where he roomed with Duncan McKenzie, "He never stopped talking", joked Ian. The second was Mackay's last game, a dull 0-0 draw with Hull City. He left the team in sixth place, two points off a promotion spot.

As usual, the club turned to Bill Anderson to assume the managerial duties, whilst they began the search for a successor.

As it turned out, the Forest revolution could have begun a year earlier than it eventually did, as Stuart Dryden made an audacious attempt to lure Brian Clough and Peter Taylor to the City Ground. Brian was open to the idea but the Forest committee weren't ready, "We don't want success at any price," Jim Willmer warned Brian Appleby. Brian Clough was asked to formally apply for the job, but didn't and shortly afterwards ended up on the south coast with Brighton. Had the Reds blown their opportunity ?

At the Aston Villa game in October, there were chants for Forest to appoint Clough and the Football Post editor agreed with them. Harry Richards said in his column several weeks later, 'When Clough wasn't appointed, it was a real missed opportunity', and lots of others agreed with him. D Caygill, Attenborough, 'The committee have done what everybody expected them to do and let Clough slip through

Neill Martin in action against Blackpool.

Ian Bowyer fires home against Middlesbrough.

Forest apply the pressure but County hold on.

McKenzie lifts the ball over the Cardiff keeper and into the net

REDS WIN A SUNDAY THRILLER

Goals that started it . . .

Forest went one up (left) when Martin scored in the second minute — and two up when skipper Sammy Chapman in the 31st, sent in a shot which a Bristol defender deflected. Right: Eadie, the Rovers' keeper dives in vain to prevent the ball going in.

FOREST-4 ROVERS-3

UP, DOWN, THEN FOREST STORM BACK IN CUP

Lyall penalty — and winner by Martin

Hindley in agony . . .

After 20 minutes second half play, with Forest a goal down, Peter Hindley was carried off in agony after colliding with Jim Barron as both raced to cut off a Rover's attack. Later it was announced that Hindley's injuries were not serious.

THE Nottingham public gave Sunday soccer a big welcome to the City Ground yesterday. The largest attendance since Forest's First Division days turned out to watch them beat Bristol Rovers.

Despite opposition from several quarters to the match being staged on the recognised day of rest, 23,456 packed the ground which just about doubles the average home attendance for the season.

Last time that figure was bettered was when Manchester United were held to a goalless draw in one of Forest's final First Division appearances.

Delighted chairman Jim Willmer, who has campaigned for the introduction of Sunday football for many years, said: "It was an even bigger crowd than I expected.

"We were hoping for something in the region of 20,000 and I am sure that it justifies what we have been saying for years. Equally, I am convinced that the attendance would have been 7,000 less if the game had been played on Saturday.

"It is impossible to say whether the figure was unduly influenced by the nice weather or if people came along because of the novelty of Sunday football but there were certainly many people at the game who would not have been able to watch it on Saturday.

"Something has to be done to get the crowds back to football and I think today's experiment has been a definite step in the right direction."

He added that the club would now make an early approach to Manchester City for the fourth round tie to be played on Sunday, January 27, providing the Football Association will again give permission for the switch.

THE superlatives were being thrown freely around hours after the end of this Sunday epic FA Cup tie, which saw Nottingham Forest clinch a glittering Fourth Round clash with Manchester City at the City Ground.

At one time it looked easy for Forest at another it appeared as though they were facing certain defeat. But in the end the Reds battled through to send a 23,000-plus crowd into raptures in a game that is not likely to be bettered on this season's Wembley trail.

It was short of nothing. There was glamour, goals and guts and when you think about those characteristics, there was a bit of each from Forest's matchwinner, Neil Martin.

The 33-year-old Scot, who must have thought a time or two that his glory days were long over, was the player who received the hero's reception at the end of this pulsating match.

INJURY

But afterwards Martin, who started the scoring and completed it, revealed that from the first ten minutes he had suffered a recurrence of the thigh injury that threatened to keep him out of the match in the first place.

"I felt it very early in the game but I wanted to keep

by John Lawson

going and it worked out all right," said Martin.

But there was one time in the match, with Rovers turning a two goal deficit into a 3-2 lead, when the unbeaten Third Division leaders looked capable of marching on.

"It looked bad for us then," admitted Martin. "But we got the penalty and that changed the game around again. We only had ourselves to blame, though, because when we were leading 2-0 the chance was there to make the game really safe."

STUNNED

He was dead right, but Rovers, subjected to chants of "What's it like to be outclassed," drew on reserves of character to stun Forest

with a three-goal burst either side of half-time.

"It didn't surprise me that we came back from two goals down," commented Rovers captain Mike Green. "I knew we could keep going and that we might get the breaks and that's the way it turned out.

"You could sense the way the game was going when we were ahead that Forest had just about given their lot. They had to push right forward and were leaving spaces at the back.

"But they got the penalty and the game was wide open. We're not arguing about the penalty but we did think he'd lost control when he went down," he added.

The penalty was the crucial turning point of the game and, ironically, it might never have occurred had Forest defender Peter Hindley not been stretchered off with a leg injury.

COLLISION

Hindley was injured 20 minutes into the second half after colliding with Jim Barron and with Forest trailing 3-2 it looked curtains.

But Miah Dennehy, who has been turning in some great performances for the reserves, came into the game to add another dimension to Forest's attack and it was from his pass that George Lyall went through to be floored for the penalty.

It was a game crammed full of incident and the action started in the 85th second.

John Winfield, who had a lot of space in which to work in the early stages, floated over a cross from the left. Ian Bowyer headed it down and Martin did the rest from close range.

Martin could easily have had a second after 18 minutes when a beautifully flighted ball from Sammy Chapman completely deceived the Rovers defence and then John Cottam put the ball over the top after Jim Eadie had fumbled a Lyall free-kick.

DESERVED

With Chapman again looking the part in midfield, Forest continued to take the game to Rovers and in the 31st minute they got a deserved second goal.

Bowyer, playing as if he'd walk through a minefield if he was asked to, swung the ball into the middle. Eadie punched unconvincingly away and Chapman rattled in a shot which deflected off Frankie Prince and into the net.

Rovers players said that the ball was well covered until it hit Prince but the Bristol midfield man got his own back in first half injury time when he started the Eastville recovery.

There seemed no danger for Forest when Prince, who admitted later that he was aiming for John Rudge's head, floated a centre from the edge of the area into the Forest net.

INCREDIBLE

Jim Barron, however seemed badly at fault and the second half was only five minutes old when the Forest keeper was beaten again.

He came out to push

Managers' quotes

ALAN BROWN: "I could have cried when we went behind but it was tremendous the way we came back to win. We had so many battlers. I was pleased for the supporters and I'm a happy man myself."

DON MEGSON: "It must have been a great game for supporters and while I'm disappointed in the result, I'm not with the performance. I've no complaints about the penalty but I did think the player had lost control when he went down."

Move caused few problems —Ken Smales

Forest secretary Ken Smales said that in terms of administration the move to Sunday caused few problems.

"The fact that team-sheets had to be sold at turnstiles meant that it took that much longer to get each person through and this built up slightly," he said.

"Biggest problem was the 2 p.m. kick-off. There was a tremendous rush in the last 10 minutes and many people missed the start of the match."

Mr. Smales added that a few people tried to gain free admittance - to which they were legally entitled. "They were abusive and we did not let them in."

'Dunc' puts one wide

It might have been another Forest goal . . . Duncan McKenzie, in full cry, makes an all-action picture on his own. But his header went wide.

NOTTINGHAM FOREST FOOTBALL CLUB

Official Team Sheet

FOOTBALL ASSOCIATION CHALLENGE CUP
ROUND THREE

SUNDAY, 6th JANUARY, 1974—CITY GROUND

NOTTM. FOREST Red Shirts White Shorts		BRISTOL ROVERS Blue/White Quarters White Shorts
Jim Barron	1	Jim Eadie
Liam O'Kane	2	Trevor Jacobs
John Winfield	3	Lindsay Parsons
Peter Hindley	4	Mike Green
John Cottam	5	Stuart Taylor
Paul Richardson	6	Frankie Prince
Duncan McKenzie	7	Gordon Fearnley
George Lyall	8	Tom Stanton
Neil Martin	9	Alan Warboys
Martin O'Neill	10	Bruce Bannister
Ian Bowyer	11	Colin Dobson
Tommy Jackson	12	John Rudge

REFEREE **Mr. J. HUNTING** (Leicester)
LINESMEN **Mr. P. J. RICHARDSON** (Lincoln)
Mr. G. A. ROSE (Leicester)

25p. JUVENILE

THANK Y... YOUR SUPPORT!

★ STAR BARGAIN ★
1971 TRIUMPH 1500 SALOON. Finished in Wedgwood Blue with blue interior, fitted wing mirrors, one owner from new, absolute gift at £800.
HOOLEYS GARAGE
DERBY ROAD, NOTTINGHAM.

EVENING POST

PRICE 3p

NOTTINGHAM, FRIDAY, JANUARY 25, 1974

No. 29,746

Saturday work option

3-DAY WEEK GOES ON

THE THREE-DAY week is to continue — but with an option on Saturday working from next week.

Announcing this in the Commons today, Energy Minister, Mr. Patrick Jenkin, said firms on the Thursday to Saturday rota would have the option of using electricity on Wednesday to Friday.

CITY CALL FOR ENERGY TALKS

'Notts vote

LEADERS of Nottinghamshire's 34,000 miners today predicted that their members would vote in favour of a strike, even though they themselves opposed a strike ballot at yesterday's meeting of the NUM executive.

'Boom'

their fingers'. D Smith, Arnold, 'The club have shown a lack of vision and timidity'.

Whilst Jim Willmer speaking on the club's behalf said, "We have had thirty two applications for the job, Clough was not amongst them. We hadn't approached him, we didn't think he would be interested".

Bill Anderson worked the oracle once more. Three successive wins, away at Palace, the first away win since he was last in charge, followed by a 3-0 win over Fulham and a 2-0 win against Carlisle.

Meanwhile power cuts were now being extensively implemented across the country and this meant early kick offs, as clubs weren't allowed to use floodlights.

Then the club dropped the bombshell that Allan Brown had been appointed as new manager. No disrespect to Brown, but he didn't fill any of the so called criteria that the club claimed they were looking for in a candidate. His managerial experience consisted of distinctly average spells with Luton, Torquay and Bury. He was old school personified. Jim Willmer in welcoming the manager hoped that he could provide good entertaining football and satisfactory results, whilst Brown said, "I am a quiet man, who will work hard for this club". Indeed, if this was the level of everyone's ambitions, no wonder Clough wasn't wanted.

The players have little to remember Allan Brown by. John Winfield says, "You hardly noticed him, he had no charisma or spark", whilst George Lyall adds, "He didn't seem to have any new ideas". John Robertson and Martin O'Neill both had no time for him, neither player seemed to be Brown's type of player.

Lifelong supporter Harry Durose wrote that, 'He was struggling to keep his long span of supporting the Reds going'.
Allan Brown's first game in charge was a goalless draw at Sunderland. He had been fortunate to inherit a team in a healthy league position, normally a manager would be brought in to replace a struggling one. Brown was also lucky that he had Duncan McKenzie. The manager recognized the situation for what it was and to his credit kept changes to a minimum.

Another point away from home at Cardiff was followed by his first defeat as manager at the hands of Middlesbrough, the last of three successive away games. The 1-0 defeat was not helped by the dismissal of Liam O'Kane, "It was a very icy pitch and I slid in to take the ball, the referee couldn't have seen what had happened because he came over and sent me off for foul play, I hadn't touched the fella. We appealed the decision and I was vindicated when it was over ruled, but we had still lost the game".

The following week, two ex Reds announced that they were being forced into early retirement. Terry Hennessey was unable to continue after a combination of knee and achilles problems, he was finished at thirty one. Whilst Ian Moore at the age of only twenty nine had to call it a day after his ankle problems had been spectacularly mishandled by the Manchester United medical team.

The Christmas period saw the two sides of Nottingham Forest support that we still see today. Only 9,000 attended the year's last home game with Bolton, an entertaining 3-2 win, before almost double that figure attended Meadow Lane to support the Reds in a 1-0 victory, courtesy of a George Lyall penalty. Then, despite the difficulties of travelling, another 5,000 fans made the trip to Hillsborough for the game against Sheffield Wednesday, a 1-1 draw, that saw McKenzie's barren run of six games without scoring end, when he struck the equalizer. Forest have always seemed to have large numbers of fans prepared to follow the team away, even if they don't go down to the City Ground.

This season, the FA Cup draw was made live on television for the first time. The Reds appeared to have a good home tie with Third Division Bristol Rovers, however the game wasn't as easy as it might have looked on paper, as Rovers were having one of their finest seasons, knocking in goals for fun on the way to winning the title. Their forwards Alan Warboys and Bruce Bannister were prolific. They were also to give Brian Clough and Peter Taylor their most humbling experience as football managers when they visited Brighton at the Goldstone Ground and left with an 8-2

The Reds' Youth Team that took part in the Bremen Tournament.

Left to right : Mickie Woods, Lee Young, Tony Woodcock, David Hunter, Bobby Heddon, Barry Towill, Keith Brown, Viv Anderson, Trevor Moden, John Middleton, Peter Wells

victory. The cup tie was also given extra significance when the Football Association allowed the fixture to be put back twenty four hours and be played on a Sunday. Forest had for many years advocated Sunday football and this gave the club the opportunity to put the theory to the test. The country was currently under a three day working week due to industrial action by the Power Company workers. Cuts were implemented on a rota basis and Nottingham had been designated to have a Saturday working day, which would have meant that many fans would have been unable to attend.

There was a further problem in that due to the 'Lord's Day Observant Act', clubs were not allowed to charge for admission on a Sunday, but they got around this by selling team sheets outside the ground for an inflated price, (the same price that admission would have been) and then you presented this paper at the turnstiles to gain entrance. Ken Smales used his contacts in the Rugby League world to ensure things ran smoothly (that sport had embraced Sunday fixtures for several years). The game itself was an absolute cracker, played out before a crowd in excess of 23,000, the highest at the City Ground since relegation and totally justifying the decision to move the game. Forest raced into an early two goal lead before Rovers struck three times in seventeen minutes either side of half-time to turn the game on its head. However, with Ian Bowyer leading from the front, Forest forced their way back into the game when Lyall won, and then scored from the penalty spot. The perfect ending for Forest came just minutes from full time, as Neil Martin rounded things off with the winning goal, heading in from a corner. It was by far the best atmosphere at the ground for years.

By now the younger Reds' fans were congregating in the East Stand, occupying the terracing around the last entrance before the Bridgford End, but it was still strange to see and hear the famous Trent End much quieter than in past years, as it was filled by a different type of supporter.

Ken Smales

'This was a fine Sunday sermon', wrote Red Reg. The draw for the next round had already been made by the time of kick off against Rovers, so both teams knew that a glamour game against Manchester City awaited the winners. Whilst this was something for the fans to look forward to, league matters now needed to take precedence. Despite a few stutters, Forest still found themselves handily placed in fifth, with a local derby at home to West Brom up next. In what turned out to be Peter Hindley's last appearance, they were brought sharply back down to earth with a 4-1 drubbing, could the Reds maintain a promotion challenge whilst they were still in the cup?

The FA once more allowed the club to stage the cup game on a Sunday after Manchester City raised no objections. Forest were rewarded with a magnificent attendance of 41,472, all the better because the away team only brought a couple of hundred followers and they were easily accommodated on the terracing in front of the Main Stand, the Bridgford side of the tunnel. It was also reported that several prisoners from Manchester prison were allowed to attend, but after the result, this was surely seen as part of their punishment.

It was a game that was forever to be known as 'McKenzie's Match', as he produced a breathtaking display of individual skill that outshone anything that City stars such as Marsh, Lee or Summerbee could produce. McKenzie's magic helped the Reds to an early two goal lead before the action in the last minute of the first half provided the memory of a lifetime for those present. Collecting the ball on the right wing, he nonchalantly beat the full back Willie Donachie, then nut-megging Tommy Booth, tricking his way past Mike Doyle, evading Tony Towers before squaring the ball back for Bowyer to fire home. Fans relating the goal afterwards would swear that he also dribbled out into the Main Stand car park, sat on the ball before re-entering the pitch down by the corner flag, such was the impact that goal had. Colin Barrett who was in the City side at the time playing right back remembers he got a dressing down from the manager, (he often thought he was made scapegoat), even though he was on the other side of the pitch. John Robertson jokes that despite all his success in football, fans still want to talk to him about that goal.

It was a particularly sweet moment for Ian Bowyer. Speaking after the game he said, "I've waited a long time to play against City, but it was worth waiting for". This was a low key response, but speaking many years later it is clear how much that result and goal meant to him. "I had endured such a difficult time at City, the

'WE ALL AGREE, DUNCAN McKENZIE IS MAGIC!'...

FOREST-4 CITY-1

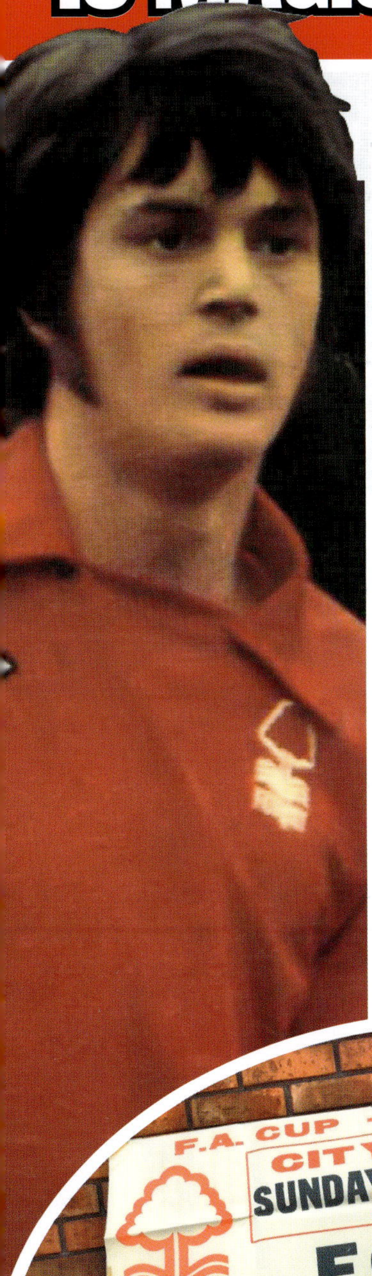

NOTTINGHAM FOREST 4
MANCHESTER CITY 1

WITH Duncan McKenzie in his most magical mood, Nottingham Forest blazed their way through to the last 16 of the FA Cup yesterday with a performance that will be long remembered by a captivated 40,000-plus crowd.

By JOHN LAWSON

It was McKenzie at his scintillating best as he produced a 45-minute performance that bettered anything City's international class stars could muster among them during the entire match.

He created wholesome havoc in a Maine Road defence that is supposed to have become one of the tightest in the First Division since Ron Saunders took over as manager.

GENIUS

And it was his genius that gave Ian Bowyer, the player who had to leave City because they could not guarantee him first team football, so much satisfaction.

Bowyer scored twice from openings by McKenzie, who hit one of the others and laid on the fourth for George Lyall.

"I've waited a long time to play against City, but it was worth waiting for," said the delighted Bowyer after the match.

"It was tremendous to score a couple of goals but you've got to hand it to Duncan. What a player! They are one of the best sides in the country and he tore them to shreds," Ian added.

McKenzie, whose unpredictable skills had City in a dither from the start, sliced open the Manchester defence in the 17th minute to begin Bowyer's bonanza.

ball on the right, he slipped past the City full back with nonchalant and contemptuous ease, nut-megged Booth, beat Mike Doyle and pushed the ball between another defender and MacRae for Bowyer to accept the simplest of tasks.

Up to that point City, who had lost Rodney Marsh in the 36th minute with an ankle injury, had produced none of their positive and imaginative forward play.

But in the final act of the half Colin Bell, in Richardson's pocket for the rest of the 45 minutes, rapped a shot against the post to remind Forest they still had a game on their hands.

Had that gone in, it might have been a different game because City's second half fight back would have been so much more threatening.

FOILED

With Bell moved into an attacking role to free him from Richardson, City strung together their moves much more effectively and they might have had more reward than Frank Carrodus's 72nd minute headed goal from Summerbee's free kick.

Before that Carrodus had [illegible] foiled by Barron, who [illegible] out the second half [illegible] of the dam- [illegible] form has [illegible] tion.

FOOTBALL POST

LOCAL RESULTS

Forest	5	Middlesbro'	1
Hull City	1	Notts. Co.	0
Derby Co.	1	Newcastle	0
Q. P. Rangers	0	Leicester C.	0

Vol. LXV No. 24 NOTTINGHAM, SATURDAY, FEBRUARY 2, 1974 Price 3p

CUP-HAPPY FOREST ROCK THE LEADERS

JOHN LAWSON at the City Ground

CUP-HAPPY Nottingham Forest gave their promotion chances a great uplift here this afternoon when they hit Division One-bound Middlesbrough with a tremendous three-goal blast in the first half.

Attendance: 18,799

fans really made my life miserable, so when those goals went in it was like a relief". Ian celebrated his first goal with an extravagant somersault.

With the job seemingly done by half-time, it was inevitable that the second half would be less intense, City pulled a goal back, but the Reds had the final word when George Lyall fastened onto another McKenzie pass to fire past MacRae to complete a 4-1 rout. Even Francis Lee said that Duncan McKenzie's performance was one of the finest he had seen. This inevitably led to speculation about the future of the Forest star. Six days later Forest entertained runaway leaders Middlesbrough, unbeaten for twenty four games under the leadership of Jack Charlton. The game was played on a Saturday, as for some reason Boro' refused Forest's request to move the game and this resulted in a disappointing attendance of 18,000.

'Cup happy Forest rock the leaders', was the headline after Forest tore Middlesbrough apart with a sensational 5-1 victory. A great team performance, that also featured a blockbusting right foot wonder goal from John Winfield, who told me, that despite playing virtually his whole career on the left, he preferred using his right foot. Duncan McKenzie might not have scored, but again he controlled the game.

Allan Brown declared that he was delighted with his team, but added, perhaps dangerously, that he didn't want to make any signings, as he was worried that new faces could upset team morale.

Confidence was now sky high, so it was massively disappointing when another huge following saw the Reds fall 2-1 to struggling Preston at Deepdale, Forest missing out on a point when Tommy Jackson failed with a last minute penalty.

Before the fifth round tie with Portsmouth, long serving Peter Hindley was allowed to join Coventry City for a small fee, but such was the regard in which he was held, Peter was granted a testimonial match to be held at the end of the season. Once again the Portsmouth game was to be held on a Sunday. M Harris, Newthorpe commented, 'I realise that Sunday football looks like it is here to stay, so would it be possible to have some hymn singing before the games?'

The match itself was a tight and tense affair settled by a disputed penalty from Duncan McKenzie. Portsmouth were fuming when Eoin Hand was ruled to have fouled Bowyer. Ian with a smile remembers, "Perhaps it was a soft decision, but we all thought we had two clear handball claims earlier in the game that weren't given, so perhaps justice was done".

McKenzie who took the penalty was only given the job because George Lyall was missing through suspension and Tommy Jackson had missed one the week before. Allan Brown had organized a penalty competition, won by Duncan, during the week running up to the game. McKenzie said, "My knees were shaking as I went to take it and as I stepped forward, I hadn't even thought what I was going to do, still it went in".

George Lyall saw the game from the stand, although he had thought about not going, "I hated watching games, for this one I was a bag of nerves, I must have chewed my nails down to the quick. It was just a relief when Duncan put the penalty away". The reward for beating Portsmouth was a trip to the North East and a game against Newcastle, but with three weeks until the game the manager had to remind his players that the league was the priority as they appeared to be struggling with more mundane fixtures. Martin O'Neill, not for the first or last time in his career, was in dispute with the manager, a training ground incident had led the club to discipline him. Harry Richards in the Football Post offered his opinion, before Martin himself wrote to the editor, telling him to keep his nose out. Martin was upset at being left out, so he asked for a transfer, although the manager still picked him for the cup game.

Before the Newcastle game, Orient were beaten at home 2-1, although both sides ended the game with ten men as Jackson and Heppolite were sent off for fighting. Forest's last game before the Newcastle encounter was another intense affair against Notts County before 30,000 fans. The Magpies came determined to win a point and the blanket defence they employed seemed to work as they escaped with a 0-0 draw.

Forest had sold 13,000 tickets for the cup tie and five trains and hundreds of coaches ferried supporters to the North East. Although Forest knew that Newcastle would be tough opposition, there was real confidence that they could get a result. George Lyall was now back, "We really thought that we had the players to win up there, the game was billed as a shootout between the two Macs, Malcolm Macdonald for the Geordies, but our Duncan was something different". The game turned out to be one of the most controversial FA Cup ties in the history of the game. Forest took the attack to Newcastle and were rewarded with an Ian Bowyer goal after just ninety seconds. Newcastle responded with a period of intense pressure that led to an equalizing goal from David Craig, but the Forest players were beginning to realise that there was nothing to fear and defensively Chapman and Serella were marking danger man Macdonald out of the game. It was no surprise that the Reds regained the lead before half-time, what was surprising was that it was Liam O'Kane, with his

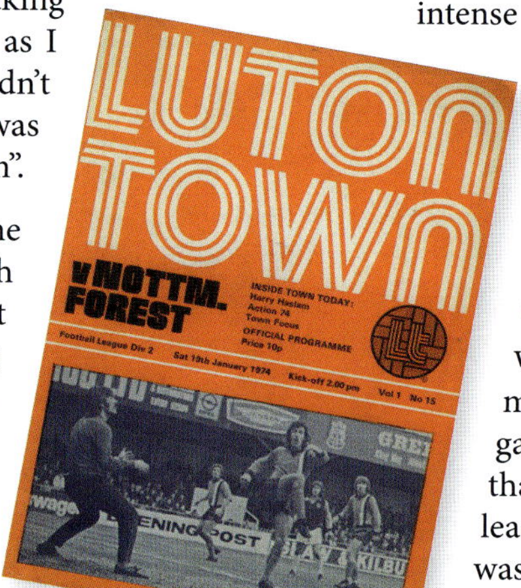

REDS 'SPOT ON' THE TRAIL TO WEMBLEY

FOREST-1
POMPEY-0

Sammy Chapman — Joe Harvey will have noted his strength.

DUNCAN McKENZIE has now scored 19 goals this season for Forest. Some have had the trademark of genius, others have been less flamboyant. But none have carried as much weight and importance as the easiest of the lot in yesterday's fifth round FA Cup tie with Portsmouth.

By John Lawson

In simple terms, McKenzie's match winning 58th minute precision penalty takes Forest past another hurdle on the Wembley trail and sets them up for a sixth round bonanza tie with pot-seeking Newcastle United at St. James's Park on March 9.

But the story behind McKenzie's penalty holds more irony than you would normally find in a full Football League programme. And soccer is noted for its paradoxical twists.

With George Lyall suspended and after Tommy Jackson's miss from the spot at Preston last Sunday, manager Allan Brown had to decide who would have the penalty job if one came along.

COMPETITION

In midweek Forest even had a penalty competition, which McKenzie won. But in a practice match later in the week McKenzie had a penalty SAVED by Reds reserve goalkeeper Dennis

player made the most of it but that's football. You just have to accept these sort of things.

"It was disappointing for us though. We knew we were in for a battle here but we felt we had weathered the storm at the start of the first half and were doing exactly the same in the second until the penalty. We are all sick about it."

APPEALS

Twice earlier in the game Forest had appealed unsuccessfully for penalties. Paul Went and Phil Roberts survived handling offences in the crucial five minute period before half time and Neil Martin, who led the protests, argued: "I was sure they were penalties — but I didn't think the one we got was!"

The penalty apart, this was always an interesting and exciting game but there was no time when it boiled

DONOVAN'S SELECTIONS

SEDGEFIELD

1.30	Star Award	3.00	STAPLE OAK
2.00	Blonde Viking	3.30	Verona's Inn
2.30	Kirwaugh	4.00	Thundergold

Double: BLONDE VIKING and STAPLE OAK

Duncan McKenzie sends Portsmouth goalkeeper Milkins the wrong way as he scores from the penalty spot to put Forest in the FA Cup quarter finals.

Fulha

NOTTS. COUNTY have not managed t win in seven Leagu visits to Craven Co tage since the war - and they never looke likely to change th course of history two second-half goa left Fulham victo ous on Saturd writes TER BOWLES.

Two goals undere mated the differe between the te Fulham were al worth both po hough in fact they not complete their orm until seven mi rom the end.

That was when Le ett, for so long one c ion Two's most co players, helped cli uccess with one f brilliance.

Troubled by a train, he had succu he close attent defender Bill Brin remained anonymous until collecting pass on the left touch line.

Nodded

Then, after losing Steve Carter, Barrett fought his way to the by-line and when Jimmy Conway nodded down his cross, Viv Busby found time to turn and

Mackay right not to go to

piled on pressure and Gregory was narrowly out with two easy chances.

Grantham shocked

The Reds robbed by the referee once more, as he disallows a Forest goal, in the cup replay.

first and only goal for the club who hooked the ball home with his left foot no less.

Forest were now on top and McKenzie began to flourish, showing his class with feints and dribbles, whilst the team knocked the ball around with confidence. The game looked over when McKenzie was pulled down for a penalty after half-time. Newcastle's Pat Howard made things even worse by getting himself sent off for arguing with the referee and despite a long wait, George Lyall coolly scored in front of the thousands of Reds fans behind the goal. Almost immediately there were disturbances behind the opposite goal, the Leazes End. Several United fans got onto the pitch, determined to stop play and before long, hundreds joined them as police struggled to maintain order. Eventually they charged the length of the pitch towards the Forest supporters punching several Reds players along the way, including Dave Serella who was badly shaken, whilst Forest's Geordie keeper Barron, got close to the Newcastle players for safety. Referee Gordon Kew was left with no option but to take the players off and give the police chance to restore order.

Looking back now, it is hard to imagine the blasé attitude the authorities took to the situation. The Forest players were shell-shocked, George Lyall recalls the mood in the dressing room, "We just sat around for about ten minutes and then they told us we had to go out again, we had some players who were really shaken up, but no-one asked us our opinion".

The atmosphere in the ground was tense, 3-1 up and against ten men Forest should have gone through, but with malevolence in the air, anything was possible. Recalling the events now, Ian Bowyer almost blames the players themselves for not being professional enough to see the job through. However, what was certain though, Newcastle raised their game and helped by a couple of goalkeeping errors and a limp performance from an obviously intimidated referee, the Magpies turned the game on its head with three goals in seventeen minutes. For anybody to imply that the events of that afternoon had not influenced the result was inconceivable, but that was what Newcastle did. John Tudor claimed that they had been 'unlucky' in the past, but this time 'luck' was on their side. Jim Barron had made some mistakes but as he says, "I couldn't stand back and position myself properly because of the crowd and I had to keep one eye looking out for missiles".

Anyone would have thought that the FA would announce their own enquiry, but times were different back then and it was left to Reds' chairman Jim Willmer to send off a telegram to the FA with an official complaint. Although most of the football world sided with Forest, some thought it was sour grapes and many thought there was little chance of the appeal succeeding.

The FA announced that the appeal would be heard by the four most senior members of the Football Association under the auspices of Lord Stevens. Nottingham Forest would send a delegation of four including Jim Willmer, Allan Brown, Ken Smales and Dave Serella who would give a first hand account of what happened on the pitch. Newcastle would be sending their chairman Lord Westwood, manager Joe Harvey and captain Bob Moncur. Lord Westwood was himself one of the most high ranking members of the FA and there were many who thought that there was going to be a clear conflict of interest.

As it turned out, the Appeals Committee only needed ninety minutes before they announced that the result of the game would be declared void and the cup tie would be replayed at Goodison Park Everton, the following Monday. Once more thousands of Reds' fans made the journey to Merseyside and saw the team robbed again. Ian Bowyer explains why the players felt so aggrieved, "We had been working on a free kick routine that involved looking like we had messed up, several players converging on the ball at the same time, it worked like a dream and I rifled the ball home. We couldn't believe it when the referee disallowed it for ungentlemanly conduct". The game ended 0-0, but at least Forest would now have a home game to try and finish the job.

There was disbelief all round when the FA announced that the replay would again be held at Everton, meaning that the Reds would be the first ever team to play three games away in the same round of the cup. It transpired that Lord Westwood had appealed to his fellow members on the FA Executive Committee that the Newcastle players would not be safe in Nottingham, as the fans would be looking for revenge. The FA agreed, so a third game was scheduled for the Thursday again at Everton and despite matching their Division One opponents once more, Malcolm Macdonald scored the only goal of the game.

The terraces at football grounds were lawless places at this time, much like the battlegrounds of industrial disputes. This incident was not an isolated one, every week disturbances were reported. There was rough play on the pitch and things came to a head that same week when referee Clive Thomas was forced to order both teams in the Manchester derby to the dressing room after Lou Macari of United and Mike Doyle of City refused to leave the pitch after being sent off.

This whole affair was to have a detrimental effect on the Reds' season. They had already slipped behind after losing fixtures to the cup run, but as George Lyall explained, "There was just a feeling of anti-climax, we were Second Division players

REDS GO OUT AS THE MOB SHAMES TYNESIDE

Guilty glory for Newcastle

I LOST count of the number of people who sympathised with Nottingham Forest manager Allan Brown and his shell-shocked players as the bitter incredibility of Saturday's Cup exit defied objective reasoning, writes JOHN LAWSON.

The condolences will continue throughout this week as football fans everywhere deplore the manner in which the intimadatory Tyneside crowd dragged Newcastle back to a 4-3 victory in this infamous sixth round tie.

It was a sad day for me personally. As a youngster I stood many times behind the goal from which the rioting fans came to turn St. James's Park into an ugly, appalling battleground.

Police fought with the hooligan hundreds and as the teams fled to the safety of the dressing rooms, one of the Forest players was kicked and then punched in the face.

Fortunately, Forest supporters, so often criticised for their violent outbursts, did not accept the idiotic bait and eventually some semblence of equilibrium was restored.

The tragedy was that the innocent saw their team suffer and the guilty were able, to g... sen... of a...

never, even in such trying conditions, have allowed their position of overwhelming s... to deteriorate so...

Manager ... spoken in his ... of the Newca... nowledged t... were not ... enough whe... on," he said ... the most ... moment of ... career.

"We di... half-time ... page we ... our game ... off."

Captain Sammy Chapman, wearing the look of a man who had seen his soccer ambitions d... amid the hor... otic second ... have never b... my life."

He summed ... ings of Trent... player who cou... sympathy in hi...

...s Clark and Craig clear a Forest attack with McKenzie in close attendance.

...nd white as the Geor... ...uled themselves dramat... ...lly level before scoring ... winner in the last ...ute.

...the inquest started into Forest's demoralising collapse, the actions of the turbulent crowd dominated conversation on the long journey home.

The fact remains, however, that the Reds should ...

...pathy ... cause of West ... egative approach, ... t to cement a place in Europe they must do a lot better than this.

Forest's goals ca... an Ian Bowyer ... inside 90 seconds, left foot shot ... O'Kane — his first ... for the club — a... Lyall's penalty ... had held dow... McKenzie.

for Europe . . ? Not ...

Rug... beat

FANS OWN UNION IS BACKING THE REDS

by PETER FRATER

SO-CALLED soccer fans showed what they are capable ... when they disrupted the Newcastle-Forest Cup tie ... the real supporters want to show what they can do ... that justice is done.

FA CONSIDER FOREST'S CUP PROTEST

by TERRY BOWLES

... FA Cup committee today received an appeal from Nottingham ... concerning their unsatisfactory exit from the competition ... could lead to the club finding themselves involved in the ... draw after all.

Monday's the day

FA RULING: FOR REDS

NEWCASTLE were this afternoon ordered to replay last Saturday's FA Cup quarter-final against Nottingham Forest.

In an unprecedented step, the special four-man commission formed to consider Forest's appeal against the outcome of the match decided that the Second Division club were justified in their complaint.

The official statement read out by FA secretary Ted Croker, said: "I have to announce ... the commission have carefully considered all the evidence and the match will be ...

'Watchdog'

Local people among M1

THOUSANDS HIT THE CUP TRAIL

All set to shout for Forest . . .

Olive's first ever win

BUT SHE NEARLY

REDS' CRUCIAL BID FOR CUP JUSTICE

by TERRY BOWLES

...cott aims for ...peat display

DUNCAN McKENZIE

LIAM O'KANE

Nottm. Forest

Frank Wignall and Joe Baker pictured alongside John Winfield on the evening of his testimonial game.

John Winfield alongside Forest Secretary Ken Smales and Peterborough manager John Barnwell, on the stage of the Heart of the Midlands as the player completes his move to the Posh.

who had a once in a career opportunity to reach an FA Cup semi-final against Burnley, everybody in our team would have backed us to beat them".

The Reds were forced to play a league game away at Fulham just two days after losing to Newcastle, a tired looking Forest slipped to a 2-0 defeat. The Londoners had new signing Bobby Moore in defence.

After the successful introduction of the new club badge, there were serious discussions about whether the club should be known as just Forest and drop the Nottingham as Orient had done. Luckily sanity prevailed and the idea was kicked out. On a positive note, the club announced plans to expand the supporter's groups and make match tickets available from outlets around the county.

A home victory 2-0, courtesy of a couple of goals from George Lyall was the only bright spot with only two further points being gained from the next five fixtures. With the worst results being an undeserved 2-1 home defeat to a relegation bound Crystal Palace.

The promotion dream finally died over three fixtures played in four days over Easter. The small squad were unable to cope with fatigue and injury. Allan Brown was now in desperate need of some quality reserves. Unbelievably the fixture list took the Reds up to Carlisle on the Friday, followed by a fixture 400 miles away at Bristol City the next day before the return game against the same opposition on the Monday. George Lyall recalls the trip home from Bristol, "The manager knew we were knackered and let us have a few beers on the coach, how they expected us to play after that journey I will never know". Other players remember that journey home as being the day Allan Brown's authority was severely tested. Those players sitting at the back gradually got merrier and then began impersonating the manager, before beginning a game where they tried to roll bottles down the aisle.

With one eye on next season the manager took the opportunity to introduce some youngsters. Dennis Peacock replaced Barron in goal, on merit Brown said, his kicking was particularly good, whilst Tony Woodcock made his debut away at Aston Villa in a 3-1 defeat.

Duncan McKenzie finished the season on a high, scoring in five consecutive matches to end with 28 goals, two away at Portsmouth in the final game was a great send off, coming two days after the National Emergency had ended. A rejuvenated John Winfield made the most appearances, fifty in total and fully deserved his testimonial game against Leicester that saw an emotional return for Joe Baker and Frank Wignall, re-united in the Forest attack. However special mention should be made for Liam O'Kane who had been splendidly consistent all season. Forest ended the season in seventh place, only four points off a promotion spot after taking only eight points from a possible twenty after the disappointing cup exit. The impossible playing demands on them at the end of the season, allied with the small squad had finally put paid to any promotion hopes.

What if they hadn't embarked on a cup run? What if the manager had strengthened the team?

We will never know, but the biggest problem facing the club at this time would be, can they keep hold of Duncan McKenzie?

FACTS and FIGURES

Aug 20th 1973, F, A, v. Lincoln City, Loss 0-2, AT 2,661, Barron, O'Kane, Winfield, Serella, Cottam, Jackson, McKenzie, Lyall, Martin, O'Neill, Dennehy, SUB Woodcock.

Aug 25th 1973, H, v. Luton Town, Win 4-0, Scorers Jackson 2 (1Pen), Martin, McKenzie, AT 10,792, Barron, O'Kane, Winfield, Serella, Cottam, Jackson, McKenzie, O'Neill, Martin, Lyall, Dennehy.

Sept 1st 1973, A, v. Oxford United, Loss 0-1, AT 7,861, Barron, O'Kane, Winfield, Serella, Cottam, Jackson, McKenzie, O'Neill, Martin, Lyall, Dennehy, SUB Galley.

Sept 8th 1972, H, v. Sheffield Wednesday, Win 2-1, Scorer McKenzie (2), AT 13,452, Barron, O'Kane, Winfield, Chapman, Cottam, Galley, McKenzie, O'Neill, Martin, Lyall, Dennehy, SUB Richardson.

Sept 11th 1973, A, v. Hull City, Draw 0-0, AT 8,134, Barron, O'Kane, Winfield, Chapman, Cottam, Lyall, McKenzie, O'Neill, Martin, Hindley, Dennehy.

Sept 15th 1973, A, v. West Bromwich Albion, Draw 3-3, Scorers McKenzie (2), Martin, AT 14,799, Barron, O'Kane, Winfield, Chapman, Cottam, Lyall, McKenzie, O'Neill, Martin, Hindley, Dennehy, SUB Richardson.

Sept 18th 1973, H, v. Swindon Town, Win 2-0, Scorer McKenzie (2), AT 11, 031, Barron, O'Kane, Winfield, Chapman, Cottam, Lyall, McKenzie, O'Neill, Martin, Hindley, Dennehy, SUB Galley.

Sept 22nd 1973, H, v. Preston North End, Draw 1-1, Scorer O' Neill, AT 12,958, Barron, O'Kane, Winfield, Chapman, Cottam, Lyall, McKenzie, O'Neill, Martin, Hindley, Dennehy, SUB Galley.

Sept 29th 1973, A, v. Bolton Wanderers, Loss 0-1, AT 15,388, Barron, O'Kane, Winfield, Chapman, Cottam, Lyall, McKenzie, O'Neill, Martin, Galley, Richardson, SUB Jackson.

Oct 2nd 1973, A, v. Swindon Town, Draw 0-0, AT 6,353, Barron, O'Kane, Winfield, Chapman, Cottam, Lyall, McKenzie, O'Neill, Galley, Peplow, Jackson.

Oct 6th 1973, H, v. Millwall, Win 3-0, Scorer Lyall, McKenzie (2), AT 11,387, Barron, O'Kane, Winfield, Chapman, Cottam, Lyall, Peplow, O'Neill, Galley, McKenzie, Jackson.

Oct 10th 1973, LC, A, v. Millwall, Draw 0-0, AT 8,763, Barron, O'Kane, Winfield, Chapman, Cottam, Lyall, McKenzie, O'Neill, Galley, Peplow, Jackson.

Oct 13th 1973, A, v. Orient, Loss 1-3, Scorer Lyall, AT 8,346, Barron, O'Kane, Winfield, Chapman, Cottam,. Lyall, Peplow, O'Neill, Galley, Martin, Jackson, SUB Dennehy.

Oct 16th 1973, LC, H, v, Millwall, Loss 1-3, Scorer Martin, AT 9,241, Barron, O'Kane, Winfield, Chapman, Cottam, Lyall, McKenzie, O'Neill, Martin, Peplow, Jackson, SUB Galley.

Oct 20th 1973, A, v. Blackpool, Draw 2-2, Scorers McKenzie, Bowyer, AT 8,101, Barron, O'Kane, Winfield, Chapman, Cottam, Lyall, McKenzie, O'Neill, Martin, Jackson, Bowyer, SUB Galley.

Oct 23rd 1973, H, v. Hull City, Draw 0-0, AT 10,392, Peacock, O'Kane, Winfield, Chapman, Cottam, Lyall, McKenzie, O'Neill, Martin, Jackson, Bowyer.

Oct 27th 1973, H, v. Aston Villa, Loss 1-2, Scorer McKenzie, AT 17,718, Barron, O'Kane, Winfield, Chapman, Cottam, Jackson, McKenzie, Lyall, Martin, O'Neill, Bowyer, SUB Richardson.

Nov 3rd 1973, A, v. Crystal Palace, Win 1-0, Scorer McKenzie, AT 22,075, Barron, O'Kane, Winfield, Chapman, Cottam, Jackson, McKenzie, Lyall, Martin, O'Neill, Bowyer.

Nov 10th 1973, H, v. Fulham, Win 3-0, Scorers Jackson, Bowyer, Martin, AT 10,530, Barron, O'Kane, Winfield, Chapman, Cottam, Jackson, McKenzie, Lyall, Martin, O'Neill, Bowyer.

Nov 17th 1973, H, v. Carlisle Island, Win 2-0, Scorers Martin, McKenzie, AT 11,153, Barron, O'Kane, Serella, Chapman, Cottam, Richardson, McKenzie, Lyall, Martin, McIntosh, Bowyer.

Nov 24th 1973, A, v. Sunderland, Draw 0-0, AT 22,252, Barron, O'Kane, Serella, Chapman, Cottam, Richardson, McKenzie, Lyall, Martin, McIntosh, Bowyer.

Dec 8th 1973, A, v. Cardiff City, Draw 1-1, Scorer Lyall (Pen), AT 10,312, Barron, O'Kane, Winfield, Chapman, Cottam, Richardson, McKenzie, Lyall, Martin, McIntosh, Bowyer, SUB O'Neill.

Dec 15th 1973, A, v. Middlesbrough, Loss 0-1, AT 16,764, Barron, O'Kane, Winfield, Chapman, Cottam, Richardson, McKenzie, Lyall, Martin, O'Neill, Bowyer.

Dec 22nd 1973, H, v. Bolton Wanderers, Win 3-2, Scorers Bowyer (2), Cottam, AT 9,498, Barron, O'Kane, Winfield, Chapman, Cottam, Richardson, McKenzie, Lyall, Martin, O'Neill, Bowyer.

Dec 26th 1973, A, v. Notts County, Win 1-0, Scorer Lyall (Pen), AT 32,130, Barron, O'Kane, Winfield, Hindley, Cottam, Richardson, McKenzie, Lyall, Martin, O'Neill, Bowyer.

Dec 29th 1973, A, v. Sheffield Wednesday, Draw 1-1, Scorer McKenzie, AT 16,210, Barron, O'Kane, Winfield, Hindley, Cottam, Richardson, McKenzie, Lyall, Martin, O'Neill, Bowyer, SUB Jackson.

Jan 1st 1974, H, v. Oxford United, Draw 1-1, Scorer Bowyer, AT 15,079, Barron, O'Kane, Winfield, Chapman, Cottam, Hindley, McKenzie, Lyall, Galley, O'Neill, Bowyer.

Jan 6th 1974, FAC, H, v. Bristol Rovers, Win 4-3, Scorers Chapman, Lyall (Pen), Martin (2), AT 23,456, Barron, O'Kane, Winfield, Chapman, Cottam, Hindley, McKenzie, Lyall, Martin, O'Neill, Bowyer, SUB Dennehy.

Jan 12th 1974, H, v. West Bromwich Albion, Loss 1-4, Scorer McKenzie, AT 15,301, Barron, O'Kane, Winfield, Chapman, Cottam, Hindley, McKenzie, Lyall, Martin, O'Neill, Bowyer, SUB Dennehy.

Jan 19th 1974, A, v. Luton Town, Draw 2-2, Scorers Richardson, McKenzie, AT 11,888, Barron, O'Kane, Winfield, Chapman, Cottam, Richardson, McKenzie, Lyall, Martin, Jackson, Bowyer, SUB Serella.

Jan 27th 1974, FAC, H, v. Manchester City, Win 4-1, Scorers McKenzie, Lyall, Bowyer (2), AT 41,472, Barron, O'Kane, Winfield, Chapman, Cottam, Richardson, McKenzie, Lyall, Martin, Jackson, Bowyer.

Feb 2nd 1974, H, v. Middlesbrough, Win 5-1, Scorers Winfield, Lyall (2)(1Pen)), Martin,

Second Division 1973-74

		Pld	W	D	L	F	A	Pts
1	Middlesbrough	42	27	11	4	77	30	65
2	Luton Town	42	19	12	11	64	51	50
3	Carlisle United	42	20	9	13	61	48	49
4	Orient	42	15	18	9	55	42	48
5	Blackpool	42	17	13	12	57	40	47
6	Sunderland	42	19	9	14	58	44	47
7	FOREST	42	15	15	12	57	43	45
8	West Bromwich Albion	42	14	16	12	48	45	44
9	Hull City	42	13	17	12	46	47	43
10	Notts County	42	15	13	14	55	60	43
11	Bolton Wanderers	42	15	12	15	44	40	42
12	Millwall	42	14	14	14	51	51	42
13	Fulham	42	16	10	16	39	43	42
14	Aston Villa	42	13	15	14	48	45	41
15	Portsmouth	42	14	12	16	45	62	40
16	Bristol City	42	14	10	18	47	54	38
17	Cardiff City	42	10	16	16	49	62	36
18	Oxford United	42	10	16	16	35	46	36
19	Sheffield Wednesday	42	12	11	19	51	63	35
20	Crystal Palace	42	11	12	19	43	56	34
21	Preston North End	42	9	14	19	40	62	*31
22	Swindon Town	42	7	11	24	36	72	25

Bowyer, AT 18,799, Barron, O'Kane, Winfield, Chapman, Cottam, Richardson, McKenzie, Lyall, Martin, Jackson, Bowyer.

Feb 10th 1974, A, v. Preston North End, Loss 1-2, Scorer McKenzie, AT 13,486, Barron, O'Kane, Winfield, Chapman, Cottam, Richardson, McKenzie, Lyall, Martin, Jackson, Bowyer.

Feb 17th 1974, FAC, H, v. Portsmouth, Win 1-0, Scorer McKenzie (Pen), AT 38,589, Barron, O'Kane, Winfield, Chapman, Cottam, Richardson, McKenzie, O'Neill, Martin, Jackson, Bowyer.

Feb 23rd 1974, A, v. Millwall, Draw 0-0, AT 8,833, Barron, O'Kane, Winfield, Chapman, Serella, Richardson, McKenzie, O'Neill, Martin, Jackson, Bowyer.

Feb 26th 1974, H, v. Orient, Win 2-1, Scorers Lyall, Martin, AT 16,632, Barron, O'Kane, Winfield, Chapman, Serella, Richardson, McKenzie, Lyall, Martin, Jackson, Bowyer.

Mar 3rd 1974, H, v. Notts County, Draw 0-0, AT 29,962, Barron, O'Kane, Winfield, Chapman, Serella, Robertson, McKenzie, Lyall, Martin, Jackson, Bowyer.

Mar 6th 1974, FAC, A, v. Newcastle United, Loss 3-4, Scorers O'Kane, Lyall (Pen), Bowyer, AT 52,551, Barron, O'Kane, Winfield, Chapman, Serella, Robertson, McKenzie, Lyall, Martin, O'Neill, Bowyer.

Mar 16th 1974, H, v. Blackpool, Win 2-0, Scorer McKenzie (2), AT 15,724, Barron, O'Kane, Winfield, Chapman, Serella, Richardson, McKenzie, Lyall, Martin, Robertson, Bowyer.

Mar 18th 1974, FAC, N, Goodison Park, v. Newcastle United, Draw 0-0, AT 40,681, Barron, O'Kane, Winfield, Chapman, Serella, Richardson, McKenzie, Lyall, Martin, Robertson, Bowyer.

Mar 21st 1974, FAC, N, Goodison Park, v. Newcastle United, Loss 0-1, AT 31,373, Barron, O'Kane, Winfield, Chapman, Serella, Richardson, McKenzie, Lyall, Martin, O'Neill, Bowyer.

Mar 23rd 1974, A, v. Fulham, Loss 0-2, AT 8,884, Barron, O'Kane, Winfield, Chapman, Serella, Richardson, McKenzie, Lyall, Martin, Jackson, Bowyer, SUB O'Neill.

Mar 26th 1974, H, v. Portsmouth, Win 2-0, Scorer Lyall (2), AT 14,040, Barron, O'Kane, Winfield, Chapman, Cottam, Richardson, McKenzie, Lyall, Martin, Robertson, Bowyer.

Mar 30th 1974, H, v. Crystal Palace, Loss 1-2, Scorer Lyall (Pen), AT 16,340, Barron, O'Kane, Winfield, Chapman, Serella, Richardson, McKenzie, Lyall, Martin, Robertson, Bowyer.

April 6th 1974, H, v. Sunderland, Draw 2-2, Scorers Richardson, McKenzie, AT 18,044, Barron, O'Kane, Winfield, Chapman, Serella, Richardson, McKenzie, Lyall, Martin, Robertson, Bowyer, SUB Galley.

April 12th 1974, A, v. Bristol City, Loss 0-1, AT 13,125, Peacock, O'Kane, Serella, Chapman, Cottam, Richardson, McKenzie, Lyall, Martin, Galley, Bowyer, SUB Dennehy.

April 13th 1974, A, v. Carlisle United, Loss 1-2, Scorer McKenzie, AT 9,258, Peacock, O'Kane, Winfield, Chapman, Cottam, Serella, McKenzie, Lyall, Bowyer, O'Neill, Dennehy, SUB McIntosh.

April 16th 1974, H, v. Bristol City, Draw 1-1, Scorer McKenzie, AT 12,756, Peacock, O'Kane, Winfield, Chapman, Cottam, Jackson, McKenzie, Lyall, Galley, McIntosh, Bowyer.

April 20th 1974, H, v. Cardiff City, Win 2-1, Scorers McKenzie, Lyall, AT 11,138, Peacock, O'Kane, Winfield, Chapman, Cottam, Richardson, McKenzie, Lyall, Galley, Martin, McIntosh.

April 24th 1974, A, v. Aston Villa, Loss 1-3, Scorer McKenzie, AT 12,439, Peacock, O'Kane, Winfield, Chapman, Serella, Richardson, McKenzie, Lyall, Galley, Woodcock, O'Neill.

April 27th 1974, A, v. Portsmouth, Win 2-0, Scorer McKenzie (2), AT 11,765, Peacock, Serella, O'Kane, Chapman, Cottam, Richardson, McKenzie, Lyall, Martin, Woodcock, Jackson.

May 6th 1974, CC, H, v. Notts County, Win 3-2, Scorers Richardson, Lyall (2), AT 9,122, Peacock, Serella, O'Kane, Chapman, Cottam, Richardson, McKenzie, Lyall, Martin, Woodcock, Jackson, SUB O'Neill.

May 13th 1974, F,H, v. Leicester City, Draw 1-1, Scorer Baker, AT 7,824, Peacock, Serella, Winfield, Chapman, Cottam, Richardson, Robertson, Galley, Baker, Wignall, Bowyer, SUBS Anderson, Woodcock.

Back Row: John Galley, John Winfield, John Cottam, John Robertson, Bob Chapman, Jim Barron, Liam O'Kane Dave Serella, Paul Richardson, Neil Martin, Peter Hindley

Front Row: Martin O'Neill, Barry Lyons, Tommy Jackson, George Lyall, Miah Dennehy, Jimmy McIntosh, Alan Buckley, Duncan McKenzie

The previous season could be considered a success. Although ultimately falling short in both league and cup, there had been lots of promising signs, not least the growth in attendances, particularly for the cup run that had shown interest was still there, it just needed to be re-kindled.

In the fan's eyes it was essential that the Reds held on to Duncan McKenzie if at all possible. Duncan as far as he was concerned, said he was happy to stay if the terms were right, but to him it appeared as if he was being pushed out of the door. He had talks in mid June with Brown about terms for a new contract and although there was a gap between McKenzie's demands and Forest's offer, it was considered bridgeable. However when an expected new offer wasn't forthcoming the delay obviously angered the player, who wasn't short of offers and led to further newspaper speculation that he would be sold. This situation dragged on into July and when, a week after, a further meeting with Jim Wilmer the chairman, (not attended by Brown who had rudely disappeared on holiday) the manager still hadn't made contact, McKenzie thought enough is enough and turned up at the City Ground asking for his National Insurance cards as his contract had ended. Unlike today, the club would still hold the player's registration, so effectively the player was in limbo or as the club described it, 'on strike'. Secretary Ken Smales had no option but to hand over the cards. From Duncan's point of view, "We had a great bunch of lads and with a little bit of investment I could see us challenging the next season, but I couldn't accept or understand what the club were playing at". McKenzie claimed he was ready to quit football and by the time Brown eventually went to visit the player at his Borrowash home, the relationship was damaged beyond repair. Forest released a statement declaring that, 'They were disappointed the player had turned down the generous offer that the club had made and now, they were reluctantly prepared to listen to offers for him'.

Spurs were first to show their hand, offering a deal, cash and a player, forward Martin Chivers, but Chivers himself turned down the move, saying he didn't want to drop down a division. Derby under the managership of Dave Mackay also came in with a player plus cash offer, the player being Kevin Hector, but this was refused. Birmingham City and Everton were also said to be interested, but as August came and the season grew closer, it looked as

74-75

NOTTINGHAM FOREST FOOTBALL CLUB

DIVISION TWO 1974 - 75

Back row, left to right: PAUL RICHARDSON LIAM O'KANE DAVE SERELLA DENNIS PEACOCK IAN BOWYER BOB CHAPMAN JOHN COTTAM

Middle row, left to right: JOHN GALLEY MARTIN O'NEILL MIAH DENNEHY JOHN ROBERTSON GEORGE LYALL NEIL MARTIN TOMMY JACKSON

Front row, left to right: VIV ANDERSON JIMMY McINTOSH TONY WOODCOCK GARY DULSON

Ian Bowyer beats Frank Clark to put the Reds ahead.

Dave Jones scores against Portsmouth.

Neil Martin jumps for joy after opening the scoring against Millwall.

Martin O'Neill goes close to adding a second against the Geordies.

FOREST START WITH BORE DRAW...

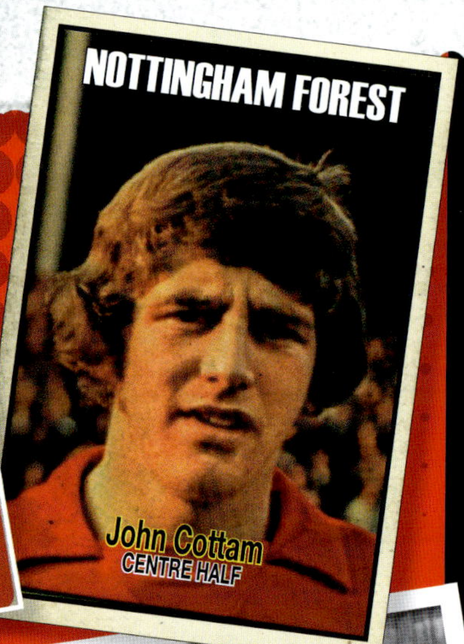

John Cottam challenges in the season's opener against Bristol City.

Bowyer nets the winner against Oxford United.

More action from the Bristol City game.

John Carter
The club's first Commercial Manager

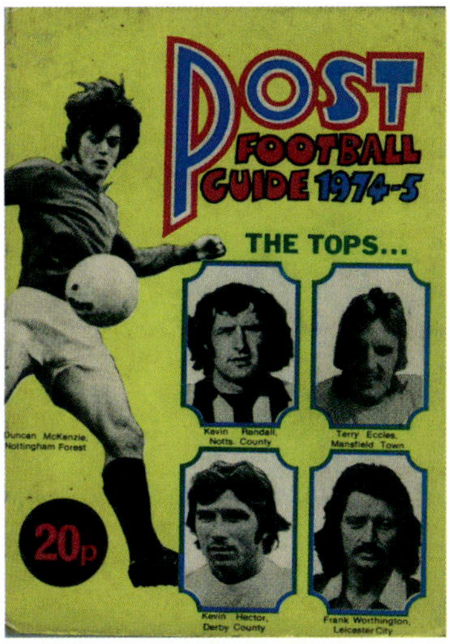

if McKenzie would remain at the City Ground. Meanwhile Brian Clough, newly installed as Leeds' manager was looking for a marquee signing to show his intent to change the club's style and philosophy.

After making contact with the player, he told him not do a thing whilst he sorted out the move. Clough made contact with Jim Wilmer at Walsall where Forest were playing a pre-season fixture and terms were quickly agreed, Forest receiving a fee of £240,000 for their star player. Forest immediately splashed £85,000 on Dave Jones from Bournemouth, he could play full back or centre half, the position he was earmarked for, but the move was not to be a success and as is the Forest way, he was sold on for a significant loss eighteen months later.

In the meantime, it was hoped that Miah Dennehy would be the player to step into McKenzie's boots. Miah had shown some promise, but asking him to make the huge step up to replace a legend wasn't fair. Then Brown tried for a couple of quality, experienced players, agreeing a fee with Manchester City for Francis Lee, only for the player to say he wasn't interested in moving, although he must have changed his mind a few weeks later, when he turned up at Derby. Next Brian Clough allowed them to talk with international full back Terry Cooper, but this time the Leeds' Board scuppered the deal. The club were trying, but for whatever reason just couldn't get these deals over the line.

There was movement out of the club however, long serving defender John Winfield joined ex team mate John Barnwell at Peterborough, signing the forms on the stage at the Heart of the Midlands nightclub during an end of season club event. John had made over four hundred appearances, scoring five goals during almost 15 years at the City Ground. The club also bid farewell to keeper Jim Barron who joined Swindon, opening the way for one of several promising young keepers at the club to claim the position.

Things were also happening off the pitch, long serving committee man Jack Glenn stepped down after twenty five years grand service, whilst Physio Bob Davies and trainer Bert Johnson were let go and replaced by Peter Blakeley and John Sheridan. Bob Davies had seemed part of the furniture, always immaculately dressed in shirt tie and a white lab coat. In these hi-tech days it is hard to imagine the primitive equipment that made up the treatment room back then. George Lyall remembers the great big ultra violet lamp and 'electro magnetic' muscle machine.

In an effort to boost off field income, the club appointed their first Commercial Manager, John Carter, and one of his first tasks was to announce the installation of an answer phone system that fans could call to listen to ticket information and club news. Due to the success of transporting fans by rail to Newcastle, the idea was expanded and the club looked to run specials to as many away games as possible. Forestrail was born and for a twenty five pence fee you could join the away travel club. John Carter was a familiar sight at the station selling extra tickets (cash and standing room only!) for latecomers. He was also determined to re-invigorate the supporter's clubs, recognizing that the club had turned its back on the most loyal fans, immediately new branches were formed in Clifton and Carlton.

Railings were now installed along the East and Bridgford terraces in an attempt to further curtail supporters from charging around, as behaviour had declined once more with success and bigger attendances.

The most surprising news came after a group of members once more proposed a change of club name, dropping the Nottingham out of the title in a sordid attempt to 'modernise' the club. A vote was taken at the club's AGM, but luckily it was easily defeated. A similar proposal at West Bromwich Albion was also defeated but successful at Leyton Orient, who would now be known just as Orient.

Pre-season consisted of three local matches, away at Port Vale and Walsall, before a home game with Leicester, which was marked once more by trouble on the Bridgford terraces.

The season's opener was a home encounter with Bristol City. Not only were the Reds without McKenzie, but they were also missing Martin O'Neill and Ian Bowyer, who once more were in dispute with the club over terms. Tony Woodcock was given an early opportunity to cement a place, but failed to grab the opportunity.

The game ended 0-0 with chances few and far between, a poor crowd of only 11,000 disillusioned supporters bothered to turn up and watch Dave Jones make his debut. This was followed by two away defeats at Millwall and Portsmouth and worryingly no goals were scored.

The first victory came at home to Millwall 2-1, Neil Martin and Ian Bowyer scoring, but already the attendance figure had slipped below 8,000, the optimism of the previous season already seemed a lifetime ago and when Oxford left with the points four days later there was despair all round. Only three points from the first five games. Ian Bowyer recalls that period, "After just missing out the previous season, we had high hopes of having a good

Neil Martin slides home against Fulham.

Ian Bowyer cracks home the first goal against York City.

George Lyall sends the Bristol Rovers' keeper the wrong way from the penalty spot.

Miah Dennehy celebrates scoring the winner against Oldham.

Ian Bowyer in an ariel challenge with the Norwich defenders.

MIAH DENNEHY
Nottingham Forest

NOBBY STILES
Preston North End

BARRY BUTLIN
Nottingham Forest
GOAL

Paddy Greenwood

season, but with Duncan leaving and the penny pinching attitude of the club, morale had fallen. The manager seemed out of his depth and unable to handle the situation". Martin O'Neill was also scathing about Brown, "He didn't do anything for me, he seemed to be stuck in the past, there seemed no hope with him around". There's a story that the players tell about the manager. Allan Brown was concerned about lateness, so gathered the players together and told them that he was introducing a fine system of 20 for each time a player was late. "£20 is a bit steep boss", "no, 20p", replied the manager and with this Neil Martin handed over £1 and left saying, "I'll see you next week". The manager himself responded through the press with a furious attack on players he labelled as cheats and a disgrace to their profession.

Unbelievably Manchester United had been relegated the previous season and to think that only seven years before, both Reds had gone head to head for the Division One title. They had made a good start and were looking to make an immediate return to the top flight, but their fans seemed determined to derail this prospect. The club were taking huge followings to away games and despite victories, they were causing havoc at almost every ground they visited. This game would give Forest an early opportunity to test out their promotion credentials when they were due to visit Old Trafford in the first week of September. They rose to the occasion and returned with a point following a 2-2 draw and a fine performance, the re-instated Bowyer and Cottam were the scorers.

As is the way with football, fate had presented Forest with an early opportunity for revenge when they were paired with Newcastle United in the second round of the League Cup at the City Ground. A pitifully small away following saw United escape with an undeserved 1-1 draw, Bowyer netting for the Reds, the fourth game in succession that he had scored. Forest went out after a replay.

Viv Anderson recalls the away fixture with Newcastle in his autobiography, although he wrongly credits Dave Mackay as being the manager, rather than Allan Brown, 'In only my second game for Forest I was subjected to a mass taunt. As soon as the crowd got sight of me, the baiting started, I froze. I told Dave Mackay (sic) that I didn't want to play. He took me aside and didn't mince his words, "If you want to be a footballer son, you've got to learn to cope with stuff like this". I played'. In between those cup ties, Hull City were crushed 4-0, the evergreen Neil Martin scoring a brace. However, the team's inconsistency was exposed four days later with a loss to Portsmouth, 2-1 at the City Ground, before another victory 3-2 at Sheffield Wednesday that saw a league debut at right back for Viv Anderson and a pitch invasion by Forest fans who stormed across the pitch from the Leppings Lane End to 'take' the Kop. Neil Martin newly restored to the side had contributed four goals in three games and at last gave the attack a focal point.

Despite the increase in goals scored, Brown was still determined to add to the strike force and eventually he was able to announce a signing. Barry Butlin would be joining from Luton Town for a club record of £122,000, a fee that was to show the spiralling rise of player acquisition and Forest's desperation. Almost all the McKenzie transfer money had now been spent, to what end?

Despite scoring on his home debut, a 3-1 defeat to Norwich, (Chapman was also sent off), Butlin's signing was not to have the desired impact, this was the striker's only goal in his first twelve outings.

The Reds made another signing shortly afterwards, with the low budget £10,000 capture of Barnsley's Paddy Greenwood to fill the troublesome left back spot. This allowed the manager to move Dave Jones alongside Sammy Chapman to his preferred position in the heart of the defence.

The letters page of the Football Post was not complimentary to the Reds, the general consensus was that the transfer money had been squandered, whilst old timers

EVENING POST

NOTTINGHAM, FRIDAY, JANUARY 3, 1975

PRICE 4p

No. 30,024

QUALITY USED CARS

CLOUGH TIPPED FOR TOP JOB

● RIGHT: ALLAN BROWN — deposed manager

● CENTRE: Brian Clough — tipped for the vacant position

● FAR RIGHT: Jim Willmer, the Forest chairman

FOREST SHOCK: BROWN IS OUT

such as Harry Durose were saddened not only by the decline on the pitch but the bad behaviour off it. Leicester fan A.L.F took great delight in winding up Forest fans, encouraging them to visit Filbert Street to see stars such as Keith Weller and Jon Sammels.

FOREST ARE ALL SET FOR TALKS WITH CLOUGH

By JOHN LAWSON

ALLAN BROWN was today dismissed from the Nottingham Forest managership just over 13 months after taking on the job of steering the club back into the First Division.

Notts. in new kit – thanks

The chances of Forest landing such a high profile manager at the start of the campaign had seemed remote at best. Brian Clough had gained his reputation as one of

Allan Brown continued to chop and change the team in search of some consistency, but there never seemed to be a place for Martin O'Neill or John Robertson, whose relationship with the manager had completely broken down. Martin was once left out by the manager after a training ground incident, the reason being, 'the player did not do as he was told'. This period just seemed to be win a game, lose a game, the season just seemed to be drifting by in front of 10,000 or so apathetic supporters. However behind the scenes, some of the fine work being done by Alan Hill with the younger players was already bearing fruit. Eighteen year old Viv Anderson was followed into the first team by seventeen year old John Middleton who replaced Dennis Peacock in goal, with more fine prospects like Bryn Gunn waiting for their chance. Two successive away victories at Southampton and West Brom briefly raised hopes. John Middleton came in for his debut away at the Hawthorns as the Reds' youngest ever keeper and despite a shaky start he made a good impression and was to hold onto the shirt for the rest of the season. Long considered to be the most promising keeper on the books, Middleton was fast tracked into the side after a series of errors by Dennis Peacock, he was also a good enough outfield player to be offered trials as well. The team lacked flair and seemed to mirror the fans opinion of the manager. George Lyall says, "It was really a nothing period for the team, but I was pleased with my own form. At one stage it looked as if I would be joining Newcastle but they signed Tommy Craig instead. If the club hadn't acted we would have been involved in a relegation battle that season".

A loss at Bolton was followed by a win against Oldham before a loss at Cardiff. So it went on, one goal a game if you were lucky, turgid uninspiring football.

Always a Red, summed up many fans frustrations when he wrote, 'Watching football is supposed to be fun, but visiting the City Ground at the moment is like a trip to the dentists'.

Off the pitch, the supporter's club arranged their annual social evening, where the players and fans would take part in a variety of games including cribbage, dominos and darts. In the absence of reigning champion Duncan McKenzie, Paddy Greenwood and Ian Bowyer fought it out for the darts title, Bomber eventually coming out on top. Trent buses once more announced that they were suspending transport for away games after continued vandalism to vehicles meant it just was not economic to continue the service.

The visit of York City to Nottingham in November, saw a return for old favourite Barry Lyons. However, it was not to be a happy return as Forest managed to hold on for a slim 2-1 victory with goals from Bowyer and Richardson. There was by now a trickle of younger fans returning to the Trent End, the lack of away fans and the wider open spaces of the East Stand terraces made it hard to create any kind of atmosphere.

The away following for the December game at Orient was boosted by the Evening Post running a subsidized 'shopping train' to London on the same day. On the train it appeared as if there were more football fans than shoppers. The game itself

WELCOME...

Brian Clough Talking...

When I was first asked to write this article my initial reaction was to say "No" because a football manager's job is not about writing notes for a match programme.

But it is the first opportunity I have had to introduce myself to you so here I am for the first — and last — time this season.

I know from the reaction there has already been to my arrival at the City Ground that something special is expected of me. But if you want wild promises of First Division football, big signings, and glamour in the near future . . . forget it!

I'm not making predictions outside saying that I will be trying my utmost to put the big and beautiful city of Nottingham back on the football map.

The club has gone places in the past but so much has gone wrong, too many bad decisions have been made and not enough work put in.

One of the greatest tragedies to my mind is the way quality players have been allowed to leave over the last five or six years.

None of that would have happened had I been here unless there was a clear indication of the player not having his heart in the club.

It does not need a ready reckoner to assess that close on £1,000,000 worth of talent has left Forest for one reason or another.

There is no purpose at all in reflecting what might have been however, but take it from me — the transfer door is now firmly bolted as far as class players are concerned.

Of course, I was responsible for taking the last pearl from Forest's oyster when I signed Duncan McKenzie for Leeds. He is a very fine player and one that I would give a lot to have with me now. I would also have loved to have had the job of sorting out the problems he obviously had here.

Nobody knows why he made his stand against Forest better than me. He must have been frustrated with what was happening and I can imagine his feelings were similar to

yours. You had run out of patience because of what had gone wrong in the past and run out of hope for the future.

I will be trying to give you something to look forward to but there is no cash at the bank to buy players so hard work is the priority.

The first responsibility to improve things is mine but players must respond to me and show they are willing to work, listen, and learn.

There will be no pressure on them to win because results are not their worry. I want them to apply themselves to their profession and that happens to be football.

The players and I have had a successful start together at Tottenham and Fulham and not, in my wildest dreams, did I expect to kick-off with two wins. It was great to meet up with Bobby Moore at Craven Cottage last week. I still have tremendous admiration for him and was sorry he was not able to join me at Derby.

Today we are attempting to make it three wins in a row against Orient — a team who showed they are not short of ability in the Cup-ties with Derby. I understand they are the unluckiest team to be knocked out of the Cup for many a year.

So it will be far from easy for us because George Petchey has worked wonders at Orient. He has not bought any £100,000 players but they will be a tough side to beat.

You, the supporters, can help by encouraging the side. But, as I have said in the local paper, I have no time for football "yobs" who come along to cause bother.

After Manchester United, Forest's hot-heads have one of the worst reputations in football and I aim to end that. My message to trouble makers is simply: "Get lost!"

To the well-behaved majority, I hope we have a successful time together and it is my intention to get to know you a lot better over the coming months.

I am not a manager who sits in his ivory tower all day long. I am a "half a beer and fish and chips" man.

I know I have got the name as soccer's "big mouth" but, deep down, I am an ordinary bloke doing a job of work!

MARTIN GIVES CLOUGHIE DREAM START...

Neil Martin gives Brian Clough a great start as new Forest Manager as he heads home the winner against Spurs.

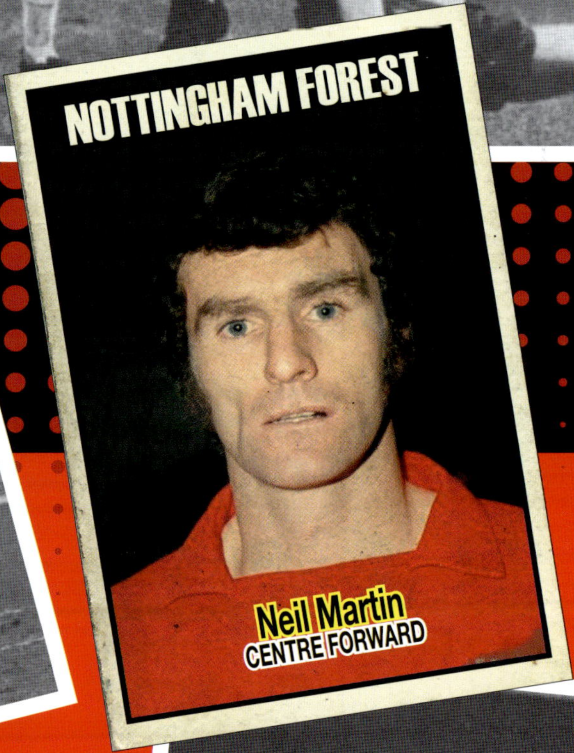

Barry Butlin curls in the second goal against Aston Villa.

Miah Dennehy nets from close range against Bolton.

Butlin goes close to heading home an equaliser against Villa.

finished all square, but Dave Jones added to the teams poor disciplinary record by getting himself needlessly sent off.

There were a couple of outgoing transfers to report, John Galley was allowed to join Peterborough on loan before clinching a transfer to Hereford, John hadn't featured in the first team since the Newcastle cup defeat. Whilst Dave Serella left on a free transfer to link up once more with ex team mate Doug Fraser at Walsall.

Unbeknown to fans, things were happening behind the scenes. Some of the committee members were not happy and had decided to take matters into their own hands. Fred Reacher had originally raised the idea, but being a new boy on the committee, had quickly backed down when he realized the resistance he would meet. Therefore it was left to Stuart Dryden to approach the now, out of work Brian Clough to see whether he would be interested if the manager's position became vacant. When the answer came back affirmative, the others on the committee had to be persuaded that this was an opportunity not to be missed.

Despite a 3-1 Boxing Day victory at Hull, the excuse to sack the manager came after a humiliating 2-0 home defeat to Notts County, that left them below their neighbours in thirteenth place.

Vice Chairman Brian Appleby distanced himself from the approach to Brian Clough, by authorizing Stuart Dryden along with Derek Pavis to sort out a deal. Chairman Jim Wilmer was one of those that thought that success was not worth the risks that Brian Clough brought. He along with other committee members had watched aghast at the antics that Clough had got up to at Derby, but he was sidelined on this occasion. Dryden recalls, "Brian Appleby thought Clough and Taylor were 'riff-raff', they might be the best at their jobs, but they were still 'riff-raff'". The two Brians hated each other. Appleby and the new manager could be considered polar opposites, socialist Brian Clough and the wealthy Tory and member of the establishment Brian Appleby. To be fair though, Appleby knew what had to be done, "This man is coming to Forest, at the moment we are one of the most unprogressive clubs in the country."

Dryden and Pavis met Brian for lunch, where details of his contract were thrashed out and all parties shook hands and looked forward to a new beginning. However, Cloughie's appointment wasn't universally welcomed by everyone at Forest. After all he had been a thorn in the club's side for years when he was at Derby, some of the Reds' best players ending up with him at the Baseball Ground and it was also only five months since he had taken Duncan McKenzie to Leeds. Ken Smales, the long serving Forest secretary had not always been complimentary about the new manager, the Ian Moore transfer saga still lingered in the memory, but as it turned out, they became the closest of work colleagues, both blunt speaking Yorkshireman, Clough really came to appreciate the professionalism of the secretary.

Brian Clough also took careful aim at those he blamed for the club's predicament, "This club has gone places in the past, but so much has gone wrong, too many bad decisions have been made and not enough work put in". It was clear, that as many supporters had known for years, the Forest Committee generally weren't worth a light. Later he particularly poured scorn on chairman Jim Wilmer. "I have never met anyone that looked less like a chairman than that man". Asked where he would put him on a list of chairman that he had worked for, he said, "He wouldn't even make it onto the list".

The manager was all business for his first meeting with the players. If you believe the stories, marching into the changing rooms he flung his jacket, landing it perfectly on a peg. "Sammy, it's cold enough in here to freeze the balls off a brass monkey", was his ice breaker, before continuing, "I have in my pocket a list of players for the game at Tottenham that will be put up after our training session and another thing, you will not wear tracksuit bottoms for training, because we don't wear them for matches".

Martin O'Neill proudly remembers being

Brian Clough enjoys a glass of champagne as he is welcomed to the City Ground by :
L to R : Ken Smales, Jack Levy, Stuart Dryden and Brian Appleby

Butlin rises, but cannot hit the target against Manchester United.

Too late for Lyall as the Cardiff keeper dives on the ball.

Fourth round cup action against Fulham.

Goal mouth action from the Orient game.

singled out, "O'Neill you will be coming with us", (Martin had been frozen out under the previous manager) things were now clearly going to be a lot different and with that they were off down the embankment to the grassy public area that passed for a training ground back then, leaving the press to hang around drinking coffee until he returned.

Brian Clough used those first press interviews to benefit the club, charging journalists a fee that he used to buy a new cooker for the kitchen staff and new ultra scan unit for the treatment room. The manager knew the importance of the team within a team, he always preached the need for everyone within the club to be pulling in the same direction and woe betide anyone he thought wasn't feeling the same pain of defeat that he was.

The chances of Brian Clough ending up at Nottingham Forest must have been a million to one only a few months before, when Brian had taken over at reigning champions Leeds United from Don Revie. As fate would have it though, Nottingham Forest were to reap the benefits, and Clough with the financial security the dismissal had given him, would ensure that he didn't make the same mistakes he had made at Derby and Leeds. Look out chairman and committee.

Another to benefit from this appointment was Evening Post journalist John Lawson. Let him take up the story, "On his first day, there was the obligatory press conference. Normally these were attended by two men and a dog, but of course on this occasion all the 'big hitters' from the national dailies turned up. I was determined to stand out, so I asked as many questions as possible. Eventually Brian said, "Oi you, are you local journalist?", "Yes" I replied, "Well keep your mouth shut and come and see me afterwards". We didn't click straight away, in fact I remember talking to my wife several months later and saying that I didn't think he liked me. Then suddenly we were off and running, I think he was just testing me out." It's very important that a local journalist who often travelled with the team and was privy to certain things, knows how to keep confidences. It would have been easy to pass something onto a national, but that would have been the end not only with the manager but the players as well.

Brian Clough's arrival had an immediate effect off the pitch. He himself welcomed new supporters to the ticket office as £4,000 worth of season tickets were sold

John McGovern and John O'Hare sign on the dotted line

in the first few days and new 'Pools' agents were recruited. Ken Smales commented, "Everyone had a spring in their step, it was great to come to work".

Brian Clough's first game in charge was the Third Round FA Cup replay at White Hart Lane, after the first game had ended in a draw. Unusually he watched the game from the Director's Box, preferring that position to run his eye over his new team. The team line up for this first game makes interesting reading;

Middleton, O'Kane, Greenwood, Chapman, Jones, Richardson, Lyall, Martin, Butlin, Bowyer and O'Neill. Sammy Chapman who was well respected by the other players was re-instated as captain. A team of decent enough pro's, but hardly inspiring. Neil Martin had the honour of heading home the first and winning goal of his reign, a 1-0 victory. The new boss was caught punching the air when the goal went in. It was a decent performance in the circumstances and the dressing room post match photographs show an ebullient manager celebrating with his players.

The journalists were quick to laud the 'Clough effect', predicting that Forest would now fly and could even make a late burst for promotion. The manager was not fooled however, he knew that the players would find their true level and that it would probably be quite low.

Clough had arranged for the team to stay over at Bisham Abbey, the Football Association training headquarters for a few days, not only to prepare for Saturday's game at Fulham, but also to give the manager more opportunity to get to know the players.

On taking up the managerial position, Clough's first call had been to veteran trainer Jimmy Gordon, who was now working at Rolls Royce after being dismissed from Leeds. Jimmy didn't take much persuading to join him.

Jimmy's first impressions were not encouraging, "They are not a bad set of lads, but they are pretty average", he told the manager. Jimmy was a perfect buffer between the manager and the players and he immediately gained their trust and respect for the honest and sincere approach he adopted. This didn't mean he was a pushover but he knew when to keep his counsel. He could also see that many of the players were overawed by Brian Clough, some might say frightened and this could be a problem.

The Reds followed up the win at Tottenham with another 1-0 victory at Craven Cottage, Butlin scoring, but in truth the win came courtesy of an outstanding performance from John Middleton.

A crowd of 17,000, well above average saw the first home game of the new era against Orient, but many of them weren't there to see a late comeback, two goals in the last four minutes from Paul Richardson earning an undeserved point, as a poor performance had seen them fall two goals behind. The corner of the Main Stand and Trent End unusually full for the final minutes, as fans making their way along the embankment, dashed back in when

AROUND AND ABOUT

Heanor Branch visit the City Ground

The Heanor Branch of the Sportsmen's Club were guests of the Forest on Sunday, 25th August. Two coach-loads of members were met by Mr. G. Macpherson and Mr. J. Carter and were conducted round the club premises.

At the conclusion of the visit the Annual General Meeting was held on the premises and the officials were elected with J. Weston (Chairman) and E. Birkin (Secretary).

Arrangements have now been made for a private 'bus for members to leave Heanor Market 1¼ hours before kick-off time for home matches.

We have some new supporters in Pittsburgh USA.

Kitchen staff take delivery of their new cooker courtesy of Brian Clough.

Forest present new tracksuits for Nottingham boys

Pictured Manager Allan Brown & keeper John Middleton plus to the front young Russell Slade.

Ted Ralph, Ground Manager hands over the keys to son Chas Ralph on his retirement.

Neil Martin soars, but heads wide against Orient in Brian Cloughs' first game

the first goal entered the net. There was plenty of activity off the pitch as trainer John McSeveny was released along with long serving assistant manager Bill Anderson. Bill had been brought in by ex manager John Carey in the mid sixties, a quietly spoken but knowledgeable man, he had stepped up to help the club on many occasions, but with the new approach he was the past, not the future.

Clough might have settled into the position, but he quickly realised that a shortage of cash was going to be an issue, regularly using the press to chide the committee about what he saw as a lack of courage. Supporters were living in 'Fantasy land' if they thought he could take this group of players up the table. In fact privately he told John Lawson that the club was in a relegation battle and would do well to survive. Dark thoughts also surfaced, that he might have made a mistake in coming to the City Ground, it was going to be a constant battle to change the timid streak that seemed to run through the club. As the team's form declined, Clough told supporters, "The only thing this club has going for it right now, is me".
Dissatisfied players were also given short shrift, "Anyone who doesn't want to be here, I will personally convey them to their next club", although the actual words he used were a little more direct.

Clough was often asked whether he would make an attempt to lure Peter Taylor to join him, "Absolutely no point", he said, "with no money available Taylors' strengths would be useless here".

In fact the manager did make a new signing. Local lad, Bert Bowery, a big bustling centre forward joined from Worksop for a small fee.

In one of his first conversations with the manager, John Lawson had been asked by Clough to 'mark his card' about anyone at the club he thought might have potential. John Lawson had long been a fan of John Robertson and wasted no time in pushing the case for his inclusion and shortly afterwards, he was to be brought back for the four game FA Cup saga against Fulham. The first game in London finished goalless before another draw, back in Nottingham, Martin scoring once more before an encouraging crowd of 25,000. However, the evening ended on a sour note as Reds' full back Paddy Greenwood was carried off with a broken leg.

With his pressing need for transfer funds, the manager knew how important a cup run could be, so there was disappointment when the toss of a coin meant the second replay would be held at Craven Cottage, but Forest were rescued when a great free kick from Robertson earned them another replay. Disappointingly though, the Reds tumbled out of the competition 2-1 in front of another big crowd at the City Ground. Fulham in fact were to go all the way this season, losing to West Ham in the final.The league form became so poor over the next couple of months that some supporters said it was even worse than under Brown.
The squad was rotated to no avail as the team went twelve league games without a win. The club had no left back, Paul Richardson was forced to fill in and to make matters worse, they weren't scoring goals either. Drastic action was required. Brian Clough went to the committee to spell out the situation and they agreed, all be it reluctantly, to sanction a couple of signings. The manager knew where he could pick up a couple of bargains, good players and the right sort as well.

John McGovern and John O'Hare had followed Clough to Leeds United, but after he had left they were marooned, no chance of playing, with their careers virtually on hold. John McGovern recalls, "When I heard that the manager had taken over at Forest, I hoped he would come in for me. Leeds were trying to push me out, first to Carlisle, then Norwich, but I wanted my next club to be one chosen by me. Brian contacted me and told me not to sign for anyone whilst he was sorting out the money side, I did get a bit twitchy at one time but he was as good as his word".

He continues, "When Forest agreed terms with Leeds for my transfer, I would have crawled on my hands and knees to rejoin the gaffer. My wife knew this and warned me that I should hold out for a good wage and don't come back if you don't. In the end the manager explained that the club couldn't afford much and I found myself signing for less money than I was on at Leeds". It was pretty much the same story for John O'Hare, taking a wage drop to get his career moving again. Whereas McGovern had endured a particularly nasty time at Elland Road, things hadn't been quite so bad for O'Hare, who knew many of the players from his time playing for Scotland, but he too was glad to get away. The fee for the pair was an absolute bargain at £60,000, less than half the amount United had paid only seven months previously.
John McGovern made his debut at home to Cardiff, a 0-0 draw, whilst a slight niggle meant that O'Hare had to wait until the

IAN
BOWYER
Nottingham
Forest
GOAL
FOREST

following week to make his bow. O'Hare didn't take long to open his Forest account, scoring in the home 3-2 defeat to Aston Villa, his second appearance.

You could see what O'Hare brought to the team, brave as a lion, he held the ball up and brought others into the game, as well as contributing goals, but opinion was immediately divided amongst supporters about the merits of John McGovern (as it would be throughout his Reds' career). Spindly, lightweight, not good in the air, not a great passer, didn't score goals. Brian Clough said he had brought him to show the others how to play, but much of the hurly burly Division Two football seemed to pass him by.
By the time Forest picked up their next victory, twelve games had passed and the club were a perilous three points off the relegation zone. If it wasn't for the poor quality of the teams at the bottom, they would have been in far worse trouble.

In the circumstances, it might not have been spectacular, but George Lyall's penalty winner in a tense encounter against rock bottom Sheffield Wednesday was desperately needed. Surprisingly Tony Woodcock at this time played a couple of games wearing the number eleven shirt. History had seemed to show that Woodcock had not featured in the manager's thoughts, but he clearly had done something to merit a couple of starts.

Supporters however weren't impressed by what they were seeing, the Football Post contained many scathing letters;
'The least skilful team I have seen in 50 years'. Red Robin, Lowdham. 'Can anybody tell me what McGovern brings to the team?' S. Marshall,Nottingham.
The last home game before this victory had seen Forest lose 1-0 at home to Manchester United, in a game that was more controversial for what happened off the pitch than on it. United fans had been causing disorder at every away game and in order to minimise the risk of trouble, the fixture had been made all ticket and to the consternation of diehards, the United fans had been allocated the Trent End, as it was thought that it would be easier to contain them, rather than allowing fans to clash on the East Stand terraces as had happened only weeks before when Villa were the visitors. Despite the fact that younger fans had already moved out of the Trent End, there was real anger, defending the Trent End against 'invaders' was still a strong memory and the thought that it could just be handed over to hated rivals was sickening. In the end the game inside the stadium passed off peacefully enough but outside there were many violent incidents. This caused Brian Clough to say, "I know we have a violent minority that support this club, but I would rather play in front of only 2,000 if they would stay away".

If it was hoped that the Wednesday game might prove to be a turning point, and herald a strong end to the season, fans would be disappointed. This was followed by a heavy 4-2 defeat away at lowly Bristol Rovers, Brian Clough caned all the players bar one for their performance. The exception being Paul Richardson as the manager bent down to unlace his boots after the game. "But I played crap," said Paul. "But at least you put the effort in, not like these other buggers", he said as an explanation.

During half time of the Rovers game Clough took John Robertson to task, "When did you ever get in their box", he asked, "where's your courage and I am not just talking about physical courage but mental courage. Demand the ball". The manager could excuse some things but lack of effort, never. The players were always surprised that he could recall small

John Middleton collects the ball against Bristol Rovers

incidents from games, the time you didn't track back, the wrong option taken, he never seemed to miss anything. To most of the players, the manager seemed typically Clough, the one that they had seen on television, but to the two Johns, as they shared a car to training each morning, they saw that the fire wasn't as great as it had been, there was something missing, a certain amount of going through the motions. His ego certainly would have expected to be challenging for honours, not scratching around at the bottom of the league, after all, who would be interested in the opinions of that type of manager? The inference being that until Clough and Taylor were re-united, neither would ever be as successful individually as they were as a partnership.
Martin O'Neill has always had the reputation for speaking his mind and as he doesn't mind admitting now, sometimes a bit too clever for his own good. Sometimes he spoke without thinking, he tells one such story. "There was a meeting at the club for all the players and management with a boot supplier, where we were supposed to choose boots for next season, I stupidly said I suppose this means I will be here next season, the look the manager gave me I cannot describe".

Unknown to supporters, John McGovern had been carrying a pelvic injury that needed an operation, or at least a good rest. He had gone to see the manager who in no uncertain terms told him he was playing for the rest of the season, "But I can't run gaffer". "You never could", was the scathing reply. In fact McGovern lasted until the penultimate game of the season, a 3-0 defeat at Norwich, by this time the club was safe and Jimmy Gordon who was in charge of the team whilst the manager was away scouting, took pity on him and subbed him after he clearly couldn't continue any more.

The season at last finished with a 2-1 victory at the Hawthorns, an experimental looking side containing John Cottam, Jimmy McIntosh, Jim McCann and Tony Woodcock took the points after a brace from Barry Butlin. Thank God it was over.

Forest finished in sixteenth place, only twelve wins and forty three goals to show from the season. A comfortable six point gap from the bottom three but it hadn't felt comfortable at any stage.

Neil Martin had finished top scorer despite only making twenty six starts and none since February. The squad was unbalanced and needed an overhaul, but would money be made available? Those fans that had been expecting a miracle had been left disappointed, but some people were optimistic. John McGovern was one, "Although we had been poor, there were good signs that some of the young players could step up and there were a few good pro's, anyway, I knew it would only be a matter of time before the gaffer sorted it out". So surely next season had to be better?

FACTS and FIGURES

Aug 10th 1974, F, H, v Leicester City, Loss 1-3, Scorer Dennehy, AT 7,842, Peacock, Serella, O'Kane, Chapman, Cottam, Richardson, Dennehy, Lyall, Martin, O'Neill, Bowyer.

Aug 17th 1974, H, v. Bristol City, Draw 0-0, AT 11,339, Peacock, O'Kane, Richardson, Chapman, Cottam, Jones, Dennehy, Lyall, Martin, Robertson, Bowyer, SUB Woodcock.

Aug 19th 1974, A, v. Millwall, Loss 0-3, AT 7,533, Peacock, O'Kane, Jones, Chapman, Cottam, Richardson, Dennehy, Lyall, Galley, Robertson, Woodcock, SUB Bowyer.

Aug 24th 1974, A, v. Portsmouth, Loss 0-2, AT 11,349, Peacock, O'Kane, Jones, Chapman, Cottam, Richardson, Dennehy, Lyall, Galley, Woodcock, Jackson, SUB Serella.

Aug 27th 1974, H, v Millwall, Win 2-1, Scorers Martin, Bowyer, AT 7,957, Peacock, O'Kane, Jones, Chapman, Cottam, Richardson, Dennehy, Lyall, Galley, Martin, Jackson, SUB Bowyer.

Aug 31st 1974, H, v. Oxford United, Loss 1-2, Scorer Bowyer, AT 9,257, Peacock, O'Kane, Jones, Chapman, Serella, Richardson, Dennehy, Lyall, Martin, Bowyer, Jackson, SUB Galley.

Sept 7th 1974, A, v. Manchester United, Draw 2-2, Scorers Bowyer, Cottam, AT 40,671, Peacock, O'Kane, Jones, Chapman, Cottam, Richardson, Dennehy, Lyall, Martin, Bowyer, O'Neill, SUB Serella.

Sept 10th 1974, LC, H, v. Newcastle United, Draw 1-1, Scorer Bowyer, AT 14,183, Peacock, O'Kane, Jones, Chapman, Cottam, Richardson, Dennehy, Lyall, Galley, Bowyer, O'Neill, SUB Robertson.

Sept 14th 1974, H, v. Hull City, Win 4-0, Scorers Martin (2), Lyall, O'Neill, AT 9,437 Peacock, O'Kane, Jones, Chapman, Cottam, Richardson, Dennehy, Lyall, Martin, Bowyer, O'Neill, SUB Robertson.

Sept 17th 1974, H, v. Portsmouth, Loss 1-2, Scorer Jones, AT 9,534, Peacock, O'Kane, Jones, Chapman, Cottam, Robertson, Dennehy, Lyall, Martin, Bowyer, O'Neill, SUB Jackson.

Sept 21st 1974, A, v. Sheffield Wednesday, Win 3-2, Scorers Martin (2), Bowyer, AT 15,449, Peacock, Anderson, Jones, O'Kane, Serella, Jackson, Dennehy, Lyall, Martin, Bowyer, O'Neill.

Sept 25th 1974, LC, A, v. Newcastle United, Loss 0-3, AT 26,228, Peacock, Anderson, Jones, O'Kane, Serella, Jackson, Dennehy, Lyall, Martin, Bowyer, O'Neill, SUB Richardson.

Sept 28th 1974, H, v. Sunderland, Draw 1-1, Scorer Lyall (Pen), AT 14,885, Peacock, Anderson, Jones, O'Kane, Serella, Richardson, Dennehy, Lyall, Martin, Bowyer, O'Neill.

Oct 2nd 1974, A, v. Aston Villa, Loss 0-3, AT 20,357, Peacock, Anderson, Jones, O'Kane, Serella, Richardson, Dennehy, Lyall, Butlin, Bowyer, O'Neill.

Oct 5th 1974, A, v. Southampton, Win 1-0, Scorer Jackson, AT 16,042, Peacock, O'Kane, Greenwood, Chapman, Jones, Richardson, Dennehy, Martin, Butlin, Bowyer, Jackson.

Oct 12th 1974, H, v. Norwich City, Loss 1-3, Scorer Butlin, AT 13,613, Peacock, O'Kane, Greenwood, Chapman, Jones, Richardson, Dennehy, Martin, Butlin, Bowyer, Jackson, SUB Lyall.

Oct 19th 1974, A, v. West Bromwich Albion, Win 1-0, Scorer Richardson, AT 13,868, Middleton, O'Kane, Greenwood, Chapman, Jones, Richardson, Dennehy, Lyall, Butlin, Bowyer, Martin, SUB Jackson.

Oct 26th 1974, H, v. Bristol Rovers, Win 1-0, Scorer: Martin, AT 11,495, Middleton, O'Kane, Greenwood, Serella, Jones, Richardson, Dennehy, Martin, Butlin, Jackson, Lyall, SUB Woodcock.

Nov 2nd 1974, A, v. Bolton Wanderers, Loss 0-2, AT 12,711, Peacock, O'Kane, Greenwood, Serella, Jones, Richardson, Dennehy, Martin, Butlin, Jackson, Lyall, SUB Anderson.

Nov 9th 1974, H, v. Oldham Athletic, Win 1-0, Scorer Dennehy, AT 10,127, Middleton, O'Kane, Greenwood, Cottam, Jones, Jackson, Dennehy, Martin, Butlin, Lyall, O'Neill.

Nov 16th 1974, A, v. Cardiff City, Loss 1-2, Scorer Martin, AT 9,279, Middleton, O'Kane, Greenwood, Chapman, Jones, Jackson, Dennehy, Martin, Butlin, Lyall, O'Neill, SUB Richardson.

Nov 23rd 1974, H, v. York City, Win 2-1, Scorers Bowyer, Richardson, AT 10,047, Middleton, O'Kane, Greenwood, Chapman, Jones, Jackson, Dennehy, Martin, Bowyer, Lyall, Richardson, SUB Butlin.

Nov 30th 1974, A, v. Orient, Draw 1-1, Scorer Bowyer, AT 5,217, Middleton, O'Kane, Greenwood, Chapman, Jones, Richardson, Dennehy, Jackson, Butlin, Martin, Bowyer, SUB Cottam.

Dec 7th 1974, H, v. Fulham, Draw 1-1, Scorer Martin, AT 10,057, Middleton, O'Kane, Greenwood, Chapman, Jones, Jackson, Dennehy, Martin, Butlin, Bowyer, Richardson, SUB Woodcock.

Dec 14th 1974, A, v. Bristol City, Loss 0-1, AT 10,006, Middleton, O'Kane, Greenwood, Chapman, Jones, Richardson, Dennehy, Martin, Butlin, Bowyer, O'Neill, SUB Robertson.

Dec 21st 1974, H, v. Blackpool, Draw 0-0, AT 8,480, Middleton, O'Kane, Greenwood, Chapman, Jones, Richardson, Dennehy, Lyall, Butlin, Bowyer, O'Neill, SUB McIntosh.

Dec 26th 1974, A, v. Hull City, Win 3-1, Scorers: Martin (2), Butlin, AT 12,278, Middleton, Serella, O'Kane, Chapman, Jones, Richardson, McIntosh, Martin, Butlin, Bowyer, Lyall.

Dec 28th 1974, H, v. Notts County, Loss 0-2, AT 25,013, Middleton, Serella, O'Kane, Chapman, Jones, Richardson, McIntosh, Martin, Butlin, Bowyer, Lyall, SUB Dennehy.

Jan 4th 1975, FAC, H, v. Tottenham Hotspur, Draw 1-1, Scorer Jones, AT 23,355, Middleton, Anderson, Greenwood, Chapman, Jones, O'Kane, Dennehy, Lyall, Butlin Bowyer, Richardson, SUB Martin

Jan 8th 1975, FAC, A, v. Tottenham Hotspur, Win 1-0, Scorer Martin, AT 27,996, Middleton, O'Kane, Greenwood, Chapman, Jones, Richardson, Lyall, Martin, Butlin, Bowyer, O'Neill, SUB Cottam.

Jan 11th 1975, A, v. Fulham, Win 1-0, Scorer Butlin, AT 9,159, Middleton, O'Kane,

Second Division 1974-75

		Pld	W	D	L	F	A	Pts
1	Manchester United	42	26	9	7	66	30	61
2	Aston Villa	42	25	8	9	79	32	58
3	Norwich City	42	20	13	9	58	37	53
4	Sunderland	42	19	13	10	65	35	51
5	Bristol City	42	21	8	13	47	33	50
6	West Bromwich Albion	42	18	9	15	54	42	45
7	Blackpool	42	14	17	11	38	33	45
8	Hull City	42	15	14	13	40	53	44
9	Fulham	42	13	16	13	44	39	42
10	Bolton Wanderers	42	15	12	15	45	41	42
11	Oxford United	42	15	12	15	41	51	42
12	Orient	42	11	20	11	28	39	42
13	Southampton	42	15	11	16	53	54	41
14	Notts County	42	12	16	14	49	59	40
15	York City	42	14	10	18	51	55	38
16	FOREST	42	12	14	16	43	55	38
17	Portsmouth	42	12	13	17	44	54	37
18	Oldham Athletic	42	10	15	17	40	48	35
19	Bristol Rovers	42	12	11	19	42	64	35
20	Millwall	42	10	12	20	44	56	32
21	Cardiff City	42	9	14	19	36	62	32
22	Sheffield Wednesday	42	5	11	26	29	64	21

Greenwood, Chapman, Jones, Richardson, Lyall, Martin, Butlin, Bowyer, O'Neill.

Jan 18th 1975, H, v. Orient, Draw 2-2, Scorer Richardson (2), AT 17,582, Middleton, O'Kane, Greenwood, Chapman, Jones, Richardson, Lyall, Martin, Butlin, Bowyer, O'Neill.

Jan 28th 1975, FAC, A, v. Fulham, Draw 0-0, AT 14,846, Middleton, O'Kane, Greenwood, Chapman, Cottam, Robertson, Lyall, Martin, Butlin, Bowyer, O'Neill.

Feb 1st 1975, A, v. Oldham Athletic, Loss 0-2, AT 10,736, Middleton, O'Kane, Greenwood, Chapman, Cottam, Robertson, Lyall, Martin, Butlin, Bowyer, O'Neill.

Feb 3rd 1975, FAC, H, v. Fulham, Draw 1-1, Scorer Martin, AT 25,361, Middleton, Jackson, Greenwood, Chapman, Cottam, Robertson, Lyall, Martin, Butlin, Bowyer, O'Neill, SUB Dennehy.

Feb 5th 1975, FAC, A, v. Fulham, Draw 1-1, Scorer Robertson, AT 11,920, Middleton, O'Kane, Richardson, Chapman, Cottam, Robertson, Lyall, Martin, Butlin, Bowyer, O'Neill.

Feb 8th 1975, H, v. Bolton Wanderers, Loss 2-3, Scorer Dennehy (2), AT 11,922, Middleton, Jackson, Richardson, Chapman, Cottam, Robertson, Lyall, Dennehy, Butlin, Bowyer, Anderson.

Feb 10th 1975, FAC, H, v. Fulham, Loss 1-2, Scorer Chapman , AT 23,240, Middleton, O'Kane, Richardson, Chapman, Jones, Robertson, Dennehy, Lyall, Martin, Bowyer, O'Neill.

Feb 14th 1975, A, v. York City, Draw 1-1, Scorer Lyall, AT 7,666, Middleton, O'Kane, Richardson, Chapman, Jones, Robertson, Lyall, Anderson, Martin, Bowyer, O'Neill.

Feb 22nd 1975, H, v. Cardiff City, Draw 0-0, AT 12,806, Middleton, Anderson, Richardson, O'Kane, Cottam, McGovern, Lyall, Robertson, Martin, Bowyer, O'Neill.

Feb 28th 1975, A, v. Oxford United, Draw 1-1, Scorer Lyall, AT 7,602, Middleton, Anderson, Richardson, O'Kane, Jones, Robertson, Lyall, McGovern, O'Hare, Butlin, Bowyer.

Mar 8th 1975, H, v. Aston Villa, Loss 2-3, Scorers O'Hare, Butlin, AT 20,205, Middleton, Anderson, Richardson, O'Kane, Jones, Robertson, Lyall, McGovern, O'Hare, Butlin, Bowyer, SUB Woodcock.

Mar 15th 1975, A, v. Sunderland, Draw 0-0, AT 30,812, Middleton, Anderson, Richardson, O'Kane, Jones, Robertson, Lyall, McGovern, O'Hare, Butlin, Bowyer.

Mar 22nd 1975, H, v. Manchester United, Loss 0-1, AT 21,893, Middleton, Anderson, Richardson, O'Kane, Jones, Robertson, Lyall, McGovern, O'Hare, Butlin, Bowyer.

Mar 25th 1975, A, v. Notts County, Draw 2-2, Scorer Lyall, Butlin, AT 20,303, Middleton, Anderson, Richardson, O'Kane, Jones, Robertson, Lyall, Chapman, O'Hare, Butlin, Bowyer.

Mar 29th 1975, A, v. Blackpool, Draw 0-0, AT 11,640, Middleton, Anderson, Richardson, O'Kane, Jones, Robertson, Lyall, Chapman, O'Hare, Butlin, Bowyer.

Apr 1st 1975, H, v. Sheffield Wednesday, Win 1-0, Scorer Lyall (Pen), AT 14,077, Middleton, Anderson, Richardson, O'Kane, Jones, Robertson, Lyall, Chapman, O'Hare, Butlin, Woodcock.

Apr 5th 1975, A, v. Bristol Rovers, Loss 2-4, Scorers Lyall, O'Hare, AT 9,648, Middleton, O'Kane, Richardson, Chapman, Jones, Robertson, Lyall, McGovern, O'Hare, Butlin,Woodcock.

Apr 12th 1975, H, v. Southampton, Draw 0-0, AT 11,554, Middleton, O'Kane, Richardson, Chapman, Cottam, Robertson, Dennehy, McGovern, O'Hare, Butlin, Lyall.

Apr 19th 1975, A, v. Norwich City, Loss 0-3, AT 24,302, Middleton, O'Kane, Richardson, Chapman, Cottam, Robertson, Dennehy, Lyall, O'Hare, Butlin, McGovern, SUB Anderson.

Apr 26th 1975, H, v. West Bromwich Albion, Win 2-1, Scorer Butlin (2), AT 11,721, Middleton, Anderson, O'Kane, Chapman, Cottam, Richardson, McIntosh, O'Neill, McCann, Butlin, Woodcock, SUB Robertson.

May 8th 1975, CC, H, v Notts County, Loss 0-1, AT 8,291, Wells, Anderson, O'Kane, Chapman, Cottam, McIntosh, Lyall, O'Neill, McCann, Butlin, Woodcock.

Back Row: R.O'Brien, L.O'Kane, B.Stubbs, R.Brown, D.Peacock, S.Chapman, J.Brindley, D.Jones

Middle Row: J.Wheeler, E.Probert, P.Richardson, K.Randall, P.Greenwood, D.Needham, B.Butlin, A.Mann, N.Martin, J.Sheridan

Front Row: G.Lyall, D.Masson, T.Jackson, I.Scanlon, I.Bowyer, J.Nixon, M.Dennehy, L.Bradd

It was mission accomplished, as far as Brian Clough was concerned, relegation had been avoided. Now it was hoped that real progress could be made and this was reflected in season ticket sales for the upcoming campaign that reached their highest total for years, as fans thought Cloughie would now wave his magic wand.

The manager knew differently however, as he knew how far away the team was from competing. Anyway, he set about clearing the decks as Tommy Jackson, Neil Martin and Steve Baines were all given free transfers. Jackson, who many committee members rated as a player, surprisingly ended up at Old Trafford, but the manager couldn't care less what they thought. A small fee was obtained for Miah Dennehy who left for Walsall after failing to make any real impression.

At the club's AGM, Brian Appleby replaced the hapless Jim Willmer. It was also suggested by fans that the committee might like to put their hands in their own pockets to provide Brian Clough with a transfer fund, but this idea did not prove to be popular with them. There had been various schemes suggested about raising interest free loans, but this also didn't come to anything. This caused the manager to question whether the people at Nottingham Forest really wanted a top flight club, after all, how could he compete with the big spenders if he had no money?

The growing success story of the youth development at Nottingham Forest was illustrated by John Middleton, who had made his debut aged only seventeen and had been one of the few bright spots of the previous season. He further enhanced his and the club's reputation when he helped Young England win the Mini World Cup played in Switzerland during June. John played in all five games.

Despite the lack of cash, the manager pulled off what turned out to be a master stroke when he persuaded Frank Clark to join him. Frank had surprisingly been released by Newcastle despite making over thirty appearances and captaining the team during the past season. A local reporter from the North East alerted Clough to his availability. The lack of a left back had bothered the manager since he had taken over. Paul Richardson a mid-fielder had filled in that position for the final fourteen games at the end of the season. Frank himself recalls the move, "I thought I was doing alright at Newcastle, I was just expecting next year's contract to appear as it always had done before, so

75-76

NOTTINGHAM FOREST FOOTBALL CLUB

DIVISION TWO 1975 - 76

Back row, left to right:

JIMMY GORDON (Trainer) PAUL RICHARDSON IAN BOWYER LIAM O'KANE DENNIS PEACOCK JOHN MIDDLETON VIV ANDERSON MARTIN O'NEILL JOHN ROBERTSON JIMMY McINTOSH BRIAN CLOUGH (Manager)

Front row, left to right:

JOHN McGOVERN DAVID JONES JOHN O'HARE BARRY BUTLIN BOB CHAPMAN GEORGE LYALL FRANK CLARK JOHN COTTAM

Clark explains his hopes for Forest

ALTHOUGH he prefers to talk about the future not the past, there is no disguising the bitterness Frank Clark feels about the way he was discarded by Newcastle.

By John Lawson

But the Nottingham Forest defender writes the close season episode off as an unfortunate experience after almost 13 years on Tyneside.

Now, he's aiming to prove Newcastle were wrong about his ability to continue as one of the country's most accomp-

"From the minute he first walked out in a Forest shirt he gave us stability in defence and he has qualities that rub off on those around him."

But it's not only his experience — he has more than 400 League games

De
t
los

**DERBY C
Park this
the form t
ionship las**

Since the
performance
Charity Shie
Wembley the
been more to
age, than
optimism for
European Cu
with Slovan B
lava, on Septemb
The Rams' ba
has made mista
midfield has yet
well as a unit
front three hav
little concerte
despite the th
against 10-ma

when the manager told me I was finished it came as a bolt from the blue. In reality I had become set in my ways, I was a local lad, who had barely travelled, so after the initial shock I decided that this was an opportunity and to be positive about the situation. I could have stayed locally with Hartlepool, but eventually I was set to sign for an ex-team mate Stan Anderson at Doncaster, that was until I received a message from Brian to not sign anything". Frank already knew Brian Clough having played in his testimonial game at Roker Park after injury had finished his career at Sunderland back in 1963. "When I met the boss I told him I fancied playing centre half, I had played several times there for Newcastle and thought to myself this is pretty easy, less running about and this could extend my career, but I was told in no uncertain terms that it was left back for me. The rest is history".

Brian Clough believed in a tough pre-season, getting all the hard work done early, before relying on conserving energy between games. Frank Clark again recalls a conversation he had with the boss. "There were very few players back then who played on well into their thirties and the consensus was the older you got, the more you should train. Brian was ahead of the game, he practically ordered me to do less, get more rest and where previously at Newcastle I was considered injury prone I now went two seasons without missing a game. There was one occasion where we had been given the day off so I decided to go for a run around Lowdham where I lived. Someone phoned the manager to tell him. The next day he had a right go at me, "When I tell you to have a day off you do it" he said. At Forest I barely missed a game so he was right, as he was about many things".

Jimmy Gordon put the players through their paces around Wollaton Park before they set off for Germany to play five games. The club lost only one game out of the five, scoring 13 goals and conceding only 2. The fifteen man squad contained youngsters Tony Woodcock, Jim McCann and Ian Miller as replacements for the more experienced Bowyer, O'Neill and Robertson who were left behind due to more contract disputes. In fact Ian Bowyer took the club to a tribunal where he faced off against the manager at the FA's headquarters in London, earning his respect Ian thought, for standing his ground. After the players returned to England, all three re-signed and joined team mates for a quick trip to Ireland for a couple of games to complete preparations. This was the first occasion when John Robertson was pushed wide left and performed creditably, a foretaste of what was to come.

For this season the club decided to adopt yellow for their away kit and for the first time replica kits would now officially be available to buy from the small club shop.

On the eve of the first game Clough declared that anybody who thought this team would win promotion was 'Bonkers', labelling them as, 'No hopers', perhaps not the kind of statement the fans wanted to hear, but honest. He also told the players in no uncertain terms that it was time they started paying their way. The club needed an 18,000 attendance to break even, but rarely came near, starting the season off with a gate of only 13,083, even this crowd size caused problems as the club were down twelve turnstile operators due to staff holidays and a cricket match at Trent Bridge. Newly promoted Plymouth Argyle were the first day opponents and they were easily brushed aside 2-0, with the honour of scoring the season's first goal of the new campaign going to Mickey Horswill the Argyle mid-fielder who lobbed the ball over his own keeper, with O'Hare wrapping things up for the Reds. The major talking point however was the sight of Brian Clough charging down the touchline to remonstrate with Forest fans who were fighting with supporters from Plymouth in front of the Main Stand, "We don't want scum at our games", declared

Mickey Horswill the Plymouth midfielder heads past his own keeper to put the Reds one goal up.

Brian Clough charges down the touchline as Forest fans spill on to the pitch against Plymouth.

Vol. LXVII No. 1 NOTTINGHAM, SATURDAY, AUGUST 16, 1975 Price 6p

O'HARE HELPS REDS TO WINNING START

John O'Hare dives in vain against Notts County.

Ian Bowyer fails to find the target from a tight angle against Bolton.

John O'Hare cooly slots the ball under the Saints' keeper.

O'Neil fires home the first goal against Southampton.

John Robertson has his penalty saved by Wealands the Hull keeper.

But Robbo heads home the rebound.

More penalty agony as Robertson misses another spot kick against Hull.

IT'S AGONY! REDS PAY THE PENALTY

FOOTBALL

TERRY CURRAN - NOTTINGHAM FOREST

Alan Hill chats with a delighted Terry Curran after he completes his move to Forest.

the manager. Clough had again expressed an interest in Tommy Booth, the Man City centre half, but got nowhere, so he began the season with the regular pairing of O'Kane and Chapman but after an early season injury to O'Kane he was forced to do a reshuffle.

The Reds followed the Argyle game up with League Cup victory at Rotherham, where Gunn and Anderson provided the club's youngest ever full back pairing. Half-time entertainment was unusual, a carpet carrying race between home and away supporters, the idea of the match sponsors Carol Aston Carpets. The Saturday saw an away draw at Portsmouth, where George Lyall incurred the manager's wrath by firing a penalty high and wide when the Reds were one up, made even worse when Portsmouth equalised with five minutes remaining. The second leg of the League Cup tie saw Forest advance comfortably, thrashing Rotherham 5-1, two each for Lyall and Richardson, plus one from Bowyer. Liam O'Kane recalls an incident after the Pompey game, "I had been chatting with the manager for a few weeks about a contract extension, but I was not totally happy about what was being offered, so I hadn't signed. As luck would have it in the next match at Portsmouth I went off with what looked like a serious injury. On the bus journey home, Brian comes down the bus, stops next to me and says, "I bet you wish you'd signed that contract now". He was only joking but he had made his point". Despite what had looked like a promising start to the season, clearly apathy abounded as only 19,000 fans bothered to turn up for the local derby against Notts. In a poor game, County left with the points after Les Bradd snatched a last minute winner. The manager was furious, losing to your 'small time' neighbours was not acceptable. Bryn Gunn made his league debut at left back, whilst Clough was forced to move Clark to centre half to replace O'Kane. George Lyall who had scored two goals in the Rotherham victory and thought that he was playing okay was surprisingly left out and after asking the manager for the reason, was told he had no future at the club.

Prior to the Notts game, Clough wheeling and dealing had pulled off what he thought was a master stroke. Winger Terry Curran, was signed from Doncaster Rovers in a cash and player exchange deal involving keeper Dennis Peacock and Ian Miller moving the other way. The manager told supporters that they would be excited by this player and despite a nervous debut, there were glimpses of real pace from the winger. Indeed, with Viv Anderson playing behind Curran, this looked very promising, in a line-up that contained only four players from Clough's first game in charge and a definite move towards a more youthful looking team.

The manager in an interview with John Lawson declared that he was trying to change the club's attitude, "We must develop youth, for too long the best youngsters have been allowed to leave, the club has always had it's best times when the team contained home grown talent".

The team's form had slipped into mediocrity and this meant that not even Brian Clough was above criticism; A.E Dexter, Sneinton pulled the manager up about what he saw as denigrating comments about the players, that is apart from McGovern and O'Hare. He also suggested that the team would be improved by playing Lyall instead of McGovern. On a similar note, A. Gibson, Bramcote, said, 'Clough's blue eyed boy McGovern is not in the same class as Lyall'.

After a League Cup victory over Plymouth, the manager turned on those fans chanting for George Lyall to come on as substitute, "I will never be swayed by supporters, if we had been down to eight men I wouldn't have put him on".

During a run of four consecutive home defeats, John Robertson had the unfortunate experience to miss two penalties in one game against Hull, although he did manage to bundle home the rebound after the first was saved. John had been given the responsibility after Lyall's penalty miss earlier in the season. Robertson himself was not that upset when this role was handed over to Terry Curran. Worse still in the Hull game, Robbo had endured barracking from sections of the crowd, who saw him as overweight and lazy. The manager also

Football Post, Saturday, September 13, 1975

BRIAN CLOUGH ON SOCCER

City gates are appalling, so...

IF EVER I needed convincing that Nottingham possesses the most fickle and apathetic football supporters this side of Hong Kong, I saw the evidence this week.

And I am not only thinking about the attitude of the City's fans to what is going on at Nottingham Forest's side of the Trent.

Spare a thought for Notts. County across the river. They forced their way to the top of the Second Division last Saturday and there were just 8,005 people there to see them do it.

That appalling figure was a smack in the eye for all of us trying to put Nottingham on the football map.

MYTH

Ever since I arrived in the city people have been telling me what a great football-minded place it is. My answer

Come on you fans—give us a chance

If I am wrong, where on

● Two former managers

responded to the terrace criticism of John McGovern by making him captain instead of Sammy Chapman, it was for just one match, but again he was laying down a marker about who was in charge.

Fans were disappointed with what they might have perceived as slow progress, but closer examination shows the building blocks of the future being put in place, however, obviously with Brian Clough as your manager, expectations were always going to be higher than normal. Brian Clough himself appealed, 'Come on you fans, give us a chance'.

Dave Jones who had never impressed the manager was allowed to join Norwich for a fee of £55,000, but the money was to stay in the bank whilst Clough shuffled the pack. According to Clough, financial pressure to balance the books meant that he had to send Barry Butlin out on loan to Brighton, although this might have been a smokescreen to help out his old mate Peter Taylor who was manager there. The unwanted George Lyall came on as a substitute to grab an 88th minute winner at Oxford, a game that also saw Ian Bowyer display his versatility as he had to spend half the game in goal as a replacement for John Middleton who had broken his nose in a collision. George remembers this period with disappointment, "I really think that I should have been given an opportunity to tie down a first team place, I don't think that I let the manager or team down, but it was only a matter of time until I left, the only question would be where to".

Two further home defeats followed to Charlton and Bolton, part of a run of four consecutive home losses and there was also a 4-2 thrashing at Bristol Rovers where Forest were spectacularly awful against a team propping up the table.

Ken Smales recalled conversations with the manager from this time, "He really was despondent at times, he didn't understand how some players couldn't master even the basics". As a sign of how desperate he was, the manager was forced to turn to John Cottam in an attempt to bring some solidity to the defence. Trying to protect youngsters Anderson and Gunn from the mess that surrounded them, he rotated each player in one of the full back spots. On paper the team looked quite strong, but for whatever reason it just wasn't gelling. Terry Curran was given a run out with the reserves in an attempt to boost his confidence and he responded with two goals against Coventry.

Forest exited the League Cup at Maine Road, 2-1 in favour of Man City, an unhappy first return back for Ian Bowyer although City manager Tony Book admitted his team had been lucky. After this game Clough took the opportunity to withdraw Bryn Gunn from the firing line altogether. Although he had been playing well, on this particular evening he had a torrid time against the emerging Peter Barnes. This positive performance was quickly forgotten days later after another abject display in a goalless draw at Fulham, Sammy Chapman was sent off and there was also a one and only loan appearance for Dave Sunley from Sheffield Wednesday, who was anonymous throughout and sent back to his parent club early. Chapman's sending off turned out to have a favourable consequence as John McGovern was moved into the back four to replace Sammy and looked so at ease that the manager paired him with Chapman in future games after he had returned from suspension. With this result, the Reds actually found themselves in the relegation zone with only seven points from ten games.

For the next game the manager restored the out of favour pair Barry Butlin and Martin O'Neill to the side and used McGovern as a sweeper. The result was an encouraging 3-1 victory over Southampton who were outclassed. 'Home joy at last for slick Forest', was the newspaper headline. Butlin combined well with O'Hare for the first, followed by a great solo effort from O'Neill, who cut in from the right and rifled home a twenty yard blockbuster.
The defence immediately had a more solid

Barry Butlin lashes home the winner against Bristol City.

Butlin turns the ball in to the Carlisle United net.

Vol. LXVII No. 14 NOTTINGHAM, SATURDAY, NOVEMBER 15, 1975 Price

QUICK-FIRE BUTLIN WINS IT FOR REDS

Barry Butlin takes the applause after his early goal.

Butlins winner against York City.

Action from the Portsmouth game.

John O'Hare with his second against Carlisle.

Terry Curran nets his first Forest goal against Carlisle.

Action from the Peterborough cup game.

IAN BOWYER

FRANK CLARK & BERT BOWERY

FOREST

DAVID JONES
Nottingham Forest

VII No. 25 NOTTINGHAM, SATURDAY, FEBRUARY 7, 1976 Price 6p

GOAL-HAPPY REDS CRUSH BLACKPOOL

Barry Butlin scores the second goal against Blackpool.

Ian Bowyer completes the scoring against Blackpool.

Ian Bowyer goes close against Sunderland.

O'Hare with the winning goal against Sunderland.

Butlin heads home against Oldham.

O'Neil scores his first against Oldham.

Bowery boy brings Forest more goal punch

ANOTHER JOHN CHARLES . . . the description is not one you could lightly relate to any players since the departure from the soccer scene of the great Welsh giant.

By John Lawson

But it was a tag once placed on Bert Bowery, the Nottingham Forest hopeful who arrived on the League scene in such exciting style last Saturday.

The man who made the comparison was former City Ground star Jack Burkitt, who knows more than most about Bowery's quiet development recent years.

the qualities needed to be a front player so we switched him around and he's stayed there since."

While he was piling up the goals for the Methodists' side, Bowery was recommended to Hereford, then ... by Notts County ... Addison.

Forest manager Brian Clough, having had recommendations about Bowery's potential, made him his first signing at a meagre £2,000 but his progress at the City Ground has been far from dramatic.

DECISION

In fact, earlier this season he would have move... to the Northern ... with ...

...ERT BOWERY

Brian Clough along with players, Paul Richardson, John O'Hare, Tommy Jackson and Viv Anderson, pictured at Bramcote swimming baths for a sponsored swim.

look about it, McGovern's ability to read the game more than made up for his lack of physical presence and aerial prowess. A couple of clean sheets followed in goalless draws against Luton and Oldham, before Carlisle were beaten 4-0, a season's first goal for Butlin, two for O'Hare and a welcome first ever first team Forest goal for Terry Curran from the penalty spot. Terry had played several more matches for the reserves in an attempt to further expand his knowledge of the game and what it meant to be a team player. He had been very inexperienced when he had joined Forest, having barely playing twenty first team games for Doncaster.

A three goal defeat at promotion chasing Sunderland was quickly forgotten after further improvement was shown in wins over Bristol City, Butlin netting the winner and then the team's finest victory for years, 3-0 away at Southampton. Paul Richardson was an ever present and outstanding performer, who inexplicably was to fall out of favour shortly afterwards. Brian Clough and the team had travelled with supporters on Forestrail to the Southampton game and then further surprised everyone including Hampshire police when Cloughie declared that as it was such a nice day, they would walk to the ground with the fans. Meanwhile over the river, Jimmy Sirrell left Notts County to join Sheffield United, which meant Ron Fenton was promoted to the manager's role. After a horrible training ground accident for John Middleton that resulted in a broken leg, the Reds were lucky to have a capable replacement in another highly rated young keeper called Peter Wells. He was drafted in for his League debut in a 1-0 home success against York and he produced a fantastic last minute save to keep a clean sheet and earn a standing ovation.

Some of the players were the subject of unfair criticism, every team seemed to have a fan's scapegoat. Ken Smales unusually was allowed to use his column in the programme to talk about a wide range of subjects that bothered him in his own inimitable style and on this occasion he came to the defence of John Robertson. 'He might not be fast, but he never gives the ball away and he has great vision, give him a chance and he could turn out to be special'.

Brain Clough presents the inaugural Forest Bowl Trophy

Brian Clough again asked the committee to give him some money, "I have a novice goalkeeper, two young full backs and not enough forwards in my squad, we need re-enforcements", was his plea.

There was high praise from all quarters for the work done by Alan Hill with the youth set up. The Brian Clough name, certainly helped when trying to recruit youngsters. The manager was always on hand Sunday mornings to meet parents and assure them that their 'bairns' would be well looked after. It also helped that so many youngsters were getting first team opportunities at this time. Forest launched their own local school's competition called 'Forest Bowl' to ensure that they had first sight of any promising local youngsters.

Surprisingly after what had looked like and felt like an average start, a 0-0 draw with Orient during the first week in January, meant the Reds found themselves only five points off third place, although behind Notts County and Sunderland who were well clear at the top.

The club had been invited on a mid season break to play Qatar, John McGovern said it would do his lumbago good. They were met at the airport by Frank Wignall who was employed by the Qatari Football Association. He broke the news that the country did not allow alcohol, but one enterprising individual who shall remain nameless sorted something out and the manager's room, number 103, was a popular destination with enquiries about his health. Within the club there were doubts about the advisability of such

POST

Carlisle Utd...1 Notts Co. 2
Burnley ....1 Derby Co. 2
Mansfield Tn.1 Gillingham 1

LXVII No. 22 NOTTINGHAM, SATURDAY, JANUARY 17, 1976 Price 6p

GOAL AT LAST BUT REDS ARE BEATEN

Fans clash

Violence flared at the City Ground before the kick-off in this afternoon's game between Forest and Chelsea.

Rival fans clashed on the terraces and a number were led from the ground by police.

There was more crowd disturbance when the game got under way and several young supporters were hurt in more outbreaks of fighting.

ton curled in a centre and full-back Locke, under pressure from Clarke, still managed a diving header, which was only just wide.

Almost three minutes of injury time was added to the first half and although Chelsea kept plugging away.

a trip at that time in the season, but the money the club received for going would come in useful. This trip turned out to be George Lyall's last outing for the club as a surprisingly low offer of only £20,000 was accepted from Hull City. George was still a crowd favourite, a real bundle of energy and enthusiasm, one hundred and thirty six appearances and twenty nine goals paid testament to that.

However financially beneficial the trip to Qatar may have been, all those doubts about the physical drain on the players, appeared to be proven right when it seemed to have a negative effect, particularly obvious when they lost 1-0 at home to Portsmouth, less than twenty fours after arriving home.

The manager defended his position, "At present there are some people who are intent on destroying us, but I for one am above their criticism and will prove it. I am going to get together the kind of side that will force people to encourage a team. Whenever some of them open their mouths at the moment, only rubbish comes out". It seemed as if a few people even inside the club were waiting for Brian Clough to fall flat on his face just so they could say, "I told you so". But this was fighting talk from the manager. Although there was no immediate reaction from the players as this was followed by two more defeats 1-0 to Plymouth, and a Boxing Day loss to West Brom. No goals had now been scored in three games. As was so often the case, the manager produced a rabbit from the hat when he handed young West Indian striker Bert Bowery his debut for the away game at Blackburn. Bert was built like a heavyweight boxer and in the days when black players were still considered a novelty, he certainly stood out. Having made his name on the local scene with Mapperley Methodists, Forest signed him for a nominal fee from Worksop Town. He was to make an immediate impression, banging in two goals in an impressive 4-1 victory played only twenty four hours after the Albion game. Forest fans again invaded the pitch as they charged across to fill the Rover's home end.

Terry Curran

Bowery was to keep his place for the two FA Cup games against Peterborough United. Forest yet again were astute in asking the FA if they could bring the tie forward to Thursday 1st January (two days before the official date) and were rewarded with an outstanding attendance in excess of 31,000. An even contest saw the teams play out a 0-0 draw. Both clubs knew by the time of the replay, that the winners would visit Old Trafford in the next round, a sure fire money spinner, but despite constant pressure in front of a massive away following, Forest couldn't score and fell to a sucker punch goal from John Cozens.

In these days of multi media outlets and trigger happy chairman, it is conceivable that Brian Clough might not have survived this period. Results and performances were not good enough and questions about team selection and tactics were often aired through the letters page of the Football Post.

The thoughts of John McGovern and John O'Hare who had seen the best of Brian Clough are particularly relevant. Both thought that the manager was not sparking as he had done previously, outwardly and to the other players this was not so apparent, but there just seemed to be a little something missing. For a manager of Brian Clough's ambition and abilities, scratching around at the bottom of Division Two was not the place to be. No-one was to know it, but the nadir had been reached and the only trajectory now was upwards.

After a 1-0 defeat by a George Lyall inspired Hull City, there were violent scenes on the wide open spaces of the Bridgford End terraces for the next home game as Chelsea won 3-1. The police were unable to exercise any control and trouble continued throughout the game whilst many supporters used this as an excuse to leave. Now begun a run of results and performances that would carry on for the next five years. It was as if a switch had been clicked on, as the team lost only two games out of fifteen until the end of the season. Goals began to flow, clean sheets followed and at one stage it looked like an unlikely promotion push was possible.

A vital part of this turn-around was the form of Terry Curran. He had shown

JOHN MIDDLETON - NOTTINGHAM FOREST

BARRY BUTLIN

PETER WELLS

VIV ANDERSON & BRYN GUNN

FOREST

what he was capable of in patches, but after a stop start season caused by illness and injury, playing in a more consistent and stable team, he caught fire. Burnley who were struggling to survive in Division One made an audacious attempt to take him on loan, but this was immediately turned down by the manager. John Robertson was now permanently pushed out wide left and into the number eleven shirt, whilst Bowyer and O'Neill formed a strong centre partnership.

Despite his disciplinary problems, the manager had a soft spot for Sammy Chapman, who although he lacked pace, could read the game well. Clough knew that every team needed steel, the trick was not to let this spill over into indiscipline. The manager had read him the riot act after his sending off at Fulham and for this season and the next, Sammy's record was much improved. Cloughie said that he wished he had got hold of him when he was younger, he could have made him an International. Glyn Saunders at seventeen was the latest off the youth production line when he made his first team debut in the County Cup against Mansfield, whilst at the same time, the injury to John Middleton opened up a space for Chris Woods, only fifteen and still at school, to play in goal for the reserves. Terry Curran scored his first goal from open play in the 1-1 draw at Luton, before the Reds clicked at home to Blackpool 3-0, with Curran scoring in successive games, three goals coming in a twenty minute second half spell. The major talking point was the attendance of only 8,582, no doubt Forest's home form was a factor but judging by the letters to the Football Post, the unsavoury scenes on the terraces at the previous home game also had an effect. The wind was so strong this day that several roof panels were blown off the East Stand.

Sammy Chapman had been granted a club testimonial and as well as a game to be played later in the year at the City Ground, his testimonial committee arranged a variety of money raising events. Amongst these there was a gentleman's evening at the Albany Hotel. In view of the animosity between them, many people were surprised that Brian Clough sat alongside Don Revie and referee Gordon Hill for a question and answer session that was warmly received.

The Reds followed this up with a 2-0 victory at Ashton Gate over Bristol City, goals from Terry Curran and John O'Hare, all the more impressive because

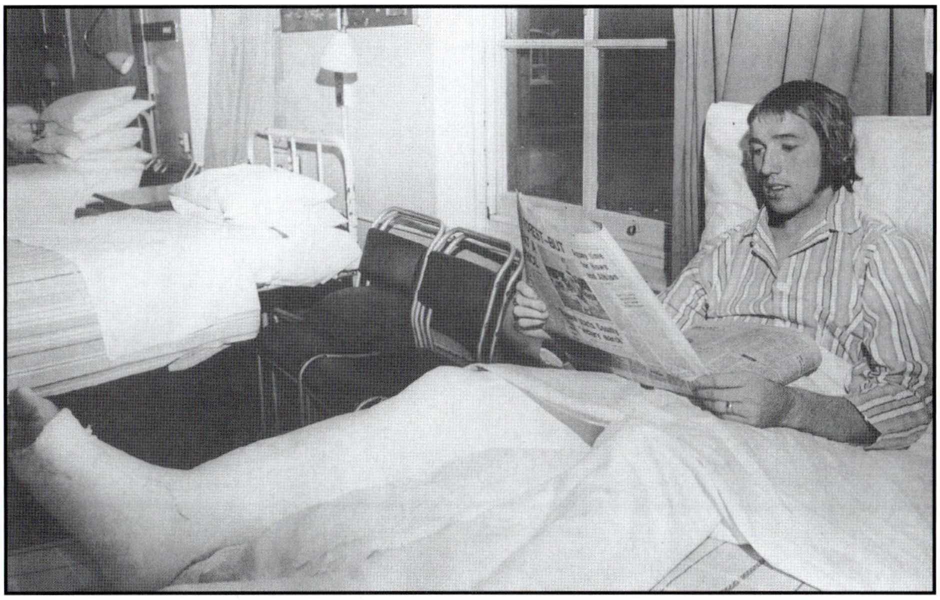

Liam O'Kane recuperates after the career threatening injury sustained at Bristol City.

the Robins were top of the table at that time. But misfortune befell Liam O'Kane once more, as he picked up the injury that would to all intents and purposes finish his career. The local Bristol press were fulsome in their praise, 'City torn apart by slick Forest team'.

The mediocre mid table position was made worse by Notts County only being one point off the top, despite losing their manager. The Reds' unbeaten run continued with a good fight back at the Valley, two late goals, including an equaliser from substitute Jim McCann earning a point, McCann earning his call up after a string of impressive performances for the reserves. Goals and good performances kept coming, supporters were treated to a highly entertaining 4-3 win over Oldham that was to form part of an eight game home winning streak, two goals for O'Neill, with Robertson and Curran causing havoc as they switched wings.

Although the manager was playing down any thoughts of a late rush for promotion, after the 1-1 draw away at Carlisle (over five hundred fans on Forestrail compared with the three hundred and fifty who followed Derby to West Ham), Clough strengthened his squad when he persuaded Colin Barrett to join on loan from Manchester City. This would add even more experience to the back four that was now settled with Clark, McGovern and Chapman. The manager had to work hard to persuade Barrett to join from Manchester City, as he initially turned Clough down. However, after a face to face meeting he overcame his reservations and signed on for the rest of the season.

The continuity of team selection was to be a major factor in this impressive run of sixteen games with only two defeats. Wells, Barrett, Clark, McGovern, Chapman, Bowyer, Curran, O'Neill, O'Hare, Butlin and Robertson was the preferred line up, in fact only two changes forced through injury, were made during the last ten matches. As Barrett arrived, Jimmy McIntosh left to join George Lyall at Hull for a nominal £5,000 fee. Bert Bowery and Tony Woodcock were also sent out on loan to Lincoln City. The relationship between Woodcock and Clough was strange in many ways. Tony was well regarded at the club and it was surprising he was never given a proper chance in the first team, particularly when they were struggling. The manager at times was cruel in the barbs he threw the player's way. Woodcock several times plucked up the courage to discuss what he thought was his best position but the manager was off hand to the point of indifference. Whether this was a ruse to bring the normally affable Woodcock out of his shell we will never know. However, it was not to be until Peter Taylor arrived, that Woodcock would get his chance and if

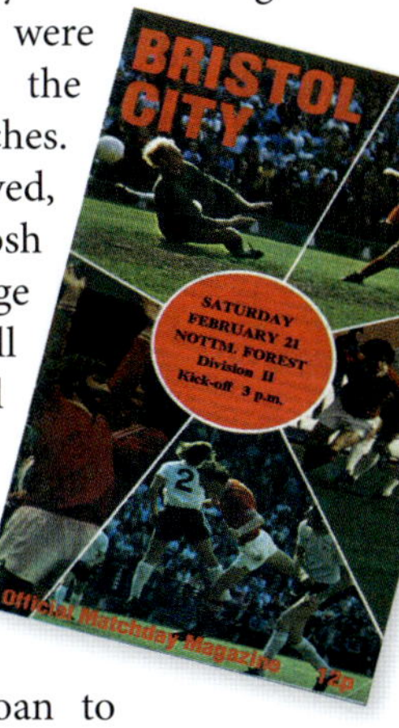

LET'S START THINKING BIG

BRIAN CLOUGH ON SOCCER

'Tell me to get promotion'

NEXT week I will be meeting the 250 members and vice-presidents who virtually control Nottingham Forest and they are sure to be asking me what I feel about our chances of promotion.

I will be disappointed if they don't tell them right down to the last detail what my feelings are on the subject.

While on recent results it is natural for

People have got to appreciate that for a club ... sion and be a power in the land, we are in a pretty unhealthy financial state. And not too much is being done about it.

I reckon if we were in a position to be challenging

... ising on the Trent.

I hope those two examples I have used give you some idea of the p... But what e... know i...

I could sign and improve the side immediately — if there was money available.

Lincoln had not been so keen to save a few bob waiting for his contract to run out, he most probably would have been allowed to leave.

Barrett made his debut in a comfortable 1-0 win at home to Fulham, but promotion fever really raised its head after League leaders Sunderland were beaten mid-week 2-1 in the season's most professional performance. Goals from O'Hare and Butlin clinched the win. With bottom of the table York up next and only five points separating the Reds from third place, there was still hope, but in the end Forest backed by another huge following, produced their most insipid display for weeks and went down 3-2 at Bootham Crescent. York scored two on the breakaway but after thousands of Forest fans again invaded the pitch, they clawed their way back into the game, until they were caught once more in the 84th minute chasing a winner.

Paddy Greenwood who had never figured after breaking his leg, was also released early from his contract to join the Boston Minuteman in America and he was joined shortly afterwards by Bert Bowery whose unsuccessful loan deal with Lincoln was cut short.

Frank Clark recalls this season, "In all honesty we were an average team and we perhaps over achieved in finishing eighth. Personally I didn't usually enjoy playing the actual matches, the pressure to win was immense, but because expectations were a little lower that season, I was able to relax a little".

Ian Bowyer, who was to finish the season as top scorer despite dropping back to midfield banged home the winner against Orient, missed by Brian Clough, as by now he was scouting throughout the Football League in search of new players.

A creditable clean sheet in an away draw with promotion chasing Bolton, was followed by a four goal hammering of Oxford, all the goals coming in the last fifteen minutes. Although Brian Clough was moved to point out the importance of Frank Clark's goal line clearance when the scores were level, that led to sustained applause from home supporters. For some reason, every Forest home goal

Paddy Greenwood pictured after he sustained his broken leg last season.

during this period was followed by mini pitch invasions and it was not until the club posted warning notices that younger fans took any notice.

The return derby against Notts at Meadow Lane attracted a significantly higher crowd of almost 30,000 than attended the early season clash. County who at one time looked favourites to clinch a promotion spot had faltered badly, dropping eleven points in seven games. However, they were still in with a chance, so it was a surprise when they resorted to a defensive formation to grind out a goalless draw.

Colin Barrett who had been sceptical about coming to Nottingham now joined on a permanent deal. He had made several errors, but otherwise he looked a useful addition.

After a loss to West Brom, Forest ended the campaign with two more home wins, 1-0 against Blackburn and an emphatic 3-0 victory over Bristol Rovers, three goals in the last half an hour from O'Hare and two from Bowyer gave the Reds some revenge for the mauling they had been given at Eastville earlier in the season.

Just one more game to mention, Sammy Chapman's testimonial match against Don Revie's 'All star XI' that saw the return, of not only Joe Baker but also Duncan McKenzie to the City Ground. As the game ended, thousands invaded the pitch to congregate in front of the Main Stand, refusing to leave until Duncan came out to acknowledge the crowd singing, 'Bring back our Duncan to us'. As the crowds drifted away, the rumours started that he was going to return. Just like so many rumours, it turned out to be just wishful thinking.

The Reds for the second year running had finished behind County in eighth place on forty six points, but Brian Clough, not usually bothered by happenings over the river was in bullish mood, when he declared that if you had a few bob to spare, put it on Forest to finish above their neighbours next season. 'We will be ahead of them once more', he declared.

The Reds' team was by now almost unrecognisable from the poor outfit he had taken over. The deadwood had been cleared out and with some astute purchases and the progression of the younger players, optimism was increasing. So when Brian Clough made his finest capture in July 1976 everything was surely set for lift off.

Action from the Orient game.

Robertson completes the rout of Oxford.

More action from the Orient game.

Curran fires home from the penalty spot against Oxford.

REDS GOAL-SPREE SHATTERS OXFORD

Staff and players travel on Forestrail to West Brom.

Martin O'Neill flies down the wing at West Brom.

Ian Bowyer chats to Commercial Manager John Carter.

Robbo and Curran celebrate with young Forest supporters.

FACTS and FIGURES

Aug 16th 1975, H, v. Plymouth Argyle, Win 2-0, Scorers O'Hare, Horswill (OG), AT 13,083, Middleton, Anderson, Clark, Chapman, O'Kane, McGovern, Lyall, Richardson, O'Hare, Robertson, Bowyer.

Aug 19th 1975, LC, A, v. Rotherham United, Win 2-1, Scorers Chapman, McGovern, AT 4,912, Middleton, Anderson, Clark, O'Kane, Chapman, Richardson, Robertson, McGovern, O'Hare, Bowyer, Lyall.

Aug 23rd 1975, A, v. Portsmouth, Draw 1-1, Scorer Bowyer, AT 10,655, Middleton, Anderson, Clark, O'Kane, Chapman, Richardson, Robertson, McGovern, O'Hare, Bowyer, Lyall, SUB O'Neill.

Aug 27th 1975, LC, H, v. Rotherham United, Win 5-1, Scorers Richardson (2), Bowyer, Lyall (2), AT 7,977, Middleton, Anderson, Gunn, Clark, Chapman, Richardson, Robertson, McGovern, O'Hare, Bowyer, Lyall.

Aug 30th 1975, H, v. Notts County, Loss 0-1, AT 19,757, Middleton, Anderson, Gunn, Clark, Chapman, Richardson, O'Neill, McGovern, O'Hare, Robertson, Bowyer.

Sept 6th 1975, A, v. Chelsea, Draw 0-0, AT 21,323, Middleton, Anderson, Gunn, Chapman, Clark, Robertson, Curran, McGovern, O'Hare, Richardson, Bowyer.

Sept 10th 1975, LC, H, v. Plymouth Argyle, Win 1-0, Scorer Bowyer, AT 8,978, Middleton, Anderson, Gunn, Clark, Chapman, Richardson, O'Neill, McGovern, O'Hare, Bowyer, Robertson, SUB Lyall.

Sept 13th 1975, H, v. Hull City, Loss 1-2, Scorer Robertson, AT 12,191, Middleton, Anderson, Gunn, McGovern, Chapman, Clark, Curran, Richardson, O'Hare, Robertson, Bowyer.

Sept 20th 1975, A, v. Oxford United, Win 1-0, Scorer Lyall, AT 5,318, Middleton, Anderson, Gunn, Clark, Chapman, Richardson, Curran, McGovern, O'Hare, Robertson, Bowyer, SUB Lyall.

Sept 24th 1975, H, v. Charlton Athletic, Loss 1-2, Scorer Robertson, AT 10,588, Middleton, Anderson, Gunn, Clark, Chapman, Richardson, Curran, McGovern, Bowyer, Lyall, Robertson.

Sept 27th 1975, H, v. Bolton Wanderers, Loss 1-2, Scorer Lyall, AT 10,780, Middleton, Gunn, Clark, McGovern, Cottam, Chapman, Curran, Richardson, Bowyer, Lyall, Robertson.

Oct 4th 1975, A, v. Bristol Rovers, Loss 2-4, Scorers Robertson, Bowyer, AT 7,698, Middleton, Gunn, Clark, McGovern, Chapman, Cottam, Curran, Richardson, O'Hare, Robertson, Bowyer, SUB Lyall.

Oct 10th 1975, LC, A, v. Manchester City, Loss 1-2, Scorer Bowyer, AT 26,536, Middleton, Gunn, Clark, Chapman, Cottam, Richardson, O'Neill, McGovern, O'Hare, Bowyer, Robertson.

Oct 11th 1975, A, v. Fulham, Draw 0-0, AT 10,149, Middleton, Anderson, Clark, Chapman, Cottam, Richardson, Curran, McGovern, Sunley, Lyall, Bowyer, SUB O'Hare.

Oct 18th 1975, H, v. Southampton, Win 3-1, Scorers Cottam, O'Neill, O'Hare, AT 12,677, Middleton, Anderson, Clark, McGovern, Cottam, Richardson, Curran, O'Neill, O'Hare, Butlin, Bowyer.

Oct 21st 1975, H, v. Luton Town, Draw 0-0, AT 12,290, Middleton, Anderson, Clark, McGovern, Cottam, Richardson, Curran, O'Neill, O'Hare, Butlin, Robertson.

Oct 25th 1975, A, v. Oldham Athletic, Draw 0-0, AT 11,437, Middleton, Anderson, Clark, McGovern, Cottam, Richardson, Curran, O'Neill, O'Hare, Butlin, Bowyer.

Nov 1st 1975, H, v. Carlisle United, Win 4-0, Scorers Curran (Pen), O'Hare (2), Butlin, AT 11,894, Middleton, Anderson, Clark, McGovern, Cottam, Richardson, Curran, O'Neill, O'Hare, Butlin, Bowyer, SUB Robertson.

Nov 4th 1975, A, v. Blackpool, Draw 1-1, Scorer O'Neill, AT 5,851, Middleton, Anderson, Clark, McGovern, Cottam, Richardson, Robertson, O'Neill, O'Hare, Butlin, Bowyer.

Nov 8th 1975, A, v. Sunderland, Loss 0-3, AT 31,227, Middleton, Anderson, Clark, McGovern, Chapman, Richardson, O'Neill, Robertson, O'Hare, Butlin, Bowyer.

Nov 15th 1975, H, v. Bristol City, Win 1-0, Scorer Butlin, AT 11,583, Middleton, Anderson, Clark, McGovern, Chapman, Richardson, O'Neill, Robertson, O'Hare, Butlin, Bowyer.

Nov 17th 1975, F, A, v. Hartlepool, Draw 0-0, AT 1,398, Middleton, Anderson, Clark, McGovern, Chapman, Richardson, Robertson, Lyall, O'Hare, Butlin, Bowyer, SUB Bowery.

Nov 22nd 1975, A, v. Southampton, Win 3-0, Scorers Richardson, Bowyer (2), AT 14,245, Middleton, Anderson, Clark, McGovern, Chapman, Richardson, O'Neill, Robertson, O'Hare, Butlin, Bowyer.

Nov 29th 1975, H, v. York City, Win 1-0, Scorer Butlin, AT 13,108, Wells, Anderson, Clark, McGovern, Chapman, Richardson, O'Neill, Robertson, O'Hare, Butlin, Bowyer.

Dec 6th 1975, A, v. Orient, Draw 1-1, Scorer Bowyer, AT 5,629, Wells, Anderson, Clark, McGovern, Chapman, Robertson, Curran, O'Neill, O'Hare, Butlin, Bowyer.

Dec 9th 1975, F, A, v. Qatar National XI, Draw 1-1, Scorer Richardson, AT 3,000, Wells, Gunn, Clark, McGovern, Cottam, Robertson, Lyall, O'Neill, O'Hare, Butlin, Richardson, SUBS Bowyer, Powell.

Dec 13th 1975, H, v. Portsmouth, Loss 0-1, AT 11,343, Wells, Anderson, Clark, McGovern, Chapman, Robertson, Curran, O'Neill, O'Hare, Butlin, Bowyer.

Dec 20th 1975, A, v. Plymouth Argyle, Loss 0-1, AT 10,545, Wells, Anderson, Clark, McGovern, Chapman, Richardson, Curran, O'Neill, O'Hare, Butlin, Bowyer, SUB Robertson.

Dec 26th 1975, H, v. West Bromwich Albion, Loss 0-2, AT 19,393, Wells, O'Kane, Clark, McGovern, Chapman, Richardson, Curran, O'Neill, O'Hare, Butlin, Robertson.

Dec 27th 1975, A, v. Blackburn Rovers, Win 4-1, Scorers Robertson, Bowery (2), Bowyer, AT 10,720, Wells, O'Kane, Clark, McGovern, Chapman, Robertson, McIntosh, Bowery, O'Hare, Butlin, Bowyer.

Jan 1st 1976, FAC, H, v. Peterborough United, Draw 0-0, AT 31,525, Wells, O'Kane, Clark, McGovern, Chapman, Bowyer, McIntosh, Bowery, O'Hare, Butlin, Robertson.

Second Division 1975-76

		Pld	W	D	L	F	A	Pts
1	Sunderland	42	24	8	10	67	36	56
2	Bristol City	42	19	15	8	59	35	53
3	West Bromwich Albion	42	20	13	9	50	33	53
4	Bolton Wanderers	42	20	12	10	64	38	52
5	Notts County	42	19	11	12	60	41	49
6	Southampton	42	21	7	14	66	50	49
7	Luton Town	42	19	10	13	61	51	48
8	FOREST	42	17	12	13	55	40	46
9	Charlton Athletic	42	15	12	15	61	72	42
10	Blackpool	42	14	14	14	40	49	42
11	Chelsea	42	12	16	14	53	54	40
12	Fulham	42	13	14	15	45	47	40
13	Orient	42	13	14	15	37	39	40
14	Hull City	42	14	11	17	45	49	39
15	Blackburn Rovers	42	12	14	16	45	50	38
16	Plymouth Argyle	42	13	12	17	48	54	38
17	Oldham Athletic	42	13	12	17	57	68	38
18	Bristol Rovers	42	11	16	15	38	50	38
19	Carlisle United	42	12	13	17	45	59	37
20	Oxford United	42	11	11	20	39	59	33
21	York City	42	10	8	24	39	71	28
22	Portsmouth	42	9	7	26	32	61	25

Jan 7th 1976, FAC, A, v. Peterborough United, Loss 0-1, AT 17,866, Wells, O'Kane, Clark, McGovern, Chapman, Richardson, McIntosh, Bowery, O'Hare, Butlin, Bowyer, SUB Robertson.

Jan 10th 1976, A, v. Hull City, Loss 0-1, AT 6,465, Wells, Anderson, Clark, McGovern, Chapman, Richardson, O'Neill, Robertson, O'Hare, Butlin, Bowyer, SUB McIntosh.

Jan 17th 1976, H, v. Chelsea, Loss 1-3, Scorer Bowyer, AT 14,172, Wells, O'Kane, Gunn, Clark, Chapman, Richardson, Curran, Bowyer, O'Hare, Butlin, Robertson.

Jan 23rd 1976, CC, H, v. Mansfield Town, Win 2-1, Scorers Richardson, Bowyer, AT 4,901, Wells, Saunders, Clark, McGovern, Chapman, Richardson, Curran, O'Neill, Bowyer, Bowery, Robertson, SUB O'Kane.

Jan 31st 1976, A, v. Luton Town, Draw 1-1, Scorer Curran, AT 8,503, Wells, O'Kane, Clark, McGovern, Chapman, Bowyer, Curran, O'Neill, O'Hare, Butlin, Robertson.

Feb 2nd 1976, F, A, v. Corby Town, Win 2-1, Scorers O'Neill, O'Hare, AT 800, Wells, O'Kane, Gunn, McGovern, Chapman, Bowyer, Curran, O'Neill, O'Hare, Butlin, Robertson, SUB McCann.

Feb 7th 1976, H, v. Blackpool, Win 3-0, Scorers Bowyer, Curran, Butlin, AT 8,582, Wells, O'Kane, Clark, McGovern, Chapman, Bowyer, Curran, O'Neill, O'Hare, Butlin, Robertson.

Feb 21st 1976, A, v. Bristol City, Win 2-0, Scorers Curran, O'Hare, AT 15,302, Wells, O'Kane, Clark, McGovern, Chapman, Bowyer, Curran, O'Neill, Butlin, O'Hare, Robertson, SUB McCann,

Feb 24th 1976, A, v. Charlton Athletic, Draw 2-2, Scorers Bowyer, McCann, AT 10,655, Wells, Gunn, Clark, McGovern, Chapman, Bowyer, Curran, O'Neill, O'Hare, Butlin, Robertson, SUB McCann.

Feb 28th 1976, H, v. Oldham Athletic, Win 4-3, Scorers Curran (Pen), O'Neill (2), Butlin, AT 11,509, Wells, Gunn, Clark, McGovern, Chapman, Bowyer, Curran, O'Neill, O'Hare, Butlin, Robertson.

Mar 6th 1976, A, v. Carlisle United, Draw 1-1, Scorer (1 O.G), AT 7,153, Middleton, Gunn, Clark, McGovern, Chapman, Bowyer, Curran, McCann, O'Hare, Butlin, Robertson.

Mar 13th 1976, H, v. Fulham, Win 1-0, Scorer O'Hare, AT 11,445, Wells, Barrett, Clark, McGovern, Chapman, Bowyer, Curran, O'Neill, O'Hare, Butlin, Robertson.

Mar 17th 1976, H, v. Sunderland, Win 2-1, Scorers O'Hare, Butlin, AT 16,995, Wells, Barrett, Clark, McGovern, Chapman, Bowyer, Curran, O'Neill, O'Hare, Butlin, Robertson.

Mar 20th 1976, A, v. York City, Loss 2-3, Scorers O'Hare, (1 O.G), AT 5,571, Wells, Barrett, Clark, McGovern, Chapman, Bowyer, Curran, O'Neill, O'Hare, Butlin, Robertson, SUB McCann.

Mar 27th 1976, H, v. Orient, Win 1-0, Scorer Bowyer, AT 11,127, Wells, Barrett, Clark, McGovern, Chapman, Bowyer, Curran, O'Neill, O'Hare, Butlin, Robertson, SUB McCann.

April 3rd 1976, A, v. Bolton Wanderers, Draw 0-0, AT 22,415, Wells, Barrett, Clark, McGovern, Chapman, Bowyer, Curran, O'Neill, O'Hare, Butlin, Robertson, SUB McCann.

April 6th 1976, F, A, v. Louth United, Win 6-0, Scorers Bowyer, Curran (2), O'Hare, McCann, Butlin, AT Not Known, Wells, Barrett, Gunn, McGovern, Chapman, Bowyer, Curran, O'Neill, O'Hare, McCann, Robertson, SUBS Middleton, Richardson, Butlin, Anderson.

April 10th 1976, H, v. Oxford United, Win 4-0, Scorers Curran (Pen), O'Neill, Butlin, Robertson, AT 11,259, Wells, Barrett, Clark, McGovern, Chapman, Bowyer, Curran, O'Neill, O'Hare, Butlin, Robertson.

April 13th 1976, A, v. Notts County, Draw 0-0, AT 29,279, Wells, Barrett, Clark, McGovern, Chapman, Bowyer, Curran, O'Neill, O'Hare, Butlin, Robertson.

April 17th 1976, A, v. West Bromwich Albion, Loss 0-2, AT 26,580, Wells, Barrett, Clark, McGovern, Chapman, Bowyer, Curran, O'Neill, O'Hare, Butlin, Robertson.

April 20th 1976, H, v. Blackburn Rovers, Win 1-0, Scorer Butlin, AT 13,006, Wells, Barrett, Clark, McGovern, Chapman, Bowyer, Curran, O'Neill, O'Hare, Butlin, Robertson, SUB Richardson.

April 24th 1976, H, v. Bristol Rovers, Win 3-0, Scorers Bowyer (2), O'Hare, AT 12,127, Wells, Barrett, Clark, McGovern, Chapman, Bowyer, Curran, O'Neill, O'Hare, Butlin, Robertson.

April 26th 1976, Test, H, v. D Revie All Stars, Win 3-2, Scorers Barrett, McKenzie (2), AT 11,429, Middleton, Barrett, Clark, McGovern, Chapman, Bowyer, Curran, O'Neill, Baker, McKenzie, Robertson.

Back Row: J.Gordon, P.Richardson, I.Bowyer, L.O'Kane, D.Peacock, J.Middleton, V.Anderson, M.O'Neill, J.Robertson, J.McIntosh, B.Clough
Front Row: J.McGovern, D.Jones, J.O'Hare, B.Butlin, B.Chapman, G.Lyall, F.Clark, J.Cottam

The Summer of '76 has gone down in history as the hottest summer ever known in the United Kingdom. Sixteen consecutive days at Heathrow where the temperature reached 30 degrees, some areas not seeing rain for 45 days, hosepipe bans and the Government encouraging people to share a bath. 'What a scorcher', was the go to headline and the Government created a new department called the, 'Ministry of Drought'. The Yorkshire Ripper began his killing spree and in America the 'Son of Sam' was slaying innocent victims across New York.

Meanwhile in Nottingham something was stirring as vice chairman Stuart Dryden took a call from Brian Clough asking to meet him at Widmerpool Cricket Club and he wondered what could be so urgent. When he arrived at the venue he found a charity match taking place and with Duncan McKenzie playing he was sure that this was the reason for the meeting.

Not so. "I'm off to Cala Millor to fetch Taylor", Clough announced. Dryden reminded him that technically Peter Taylor was still Brighton's manager. "Don't worry about that", he was told. As Peter Taylor recalls, "He caught me at just the right time. We had missed out on promotion at Brighton and although Chairman Mike Bamber was happy, I realised that I was missing Brian and together we would be far stronger". Three days later Clough phoned Dryden to say the deal had been done, but until Taylor's end was sorted, to keep it quiet. Brian Appleby and Stuart Dryden then met with Peter Taylor to confirm the details of job title and wages and that just left Taylor with the difficult task of telling Brighton that he was leaving, officially resigning his post on July 16th.

What particularly stuck out for Taylor, was Appleby's realistic expectations. There were no big ultimatums, just a sensible approach, he wasn't expecting miracles but would like the club back in Division One within three years.

Peter Taylor was a Meadow's lad, he might have moved on, but he still had the Nottingham accent. He had been a supporter of Forest and County, watching both teams alternatively and had in fact joined the playing staff at the City Ground as a keeper, making several appearances, the first being on 21st April 1945 against County. Peter wasn't offered a pro contract, so he left. Frank Clark recalls his impressions of Peter Taylor. "He wasn't everyone's cup of tea, but it was definitely more fun when he was around. He used

76-77

NOTTINGHAM FOREST FOOTBALL CLUB

DIVISION TWO 1976 - 77

Back row, left to right: JOHN COTTAM GLYN SAUNDERS JIM McCANN MARTIN O'NEILL JOHN MIDDLETON PETER WELLS COLIN BARRETT VIV ANDERSON JIMMY GORDON (Trainer)

Front row, left to right: TERRY CURRAN FRANK CLARK JOHN ROBERTSON PAUL RICHARDSON BARRY BUTLIN BOB CHAPMAN JOHN O'HARE IAN BOWYER

Vol. LXXIV No. 4 NOTTINGHAM, SATURDAY, SEPTEMBER 11, 1976 Price 6p

THRILLS GALORE AS REDS ROAR HOME

Ian Bowyer scores the equaliser against Hereford.

Bomber puts the Reds ahead after a surging run.

Barry Butlin swivels to start the fightback

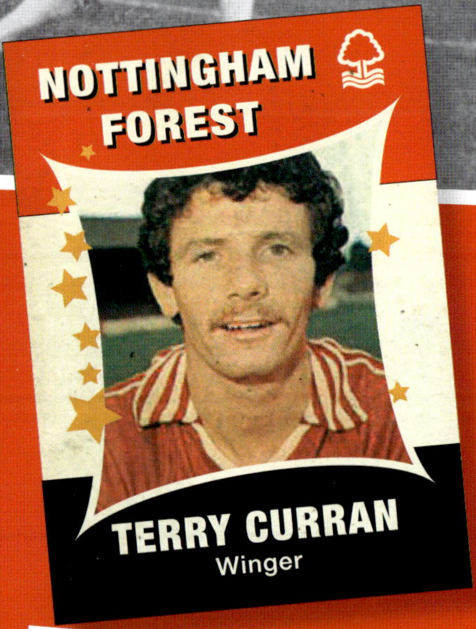

This cross shot from Robertson finds it's way into the Hereford net.

Action from the Coventry League Cup game.

More action from the Coventry game.

to get under people's skin, question them in an attempt to get more out of them. He had an idea that everyone had a vice; booze, gambling or women and he was prepared to accommodate one of them if it wasn't too extreme, but he wanted to know. In truth, I don't think he rated me, whenever he was left to pick the team he often left me out".

BRIAN CLOUGH ON SOCCER

It's great to be together again!

IF Nottingham Forest don't improve on their position of finishing eighth in the Second Division, I'll sack Peter Taylor.

I am not stirring anything up between us for saying that, just merely pointing out the high regard I have for the talent of the man who has just joined me at the City Ground.

As we enter a new season I can't for the life of me see us failing to progress further up the Second Division table. And Peter's arrival here prompts that view.

It's great to be back in partnership and to have Peter share the responsibilities of getting Forest back into the First Division.

With Taylor joining, Brian Clough announced that the club had done its best stroke of business for years. There was positive news about the club's financial position as well. After years of haemorrhaging money, losses were down to £13,000 and after all, Clough had said that there was no reason to appoint Taylor if there was no money to spend, so fans were entitled to think that the purse strings might be loosened.

At the club's AGM, Jim Willmer was surprisingly, to some, voted off the committee after twenty seven years service. In a head to head vote off against Derek Pavis he was defeated by 69 votes to 61. Immediately on taking the position, Taylor told Clough to hold fire on making any decisions about releasing players until he had run his eye over them and this was later to have an impact on the career of Tony Woodcock. Peter Taylor went to watch the reserves play a friendly at Kettering and he had been impressed by the player's performance. Speaking to him afterwards he learned that Woodcock wanted to play up front and vowed to himself to keep an eye his progression.

The anecdotes and stories about Nottingham Forest during this period have grown and grown. Tales that have been honed and refined over the years in numerous autobiographies, films and interviews have taken on a life of their own. Often retro-fitted to make greater impact, it is sometimes difficult to separate the truth from the hyperbole. Take the story of the Reds' pre-season trip to Germany and the impact that Peter Taylor's intervention had, not only on the career of John Robertson but also the history of the club. Robbo, although he had not reached the heights that would come, was an established first teamer and by now had claimed the left wing slot as his own, although outwardly he didn't always give the impression that he was making the best of his ability, either through application or lifestyle choices. Anyway, with the harsh words of the new man ringing in his ears, he finally set about applying himself to be a professional footballer. After Peter Taylor's first inspection of the squad, his first thought was, 'How did you get this lot to eighth place? They are nice lads and no trouble, but some of them are only third division players'. Brian Clough was happy to let Taylor take centre stage, encouraging him to formulate his own ideas, even delaying his own arrival in Germany by several days so that he could appraise the players unhindered. Peter Taylor was able

Brian Appleby and Stuart Dryden welcome Peter Taylor to the City Ground

to identify what talent was available at the club already and how some judicious signings would compliment them and allow it to flourish even more. By the time this season had finished, twelve players from the previous year's squad had been released and only two, Larry Lloyd and Peter Withe were added.

Immediately it seemed to John McGovern that it was as if the manager had been attached to a battery charger, he had moved up a notch, the barbs and put downs were back, "I told the other players it was now a case of when we would get promotion, not if". John also recalls an incident from the trip to Germany when the bus carrying the team went past the Olympic Stadium in Munich, "I wonder what odds you would have got then for Forest to be playing in a European Cup Final there less than three years later?".

After the pre season games in Germany, the club would get the chance of meaningful competitive pre-season action as they had been accepted to take part in the Anglo Scottish Cup, really a tournament for second ranking English and Scottish clubs, but also a chance for the club to earn a little extra money. As far as Brian Clough was concerned, there was no such thing as a meaningless match, particularly if there was a trophy at stake. Peter Taylor recalled a conversation that he had with Brian Appleby, "Peter, we would just like to win a trophy", so from then on there was no chance that the Reds wouldn't put out a strong team.

The competition began with 'round robin' games against English opposition, Notts County, West Brom and Bristol City. After a goalless bore draw at Notts, Forest racked up seven goals and two victories over their next two Division One opponents, to move through to the knockout stages. Terry Curran starting the season off as he had finished the previous one and there were also goals for Butlin and O'Hare. Sean Haslegrave was the only new face as the season began, joining for £35,000 from Stoke City, whilst Viv Anderson's injury gave Glyn Saunders a chance at full back. There was also a change in league rules, as goal difference, (goals scored minus goals conceded) was introduced if teams were level on points. The bookmakers had Forest as third favourites for promotion behind Bolton and Wolves, whilst the Sunday People in a poll of managers put Forest top of the pile.

The opening day's weather was a scorcher as Forest began their campaign against Fulham at Craven Cottage, before several thousand Reds' fans who basked in the sunshine on the open terraces. Although playing well, it took a late goal from John O'Hare to rescue a point. Peter Wells had kept the now available John Middleton out of the team and there was a debut for Haslegrave who, after a disappointing pre season being regularly substituted, again failed to impress and virtually disappeared afterwards. Charlton Athletic provided the first home opposition of the season. Another tentative performance brought only one point in a 1-1 draw, Curran scoring for the second successive game. This game marked not only Ian Bowyer's 100th league appearance for the club, but also marked the end of Paul Richardson's Reds career, as he was soon allowed to leave for Chester. There was an early chance to test out the club's promotion credentials, when newly relegated Wolves visited on the following Saturday. Despite an early boost, taking the lead through an own goal from Steve Daley, Forest were thoroughly outplayed to lose 3-1. Even Terry Curran missed the opportunity to keep his scoring run going when he failed from the penalty spot in the last minute. The game was marred by crowd trouble on the Bridgford terraces and Wolves fans were escorted out of the ground for their own safety.

There was a break from league action when Forest once again were matched with Walsall in the League Cup. The Reds came up against three old boys in Serella, Dennehy and Buckley who even gave the home side an early lead, but led by a couple of goals from Martin O'Neill, Forest eased through to the next round 4-2. John Middleton was re-instated in goal and was to keep his place for the rest of the season and Colin Barrett was preferred at right back.

Crowd trouble at the Wolverhampton Wanderers game.

Forest made it four league games without a win when they were pegged back in the 89th minute after Barrett put through his own goal at Luton, so when Hereford United made their first ever visit to the City Ground in front of the ATV cameras, fans wanted to see a convincing performance and a victory. They weren't best pleased when Forest found themselves two goals down after only twenty minutes but after Butlin had pulled one back the country got a taste of what Terry Curran was all about. Picking the ball up deep in his own half on the right touchline, he simply pushed the ball down the line and chased it and even when he was obstructed he simply went wider onto the cinder track. His cross eventually found its way to Ian Bowyer and he equalized. The second half saw a barnstorming run from Bowyer, bursting through three tackles to fire home from twenty yards and it then looked as if the points were safe after a cross shot from John Robertson found its way into the net, but immediately McNeil pulled one back which meant the crowd suffered an anxious time before the season's first league win was finally clinched.

Forest had been drawn against Kilmarnock in the knockout stage of the Anglo Scottish Cup. The tie to be played over two legs with the aggregate score deciding who would go through. The first leg was played on the 14th September in Nottingham, Forest scraping a victory 2-1, Robertson and Chapman the scorers. Surprisingly both Clough and Taylor missed the game as they were having one final look at a 'mystery striker'. Games were now coming thick and fast. A draw away at Southampton was followed by a 3-0 home defeat in the League Cup to Coventry, all three goals coming in a fifteen minute spell in the first half, in between a decent display from the Reds.

The reason for the managerial duo's absence was explained when centre forward Peter Withe was unveiled as the club's latest signing, a £45,000 capture from Birmingham City. Withe was an archetypal Taylor signing. His attributes had been overlooked by those who only saw what he couldn't do, not what he could do. Taylor had wanted to sign him for Brighton but had been unable to raise the funds. Good in the air, Taylor knew that he would thrive from the wing service Forest could give him. Brave with his back to goal, (just as Clough liked his centre forwards). Withe was much travelled, even going to South Africa at one stage to kick-start his career and at twenty five now was the time for him to make an impact.

Just as Withe's career at Forest was about to begin it seemed as if Tony Woodcock's was ending, as once more he was loaned out to Doncaster Rovers.

Withe made his debut two days after signing in a 5-1 demolition of Carlisle, it could have been more, Terry Curran once again missing from the penalty spot. This was a majestic display of attacking football, surging runs, dribbling, headers and powerful shots all contributing to a fantastic afternoon's entertainment. The Reds set off for the second leg against Kilmarnock early on Tuesday morning by bus. They had initially looked at flying but the cost was prohibitive so the eight hour road journey was undertaken,

Curran blow a stern test for Forest

Nish loss is a worry for Derby

THE LOSS of Terry Curran's speed and skill throws up a fresh challenge to Nottingham Forest as a team and — more pointedly — to certain individuals.

The knee ligament injury which keeps ...st's swashbuck...inger out of th...

BY JOHN LAWSO...

Irish international Martin O'Neill foll... two-goal display against Burnley wi... show for Forest in the Midweel... Cup Final.

only interrupted by the calls from bored players, "Are we there yet?". This journey probably explains why they went two down in the first half. It wasn't until Withe was substituted and Curran pushed down the middle that they got themselves back into the game. Curran's first goal brought the aggregate level and then his equaliser in extra time saw the Reds progress 4-3.

This was a strange period for the team, scoring goals for fun at home, they inexplicably kept failing to score away from home. Next up were Hull, with new signing Billy Bremner making a scoring debut in a 1-0 win. Boothferry Park where Hull played at that time had a railway platform built into the ground right behind the away supporters who were situated at the side of the pitch. Randall's Vandals also made an appearance, suddenly arriving at the back of the home end and causing a surge that forced home fans onto the area behind the goal.

Peter Taylor who had told Clough that Sammy Chapman had, "Shot it", had been out looking for a replacement. He had settled on Larry Lloyd who was having a poor time at Coventry. Larry had made his reputation at Liverpool where he was a formidable competitor but often talked his way into conflicts that were unnecessary. He had fallen out of favour at Anfield, so he had asked for a transfer and ended up at Coventry for a fee of £240,000. It had not taken him long to realise he had made a big mistake and this along with a niggly back injury was contributing to an attitude

Peter Taylor greets Peter Withe after had signed for the Reds'.

Often portrayed as a 'Big Time Charlie', there was much more to the player than that, but his offhand reaction when Forest came in to take him on loan only helped re-enforce the stereotyped image. Taylor recalls, "Everyone told me to avoid him, he thinks he is the big I am, but on the other hand he was big and could head a ball. Brian and I didn't mind a bit of arrogance,

Steve Burke (Centre) receives congratulations from his team mates on becoming the Reds' youngest ever first-teamer

anyway we thought we could sort him out. It turned out he needed sorting out far more than we thought, forever butting in during team talks, he seemed to think he was dealing with a couple of non league managers". Lloyd remembers his debut at Hull. "I was brought in to replace fan's favourite Sammy Chapman and it was during warm up when my name was announced that I heard booing and I realised it wasn't Hull fans but Forest supporters doing it".

Several players recall Larry on away trips regaling them with tales of life at Liverpool whilst puffing away on a huge cigar. This wasn't recalled in a nasty way, the signing of a player such as Lloyd was regarded as a sign of better things to come and he quickly made friends in the dressing room but just as an example of how he liked to portray himself. Taylor once told him, "You want to keep your trap shut, because we are the best thing that's ever happened to you". Although the player continued to always fight his corner with the management, there was only ever going to be one winner and the relationship turned out to be mutually beneficial. Going from Coventry's reserves into a progressive team must have been fun for Larry as the Reds banged six past hapless Sheffield United on his debut, when even Viv Anderson got into the act with a surging run and goal that was to be his trademark over the next few years. Again Forest drew another blank at Blackpool losing 1-0 on a day of 'Tower Power' and clashes with Newcastle fans who were there for Geordie holiday week. This result obviously gave Allan Brown the Blackpool boss great satisfaction. Two more home wins followed, the first a routine 2-1 victory over Ayr United, that saw debutant Steve Burke at 16 years and 22 days and still a pupil at Gedling Comp. become the youngest ever player to pull on the Garibaldi. The second, another heavy

John O'Hare drills home against Carlisle United.

This spectacular header from Ian Bowyer flashes past the Carlisle keeper.

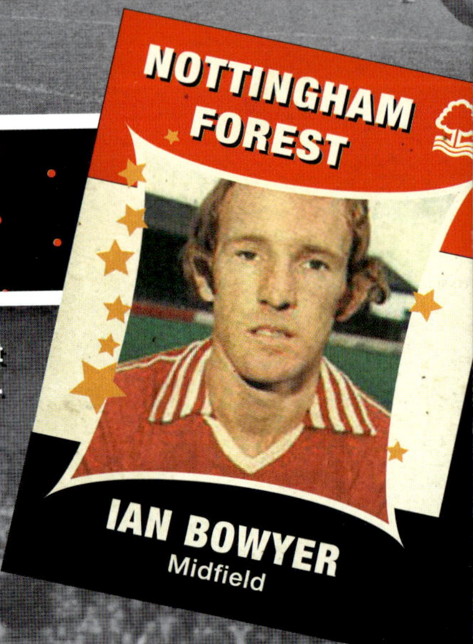

BLADES BLUNTED AS REDS HIT SIX

Peter Withe calmly places the ball past Jim Brown in the Sheffield United goal.

Viv Anderson completes the scoring as the Reds smash United.

Terry Curran slots home after rounding the Burnley keeper.

It's Butlin again!

Peter Withe triumphantly nets against Blackburn.

Ian Bowyer (just visible) fires home from close range against Blackburn Rovers.

A precision shot from Peter Withe, leaves the keeper helpless.

Withe surprisingly fires over the bar from close range against Bristol Rovers.

After neat build up Woodcock fires home the equaliser!

VIOLENCE MARS CHELSEA CLASH!!

O'Neill wrong foots Chelsea keeper Bonetti to put the Reds one up...

A desperate save from Bonetti deprives Ian Bowyer of a last minute winner.

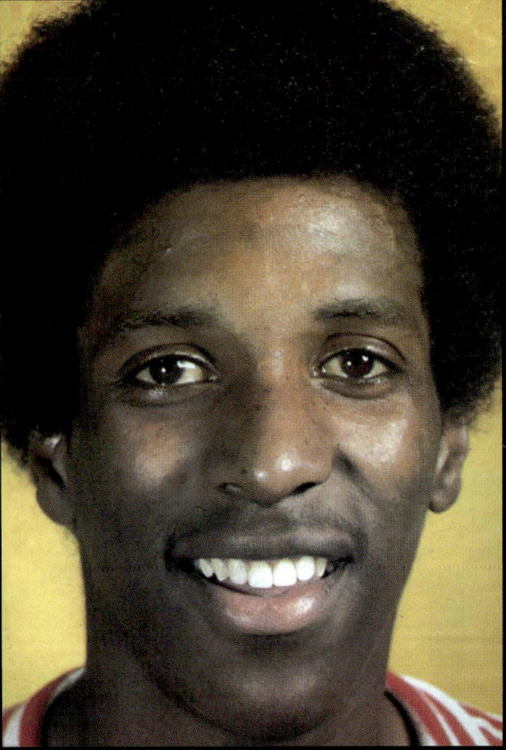
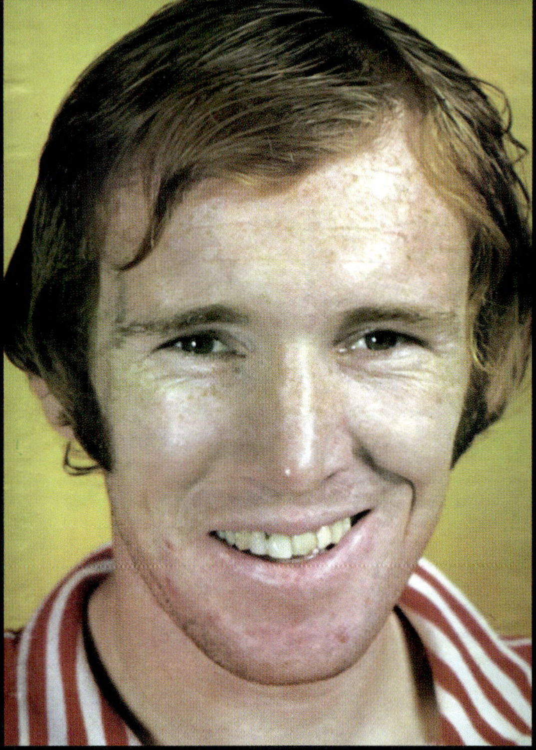

Viv Anderson | Ian Bowyer | Terry Curran

Larry LLoyd | John McGovern | John Middleton

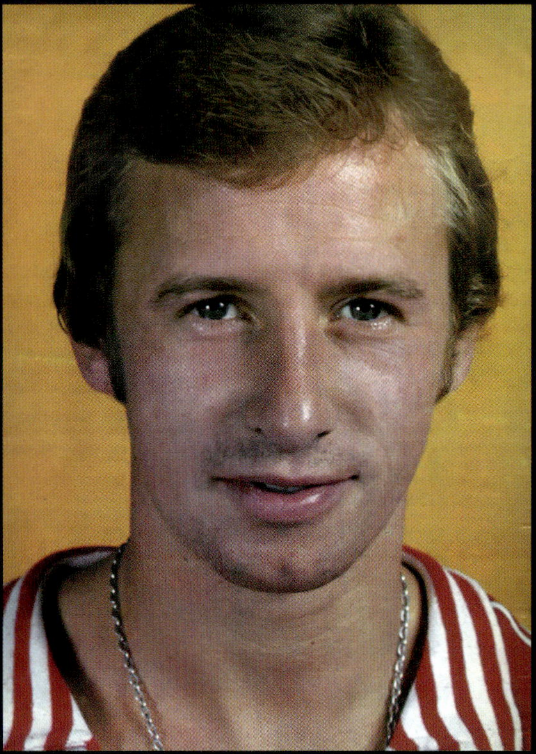

Meet the

John O'Hare | Tony Woodcock | Martin O'Neill

John Robertson | Peter Withe | Frank Clark

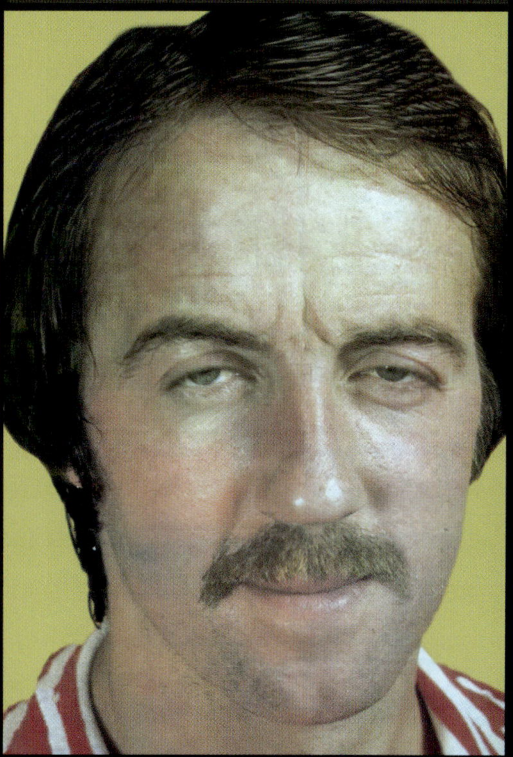

ricky Trees

Two fans stabbed in clashes

TWO soccer fans were stabbed during clashes between fans before the Nottingham Forest - Chelsea game at the City Ground this afternoon.

One stabbing occurred outside the ground, the other near a public house at Trent Bridge. Police have arrested two youths in connection with one knifing and are hunting a group of youths involved in the second incident.

Meanwhile, 15 arrests were made as more than 1,000 Chelsea fans, under heavy police escort, made their way from the Midland Station to the City Ground.

Play was also held up when dozens of fans spilled on to the pitch three minutes after kick-off. The referee ordered both teams to the dressing rooms for six minutes before re-starting.

home win, this time 5-1 over Burnley that was spoiled due to an injury to Terry Curran, that looked like it would have a negative effect on the promotion push. After helping the Reds into a 3-1 lead, Terry was carried off after sustaining a serious knee injury that would keep him out for months. John Lawson was in the manager's office after that game. "We were just sitting chatting when there was a knock on the door and Terry Curran came in and Brian, who hated being around injured players told Terry to, "Keep those bloody crutches out of my office". After a few softer words Terry left and Brian turned to me and said, "Promotion has just limped out of the door".

The Burnley game also saw the last appearance of his loan spell for Larry Lloyd, who famously when asked whether he was signing replied, "I've not seen anything here that turns me on".

Was it luck or fate that was to take a hand in the management's next big decision. After losing to Notts in the County Cup, held over from the previous season, there was another 1-0 defeat at Oldham before another long journey to Scotland for the return leg against Ayr.

Tony Woodcock had returned from his loan away and Brian Clough was persuaded by Taylor to give him a chance. Peter had watched the player several times, noted his pace and ability to turn defenders and his implacable temperament after being fouled. The manager told Taylor that this was his call. It is strange that Clough had not recognised Woodcock's potential, although he himself said he was not the best judge of a forward. Tony was well regarded by his team mates who all thought he could play.

So on a cold blustery night in Scotland the forward partnership that was to propel Nottingham Forest to the top of British football was born.

The 2-0 win in which Woodcock and Withe both scored, not only broke the run of goalless away games but highlighted immediately that as a pairing they were suited like hand and glove. It really looked as if they had played together for years. Strength and pace, the bludgeon and the rapier, Woodcock and Withe. Curran had gone, to be replaced by something even more exciting and unpredictable.

The dream of Brian Appleby that the club should win something was now in sight, only Orient stood in their path, but that was a month away and the task of closing the gap to the promotion places took precedence. Next up were Blackburn at home, only three goals this time in a 3-0 win, Chapman had been restored to the side whilst efforts continued to persuade Lloyd to join permanently. Orient were then beaten 1-0 at Brisbane Road in a dress rehearsal for the Anglo Scottish Final, Woodcock with the winner before the biggest game of the season so far took place against leaders Chelsea in front of the Match of the Day cameras in Nottingham. It felt as if the 'big time' was back.

Much to the annoyance of supporters, under police instructions, Chelsea were given the Trent End to reduce potential trouble. Many younger Forest fans had returned to the Trent End so this was a more sensitive matter now than the previous time that the police had insisted on it. The match took place in a hostile atmosphere, some Chelsea fans for some reason were allowed to wander around the perimeter before a confrontation at the corner of the Bridgford and East Stand forced the referee to suspend play whilst order was restored. Fights broke out sporadically after that. Police had their hands full before and after the game as fans clashed, newspapers described the scenes as mayhem, four stabbings were reported. Ken Smales devoted the whole of his column in the next programme to the situation. What could the club do, it had taken all precautions and done everything the police had asked. The match itself was a tight affair, a draw being a fair result, O'Neill giving the Reds an early lead before Anderson mis-controlled a cross, allowing the ball to bounce off him to Ian Britton who nodded home.

Forest were right back on track the following week with a 3-0 win in South Wales against Cardiff; Withe, Chapman and Woodcock were the scorers. This time it was the Forest supporters turn to be on the receiving end as there was little segregation at Ninian Park.

Eventually Peter Taylor was to get his man as Larry Lloyd signed for a bargain fee of only £60,000, another astounding piece of business. Those who claimed that Clough and Taylor were cheque book managers really should shut up. As Peter Taylor said, "These players were all there for people to see, if we do our homework better, then that's their fault". The spine of the team in terms of 1976 prices cost virtually nothing. John Middleton from the youth team, Larry Lloyd £60,000, John McGovern a portion of £60,000, Peter Withe £42,000 and Tony Woodcock also from the youth team.

Larry had gone back to Coventry and had in fact forced his way back into the first team, but still manager Gordon Milne didn't want him and told him to go. Larry remembers one final thing, "Word came to me that Coventry Chairman Jimmy Hill was laughing, claiming that the club had got rid of a crock. Well after winning the Championship at Highfield Road I made a point of searching him out and letting him know in no uncertain terms what I thought". Larry Lloyd made his second debut in a 4-2 win against his first club Bristol Rovers, followed by another convincing 2-0 win at Millwall that moved the Reds handily within one point of third place. The Anglo Scottish Cup Final took place in December, the first leg at Brisbane Road on the Monday finished 1-1, a John Robertson penalty for the Reds' goal.

The return game took place only two days later before just 12,000 fans in Nottingham. The Reds cruised to a 4-0 victory, the scorers, unusually were Colin Barrett with two, Sammy Chapman and

Garry Birtles

Colin Barrett

Peter Withe

Tony Woodcock

Larry LLoyd

Notts County

West Brom

Bristol City

MAGPIE

Anglo-Scottish Cup
Preliminary Round

Saturday, 7th August, 1976
Kick-off 7.30 p.m.

NOTTS COUNTY
(Black/white striped shirts, black shorts)

1—ERIC McMANUS
2—PETER RICHARDS
3—RAY O'BRIEN
4—ERIC PROBERT
5—DAVID NEEDHAM
6—BRIAN STUBBS
7—STEVE CARTER
8—DAVID McVAY
9—LES BRADD
10—ARTHUR MANN
11—IAN SCANLON
12—JOHN SIMS

NOTTINGHAM FOREST
(Red shirts, white shorts)

1—PETER WELLS
2—COLIN BARRETT
3—FRANK CLARK
4—JOHN McGOVERN
5—BOB CHAPMAN
6—IAN BOWYER
7—TERRY CURRAN
8—SEAN HASLEGRAVE
9—JOHN O'HARE
10—BARRY BUTLIN
11—JOHN ROBERTSON
12—To be announced

Referee:
Mr. J. Hunting (Leicester)

Linesmen:
Red Flag—Mr. N. Taylor (Leicester)
Yellow Flag—Mr. R. C. Jackson (Grantham)

Official Match-Day Programme
PRICE 5p

FOREST REVIEW

Official Match-Day Programme
Volume 9, Number 1
PRICE 5p

Anglo-Scottish Cup
Preliminary Round

Wednesday, 11th August, 1976
Kick-off 7.30 p.m.

Nottingham Forest
(Red shirts, white shorts)

1—PETER WELLS
2—GLYN SAUNDERS
3—FRANK CLARK
4—JOHN McGOVERN
5—BOB CHAPMAN
6—IAN BOWYER
7—TERRY CURRAN
8—SEAN HASLEGRAVE
9—JOHN O'HARE
10—BARRY BUTLIN
11—JOHN ROBERTSON
Substitutes—JOHN MIDDLETON (goal), COLIN BARRETT

West Bromwich Albion
(Blue/white striped shirts, white shorts)

1—JOHN OSBORNE
2—PADDY MULLIGAN
3—LEN CANTELLO
4—TONY BROWN
5—JOHN WILE
6—ALISTAIR ROBERTSON
7—MICK MARTIN
8—ALISTAIR BROWN
9—JOE MAYO
10—JOHNNY GILES
11—WILLIE JOHNSTON
Substitutes—To be announced

Referee:
Mr. R. Kirkpatrick (Leicester)

Linesmen:
Red Flag—Mr. M. J. Smith (Coalville)
Yellow Flag—Mr. J. E. Bray (Hinckley)

NOTTINGHAM FOREST FOOTBALL CLUB

FOREST REVIEW

Official Match-Day Programme
Volume 9, Number 2
PRICE 5p

Anglo-Scottish Cup
Preliminary Round

Saturday, 14th August, 1976
Kick-off 7.30 p.m.

NOTTINGHAM FOREST
(Red shirts, white shorts)

1—PETER WELLS
2—GLYN SAUNDERS
3—FRANK CLARK
4—JOHN McGOVERN
5—BOB CHAPMAN
6—IAN BOWYER
7—TERRY CURRAN
8—SEAN HASLEGRAVE
9—JOHN O'HARE
10—BARRY BUTLIN
11—JOHN ROBERTSON
Substitutes—CHRIS WOODS (goal), COLIN BARRETT

BRISTOL CITY
(White shirts, black shorts)

1—RAY CASHLEY
2—GERRY SWEENEY
3—BRIAN DRYSDALE
4—GERRY GOW
5—GARY COLLIER
6—GEOFF MERRICK
7—TREVOR TAINTON
8—TOM RITCHIE
9—JIMMY MANN
10—PAUL CHEESLEY
11—CLIVE WHITEHEAD
Substitutes—To be announced

Referee:
Mr. K. H. Burns (Stourbridge)

Linesmen:
Red Flag—Mr. A. D. Lewis (Willenhall)
Yellow Flag—Mr. K. J. Emsden (Sheffield)

NOTTINGHAM FOREST FOOTBA

FOREST

FOREST REVIEW
The official Match Day
Magazine of
NOTTINGHAM FOREST
FOOTBALL CLUB

ANGLO-SCOTTISH CUP, QUARTER-FINAL, 1st LEG

Kilmarnock

Tues., 14th September
Kick-off 7.30 p.m.

12p

Volume 9, Number 7

Where it all bega

John McGovern prepares to lift the trophy.

Fans celebrate in front of the Main Stand.

Bristol City

Bristol City

Bristol City

V... Anglo-Scottish Cup Winners 1976

"THE MOST IMPORTANT TROPHY I WON AT NOTTINGHAM FOREST, BECAUSE IT WAS THE FIRST".

Brian Clough

A rocket from Colin Barrett.

NOTTINGHAM FOREST

V

ORIENT

Sammy Chapman scores from close range.

MARTIN
O'NEILL
Nottingham
Forest

Robbo gives Forest the lead from the penalty spot against Southampton in the FA Cup.

Another beauty from Robbo as he fires into the roof of the Saints' net!!!

Woodcock produces our second equalising goal off the post and the back of Peter Wells...

REDS HELD BY THE SAINTS, IN SIX GOAL THRILLER...!!!

O'Neill nets the second from close range.

Moore, Best & Marsh).

Larry Lloyd glances home to break the deadlock against Fulham.

Tony Woodcock completes the scoring with an unstoppable piledriver after a brilliant solo run!

Ian Bowyer. Forest were weakened due to injuries for the second leg, both Withe and Woodcock were out so Bert Bowery was drafted in and picked up a surprise winners medal.

When Brian Clough was asked about the trophies he collected at Forest, he stated, "Of all the trophies we won, the Anglo Scottish Cup was the most important because it was the first. It was also important because it bought home to the players what we had been saying, you can win, now they could truly believe us".

In what was to be a feature of his time at the club, the success that Brian Clough was enjoying once more had brought him back into the spotlight and rumours that clubs were interested in luring him away began. Sunderland who had a big Clough connection wanted him, but the way the club had treated him after his career ending injury still rankled with Brian and there never was any real possibility that he might go. But fans were right to be wary, with echoes of Dave Mackay, could the Forest revival be scuppered before it had properly started?

There was just one final game to play against Plymouth before Christmas, the team was still without Withe and Woodcock and now also missing John McGovern. They were grateful for another goal from Colin Barrett to rescue a point, but they missed out on the psychological boost of going second, level with their next opponents Bolton. The absence of McGovern meant that Chapman and Lloyd were paired together at the back.

With the emergence of the young keeper Chris Woods, Peter Wells was now considered surplus to requirements and sold to Southampton for £8,000, where he went on to enjoy seven years on the south coast, only leaving the Saints after they had signed Peter Shilton, also from Forest.

Boxing Day fell on a Sunday that year, which meant that all the games were put back twenty four hours. Another massive following to Lancashire saw the Reds deservedly take a share of the spoils. In fact the Reds' support in a crowd of over 32,000 was so large, that Forest fans had to climb over the railings in the Lever End behind the goal, to take over more of the stand. Forest and County were due to play each other just two days later but the City Ground pitch was unplayable and the next home fixture also fell foul of the weather, so despite another trip back to Lancashire and an impressive 3-0 win at Blackburn, the Reds lost ground as rivals picked up points. Forest had once more

been paired with Bristol Rovers in the FA Cup third round. Notts County had also been drawn at home to attractive opposition in Arsenal on the same day. This meant staggered kick off times, Notts for 2.30pm and the Reds at 3.15pm. This was not the end of the problems however, the police had to mount a difficult operation to keep four sets of supporters apart and both clubs were short of gateman as many worked for both clubs. In the end the day passed off peacefully enough, Notts losing and Forest surprisingly only drawing with a team that they had outclassed before Christmas. The replay was also an unwanted extra fixture, but Forest had enjoyed the bigger attendance out of the two Nottingham clubs on the day.

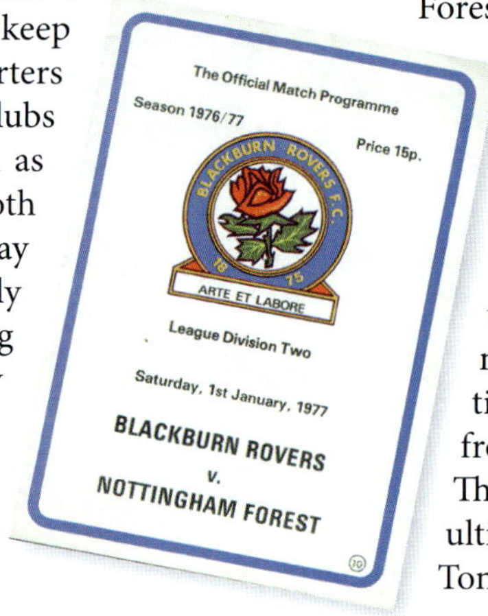

The replay three days later still couldn't produce a winner, another 1-1 draw with Woodcock scoring. It was also to prove to be the last game in an undefeated run of fourteen matches. Defeat finally coming, 2-1 at the Valley on the Friday evening, despite a performance that had Charlton manager Andy Nelson waxing lyrical about the Reds' quality.

The Rover's cup tie was emphatically decided with a 6-0 mauling at neutral Villa Park, five different scorers, Woodcock with two, Bowyer, Withe, Anderson and O'Hare with the others. The tie attracted only 5,736 fans, most of them Reds who were given the vast Holte End. This game was a milestone for Sammy Chapman who registered his 400th appearance for the club.

Fulham had enterprisingly signed up George Best and Rodney Marsh to join Bobby Moore. Although results weren't always positive, there were many outstanding and vibrant performances, with the added bonus of large crowds who turned out to see them perform. It was no different at the City Ground when over 24,000 saw the Reds win 3-0 in a game that was far different from what the score line would suggest. It took three goals in the final nine minutes to finally break the Cottagers' resistance, Lloyd, O'Neill and Woodcock were the scorers. Despite the various postponements this was the Reds' 44th game of the season and they weren't even out of January.

Forest had by now been drawn at home against cup holders Southampton, which would mean a quick return for Peter Wells. Despite opposition again from home supporters, Southampton fans were given the Trent End despite having no reputation for trouble. The tie turned out to be a classic in front of over 38,000 supporters. The game ebbed and flowed but ultimately ended in a 3-3 draw, Tony Woodcock saving the game for Forest. The replay was a real letdown, a controversial offside looking goal from Ted MacDougal proving to be the winner in a 2-1 defeat. Brian Clough would never admit it, but could the Reds have coped with any further fixture congestion if they had progressed?

The club held a gentleman's evening at the Albany Hotel, many positive speeches were made, not least by Brian Appleby who praised the work done so far and Ken Smales who commented that he couldn't remember a time when the club was so together, the growth of supporter's clubs, a golf day, members nights showed the new direction that the club was travelling.

There were a couple of tricky looking fixtures looming, firstly away at Wolves and another 2-1 defeat on a mud bath of a pitch that didn't suit either team. Forest fans were based on the vast South Bank right next to the home support and separated by only a stretch of police tape. This along with shared toilet and refreshment facilities meant that outbreaks of trouble were regular. The most disappointing result of the season so far came the following week against Luton Town, who in a thoroughly professional performance helped themselves to a 2-1 victory. This was the first game in a long while that the Reds had looked second best. Larry Lloyd had turned in the consolation goal. Forest were now four points off the pace in 5th place. The next seven days turned out to be pivotal in the history of the club, two unconnected events were to have greatest bearing on the direction that would follow.

Firstly, on the pitch Forest had an early opportunity to make up for the Luton game when Southampton were the visitors on Wednesday the 16th of February. Although they possessed great players such as Alan Ball, Mick Channon and Peter Osgood, they had not made the expected impact on the League and found themselves marooned in mid-table, but they were making progress once more in the FA Cup and in Europe. It was hoped therefore with an upcoming cup game that they might ease off in this fixture. No such luck, after taking an early lead they had no trouble in keeping Forest at arms length, as Martin O'Neill put it, "We wouldn't have scored if we had played all day".

Fate in the form of fog was to take a hand, sweeping over the ground from the Bridgford End. Fog had been common place at the City Ground, but usually from the direction of the Trent End. Older spectators couldn't recall it ever coming from the opposite end. After giving it fifteen minutes referee Roy Capey called the two managers together and told them that he had no choice but to abandon the game, thereby letting Forest off the hook. There were no complaints from Saints' manager Lawrie McMenemy. However, no sooner had the game been abandoned than the fog cleared, if the referee had just waited a little longer!

Brian Clough was now forced to come down hard on Larry Lloyd. Larry had already reached twenty disciplinary points for the season, earning him a three game ban, but when he himself spotted the player commit an off the ball foul against Southampton he felt he had to act. Lloyd was fined and dropped from the next game, before his official ban was to start. The manager explained, "I will not tolerate that sort of behaviour from any of my players, they will be left out even if it is to the detriment of the team". Can you imagine any other manager doing that? Particularly at a time of the season when everything is deemed important.

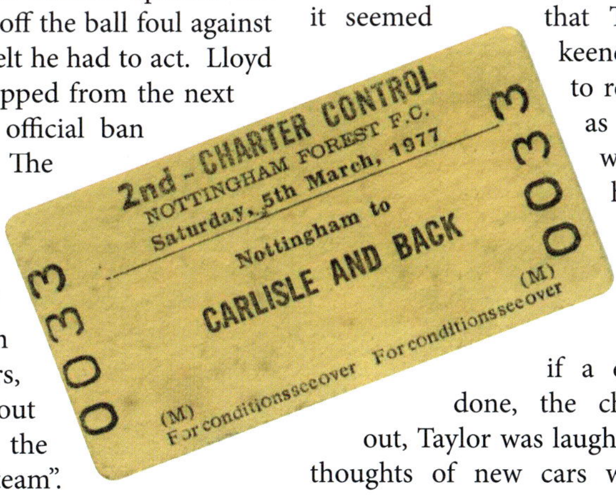

February 21st 1977. This was to be a day of intrigue, suspicion, pain and joy as Forest came close to losing the man who was to become synonymous with all the success that followed. It was the day when the world found out that Clough and Taylor had already been speaking to Derby County about returning to the Baseball Ground. It was a day of mystery, claim and counterclaim about motives, no clearer even now, especially since the main protagonists are dead. Through the mists of time autobiographies have been written, interviews given and stories changed and there is still no definitive version. Let's start with the facts. George Hardy had taken over from Sam Longson as chairman and in an attempt to court good publicity he announced that he wanted Clough and Taylor to come back to Derby. Initially using their old friend Mike Keeling to sound them out, he then approached Brian Appleby the Reds' chairman, officially to ask for permission to speak to the pair. Appleby pragmatically realized he had no choice and gave permission. From now on events are open to interpretation, one thing is clear however, Brian Clough did like being 'courted', regularly using these approaches and rumours to extract either extra money for himself or guarantees about future ambitions or funding for players.
Clough and Taylor the evening before, had gone to Hardy's house where they met Stuart Webb and Hardy himself to discuss matters. When Hardy offered the pair £17,000 pa, the same wage that they were already on at Forest, it was not a good start, Clough countered asking for another £5,000, but Hardy said he couldn't stretch to that. To those present, it seemed that Taylor was far keener than Clough to return, although as the evening wore on Clough himself seemed to be warming to the idea. At 10.00pm it looked as if a deal had been done, the champagne was out, Taylor was laughing and joking, thoughts of new cars were discussed. Clough agreed to speak the next day.

Hardy with some sort of premonition had become worried overnight and more so the next morning when he was unable to make contact with Clough.

Meanwhile Clough had gone home and it is thought that after discussions with his wife Barbara, he came round to the conclusion that he owed Forest some

Larry Lloyd pulls a late goal back for Forest at home to Luton Town.

FOG SAVES LUCKY FOREST

Withe rounds the Saints' keeper, but the ball goes wide.

Lawrie McMenemy and Jimmy Gordon with the match officials as the referee decides that the Forest Southampton game cannot continue.

Woodcock turns away after Terry Curran's effort finds the net away at Hereford.

Peter Withe blasts home against Notts County.

Withe fires home the second goal against Hull City.

Brian Clough sets off to tell Derby he's not going ...

loyalty. His enemies Longson and Webb were still at Derby and he couldn't shake the feeling that Derby were a team in decline. Down at the City Ground the day dragged on, press and TV gathered outside waiting for news. It was a big story. Clough and Taylor were ensconced in Taylor's office until finally Brian said, "Let's go and face the music because we ain't going, at least I'm not". Peter Taylor was so disappointed that he told Clough he wouldn't go to Derby with him to tell them their decision, so it was left to Jimmy Gordon to drive the manager over. On his way out, Clough stopped to tell Stuart Dryden they were staying and gave John Lawson the scoop as well.
Over in Derby nerves were well and truly jangling, the longer this went on the feeling that Clough wasn't returning grew. On his arrival at the Baseball Ground, Clough rushed past the waiting press and said that he would like to speak to Hardy alone. "I am not coming", said Clough, "You bastard, get out", replied Hardy. One final twist, as Hardy reported that allegedly Clough said that he would reconsider if he got rid of Longson and Webb, knowing full well that he didn't have the authority to do that.

On his way out Clough bumped into Colin Murphy the beleaguered Rams' boss, "Ask them for more money, I was never coming", he reportedly said. George Hardy made one last attempt to save face by phoning Brian at home that evening and offering him £50,000 to sign, but it was too late.

Clough maintained afterwards that he never had any intention of going, but just wanted to listen to what they had to offer and had been insulted when Hardy had accused him of being greedy.

There was great embarrassment around Derby, Hardy had put his neck on the block and come up short, whilst newspaper billboards around the town proclaimed, 'He's coming home' and Radio Derby were predicting a positive outcome.

There was a different atmosphere back in Nottingham as news broke. John Lawson got his front page scoop, Chris Ashley of Radio Trent, an early example of a 'shock jock' had been winding fans up about losing their manager on his 'Talkback' phone in programme. Taking calls, firstly from those that were sure they were going and then from happy fans giving him stick. Relief was the overwhelming emotion from Ken Smales, "To even contemplate the mere possibility of 'B' and 'P' leaving was enough to completely upset my metabolism. It would have been like your fiancée leaving before the wedding".

FOREST JOY AS TOP TWO SAY 'NO'

I'M STAYING says Clough

BRIAN CLOUGH and Peter Taylor are staying with Nottingham Forest. Late this afternoon, the City Ground managerial pair decided to turn down Derby County's plea to them to take over at the Baseball Ground.

The decision was reached after almost five hours of talks today between Clough and Taylor, and the Forest chairman Brian Appleby and vice-chairman Stuart Dryden.

WAITING FANS

Anxious Forest fans waited outside the ground for news, but Clough did not reveal his plans until talks with Derby vice-chairman George Hardy back at the Baseball Ground.

A delighted Mr. Dryden could not hide his elation that Clough and Taylor were to continue in their bid

FRESH HOPE AS JOBLESS TOTAL DIPS

NOTTINGHAM'S unemployment figures have dropped for the first time in months.

Brian Appleby gave the outward appearance of calm, claiming afterwards that he knew that they wouldn't leave, that it was just a case of the manager settling old scores, although someone in the office leaked out that the first thing the chairman had said on his arrival at the ground was, "Have they left yet?". Brian Clough himself wasn't totally convinced that Appleby wanted him to stay.

So what was the truth? Peter Taylor thought that there was unfinished business at Derby, Brian Clough liked the idea of a hero's return, but with old enemies in place, could it really work? John Lawson agrees with Brian Appleby that this was a chance for revenge and that Brian Clough's family influenced him, emphasizing the loyalty he should show to Stuart Dryden. To further illustrate the confusion surrounding the whole affair, John also thinks that Peter Taylor had got cold feet at the end. No-one knows for certain, but it

backed by their usual large following, many of whom had made the trip by train. There was disappointment all round, as the concession of a late equalizer after Robertson had given them the lead from the penalty spot, deprived them of all the points. What made it more painful was that Woodcock had just missed a sitter to make the game safe. In an effort to find a role for Curran, he had replaced Withe at centre forward to utilize his pace, the experiment was not repeated.

Notts County, despite losing their manager Jimmy Sirrell, had been on a great run under Ronnie Fenton (later to join the Reds) and had actually leapfrogged Forest to go into sixth place and with this form seemed more likely to achieve promotion than the Reds. Brian Clough had made great play of insisting that the Reds would finish above the Magpies this season, so it must have even more galling when County visited the City Ground and left victorious, winning 2-1 and extending the gap to three points in the process. The season's largest league attendance of over 31,000 were there to see it.

Hull City were next up and the crowd had halved within four days. There was a sense of anti-climax around the stadium. An edgy 2-0 win with goals from Withe and Woodcock calmed the nerves slightly. Garry Birtles famously made his debut wearing the number 7 shirt in mid field for this game, on Taylor's recommendation, he had a very poor game, causing the manager to say, "Gaz, if I ever think about playing you in midfield again, shoot me". Whilst telling Taylor that the player wasn't good enough and he wasn't ready.

wouldn't be the last approach for the duo, in fact the next would be only ten months later, when England came calling.

Surprisingly there was very little resentment towards the managerial duo from Reds' supporters, it would have been easy for the season to go off the rails if there had been a backlash against this brinksmanship, particularly as it involved the fans most hated rivals. Now the fixture list was kind, allowing the dust to settle. Due to postponements and other team's cup commitments there were no league games scheduled for Forest until the away game at Hereford on March 2nd, a gap of eighteen days between matches.

Clough decided that what was needed, was for the players to take a break, so they all packed up and decamped to Torremolinos, where surprisingly the team worked hard, usually the manager used these trips to re-charge the player's batteries.

Terry Curran who had by now recovered from his injury had been restored to the first team for the abandoned Southampton game and he kept his place for the visit to Hereford, scoring the all important winning goal in a tense 1-0 win, but the management weren't entirely convinced about his fitness. Also whilst he was out injured the team had adapted, John Robertson was now the main man, everything constructive seemed to be channelled down his side, whilst Martin O'Neill, although still wearing the number 8 shirt had been pushed wide right to form a great partnership with Viv Anderson down the opposite flank. O'Neill's greater work ethic and adherence to his defensive duties had secured his position.

Whilst Lloyd was serving his suspension, McGovern and Chapman were re-united in central defence with mixed results. Forest made the long trip to Carlisle

For the away game at Sheffield United, Clough paired the returning Lloyd with Chapman and moved McGovern back in to midfield. Clearly there was now a lack of speed through the middle of the defence and they could be over reliant on experience, but they were also two of the hardest defenders around and if they could keep within some bounds of responsibility, it could work. As it turned out, Sammy was to be a rock during the run in.

It didn't look that way after a 2-0 defeat at Bramall Lane, where incomprehensibly for a team with such flair, they just couldn't score despite having the majority of possession and chances. Further trouble off the pitch as hundreds of Reds' fans had infiltrated the Kop before the game and there were attempts to set fire to a refreshment hut afterwards. Forest had now slipped six points off third spot.

In an audacious move, Clough made a pre transfer deadline attempt to sign Archie Gemmill from Derby, the player was keen, but the transfer fell through, perhaps the Rams were getting their own back. So as the deadline passed, Forest were left to finish the season with what they had. Amazingly Forest were able to name an unchanged line up for the final thirteen games of the season, beginning with the re-arranged fixture against Southampton. The Saints were still mid-table and although they had been knocked out of the FA Cup they had battled through to the quarter finals of the European Cup Winners' Cup, they were certainly no mugs. On this occasion Forest made no mistake, a 2-1 victory, the first of five consecutive wins.

Next a televised 3-0 victory over Blackpool, followed in quick succession by another 3-0 win in a re-arranged game against Orient. Overnight the spark that had gone out had been rekindled, Withe and Woodcock in particular looked inspired once more.

After another professional away win 1-0 at Burnley, courtesy of a Tony Woodcock goal, Forest had clawed their way in to the third promotion spot and seemingly turned their season around, now even Wolves and Chelsea were having wobbles, the gap to top spot was only three points. The opportunity to cement their position came four days later with the visit of Bolton Wanderers to Nottingham. Considered by many good judges to be the best team in the division, although they had a reputation for wilting when the pressure was on.

Almost 25,000 were there to see a fantastic 3-1 victory to the Reds. Bolton surprised many with their defensive line up and when the game started it looked as if they would be happy with a point. Goals from O'Neill, Bowyer and Withe put the seal on a great performance. In the space of only a couple of weeks, belief had been re-kindled.

The return fixture against County at Meadow Lane was next up. A game described as a 'must win' by Fenton, in reality turned into a 'must not lose', as Notts strung out a line of defenders to stop the Reds playing, clearly fearing what might happen if it was an open game. The 1-1 draw still kept open the possibility that both Nottingham teams could be

BRIAN CLOUGH ON SOCCER

EVEN if we do win promotion — and it's still a very big "if" — I can still look back on the season and reflect on disappointments.

I'm sorry Terry—but there's no room for prima donnas

One of them was losing at home to Coventry City in the League Cup when we had the chance to prove we could match a First Division side.

Another setback was the annual home defeat by Notts County. (Next year, providing we are in the same division, we'll send them the points with the Christmas card and save them the trip).

More recently, I've had sleepless nights thinking about our defeats at Chelsea and at home to Cardiff when we have been on the brink of promotion.

But, for me personally, the biggest disappointment of all came on the day Terry Curran walked into my office and slapped a transfer request on the desk.

From that very second I told him he was available. If he wants to go to another club and if anyone's offer is acceptable to me and Forest, the door is open.

No matter how much talent he has got — and no one has more at the City Ground even if they have as much — the last thing I want is a discontented player.

His transfer request was a blow to me after signing him from Doncaster for what was, after all a pretty high fee of £75,000.

I gave him the chance to launch his career because no other top manager was willing to go to Doncaster and give them a sizeable cheque for a relatively inexperienced youngster.

So it's only natural that when he comes and tells

They can make noises in other places but any

stop people at the City Ground talking about the

more to the matter than that.

At one stage I even sent him home after one

TERRY CURR slapped a tran quest on my des me my biggest pointment of the

walking out of th like a child, I reports back season training a

Settle do

promoted. County had announced a new sponsorship deal that day with Wrangler and a two page advert in the club newspaper told fans to buy their jeans from Jeff's Fashion Centres, Jean Jeannie or Geoffrey Davis. Where are they now?

This crazy season was about to take another twist, just as it seemed the Reds had regained their form at exactly the right time. There were only six games to go and still seven teams in contention for promotion. Chelsea had been top all season until two heavy defeats at Fulham and most recently 4-0 at Charlton had meant they were displaced by Wolves on goal difference. They had not lost successive games all season but in the circumstances they could not be looking forward to the visit of Forest, as defeat could push them down to fourth place. Smoke bombs and fighting on the terraces greeted the players. Martin O'Neill scored for Forest in a tight encounter but this was not enough to stop Chelsea winning 2-1 and regaining top spot. To the amazement of some, Brian Clough allowed six of his squad to play in the Dave Needham testimonial game just two days after this match. Notts County meanwhile had drawn two games to go a point clear by the time Forest played Cardiff, whilst Bolton had ended their poor run with a home win against Southampton and a draw away at Charlton putting them right back in contention. This was nip and tuck, there was no way this wasn't going down to the last game.

The 1-0 home defeat to Cardiff was one of the most frustrating games in the club's history. Thirty attempts on goal and twenty one corners tells its own story. Forest battered away but just couldn't score and when Viv Anderson fired over the bar in the last minute there was a collective sagging of shoulders around the City Ground. Martin O'Neill recalls the dressing room afterwards, "We were devastated, even though the manager tried to put a brave face on it, he thought we had blown it too. Promotion was no longer in our own hands, even if we won every game".

Ronnie Fenton recalls his disbelief when he heard the score, "I was so convinced that Forest would win, that we changed our tactics at Luton to try and win the game but lost 4-2, in hindsight I shouldn't have". Peter Withe had often incurred the wrath of the manager. Clough hated it when he perceived that his centre forwards were not doing the job he paid them to do, avoiding going in to the penalty area to chase a goal. On the occasion of the Oldham game, he threatened to replace him with Barry Butlin, only changing his mind at the last

WE ASK

TONY WOODCOCK

ANSWERS

FULL NAME: Anthony Stewart Woodcock
BIRTHPLACE: Nottingham
BIRTHDATE: 6th December, 1955
HEIGHT: 5ft 11ins
WEIGHT: 11st
PREVIOUS CLUBS: Lincoln City and Doncaster Rovers on loan
MARRIED: No
CAR: Volkswagen
FAVOURITE PLAYER: Denis Law (past); Johan Cruyff (present)
FAVOURITE OTHER TEAM: Lincoln City
MOST DIFFICULT OPPONENT: Too many to mention
MOST MEMORABLE MATCH: My League debut . . . and the last game I scored in
BIGGEST DISAPPOINTMENT: Playing reserve soccer for 18 months after I'd broken through into the first team
BEST COUNTRY VISITED: Holland
FAVOURITE FOOD: Steak
MISCELLANEOUS LIKES: Travelling, driving, eating out
MISCELLANEOUS DISLIKES: Smoking
FAVOURITE T.V. SHOWS: Most sports programmes, Morecambe & Wise
FAVOURITE SINGERS: 10CC, Rolling Stones
FAVOURITE ACTOR/ACTRESS: Dustin Hoffman, Barbra Streisand
BEST FRIEND: I have many good friends
BIGGEST INFLUENCE ON CAREER: Bert Johnson, the ex-Forest coach
BIGGEST DRAG IN SOCCER: Not playing well
INTERNATIONAL HONOURS: Member of England Under-21 squad
PERSONAL AMBITION: To be successful outside of football and be happy and healthy
PROFESSIONAL AMBITION: To play for England
IF YOU WEREN'T A FOOTBALLER WHAT DO YOU THINK YOU'D BE? Don't know
WHICH PERSON IN THE WORLD WOULD YOU MOST LIKE TO MEET? I'd like to meet many people . . . it's difficult to mention one

minute. Withe was to enjoy a strange scoring record with the Reds, his goals coming in batches followed by periods when he didn't look as if he could hit a barn door. He didn't score that night either but the team coasted to a 3-0 victory at a subdued City Ground.

Three games to play, two away at Bristol Rovers and Plymouth before a final encounter with Millwall. Brian Clough pulled off what turned out to be a masterstroke. He had persuaded the Football League to allow Forest to bring forward the fixture with Plymouth that should have taken place on the actual final day of the season, to the Monday after the Bristol game. He pointed out to the League, that the club could save money and travel time by staying down in the West Country. Plymouth agreed and the scene was now set for Forest to have finished their fixtures and have the points in the bag giving Bolton the pressure of having to match them. The manager then arranged for a club trip to Spain leaving at the exact time the final days fixtures would be taking place.

Of course this wouldn't mean anything unless the Reds posted a points target for Bolton to aim for. Bristol Rovers back in the 1970's played at the dilapidated Eastville Stadium that they also shared with the local speedway team. During the game Forest were having a hard time of it, losing 1-0, until Forest supporters discovered that the mesh wiring around the perimeter used to stop bikes crashing into the crowd wasn't as firmly fixed as it should have been. When a section of it was pulled down, the referee called a halt whilst order was restored and on the restart a more composed Forest rescued a point with a goal from Robertson.

It had now turned into a three horse race for the last promotion spot. That same day, Bolton had beaten Hereford 3-1 to move closer and County had beaten Southampton 3-1.

Forest achieved the much needed victory against Plymouth Argyle, thanks to a winning goal from Peter Withe in a 2-1 victory. The Reds were at their best defensively and in truth easily held out Plymouth. This restored the advantage back to three points over Bolton.

The final fixture was always going to be a tense affair. Although there was hope, realistically Forest fans thought that Bolton would snatch third place with their games in hand. This game despite constant pressure from the Reds was only settled by an own goal from Millwall full back Jon Moore who headed past his own keeper, an unlikely hero in the Nottingham Forest story. Although there was the usual pitch invasion, there were not wild scenes of celebration, until news filtered through that County had lost at Burnley and Bolton had dropped a point by drawing at Luton. All of a sudden a massive feeling of optimism swept the crowd.

The situation was now clear cut, Notts County were out of it, only Bolton could now overhaul the Reds, but because of an inferior goal difference they needed at least two wins and a draw to do it.

On the Monday evening Clough fulfilling an obligation to one of his favourite players, took a full strength team over to Derby for Kevin Hector's testimonial. This resulted in a good attendance for the player, but the newspapers chose to concentrate on the crowd trouble that surrounded this so called friendly fixture.

The final fixture for Forest came the following day at Mansfield for the County Cup semi final. As Bolton were playing the same evening, thousands of fans travelled again in the hope that Bolton might drop points and they could celebrate promotion with the team. No such luck, Bolton stayed in the race with a 2-1 victory.

Bolton's last home game of the season looked tricky, at least on paper. The visitors were Wolves, but as they had already clinched the Championship, there were fears that their hearts might not be in it. No such worries though, with typical British spirit they fought hard to win 1-0, with a goal from Kenny Hibbitt. Even that does not tell the whole story as Hibbitt was forced to go in goal for the final quarter of the game due to an injury to the Wolves' keeper. Despite non-stop pressure Bolton couldn't find an equalizer.

Although they still had one fixture left, they would need to win by fourteen goals in order to deprive Forest of

It looks like Div II again for the Forest

BY JOHN LAWSON

STATISTICS as well as logic now say that Nottingham Forest are destined for at least one more season of Second Division football.

Tuesday's defeat by Notts County clearly put them firmly behind the asking rate in terms of points from matches in the run-in to the end of the season.

Before this afternoon

third respectively, both went up with 53 and the season before ... claimed

Clough adopt that style of play so those critics clamouring for more direct policy can ...

top flight but against Chelsea (27,089), Southampton in the Cup (38,284) and now Notts ... fans

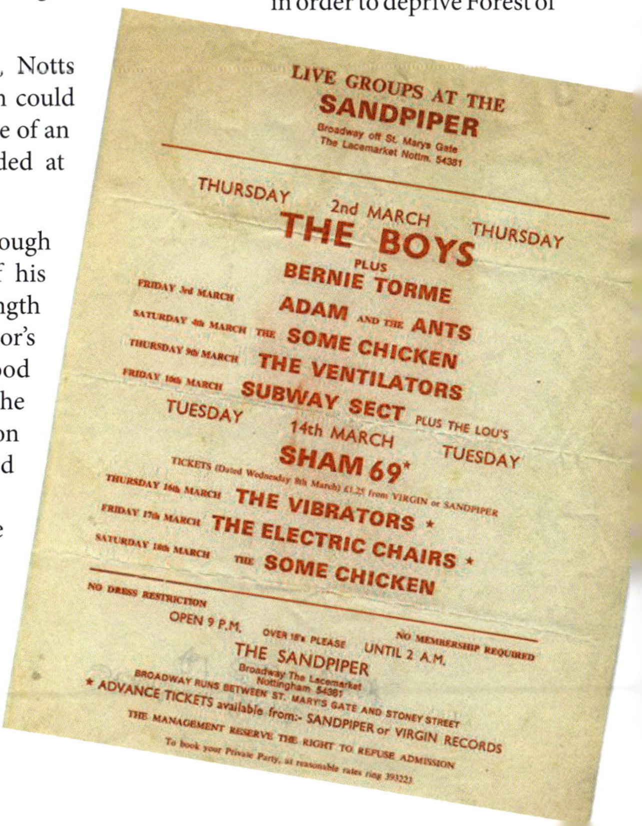

Peter Withe continues his fine scoring run with this effort against Blackpool.

Withe leaps to head home at Meadow Lane.

After rounding the keeper Tony Woodcock turns the ball in to the empty net from a tight angle.

O'Neill turns away after netting the third against Oldham.

Woodcock scores, Plymouth 0 Forest 1.

Withe heads home the winner at Plymouth.

NOW ALL THE REDS CAN DO IS WAIT...

Anderson lashes over late on against Cardiff.

This goal, turned out to be the one that clinched promotion for the Reds, Millwall full back Jon Moore heads the ball past his own keeper for the only goal of the game.

promotion, but for the Reds' fans who had travelled to Lancashire and those thousands celebrating back in the Market Square in Nottingham this was not even a consideration. The party travelling to Spain on the Saturday contained most of the squad and officials, although Peter Withe and Larry Lloyd along with Peter Taylor and Fred Reacher were to travel the next day. Garry Birtles was given a space because Sammy Chapman hadn't travelled due to a fear of flying. Boarding took place at 3.00pm, just as the game kicked off at Burnden Park and by the time they were airborne nerves were shredded. Cloughie had asked the pilot to try and follow the score but the reception was patchy and when the pilot announced that Wolves had taken the lead cheering broke out, muted until it could be properly confirmed. That was the last time they were to hear from the pilot, so nobody knew whether that meant no further goals had been scored or that he hadn't heard. Some players recall that celebrations started on the plane, but in truth it was not until the plane landed and the result was confirmed that the players really let themselves go. On landing, the manager tried several times to get through to his wife, but to no avail. In desperation he phoned Stuart Dryden's wife who answered with the immortal words that he wanted to hear, "I suppose congratulations are in order".

Tony Woodcock receives the fans Player of the Year Trophy

It was also a season of personal triumph for certain players. John Robertson had been voted by his fellow professionals into the Division Two team of the year, whilst Tony Woodcock had finally been given the chance and grabbed it with both hands and was voted 'Player of the Year' by supporters. 'Injury prone' Frank Clark had now completed two full seasons without missing a game and the legendary Sammy Chapman had fully played his part in the promotion after fifteen years service at the club. It had taken just one season for the re-united pair to return Nottingham Forest to the top flight, but what would the ambitions be; Survival? Consolidation? Or more?

Peter Taylor turned to Brian Clough, "Now we really will have to get the cheque book out".

FACTS and FIGURES

Aug 7th 1976, ASC, A, v. Notts County, Draw 0-0, AT 12,258, Wells, Saunders, Barrett, McGovern, Chapman, Bowyer, Curran, Haselgrave, O'Hare, Butlin, Roberton.

Aug 11th 1976, ASC, H, v. West Bromwich Albion, Win 3-2, Scorer Curran (2) (1Pen) Butlin, AT 7,018, Wells, Saunders, Clark, Barrett, Chapman, Bowyer, Curran, Haslegrave, O'Hare, Butlin, Robertson.

Aug 14th 1976, ASC, H, v. Bristol City, Win 4-2, Scorers O'Hare (2) Butlin (2), AT 8,527, Wells, Saunders, Clark, McGovern, Barrett, Bowyer, Curran, Haslegrave, O'Hare, Butlin, Robertson, SUB Chapman.

Aug 21st 1976, A, v. Fulham, Draw 2-2, Scorers Curran, O'Hare, AT 9,437, Wells, Saunders, Clark, McGovern, Chapman, Bowyer, Curran, Haslegrave, O'Hare, Butlin, Robertson, SUB Richardson.

Aug 25th 1976, H, v. Charlton Athletic, Draw1-1, Scorer Curran (Pen), AT 12,662, Wells, Saunders, Clark, McGovern, Chapman, Bowyer, Curran, Richardson, O'Hare, Butlin, Robertson, SUB O'Neill.

Aug 28th 1976, H, v. Wolverhampton Wanderers, Loss 1-3, Scorer Daley (OG), AT 17,222, Wells, Saunders, Clark, McGovern, Chapman, Bowyer, Curran, Barrett, O'Hare, Butlin, Robertson, SUB O'Neill.

Aug 31st 1976, LC, A, v. Walsall, Win 4-2, Scorers Barrett, Curran, O'Neill (2), AT 8,437, Middleton, Barrett, Clark, McGovern, Chapman, Bowyer, Curran, O'Neill, O'Hare, Butlin, Robertson.

Sept 4th 1976, A, v. Luton Town, Draw 1-1, Scorer Curran(Pen), AT 11,231, Middleton, Barrett, Clark, McGovern, Chapman, Bowyer, Curran, O'Neill, O'Hare, Butlin, Robertson, SUB Anderson.

Sept 11th 1976, H, v. Hereford United, Win 4-3, Scorers Bowyer (2), Butlin, Robertson, AT 12,081, Wells, Barrett, Clark, McGovern, Chapman, Bowyer, Curran, O'Neill, O'Hare, Butlin, Robertson, SUB Anderson.

Sept 14th 1976, ASC, H, v. Kilmarnock, Win 2-1, Scorers Chapman, Robertson, AT 8,911, Wells, Barrett, Clark, Anderson, Chapman, Haselgrave, Curran, O'Neill, O'Hare, Butlin, Robertson.

Sept 18th 1976, A, v. Southampton, Draw 1-1, Scorer Bowyer, AT 23,096, Middleton, Barrett, Clark, Anderson, Chapman, Bowyer, Curran, O'Neill, O'Hare, Butlin, Robertson.

Sept 21st 1976, LC, H, v. Coventry City, Loss 0-3, AT 15,969, Wells, Barrett, Clark, McGovern, Chapman, Bowyer, Curran, O'Neill, O'Hare, Butlin, Robertson.

Sept 25th 1976, H, v. Carlisle United, Win 5-1, Scorers Barrett, Bowyer (2), O'Hare, Withe, AT 12,479, Middleton, Barrett, Clark, McGovern, Chapman, Bowyer, Curran, O'Neill, O'Hare, Withe, Robertson.

Sept 28th 1976, ASC, A, v. Kilmarnock, Draw 2-2, Scorer Curran (2), AT 4,227, Middleton, Anderson, Barrett, McGovern, Chapman, Bowyer, Curran, Haselgrave, O'Hare, Withe, Robertson, SUB O'Neill.

Oct 2nd 1976, A, v. Hull City, Loss 0-1, AT 16,096, Middleton, Barrett, Clark, McGovern, Lloyd, Bowyer, Curran, O'Neill, O'Hare, Withe, Robertson, SUB Anderson.

Oct 9th 1976, H, v. Sheffield United, Win 6-1, Scorers Anderson, Bowyer (2), Curran, Withe, Butlin, AT 17,801, Middleton, Anderson, Clark, McGovern, Lloyd, Bowyer, Curran, O'Neill, Withe, Butlin, Robertson.

Oct 16th 1976, A, v. Blackpool, Loss 0-1, AT 17,089, Middleton, Anderson, Clark, McGovern, Lloyd, Bowyer, Curran, O'Neill, Withe, Butlin, Robertson, SUB Haslegrave.

Oct 23rd 1976, ASC, H, v. Ayr United, Win 2-1, Scorers Lloyd, Withe, AT 9,138, Middleton, Anderson, Clark, McGovern, Lloyd, Bowyer, Haselgrave, O'Neill, Withe, Butlin, Robertson, SUB Burke.

Oct 23rd 1976, H, v. Burnley, Win 5-2, Scorers Curran, O'Neill (2), Butlin, Robertson, AT 15,279, Middleton, Anderson, Clark, McGovern, Lloyd, Bowyer, Curran, O'Neill, Withe, Butlin, Robertson, SUB Barrett.

Oct 25th 1976, CC, A, v. Notts County, Loss 0-1, AT 9,415, Middleton, Saunders, Clark, McGovern, Chapman, Bowyer, Haselgrave, O'Neill, Withe, Butlin, Barrett.

Oct 30th 1976, A, v. Oldham Athletic, Loss 0-1, AT 10,597, Middleton, Saunders, Clark, McGovern, Anderson, Bowyer, Barrett, O'Neill, Withe, Butlin, Robertson, SUB Haslegrave.

Nov 3rd 1976, ASC, A, v. Ayr United, Win 2-0, Scorers Withe, Woodcock, AT 3,326, Middleton, Anderson, Clark, McGovern, Chapman, Bowyer, Haselgrave, O'Neill, Withe, Woodcock, Robertson.

Nov 6th 1976, H, v. Blackburn Rovers, Win 3-0, Scorers Bowyer, Haslegrave Withe, AT 12,972, Middleton, Anderson, Clark, McGovern, Chapman, Bowyer, Haslegrave, O'Neill, Withe, Woodcock, Robertson.

Nov 13th 1976, A, v. Orient, Win 1-0, Scorer Woodcock, AT 5,921, Middleton, Anderson, Clark, McGovern, Chapman, Bowyer, Haslegrave, O'Neill, Withe, Woodcock, Robertson.

Nov 20th 1976, H, v. Chelsea, Draw 1-1, Scorer O'Neill, AT 27,089, Middleton, Anderson, Clark, McGovern, Chapman, Bowyer, Haslegrave, O'Neill, Withe, Woodcock, Robertson.

Nov 27th 1976, A, v. Cardiff City, Win 3-0, Scorers Chapman, Withe, Woodcock, AT 12,741, Middleton, Anderson, Clark, McGovern, Chapman, Bowyer, O'Hare, O'Neill, Withe, Woodcock, Robertson.

Dec 4th 1976, H, v. Bristol Rovers, Win 4-2, Scorers Withe, Woodcock, Robertson (2) (1 Pen), AT 16,302, Middleton, Anderson, Clark, McGovern, Lloyd, Bowyer, O'Hare, O'Neill, Withe, Woodcock, Robertson.

Dec 11th 1976, A, v. Millwall, Win 2-0, Scorers O'Hare, O'Neill, AT 9,307, Middleton, Anderson, Clark, McGovern, Lloyd, Bowyer, O'Hare, O'Neill, Withe, Woodcock, Robertson.

Dec 13th 1976, ASC, A, v. Orient, Draw 1-1, Scorer Robertson (Pen), AT 5,058, Middleton, Anderson, Clark, McGovern, Lloyd, Bowyer, O'Hare, O'Neill, Withe, Woodcock, Robertson, SUB Barrett.

Dec 15th 1976, ASC, H, v. Orient, Win 4-0, Scorers Chapman, Barrett (2), Bowyer, AT 12,717, Middleton, Anderson, Clark, McGovern, Lloyd, Chapman, O'Neill, Barrett, Bowery, Bowyer, Robertson.

Second Division 1976-77

		Pld	W	D	L	F	A	Pts
1	Wolverhampton Wand.	42	22	13	7	84	45	57
2	Chelsea	42	21	13	8	73	53	55
3	FOREST	42	21	10	11	77	43	52
4	Bolton Wanderers	42	20	11	11	75	54	51
5	Blackpool	42	17	17	8	58	42	51
6	Luton Town	42	21	6	15	67	48	48
7	Charlton Athletic	42	16	16	10	71	58	48
8	Notts County	42	19	10	13	65	60	48
9	Southampton	42	17	10	15	72	67	44
10	Millwall	42	15	13	14	57	53	43
11	Sheffield United	42	14	12	16	54	63	40
12	Blackburn Rovers	42	15	9	18	42	54	39
13	Oldham Athletic	42	14	10	18	52	64	38
14	Hull City	42	10	17	15	45	53	37
15	Bristol Rovers	42	12	13	17	53	68	37
16	Burnley	42	11	14	17	46	64	36
17	Fulham	42	11	13	18	54	61	35
18	Cardiff City	42	12	10	20	56	67	34
19	Leyton Orient	42	9	16	17	37	55	34
20	Carlisle United	42	11	12	19	49	75	34
21	Plymouth Argyle	42	8	16	18	46	65	32
22	Hereford United	42	8	15	19	57	78	31

Dec 18th 1976, H, v. Plymouth Argyle, Draw 1-1, Scorer Barrett, AT 15,180, Middleton, Anderson, Clark, Barrett, Lloyd, Bowyer, O'Neill, O'Hare, Bowery, Chapman, Woodcock.

Dec 27th 1976, A, v. Bolton Wanderers, Draw 1-1, Scorer Withe, AT 32,630, Middleton, Anderson, Clark, McGovern, Lloyd, Bowyer, O'Hare, O'Neill, Withe, Woodcock, Robertson.

Jan 1st 1977, A, v. Blackburn Rovers, Win 3-1, Scorers Bowyer, Withe, Woodcock, AT 14,524, Middleton, Anderson, Clark, McGovern, Lloyd, Bowyer, O'Hare, O'Neill, Withe, Woodcock, Robertson.

Jan 8th 1977, FAC, H, v. Bristol Rovers, Draw 1-1, Scorer Robertson (Pen), AT 17,874, Middleton, Anderson, Clark, McGovern, Lloyd, Bowyer, O'Hare, O'Neill, Withe, Woodcock, Robertson.

Jan 11th 1977, FAC, A, v. Bristol Rovers, Draw 1-1, Scorer Woodcock, AT 12,257, Middleton, Anderson, Clark, Chapman, Lloyd, Bowyer, O'Hare, O'Neill, Withe, Woodcock, Robertson, SUB Barrett.

Jan 14th 1977, A, v. Charlton Athletic, Loss 1-2, Scorer Bowyer, AT 8,021, Middleton, Anderson, Clark, McGovern, Lloyd, Bowyer, Chapman, O'Neill, Withe, Woodcock, Robertson.

Jan 18th 1977, FAC, N, Villa Park, v. Bristol Rovers, Win 6-0, Scorers Anderson, Bowyer, O'Hare, Withe, Woodcock (2), AT 5,736, Middleton, Anderson, Clark, Chapman, Lloyd, Bowyer, O'Hare, O'Neill, Withe, Woodcock, Robertson, SUB Barrett.

Jan 22nd 1977, H, v. Fulham, Win 3-0, Scorers Lloyd, O'Neill, Woodcock, AT 24,718, Middleton, Anderson, Clark, McGovern, Lloyd, Bowyer, O'Hare, O'Neill, Withe, Woodcock, Robertson.

Jan 29th 1977, FAC, H, v. Southampton, Draw 3-3, Scorers Woodcock, Robertson (2) (1Pen), AT 38,284, Middleton, Anderson, Clark, McGovern, Lloyd, Bowyer, O'Hare, O'Neill, Withe, Woodcock, Robertson.

Feb 1st 1977, FAC, A, v. Southampton, Loss 1-2, Scorer Woodcock, AT 29,401, Middleton, Anderson, Clark, McGovern, Lloyd, Bowyer, O'Hare, O'Neill, Withe, Woodcock, Robertson.

Feb 5th 1977, A, v. Wolverhampton Wanderers, Loss 1-2, Scorer Chapman, AT 30,661, Middleton, Anderson, Clark, McGovern, Lloyd, Bowyer, O'Hare, O'Neill, Withe, Woodcock, Robertson, SUB Chapman.

Feb 12th 1977, H, v. Luton Town, Loss 1-2, Scorer Lloyd, AT 18,225, Middleton, Anderson, Clark, McGovern, Lloyd, Bowyer, Chapman, Haslegrave, O'Hare, Woodcock, Robertson.

Feb 16th 1977, H, v. Southampton, Abandoned, Middleton, Anderson, Clark, McGovern, Lloyd, Bowyer, Curran, O'Hare, Withe, Woodcock, Robertson.

Mar 2nd 1977, A, v. Hereford United, Win 1-0, Scorer Curran, AT 7,503, Middleton, Anderson, Clark, Barrett, Chapman, Bowyer, Curran, O'Neill, Withe, Woodcock, Robertson, SUB O'Hare.

Mar 5th 1977, A, v. Carlisle United, Draw 1-1, Scorer Robertson (Pen), AT 7,603, Middleton, Anderson, Clark, McGovern, Chapman, Barrett, O'Hare, O'Neill, Curran, Woodcock, Robertson, SUB Withe.

Mar 8th 1977, H, v. Notts County, Loss 1-2, Scorer Withe, AT 31,004, Middleton, Anderson, Clark, McGovern, Chapman, Bowyer, O'Hare, O'Neill, Withe, Woodcock, Robertson.

Mar 12th 1977, H, v. Hull City, Win 2-0, Scorers Withe, Woodcock, AT 15,116, Middleton, Anderson, Clark, McGovern, Chapman, Bowyer, Birtles, O'Neill, Withe, Woodcock, Robertson.

Mar 19th 1977, A, v, Sheffield United, Loss 0-2, AT 30,370, Middleton, Anderson, Clark, Chapman, Lloyd, Bowyer, McGovern, O'Neill, Withe, Woodcock, Robertson, SUB O'Hare.

Mar 22nd 1977, H, v. Southampton, Win 2-1, Scorers O'Neill, Woodcock, AT 12,393, Middleton, Anderson, Clark, Chapman, Lloyd, Bowyer, McGovern, O'Neill, Withe, Woodcock, Robertson.

Mar 26th 1977, H, v. Blackpool, Win 3-0, Scorers Withe (2) Woodcock, AT 16,658, Middleton, Anderson, Clark, Chapman, Lloyd, Bowyer, McGovern, O'Neill, Withe, Woodcock, Robertson.

Mar 29th 1977, H, v. Orient, Win 3-0, Scorers Lloyd, With (2), AT 16,267, Middleton, Anderson, Clark, Chapman, Lloyd, Bowyer, McGovern, O'Neill, Withe, Woodcock, Robertson, SUB O'Hare.

Apr 2nd 1977, A, v. Burnley, Win 1-0, Scorer Woodcock, AT 11,112, Middleton, Anderson, Clark, Chapman, Lloyd, Bowyer, McGovern, O'Neill, Withe, Woodcock, Robertson, SUB Barrett.

Apr 6th 1977, H, v. Bolton Wanderers, Win 3-1, Scorers Bowyer, O'Neill, Withe, AT 24,580, Middleton, Anderson, Clark, Chapman, Lloyd, Bowyer, McGovern, O'Neill, Withe, Woodcock, Robertson, SUB Butlin.

Apr 9th 1977, A, v. Notts County, Draw 1-1, Scorer Withe, AT 32,518, Middleton, Anderson, Clark, Chapman, Lloyd, Bowyer, McGovern, O'Neill, Withe, Woodcock, Robertson, SUB Barrett.

Apr 16th 1977, A, v. Chelsea, Loss 1-2, Scorer O'Neill, AT 36,499, Middleton, Anderson, Clark, Chapman, Lloyd, Bowyer, McGovern, O'Neill, Withe, Woodcock, Robertson.

Apr 23rd 1977, H, v. Cardiff City, Loss 0-1, AT 20,646, Middleton, Anderson, Clark, Chapman, Lloyd, Bowyer, McGovern, O'Neill, Withe, Woodcock, Robertson, SUB Butlin.

Apr 27th 1977, H, v. Oldham Athletic, Win 3-0, Scorers Bowyer, O'Neill, Woodcock, AT 17,139, Middleton, Anderson, Clark, Chapman, Lloyd, Bowyer, McGovern, O'Neill, Withe, Woodcock, Robertson, SUB Curran.

Apr 30th 1977, A, v. Bristol Rovers, Draw 1-1, Scorer Robertson, AT 8,900, Middleton, Anderson, Clark, Chapman, Lloyd, Bowyer, McGovern, O'Neill, Withe, Woodcock, Robertson, SUB Curran.

May 2nd 1977, A, v. Plymouth, Win 2-1, Scorers Withe, Woodcock, AT 13,542, Middleton, Anderson, Clark, Chapman, Lloyd, Bowyer, McGovern, O'Neill, Withe, Woodcock, Robertson.

May 7th 1977, H, v. Millwall, Win 1-0, Scorer Moore (OG), AT 23,529, Middleton, Anderson, Clark, Chapman, Lloyd, Bowyer, McGovern, O'Neill, Withe, Woodcock, Robertson.

May 19th 1977, CC, A, v. Mansfield Town, Win 2-1, Scorers Anderson, Withe, AT 9,679, Middleton, Anderson, Clark, Chapman, Lloyd, Bowyer, Barrett, O'Neill, Withe, Woodcock, Robertson, SUB Curran.

Back Row: J.Robertson, P.Richardson, M.O'Neill, I.Bowyer
Middle Row: B.Clough, C.Barrett, S.Wignall, J.Middleton, P.Wells, B.Butlin, S.Dall, J.Gordon
Front Row: T.Curran, J.McGovern, S.Haslegrave, B.Chapman, J.O'Hare, F.Clark, G.Saunders

Poolside at a hotel in Cala Millor with a drink in your hand is perhaps not the best place to have doubts about your ability or your position in the team. But those were the exact thoughts that Martin O'Neill and several of his team mates were having that May.

Larry Lloyd might have been confident of retaining his place, but O'Neill knew that the management could be ruthless when it came to team building and after all he had had several run ins with Brian Clough. Although he had played top flight football before, albeit six years previously and played International football with Ireland, could he make the step up now?

Although they had just scraped up in third place, there was no doubt in the minds of Clough and Taylor that they could fashion a team that would be competitive. In typical Taylor fashion he claimed that Forest should be looking to challenge for a place in Europe, whilst Clough sometimes would chide him for putting unnecessary pressure on themselves, he realised that this kind of statement would keep them both on their toes.

Peter Taylor was certain from early on about the players that he wanted to bring in, although the hard part might be persuading them to join a club that was predicted by all the pundits to struggle. Firstly they had to move the players out that they deemed surplus to requirements. Long serving Sammy Chapman was allowed to join Notts County on a free transfer and they got a small fee for Barry Butlin when he joined Peterborough for £20,000. Sean Haslegrave also raised £30,000 when he joined Preston in August.

The management duo were obsessed with what they called the spine of the team, believing that if you could get this area right, everything else would fall into place. Despite promotion Taylor had always harboured doubts about Chapman and also John Middleton, believing he wasn't as good as others believed. Even whilst they were at Derby they had coveted Peter Shilton and reckoned that he could be worth at least ten goals per season to the team. This went against most current thinking at that time in football, most managers didn't place the same value on keepers as they did goalscorers.

Despite their reputation for attacking football, the philosophy had always been to build from the back. If you don't concede you cannot lose and with this in

77-78

NOTTINGHAM FOREST FOOTBALL CLUB

DIVISION ONE 1977 - 78

Back row, left to right:

BRYN GUNN MARTIN O'NEILL IAN BOWYER PETER WITHE VIV ANDERSON JOHN MIDDLETON GARRY BIRTLES BARRY BUTLIN COLIN BARRETT KENNY BURNS

Front row, left to right:

LARRY LLOYD SEAN HASLEGRAVE FRANK CLARK JOHN McGOVERN JOHN ROBERTSON TERRY CURRAN TONY WOODCOCK

WE ASK John Robertson ANSWERS

FULL NAME: John Robertson
BIRTHPLACE: Uddingston, Scotland
BIRTHDATE: 20th January, 1953
HEIGHT: 5ft 7½ins
WEIGHT: 11st 10lbs
PREVIOUS CLUBS: None
MARRIED: Yes
CHILDREN: No
CAR: Viva
FAVOURITE PLAYERS: Liam Brady and Kenny Dalglish
FAVOURITE OTHER TEAM: Glasgow Rangers
MOST DIFFICULT OPPONENT: Pedro Richards of Notts County
MOST MEMORABLE MATCH: v. Derby this season. We won 3-0
BIGGEST THRILL: Getting promoted
BIGGEST DISAPPOINTMENT: Not winning Second Division Championship
BEST COUNTRY VISITED: Israel
FAVOURITE FOOD: Italian
MISCELLANEOUS LIKES: Records, films and tennis
MISCELLANEOUS DISLIKES: Gardening and washing my car
FAVOURITE T.V. SHOWS: When The Boat Comes In
FAVOURITE SINGERS: Bryan Ferry and Jeff Lynne
FAVOURITE ACTORS/ACTRESS: Clint Eastwood, Robert Shaw and Jodie Foster
BEST FRIEND: Dave Serella of Walsall
BIGGEST INFLUENCE ON CAREER: Brian Clough
BIGGEST DRAG IN SOCCER: Not playing well
INTERNATIONAL HONOURS: None
PERSONAL AMBITION: To be happy and to make money
PROFESSIONAL AMBITION: To play for Scotland and win the First Division Championship
IF YOU WEREN'T A FOOTBALLER, WHAT DO YOU THINK YOU'D BE? Don't know
WHICH PERSON IN THE WORLD WOULD YOU MOST LIKE TO MEET? Clint Eastwood

mind, they began the chase for Shilton's signature. Peter had just been relegated with Stoke City. Originally when he had joined the Potters they looked like a team going places, they had stars such as Alan Hudson and Jimmy Greenhoff propelling them to the top of the table, but in a

scenario very much akin to Forest in the late 1960's, their Board of Directors had also got cold feet and begun selling off the assets after storm damage to an uninsured stand at the Victoria Ground.

Crowds had dwindled at Stoke and they once again found themselves in a financial mess and needing to sell. They weren't prepared to sell cheap however and this coupled with the wage demands from the player, meant that the deal could not be concluded before the beginning of the season. Shilton was considered to be the highest paid player in the country on £400 per week and his agent had cannily inserted a clause linking the keeper's wages to the rate of inflation and with inflation raging, it was hitting Stoke hard.

Nottingham Forest's only major pre-season signing turned out to be a surprise in several ways. With his usual flair, Taylor's eye had fallen on Kenny Burns, a firebrand of a centre forward with Birmingham City. Although he had played at the back, he had found his niche partnering Trevor Francis in the Blues' attack, scoring over 20 goals the previous season. Taylor was fastidious when it came to wanting to know about a player's background. As we have already seen he was prepared to overlook a vice or two as long as he knew about it, and it wasn't excessive. Plenty of good experts in the game had warned him off Burns, including it is alleged, Birmingham's own chairman, but Taylor wanted to see for himself. When Taylor had told Clough who they should sign, the manager was not impressed, "I am not having an ugly bastard like that at my club", he reportedly said. Taylor assured him that he was not as bad as he was painted and would bring him the evidence.

Mid week at Perry Barr dog track, Peter Taylor along with chief scout Maurice Edwards followed the player around and they were pleased to note that Burns was only betting in small amounts whilst having a couple of halves to drink.

Brian Clough as usual, was prepared to back his partner's judgement and after several meetings with the player himself, including the oft talked about visit to a garden centre, Forest offered Birmingham City £145,000, which they gratefully accepted. Clough and Taylor were now forced to spell out the financial realities of First Division football to the Forest Chairman and committee, many of whom had been around during the calamitous late 60's period when the club had their fingers burnt signing Jim Baxter. The pair pointed out that even if they poddled around in mid-table, revenues were forecast to reach £650,000, so on this basis

Kenny Burns

a transfer kitty of £450,000 was agreed. Back to the signing of Kenny Burns. If you believe the player himself, he had no idea that he would be playing alongside Larry Lloyd, until the first training session when Jimmy Gordon handed out the bibs and told him where to play. Peter Taylor had believed that Burns best position was as a sweeper, having seen him play that

position several times for Birmingham. Not only did he have the ability to play the ball out of defence, but Taylor also reckoned he had a streak of laziness that made him unsuitable for the centre forward position.

As the club readied itself for the return to the top division, improvements to the ground were needed to comply with stricter league regulations. Extra seating for 1,139 fans was added to the terracing at the front of the Main Stand and a new segregated visitor's section was created on the terraces of the East Stand, towards the Trent End side, these would have their own toilet and refreshment facilities

The club had never had its own social club within the confines of the ground, this was rectified when the Jubilee Club, (named in honour of the Queen's Silver Jubilee celebrations that were taking place that summer) opened its doors for the first time in July. Situated behind the Main Stand, it was considered luxurious at the time and a fitting sign of the club's new status.

There were some grumbles however when the new ticket prices were announced, across the board increases of 30%, but prices were still lower than most other teams. This might have been a contributory factor to sluggish season ticket sales, although the real reason was probably the feeling that the team might struggle this season. However by the time the season started, they had smashed all previous records, sales totalled over £235,000. The match day programme price was also raised by five pence, but that could be justified by the additional four pages.

Forest now announced that they had signed a deal with major kit supplier Adidas and the shiny red shirt with its distinctive white v neck and three sleeve stripes was to be the most iconic in the club's history. The same style shirt, only in

Brian Clough and the bench celebrate Forest's third goal at Everton on the opening day.

Peter Withe soars to head home the only goal against Bristol City.

Withes' second against Derby.

Withe beats McFarland to lash home against Derby.

Tony Woodcock challenges for the ball .

GREAT START FOR THE NEWLY PROMOTED REDS!

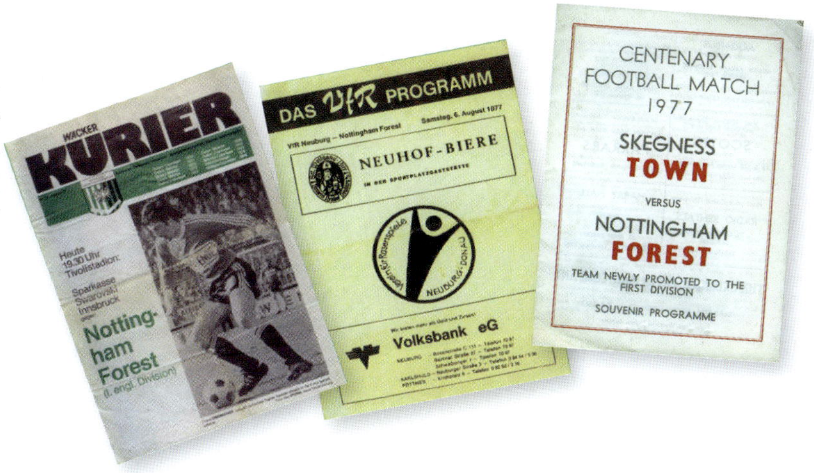

yellow and royal blue, would be used for the away kit.

It had been decided not to defend the Anglo Scottish Cup, but instead set up a training camp back in Germany and play a series of matches against a variety of opposition.

The trip to Germany started badly, the flight was delayed by two hours and then fog over Germany meant that the plane was diverted to Nuremburg airport, before permission to carry on to Munich was given. Even then the drama was not over as low cloud meant it took the pilot two passes before he was able to land. Bear in mind, this was less than twenty years since Manchester United had been involved in a catastrophic plane accident, also at Munich, so there was bound to be a feeling of nervousness as events unfolded. Arriving late at the hotel, they were met by Brian Clough who had taken the opportunity to arrive two days earlier. The players were based at the Hotel Alpenhof in Augsburg, chosen because it was centrally based for where they would play their matches, but it still meant considerable journeys by coach to get to the various venues.

The quality of the opposition that they were to face was varied, with some top flight opponents as well as a couple of regional teams.

The first game was in Switzerland against St Gallen, a Swiss First Division team, who were due to play the first game of their new season the following week. After a journey of over two hundred kilometres, the players were vociferously greeted by about fifty supporters who were to appear at every game on the tour. Forest won the game 3-2, Peter Withe knocking in a couple, before a misunderstanding when Kenny Burns turned the ball back to John Middleton who had rushed out of his net, thereby missing the ball and gifting the hosts a goal. The highlight of the tour was to be the next game against Wacker Innsbruck, quality opponents, who were due to play in that season's European Cup.

Forest fans in Switerzerland

After a beautiful journey through the Tyrolean Alps, the team arrived at the picturesque city of Innsbruck and produced such a fine display that those present were almost taken aback by the quality of play. Several weeks later Ken Smales said that people didn't believe him when he told them how well they had played, particularly if they had seen the Notts County game. A 2-0 victory was soured slightly by the broken nose suffered by Peter Withe from a defender's elbow, who then compounded things by retaliating and getting himself sent off. This performance had a significantly positive effect on the squad, they had gone head to head with one of the best teams in Europe and outplayed them.

They then remained unbeaten on tour, scoring fifteen goals and conceding only two in the remaining three games, before returning back to England and taking a full strength squad to Skegness for another game.

The last game of pre-season, was the carried over County Cup Final against Notts County played at the City Ground. The result was a hardly deserved win on penalties, after a 1-1 draw.

This was another occasion that came to have far greater significance than it in fact merited. Speaking to the players and others involved, they are convinced that this was the game that forced the management to abandon a plan to take the division by storm with two attacking wingers. In fact Terry Curran did not play in this game, his last appearance in a Reds' shirt was against Skegness. Martin O'Neill was wearing the number 7 shirt, his hard working style had won the day. Those wildly optimistic attacking plans had already been shelved in Germany.

Don Revie and Brian Clough, as everyone knew had not enjoyed the best of relationships. Revie's role in, and subsequent gloating when Clough had been sacked as Leeds' manager had a deep and profound effect on the Reds' boss. So when Don Revie announced in July that he was walking out on the England job to take a highly lucrative role in the United Arab Emirates, Clough scented blood. Revie who was to earn the soubriquet 'Don Readies' for his love of money, had besmirched the good name of English football, scuttling off in the dead of night to grab his filthy lucre. Clough never missed an opportunity to comment on what he saw as the ultimate betrayal.

The role of England manager was now vacant, the calls for Brian Howard Clough to take over were muted at first, but after Forest's impressive start to the season, they soon became a crescendo.

Very few pundits predicted anything other than a season of struggle for Forest, after all, they had only just scraped promotion. A couple of Clough allies such as John Sadler at the Sun thought that they might surprise a few teams, but the general concensus was that this rag bag outfit of misfits and youngsters would probably be for the drop. All these 'experts', somehow missed the fact that exactly the same charge had been levelled at Derby County back in 1969; Dave Mackay was over the hill, Kevin Hector who is he? Did they really think that Brian Clough and Peter Taylor didn't know what it would take to prosper in this division?

There was optimism, but also a great deal of apprehension as the team bus made its way through the crowded streets to Goodison Park for the first game of the season, with Everton as the opposition. A neat bit of symmetry, as it was on this ground five years earlier that the Reds had bowed out of the First Division. John

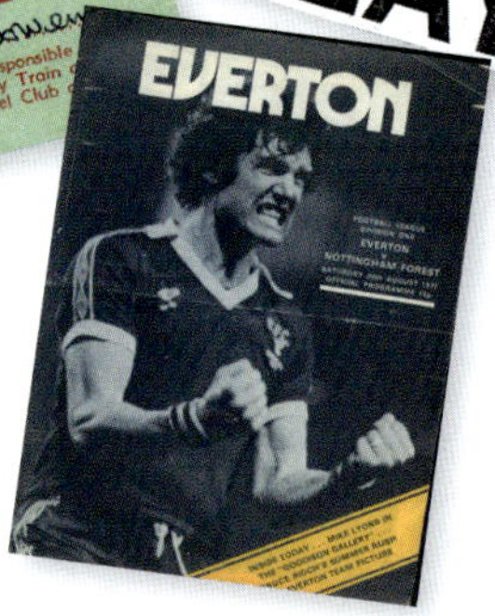

WHAT A START —BUT CLOUGH PLAYS IT COOL

FOREST, back in the big time after five years, cooly tore Everton to shreds with a mastery that must spell trouble for many more of Soccers' top set. Goals by Peter Withe and John Robertson were quickly followed by one from Everton's Jim Pearson but Martin O'Neill rammed home Forest's superiority with another in the second half.

Everton 1 Nottm. Forest 3: by DON HARDISTY

But Forest manager Brian Clough was cautious after this flying start. "We were well organised for an away team and we played reasonably well.

"It's always difficult for the home team in the first match—so much is expected. I'm very sorry for Gordon Lee (the Everton manager) ...

injured, and star striker Bob Latchford, suspended.

Trouble was also in store for their £340,000 pair of newcomers — goalkeeper George Wood made a nightmare start and Dave Thomas held his head in despair after he missed the easiest chance of the match which could have saved his side a point.

That big, brave Scot Kenny Burns was in the thick of the ...

The jolly giant from Blackpool who cost Everton £140,000 last week found his debut had turned into a nightmare with a fusilade of chances which might easily have yielded more than two goals for Forest.

Wood was cruelly exposed by his defence as Withe headed Forest into the lead from Woodcock's corner in the 31st minute. Wood saved ...

Robertson sat next to Martin O'Neill and both can remember a nerve wracking feeling that day, one that continued right through to the dressing room. However, this was when Peter Taylor came to the fore, sensing the tension he cracked jokes, told stories and had the players in stitches, so that by the time kick off came, there was a different mindset amongst the players who prepared to take the field.

Everton were expected to challenge for the title this season, this was going to be a tough game. The players recall the wall of noise that hit them when they took to the field, there were about 3,500 Forest fans packed behind the goal, but this wasn't Bloomfield Road, this was the big league. The intensity and speed with which the game started took the players by surprise, O'Neill says, "It was so fast, I didn't have time to draw breath", Woodcock recalls being clattered by Mick Lyons the giant Everton centre half. Gradually though Forest weathered the storm, Burns and Lloyd were resolute at the back and they started winning some balls. Twenty minutes in, the Reds won a corner, Robertson crossed and Withe nodded home for the opening goal of the season.

It was as if a weight had been lifted from the players' backs, all of a sudden the ball was fizzing around and it wasn't long before Robertson extended the lead with a crisp finish into the roof of the net. Forest were well on top, until they conceded in stoppage time of the first half, a warning that at this level, any lack of concentration would be punished.
The Reds dominated long periods of the second half, but they were not able to extend their lead until the 77th minute when Martin O'Neill fired home to make the game safe. Brian Clough was photographed almost regally acknowledging this goal.
He was back. The dressing room was sacrosanct as far as Brian Clough was concerned, so it was a surprise to the players when after a knock on the dressing room door, Bill Shankly, the truly legendary ex manager of Liverpool was ushered in and invited to speak to the players. The gist of his speech was to enjoy this, but don't just be in the First Division, go and win it.

The First Division not only brought with it a step up in class for the players, but also the fans. The days when big followings could just turn up and have their own way were over. There were clashes inside and outside the ground and supporters who had travelled by train had to take special buses back to Lime Street station.
Liverpool even then was not a rich city, many areas were still barren, with rubble left over from the German bombings thirty years before and these sites provided an array of missiles that were now being used to fire at these buses. The drivers must have known what was going to come, as they encouraged fans to use seats to protect themselves against the windows as flying glass showered everywhere. No buses were safe, even the bus carrying Forest officials had the back window shattered, but there was still a great cheer for the players as they walked down the station platform.

The players should have been entitled to a far bigger crowd than the 21,743 who turned up for the first home game of the season against Bristol City. They might not have been the most exciting opponents, but after five years away from the top flight, where were the fans? City had gone down 3-2 at home to Wolves in their first game and they set themselves up not to lose this one. Employing an extra mid-fielder to help stifle Forest's attacking instincts, it looked as if they might succeed, until an eighty second minute free kick from Robertson found the head of Peter Withe and he powered the ball home for the only goal of the game. It was a good start to the season, although no-one was getting carried away, newly promoted sides often enjoyed a 'honeymoon' period before finding their true level.

Third match into the season gave Forest fans the game they had been looking forward to for five years, the resumption of battles with bitter rivals Derby County. The Rams were now a team clearly on the wane, having finished the previous season in seventeenth place only three points off a relegation spot. The inexperienced Colin Murphy had been promoted to manager after they had hastily sacked Dave Mackay and without the necessary funds to bring in players to replace an ageing squad, they looked set for another season of struggle.

A crowd of over 28,000 was an improvement on the first game, but still not enough. The attendance was not helped by Derby only bringing 1,500 fans to the game. The newly opened away section was barely half full. The Forest side were unchanged apart from Terry Curran replacing Barrett as substitute. In front of the ATV cameras the Reds were immediately on to the attack and could have scored as early as the first minute, an effort from Robertson forcing Boulton in the Derby goal to dive and punch clear. The first half hour was end to end, with no direct scoring chances, until Withe pounced on a loose punch from Boulton to volley home.
The whole complexion of the game now changed as the Reds took control and when

Ian Bowyer nods home from close range against Middlesbrough.

Martin O'Neill forces the ball over the line despite the attention of the Coventry defender.

Archie Gemmill with a blockbuster against Manchester United.

Viv Anderson scores his second against Middlesbrough.

More goal action against Middlesbrough.

HEADS UP IT'S ARCHIE!!

Archie with this spectacular header, for the winner against United.

IT'S WITHE AS CITY FALL TO LATE FOREST WINNER...

Tony Woodcock fires home against Aston Villa.

Burns leaps and scores against Norwich.

Robertson tucks home the second against Aston Villa.

Peter Withe turns against Manchester City...

Then gets his shot away.

Celebrations, Forest 2 City 1.

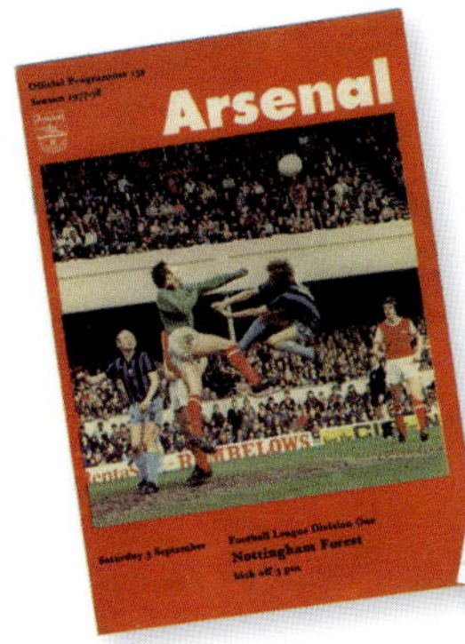

Clough on the spot as Burns is caught out

Arsenal 3
Nottm. Forest......... 0
By JEFF POWELL

TELEVISION yesterday presented Southern viewers with the evidence of the thuggery Manager of the Month Brian Clough failed to notice from his seat on the Highbury touchline.

London Weekend's *Big Match* presented a montage of fouls by Nottingham

about disciplining one of his own players.

It is a decision crucial to Forest. The fact that they

Challis) did well to give the penalty.'

Stapleton, like the perceptive young Graham Rix, the gifted Liam Brady, the competitive Trevor Ross and the miraculous Jennings, suggest that Arsenal are back in serious business as a major First Division football club. Don Howe's coaching is already harnessing the talent

McFarland limped off, the writing was on the wall for the Rams. Woodcock then gave a glimpse of the speed that made him so dangerous and as he sped past Langan the full back, the ball then rebounded to O'Neill, he calmly chipped over for Withe who hit number two. Hugh Johns the commentator was so taken by this play he announced, "That was some of the most electrifying football that I have seen in a very long time". Robbo made absolutely certain of the points, when he calmly passed the ball into the net to complete the scoring. Forest were top, the only team with maximum points. Peter Withe had scored in all three games and the team looked completely at ease in the First Division, although some journalists pointed out that Carlisle had also topped the table in 1974 and they were relegated the same season!

There was now a break from league action, with West Ham providing the opposition in the first round of the League Cup. In the pre-match build up, Frank Lampard said he had never heard of John Robertson. However, he certainly wouldn't forget him after one of the most torrid nights of football he was ever to endure. "It's not fair," he said. "The geezer can go either way". Forest hammered home five goals without reply, Withe again on the scoresheet for the fourth consecutive game.

Football journalism was very London centric at this time, with the so called big hitters such as Brian Glanville seldom venturing outside the capital and therefore basing a lot of their opinions on a skewed version of the truth. If you didn't do it in London, or they didn't see it, then it might as well have not happened.

It was against this background that the Reds ventured south to Highbury, to take on Arsenal, the first chance these 'experts' would have to see what all the fuss was about. Unfortunately it turned out to be not only the Reds' worst display of the season so far, but also a day when Burns and Lloyd crossed the line into thuggery.

There was another good following for the Reds in a crowd of 40,000, but as there was no segregation on the Clock End where the majority of Reds' fans were standing,

Alan Hill and Derek Pavis with a young Steve Hodge as he signs school boy forms with the club.

the afternoon's entertainment would again be interrupted by skirmishes. It was also on this occasion that Forest fans first experienced the white coated nut salesmen who moved around the terraces touting for business, by shouting, "Come and get your peanuts", a phrase used to this day by Forest fans to taunt the opposition, when the opponents are from London. During the three goal defeat, London Weekend cameras and commentator Brian Moore noticed a disturbance in the Nottingham Forest defensive wall as Arsenal prepared to take a free kick. Closer examination of footage the next day during the 'On the Ball' programme, clearly showed Burns headbutting Ritchie Powling, the Gunners' mid-fielder on the back of his head, as he tried to infiltrate the wall. Burns tried to laugh it off by saying he sneezed, but with Brian Clough's reputation for fair play, the newspapers were full of stories demanding that he take action, or be accused of hypocrisy.

They didn't know the manager if they thought this wouldn't happen. This incident was one of many occasions when the press tried to stir up trouble. They continually expressed a desire for a more competitive league, but when this happened, they couldn't wait to pick holes with any upstart that challenged the 'Old Order'. Before training on the following Monday, Jimmy Gordon was given the task of handing out envelopes to Burns and Lloyd containing details of the fines that they would both have to pay. Lloyd had also been caught out with another off the ball incident and Brian Clough made it clear that there was to be no repetition of this sort of behaviour.

Although, in a team meeting around this time, Larry Lloyd came close to an action that might well have brought his Forest career to an early finish, as Clough and Taylor intimated that they had thought he had ducked out of a physical challenge with Frank Stapleton when he scored. The one thing Lloyd wouldn't take from anyone, was the implication that he was a coward, so after getting to his feet he stopped only inches away from physical contact with the pair. As the other players will testify, Clough seemed to get pleasure from winding up the centre half, regularly baiting Lloyd, "Oi big head, just win the ball and give it to someone who can play".

Whilst this was happening Clough was once more trying to complete the signing of Peter Shilton. By now it looked pretty clear that Stoke weren't going to bounce straight back, so when Shilton forced the issue, they were left with no choice but to sell the player.

WHO GETS THE CLOUGH CHOP?

By DENNIS SIGNY — Leicester 0 Nottm Forest 3

THIS flowing Forest victory—without suspended top scorer Peter Withe and newcomer Archie Gemmill—leaves Brian Clough with the sort of problems many managers will envy.

Where does newcomer Gemmill slot into a free-scoring side comfortably keeping pace with the First Division leaders?

Martin O'Neill, reckoned one of the candidates to lose his place to Clough's former Derby star, scored a goal and, for my money, was Forest's hard working man of the match.

All Clough would admit was: "Gemmill and Withe will play next Saturday."

Jokingly, Clough added: "Archie may play in goal —Peter Shilton dropped one of the three shots he had to save."

Leicester manager Frank McLintock's problems—his side have lost four in a row—increased when Alan Woollett went off with ligament trouble just after half time to be replaced by Brian Alderson.

"Alan steadies the defence," he said. "For 60 minutes we played as well as we've played all season and although I am terribly disappointed with the result, there was a lot to work on."

Asked if he contemplated a comeback, McLintock said: "If Alan is out for a while, I woul dconsider it, but after 20 years as a player, I really want to concentrate on the managerial side."

Confident Forest, who have lost only once this season and scored 20 goals won this game in midfield.

Irish international O'Neill had a simple tap-in job after 18 minutes when Mark Wallington could only push aside a hard cross from Ian Bowyer.

Leicester, despite the injection of £120,000 worth of George Armstrong, Lammie Robertson, run ragged after hal

Armstrong kept L hoping with a liv play, and Waddle his use in the air tired.

Frank Worthin benefit from a t partner and a v there was litt against this so defence.

Forest threat from the star just about wo time lead them.

But when cock put a pass in fo after 66 threatened Robertson

The manager was often a law unto himself when it came to transfer dealings, previously Clough had once disrespected the Derby Board of Directors when he signed David Nish from Leicester, despite not having the authority. He had offered Leicester £250,000 for the player and presented the transfer as a 'fait accompli'. He used similar tactics with this transfer as well, taking Stuart Dryden with him to meet the Stoke chairman during a game at Goodison Park, then telling him in front of a packed boardroom, "We've just signed Shilton". With Clough and Taylor, at that time they saw everything in black and white, if you didn't support them, you were basically against them. They simplistically thought success on the field would bring riches off it, the fact that banks and accountants had to be involved was considered a mere inconvenience. Back in 1970, Derby had been banned from playing in Europe after financial irregularities were uncovered. Under Brian Appleby's watch, this was not going to happen at Nottingham Forest.

Peter Shilton

The transfer itself didn't go through until after the next game away at Wolves, because Shilton was determined to collect a loyalty bonus that he thought he deserved from Stoke. Peter Taylor considered this to be the finest signing he ever made. Support for the signing wasn't unanimous though. Taylor couldn't understand why other managers didn't place the same importance on keepers that he did and also he had to explain to Forest fans and the committee, that the signing of Shilton was an upgrade on John Middleton.

The Professional Footballer's Association (PFA) under the leadership of Derek Dougan, were trying once more to improve the situation for players. The players might have won several victories in the 1960's, but the ultimate ambition for them was to have complete freedom of movement, once you had reached the end of your contract. This was almost unanimously opposed by clubs as they felt that it was unfair that they could they lose players for nothing if a player refused to sign again, even if he was offered improved terms. The players on the other hand had voted to empower their union to use all means at their disposal, including the threat of strike action.

After the disappointing result at Highbury, it was back to winning ways the following week at Molineux, as the Reds survived a late fight back to win 3-2 against Wolves. Colin Barrett had been given the number 3 shirt after Frank Clark had been injured at Arsenal. All three of the Reds' goals were headers; Withe, Bowyer and Woodcock.

Liam O'Kane had taken the heartbreaking but seemingly inevitable decision to retire. He was rewarded by the club with a testimonial game against Leicester City. It was hoped that Peter Shilton would be signed in time to make his debut and no doubt add a few thousand to the gate, but he didn't put pen to paper until the following day. It was an unusual team that started for Forest, of course Liam O'Kane played for a period, but more interestingly, Colin Todd, Archie Gemmill and Duncan McKenzie guested in the Reds' line-up.

There was sad news on the music front, as Marc Bolan died after crashing his mini into a tree, exactly a month after Elvis Presley had also passed away.

Peter Shilton made his debut in front of a season's high crowd of 31,000 against Aston Villa. It finally looked as if the Nottingham public had woken up to what was happening down at the City Ground. Shilton kept his first clean sheet as Villa were brushed aside 2-0.

Tony Woodcock who had been married the previous Sunday, scored on his return from honeymoon.

The profile of the club and the players was rising, there was interest in several Reds players, so it was not a complete surprise when news came through that Forest had rejected a bid of £200,000 from German club St Pauli for striker Peter Withe. As Peter Taylor often said, sometimes transfers are just a matter of timing and now the Rams needed a keeper and it just so happened that Forest had a spare one. Derby also had a player the Forest management coveted in Archie Gemmill. Derby had just appointed Tommy Docherty as their new manager and there was history between him and the player, bad history. Docherty had been Scotland manager for a period in the early '70s and after an international defeat, for which he blamed Gemmill, he had frozen him out of the national squad.

One of the first things that Docherty did on taking over at the Baseball Ground was to summon the player to the hotel where he was staying and told him in no uncertain terms that he had no future at the club, as he reckoned the player's legs had gone. This suited Archie, the way was now clear for him to join Forest.

There was one more snide part of the story, that doesn't reflect well on the Derby boss. He made the player submit a written transfer request, so that he couldn't claim his share of the transfer fee. The player wanted to stay and fight for his money, but he was told he would be certain to win his case at a tribunal later anyway, and he was. In the end it turned out to be another 'steal' by Peter Taylor, Forest handed over just £20,000 and John Middleton, for the midfield dynamo, who was to give Forest two years sterling service. Archie's arrival, although good for the team, raised important questions about who would make way for him.

Three into two central midfielders didn't go. However, for the moment that wasn't an issue, as he hadn't signed in time to make his debut at Leicester and had to watch the game from the stand alongside Peter Withe, who was serving a one game ban for being sent off against Wacker Innsbruck in pre-season.

Leicester's short period of minor success in the 1970's was now well and truly over and they were sliding towards relegation. The 3-0 victory was simplicity itself, O'Neill, Woodcock and Robertson with the goals, as the 7,000 Forest fans in a crowd of only 21,000 filled both the side of the pitch and half of the Kop. The following Saturday for the Norwich game, the fans found out who would make way initially for Gemmill. Not only did he replace John McGovern, but he was also given the captain's arm band, with the manager once more signalling that no-one should take their place for granted. Gemmill did not have the best of games, in fact Clough said that the player would have to be re-educated because he had picked up so many bad habits, passing the ball square and backwards too often. Archie picked up a slight knock during this game anyway, so missed the next fixture.

Norwich City under John Bond had clearly done their homework. They detailed John Ryan to follow Robertson around and packed their mid-field. Despite this, the Norwich goal lived a charmed life as they weathered sustained pressure. Heavy rain had soaked the pitch before the start and returned soon after kick off, making second half conditions difficult. Even so, a first goal for Kenny Burns late in the game, looked to have clinched victory, but Martin Peters capitalised on a slip by Shilton, as he lost his footing on the treacherous surface, to glance home an undeserved equaliser.

four-goal Withe as Ipswich are torn apart

FOREST .... 4 IPSWICH 0

PETER WITHE, the man Ron Greenwood ignored, etched his name into the record books at the City Ground last night as the First Division woke up to the fact that Nottingham Forest are very real championship material.

The effervescent Reds simply tore apart one of the country's most professional sides with a display of ruthless aggression and flowing skill.

By dropping a point, Forest had missed out on going top of the league again, but they were given another opportunity four days later when Ipswich Town visited. Ipswich under Bobby Robson were an improving outfit, who would go on to lift the FA Cup this season, but their skipper Mick Mills made a blunder when he was quoted as saying Forest were a team of, 'Has Beens'. Mills was an experienced international right back, who should have known better than to denigrate fellow professionals. Brian Clough's team talk was now done for him, the crowd were onto Mills straight away, as were the team. He himself had a torrid evening as Robertson took him to the cleaners, worse still, Mills appeared to think that Robbo was all left foot, as he continually showed him inside and the winger took full advantage. It was also a night to remember for Peter Withe who continued his fine start by bagging all four goals, the first Forest player since Enoch West in 1907 to score four times in one match, in the top flight.

It is traditional for players scoring three or more goals in a game to be given the match ball, but Clough who was often on Withe's back declared, "He can have the ball when he has learnt how to play with it". This was only an attempt to keep the player's feet on the floor as he was given the ball after training on the Friday. Peter had now scored ten times in ten competitive games.

Forest were now top, a position that they would not relinquish for the rest of the season. This was also the first occasion in the club's history that they had ever been top of the First Division, after ten games had been played. The same evening, Notts County sacked Ron Fenton and replaced him with the returning Jimmy Sirrell.

"Hello Mr Clough, what went wrong today?", was how Ken Smales began his programme notes the week after the Reds were held to a 0-0 draw at Upton Park against West Ham. That question was not from Ken himself, but a railway guard on the train home. Aspirations were now so high that an away draw could be considered a failure. Lampard had not made the same mistake twice, learning from earlier in the season and playing far tighter to Robertson.

Off the field, the club was trying to keep pace with action on it. As the club prospered, fans clamoured for more involvement with the club. Ken Smales organised the first Nottingham Forest golf day, held at the Sherwood Forest Club. The event was attended by players , both current and old, plus members of staff and supporters. Kenny Burns showed his versatility by becoming the inaugural champion, playing off eighteen handicap.

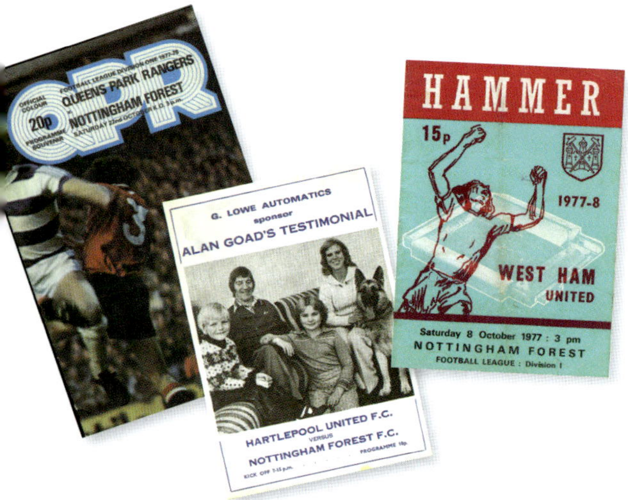

Nottingham Forest were now becoming 'Box office'. The BBC Match of the Day cameras paid their first visit of the season to the City Ground to cover the top versus second clash against Manchester City. They weren't to be disappointed as both teams put on a real show. City were quick out of the blocks and after some good pressure they took a 21st minute lead when Brian Kidd steered home. Forest were then grateful to Colin Barrett for a brilliant tackle that prevented Tueart from extending City's lead before Robertson put the ball on a plate for Woodcock to slide home the equaliser. City again started the second strongly, but sterling defensive work kept them out. Just as in the first half, Forest regained the initiative; O'Neill, Gemmill and Woodcock all going close. It looked as if the game was destined to be a draw, that was until the 86th minute when Robertson jinked his way into the penalty area and looked to have set up Woodcock from close range. Tow the disappointment of the crowd Withe nicked the ball off his toe and the opportunity seemed lost, but Withe turning as slowly as a super tanker, got a scuffed shot away, that wrong footed the bemused Corrigan in the Manchester goal and went in. The crowd went delirious and there is a fantastic picture of Ian Bowyer laughing as the players made their way back to the half way line. Ian who always enjoyed putting one over his old team, had been 'having words', with City's Asa Hartford all afternoon and was now enjoying his own moment of huge satisfaction at the outcome. Forest had faced their sternest test yet and come through with flying colours. Even the national media were forced to admit that something was stirring in the Forest. Brian Clough was not so happy, choosing his post match press conference to launch an attack on Forest fans; those who either didn't attend, shouted obscenities or didn't give the players the backing they deserved.

The following Monday saw a testimonial game for John Harris the Sheffield United manager and a story that encapsulates Brian Clough totally. As usual, Clough had sent up a full squad for a game, he chose not to attend, leaving team matters to Jimmy Gordon. The Forest players, who had a heavy workload, were taking the game quite easily and returned to the dressing room with the score at 1-1. Suddenly the dressing room door flew open and in charged Brian Clough, his face contorted with anger as he tore into the players and told them in no uncertain terms to get out there and do their job. The players with their ears burning went out and hit five goals past a surprised United. Another lesson learned, the boss expects certain standards, even when he is not there and woe betide anyone who does not live up to them. Meanwhile, The Football Association had invited applications for the role of England football manager and the public had decided that there was only one man for the job. Brian Clough used his contacts in the press to let it be known that he was interested, but he also knew that there would be significant opposition on the selection committee to his application. After all, Ron Greenwood, an establishment type figure currently held the position, albeit in a caretaker capacity. Forest returned to London for the next game, hoping to put on a good show in the capital at Queens Park Rangers. That day, on the BBC's lunchtime Football Focus programme, the presenter, ex Arsenal keeper Bob Wilson was to give Brian Clough more material with which to motivate his team. He was really only articulating what others in the game were thinking, but his choice of words seemed overly churlish, commenting that the Reds were, "Little more than a flash in the pan, a bubble that will soon burst".

Later that day, Bob Wilson saw Forest give what Peter Taylor described as, "Their best display of the season so far", not true, but by commenting on the game in such a contrary manner, Taylor was almost inciting journalists to disagree with him. Rangers were easily brushed aside though, 2-0, Kenny Burns with an exquisite free kick and Bowyer with the goals.

Post match Brian Clough joined in and took aim with both barrels, "People in the journalistic industry don't do themselves any credit at all, then that bloody Bob Wilson, who's never been a manager in his life committed the sin of saying our bubble will burst or something like that. If you don't know what you are talking about, don't talk". Ken Smales in his programme column the following week was even more strident, comparing critics to 'circling vultures' who would be waiting a long time before they could pick over the carcass. Forest had been drawn at home to Notts County in the third round of the League Cup, presenting the Magpies

with yet another chance to put one over the Reds. In a sign of how different things now were, Forest even with seventeen year old Chris Woods making his debut in place of cup tied Shilton and also missing Gemmill, brushed aside their local rivals with consummate ease, winning the tie 4-0. The first came from a penalty after the returning Sammy Chapman fouled Woodcock in the box. In the space of just four months the chasm between the two teams had become massive, players had not only absorbed the lessons of playing in the top flight, but had improved from the experience.

The main talking point of the evening however was the large billboard that greeted fans in the Trent End when they entered the ground. 'Gentleman, no swearing please, Brian'. The manager was getting fed up with the fans, not only with the hooliganism, but with the foul language emanating mainly from the Trent End and had arranged for this board to get his point over.

This was his way of trying to influence the fans behaviour, although those who were seated next to him during a game might have thought there was a touch of hypocrisy about his campaign. Anyway, for a few weeks at least, the fans responded with, "What the flippin' heck was that?", and other such variations.

Goals continued to flow when Middlesbrough came to the City Ground, they left with their tail between their legs after being thumped 4-0. Viv Anderson scoring two first half goals, one a right foot pile driver the other a replica, but with his left foot. This time it was Martin O'Neill's turn to be left out to accommodate Gemmill.

Forest's London critics were given further ammunition when they went down 1-0 at Stamford Bridge to Chelsea, a lacklustre game that was settled in the Blues' favour by a goal from Trevor Aylott. Surprisingly Woodcock and Withe had little success against a pair of lumbering centre halves in Mickey Droy and Steve Wicks. The Forest fans' mood was not helped when post match, the FA announced that Brian Clough was on the short list to be interviewed for the England position. Whether the concern over the possibility of losing the manager contributed to it, but the Reds were again below par at home against Manchester United the following Saturday. Due to continuing crowd trouble that surrounded United's away games, they had been banned from attending away fixtures and the matches had been designated all ticket. Forest had issued vouchers at the turnstiles before the cup game against Notts, but an enterprising 1,000 United fans still managed to buy tickets and they were segregated in the usual away section in the East Stand. The match was played out in monsoon like conditions, and United with the wind at their backs took a fifth minute lead through Pearson, before second half goals from Burns, and the rare sight of an Archie Gemmill header, gave Forest the points. The crowd were also treated to the unusual sight of John Robertson missing from the penalty spot.

Off the field, the Forest back room staff were bolstered by the arrival of Ron Fenton, who joined initially as a coach after being sacked by Notts County. Ron was to become one of Brian Clough's most trusted allies at the club until his retirement. Terry Curran's spell at the club also ended when he was allowed to join Derby for a lower than expected fee of £50,000, after completing a loan spell at Bury. Peter Taylor also showed he was not infallible, when luckily for the Reds, Blackpool turned down a bid of £240,000 for their centre forward Micky Walsh.

John Robertson was finally getting the national recognition that his displays deserved. James Lawton writing in the Daily Express said he was, 'Surprised that First Division managers hadn't had the gumption to identify the source of Forest's strength. Surely even a casual observer must have noted that their pale faced, dark haired 24 year old Scottish winger was the man at the heart of it. Whether he is dawdling in a deep position down the left wing or delivering balls of deep penetration early or late, he is clearly the man that matters'. He continued, 'the Middlesbrough full back John Craggs was forced to leave the pitch early recently, some said for treatment on a bruised leg, others that he was in need of some dramatic spiritual repair'.

The Leeds United game played on November 19th was a landmark occasion as it was the last league defeat Forest were to suffer, not only for this season but for over a calendar year as they remained unbeaten for forty two games. The game was a fine spectacle, only settled by one goal after a groggy Peter Shilton was beaten by an effort from Ray Hankin. It was an uncomfortable afternoon for both Brian Clough and John McGovern who were both jeered constantly by the home crowd. Ian Bowyer remembers how disappointed the players were in not getting the result that the management wanted. Forest took advantage of their position as league leaders by pulling in a flying visit to Israel to play a lucrative friendly against Maccabi Tel Aviv. Plenty of sightseeing and a 6-1 victory, but as was to be the case on numerous occasions after foreign jaunts, they were held to a 0-0 draw at home to West Brom on their return.

There was a distinct difference between going off to Spain for a few days relaxation as they often did, compared to embarking on an exhausting plane journey, coupled with a game, often returning home to play a competitive fixture with less than twenty fours preparation time. Indeed, Forest were often on the end of a surprise result after such a trip.

Chris Woods and Chick Thomson

Dave Needham

Clough perhaps didn't help his England chances when he criticised England committee member and West Brom Chairman Bert Millichip for not giving Ronnie Allen, the Baggies' manager a contract, Millichip told Clough to mind his own business. Brian Clough was using his pursuit of the England job to drum up more support for the team, suggesting higher attendances might persuade him to stay, even if he was offered the job. In fact, this seemed to work, as over £10,000 of season tickets were sold in the seven days after this announcement. Before the League Cup game against Aston Villa, the Supporter's Club mimicked Brian Clough and had their own billboard placed in front of his dugout which read, 'Brian, no leaving please, the gentlemen'. Clough gave the impression that he hadn't noticed as he strode purposefully down the touchline.

The game was all ticket at the request of Aston Villa, who had expressed concern that their fans might not gain admission, this contributed to a lower than expected attendance of 29,000 which contained fewer than 2,000 Villa supporters, although the icy and freezing conditions might also have played their part in dissuading fans. Chris Woods once more took his place in the Forest goal as the Reds tore into their opponents, netting three times in the opening 25 minutes. Robbo once more giving another full back a difficult time, on this occasion John Gidman. After adding a fourth from Tony Woodcock, Forest eased up and allowed Villa a couple of consolation goals, the second from Frank Carrodus slipped under the body of Chris Woods. However, this still couldn't spoil another almost faultless display from the sixteen year old. Forest had now progressed further than ever before in this competition. Brian Clough had taken umbrage with the way the press had reported the Albion game and decided to deal with it in his own inimitable way. Bursting into the press room after the game, he told the assembled reporters, with a few choice words, what he thought of them, before returning several minutes later to repeat it, "In case you didn't hear correctly". The Nottingham Forest defence was now looking almost impenetrable, but Larry Lloyd recalls not receiving what he thought was his due share of the praise, "The boss was always going on about Shilts this, Shilts that, how great Kenny was at reading the game, whilst me, I was always first in, I broke my nose whilst he was strolling around behind me, on his way to Footballer of the Year". Although Larry was smiling whilst he said this.

The game at St Andrews against Birmingham City didn't prove too taxing, a regulation 2-0 win. The only concern was provided by Trevor Francis of the Blues as his quick turn and powerful shot provoked Peter Shilton into what was described as a 'wonder save'. Kenny Burns was heckled on his return, particularly after he meted out some rough treatment to his ex team mate, but not close friend Trevor Francis. The Blues were managed that season by ex England boss Sir Alf Ramsey, but he was not to see the season out, resigning early in the New Year. Only one point separated Forest from their closest rivals Everton, so every game took on extra importance.

Coventry City had also been a surprise package this season, and when they turned up at The City Ground they were lying in fifth place, so were expected to provide a stiff test, but with an emphasis on attack they also leaked a lot of goals. All the goal action was condensed into a five minute spell just before half-time, O'Neill putting the Reds ahead, before Wallace pegged them back and McGovern hit the winner. Forest controlled the second half to run out 2-1 victors.

Worryingly Forest picked up their first serious injury of the season after Larry Lloyd broke his toe and with no real replacement available, it looked as if they would have to enter the transfer market. But who would be the manager to make that decision? Upper most in the thoughts of all Reds' followers was the upcoming Monday's announcement concerning the England job. Clough had been interviewed the previous week along with Ron Greenwood, Lawrie McMenemy, Jack Charlton and Dave Sexton. Brian Clough had come back from the interview in a positive mood having, he thought, charmed the selection committee. "It's ours if it's not bent", he told Taylor.

Of course it wasn't straight, the committee had already decided to give the job to Ron Greenwood, but because of the clamour for Clough, they had to be seen to go through an official process. To add insult, Clough and Taylor were later to be offered a junior position with Young England. Still, the collective sigh of relief from Nottingham could be heard for miles.

The Lloyd injury situation was solved by returning to an old transfer target. Back in August, Forest had offered £100,000 for Dave Needham the Notts County centre half, but County not wishing to alienate their supporters by selling him to the Reds, had instead done a deal with QPR.

Tony Woodcock celebrates after scoring at Old Trafford.

United 0 Forest 1

FOREST HAND MAN UTD A FOOTBALLING LESSON!

Tony Woodcock takes the ball around Paddy Roche the United keeper

Needham who was involved in a relegation battle at Loftus Road didn't take much persuading to return to Nottingham, and Rangers pocketed a quick £40,000 profit on a player they had had for only four months. The player was to make his debut in the cauldron that was Old Trafford only three days later.

It was a whirlwind start to Dave Needham's Forest career, as the player explains, "I know County refused to sell me to Forest during the summer, I can understand why. The pressure was on me to drop in straight away and do well and I was a bit apprehensive about how the fans would accept me after I had spent so long with Notts County, but there was obviously something special about Brian Clough and Peter Taylor and the idea really appealed to me".

In every Championship or cup winning campaign there is always one stand out performance, a result so good and satisfying that everyone is filled with the belief that it is really going to be their year. Nottingham Forest's came on December 17th 1977, when in front of the BBC Match of the Day cameras they produced the sort of display that killed off any thoughts that they were a, 'flash in the pan'. They took Manchester United apart, winning 4-0 in the most ruthless and clinical display seen for many a year. Barry Davies commentating, was moved to say as the players left the pitch at full time that, "United have just been buried in their own back yard". In truth, this wasn't a vintage United team, but they were always a formidable outfit at home and this was a proper hammering.

Clough said, "We gave them a lesson in skill, and at Old Trafford the place where football is supposed to count for everything". Breaking quickly and precisely, United didn't know what had hit them as Forest turned defence into attack in the blink of an eye. Dave Needham had gone from the bottom of the table and a home defeat to Newcastle, to the pinnacle and afterwards he paid tribute to his new team mates, "They couldn't have made me feel more welcome, I slotted in as if I had played with them for years".

Dave Sexton the United manager said, "They don't play with eleven men, they seem to have sixteen or seventeen". That evening Peter Taylor told the chairman, "I hope you've enjoyed the football you've seen this season because you won't see us play like that again". He had reasoned that the route to success in future would be based on meanness and method, the buccaneering style to be replaced by a strong defence and counter attack.

The way the fixtures fell that season, meant there were no further games for the Reds before the Boxing Day encounter with the league's most formidable team, Liverpool, current champions. This was to be the first of four games crammed into only eight days over the festive period. Officially over 47,000 fans paid to watch this game, but with thousands crammed around the pitch and left outside, it felt like more. Liverpool might have been in third place, but they were the benchmark against which you measured your achievements. Clough tried to boost the dressing room when he intimated that Bob Paisley had told his players that they must match the Forest player's efforts to contain them. It might have been mind games but by now the manager could tell them that Father Christmas was real and they would have believed him.

Football Post, Saturday, December 17, 1977

4-0 ROUT BY LEADERS

Forest rip United to tatters

JOHN LAWSON at Old Trafford

RAMPANT Nottingham Forest survived Manchester United's early attacking fury to reveal the class expected of ...

SCOTTISH (Premier Division)

Clydebank	0	Ayr	...
Half-time: 0-1			
Dundee U	2	Partick	
Half-time: 1-1			
Hibernian	2	Aberdeen	
Half-time: 1-0			
Rangers	3	Motherwell	
Half-time: 1-0			
St Mirren	3	Celtic	...
Half-time: 1-1			

Liverpool were the reigning League Champions and had also won the European Cup. Kevin Keegan may have left to join Hamburg, but they had replaced him with an even better player in Kenny Dalglish, so the scene was set for an encounter between the two best teams in the league. The fans weren't to be disappointed as both teams went all out. Forest though exploded into the game, Robertson quickly gaining ascendancy over Phil Neal, chances were created and missed, until finally in the 21st minute Gemmill fired home after a scintillating move. Forest continued to dominate until one moment of slack defending allowed Heighway to prod home after the ball wasn't cleared, Clough would have been seething. Liverpool, afraid of the Forest speed, used their vast experience to kill the game, judiciously time wasting and continually knocking the ball back to Ray Clemence, ('Back to Raymond', as the Trent End sang). They took all the sting out of the game and ruined what had been up to that point a great spectacle. Forest then suffered what they thought was a final piece of injustice, when referee Derek Civil turned down a stonewall penalty, after Woodcock was bundled over by Ray Kennedy. They might have only drawn, but when news came through that Manchester United had won 6-2 at Everton, it meant that the lead at the top was extended to three points.

Two days later on a snowy cold evening at St James Park, Forest barely needed to break sweat as they won 2-0, Needham who offered far more of a goal threat than Lloyd, opened his Reds' account with a near post header from a Robertson corner. Brian Clough when interviewed after the game said, "When we go away from home we have to give Shilton the match ball afterwards, because he has seen so little of it during the game".

Just three days later another comfortable away win, 3-1 at Bristol City, Needham scoring again, (the first time the club had recorded four successive away victories since 1894) meaning that Forest entered the New Year with a more than healthy five point lead at the top. Forest were backed by another massive following, (even more impressive when you remember that this was New Year's Eve), including two full trains of supporters that didn't make it back into Nottingham until after 9.00pm leaving little time for traditional celebrations.

In his programme notes for the first home game of the New Year against second place Everton, Ken Smales laid out exactly how far the club had to travel off the pitch to keep pace with success on it. The club had a pitiful 7,200 seats compared to other clubs that had over 20,000 and they would be forced during the close season to spend money on terracing, toilets and general ground improvements just to obtain a new safety licence. The training ground was a patch of land alongside the River Trent that was prone to flooding and the club had no indoor training facilities of their own. If they qualified for Europe, significant money would also have to be spent on upgrading the floodlights and the press facilities would have to be expanded. So Ken rightly pointed out that those fans who were moaning about the time it took to gain entry or waiting in tea bar queues, should perhaps, just appreciate these momentus times instead.

Everton who had suffered two heavy defeats recently, came to the City Ground determined to keep it tight, but it was to be referee Ray Toseland, who was to take centre stage with a series of baffling decisions. Firstly in the 25th minute he awarded the Reds a penalty, when nobody in the ground saw any offence. Robertson took full advantage by scoring, but it was in the second half when the referee came into his own, disallowing what many thought were two legitimate Forest goals, and then missing a clear penalty when Darracott tripped Robertson. His final act was to award a penalty to Everton, when he thought that he saw Burns handle a Duncan McKenzie header to give Ross the chance to salvage a point in the 85th minute. Even the Reds' players who were warned never to dispute decisions appealed this one. Somehow Everton had escaped with a point.

As an illustration of the spending power of clubs that the Reds were now competing against, January saw Manchester United splash out £350,000 on centre forward Joe Jordan from Leeds and Liverpool almost £400,000 on Graeme Souness, a player who Peter Taylor had long admired, but presently Forest couldn't afford.

Nottingham Forest were now attacking trophies on three fronts. Out of the next twelve games, eight would be cup ties, beginning with a home encounter against Swindon in the FA Cup. No worries about the unavailability of players for this competition, a full strength side brushed aside the Railwaymen 4-1.

It was a measure of the success that the club was now enjoying, that the visit to the Baseball Ground was no longer considered the highlight of the season. The usual big following might have been disappointed with only a draw, but Derby fans celebrated the point gained as if they had won the cup. Terry Curran who had joined Derby shortly before, had been desperate to make an impression, but save for a couple of runs he was generally held in check, whilst the other Forest 'old boy' John Middleton, had a far more impressive game in goal, keeping a clean sheet in a 0-0 draw.

THERE'S NO HOLDING HIGH-RIDING FOREST

JOHN LAWSON at the City Ground

THE skill and commitment of Nottingham Forest proved too much even for the considerable defensive qualities of title rivals Arsenal in another thrill-packed game, here this afternoon.

Attendance: 35,743

...nd, it soon became like a scene from th... around the Arsenal goal. McGovern

On paper, the League Cup quarter final away at Bury looked a potential banana skin. Bury had disposed of West Brom in the previous round, but once again Forest were in imperious form as they hardly had to break sweat to advance 3-0. Already without Lloyd, they were also unable to call on the 'cup tied' Needham. This meant a reshuffle with Barrett moving to centre back and Frank Clark coming back in at left back. The fans felt so little pressure that there was an impromptu game of football at half-time on the flat area behind the goal in front of the terracing where the Reds' supporters were based, it was all looking too easy.

There was a far bigger challenge on the following Saturday when Arsenal were the visitors. The Gunners had proved to be the only team to have outplayed Forest so far, so the Reds definitely had a point to prove. The fixture had been chosen as the feature game for Match of the Day and this would be the perfect time to re-iterate to ex Arsenal keeper Bob Wilson, the folly of his earlier remarks.

Arsenal were making steady progress in their league campaign, they were lying in fourth position only five points behind the Reds, and in mid-field possessed great talent such as Liam Brady and Graham Rix. It was important that these two players were not allowed to settle. In a barnstorming game on a mudbath of a pitch, that by today's standards would be classed barely playable, Forest ran out worthy winners. McGovern and Gemmill firstly matched their opponents and then gradually strangled the life out of them and by the end of the game they were barely a factor. After a subdued start, the game burst into life when Alan Sunderland forced Shilton into a full length save, before the Reds took a thirty fourth minute lead when Needham powered home a header from a Woodcock corner. Needham had been signed as cover for Larry Lloyd, but already his goals were becoming indispensible. Arsenal came out fast after half-time, Shilton once more called into action, before Forest launched a series of attacks themselves, Jennings twice denying Peter Withe. However, in the 64th minute Forest produced a move of breathtaking speed and simplicity to double their lead.

An Arsenal corner was picked up by Gemmill who fed Withe down the left wing, and as he made steady progress down the touchline, television viewers were treated to the sight of Archie Gemmill racing across the screen towards the Arsenal goal. "Withe hasn't seen him, ...he has now", shouted commentator David Coleman, as the ball flashed across the penalty area in a perfectly timed pass that allowed the unmarked Gemmill to slide the ball past Jennings and into the net. If ever a goal encapsulated a team, this was it. Hard work, skill and speed of thought, represented how the manager wanted to see his team play. As Martin O'Neill comments, "We had no fear that first season. We attacked away from home, there was none of this stuff about soaking up pressure, we just ran them off their feet. At home we were straight at them, just paralysing sides". Forest ended the game in complete ascendancy, only Jennings and wasteful finishing stopped Arsenal being completely humiliated.

Colin Barrett goes close with this effort at the Baseball Ground.

John Robertson curls in the opening goal against Manchester City.

The Reds go close but can't force the ball in to the Derby net.

Peter Withe scores the winner against Man City once more.

REDS MARCH ON ALL THREE FRONTS!!

Dave Needham powers home this header against Arsenal.

Not content with dominating football, the team were invited to make an assault on the 'pop charts' when alongside local group Paper Lace, they recorded a song called, 'We've got the whole world in our hands'. The lyrics paying homage to the team members and also featuring the Trent Enders, recorded during the next home game, 'Mull of Kintyre', sang by the fans can be heard on the record as it fades out. In truth this was a risky enterprise, the team had actually won nothing yet and there was plenty of time for it all to go wrong. Luckily it didn't and the song reached the dizzy heights of 24th in the United Kingdom 'Charts', before becoming a surprise number one hit in a couple of European countries, including Belgium, a damning indictment of their musical taste.

Icy weather was now sweeping the country, leaving a swathe of postponed fixtures in its wake. Forest's fourth round FA Cup game scheduled for the 28th of January against Manchester City was one of them. However, back in those days there was little interference from police about arranging fixtures, so the game was immediately rescheduled for the following Tuesday.

Forest players and management during the recording of 'We've got the whole world in our hands'.

City had now leapfrogged Everton into second place, so this was a genuine top of the table clash. Unlike the league encounter, this time it was Forest who came out hard and fast and they were rewarded with a magnificent 3rd minute strike from John Robertson who expertly curled a right foot shot into the top corner. For the next thirty minutes the Reds battered City, but with Corrigan in inspired form, they were unable to extend their advantage.

City themselves came back strongly into the game before half-time but 1-0 remained the score. The second began much as the first half ended, with City pressing, but an incredible miss from Withe on a rare foray forward should have eased things, before the centre forward made amends when he headed home at the near post from a Robertson cross. The two goal advantage only lasted two minutes as Kidd swept home from close range. You now might have expected City to push on, but it was Forest who continued to take the game to their opponents and they could easily have scored more. Although not a capacity crowd, fans were once more treated to a spectacular game and the club announced record receipts of over £50,000. The odds on Forest now completing an unprecedented treble had been slashed to only 6-1.

As the 'Pools Panel' sat again on the Saturday, it was expected that the City Ground, under water for the latter part of the week would prove unplayable for the visit of Wolves, but after three inspections, referee Derrick Richardson surprisingly gave the go ahead. The poor surface presented no problems and a routine 2-0 win with goals from Woodcock and McGovern. Colin Barrett recalls what it was like playing on such a variety of surfaces back then, "Nowadays all they play on is bowling greens, they never have to worry about the ball bouncing or being ankle deep in mud. We were still trying to play good football, trying to do the right thing, by the end of the season the only grass you might find would be out on the wings". Leeds United stood in the way of a first appearance at Wembley since 1959, in the two legged semi-final of the League Cup. The first game was to take place at Elland Road. Initially Clough and Taylor had decided to stick with the same team that had played at Bury in the previous round, but on the coach to the game they decided instead to drop McGovern back into defence alongside Burns and use John O'Hare in midfield. Leeds had scored lots of goals on route, including hitting four past Everton in the last round and this allied with the 1-0 victory over the Reds earlier in the season filled them with great confidence.

The under soil heating ensured that the game would go ahead. 8,000 Forest fans filled half of the Lowfields' terracing up to the half way line and a substantial area behind the goal that the Reds attacked in the first half. They were ecstatic when two

PAPER LACE

21st minutes gave the Reds a brilliant start. Even Eddie Gray pulling a goal back before half-time couldn't dent the confidence, although Leeds huffed and puffed they rarely created a chance. As so often in football, it was left to ex Leeds player John O'Hare to apply the coup de grace when he fired home after a six man move to give the Reds a two goal advantage in the tie. This time John McGovern could allow himself a small smile of satisfaction as he left the pitch, surely Nottingham Forest were now Wembley bound.

With matches coming thick and fast the Clough methodology of rest and recuperation came into its own. As Colin Barrett describes, "When we did train during the season, it was mostly five a sides. If we played mid week it would be see you Wednesday, without midweek game, see you Thursday. Luckily we had a group of players that didn't abuse the situation. We rarely saw the gaffer down at training, that was usually left to Jimmy Gordon, but if you saw his car or him appear, training immediately went up a notch". Weather continued to play havoc with fixtures, the game at Villa Park was called off as was the second leg against Leeds, although this was so late in the day, that many Leeds fans had arrived for the game and there were clashes between fans in the East Stand car park, until the police arrived to restore order.

The weather relented of sorts, to allow the fifth round FA Cup tie at Loftus Road to go ahead. The pitch, half of which resembled an ice rink was deemed playable, large amounts of sand were spread over the playing surface making it look like a frozen Sahara. Rangers settled to the conditions far better to take a one goal lead and it looked for long periods as if the treble dream was about to end, before Martin O'Neill popped up with a last minute

Archie Gemmill hammers home the opening goal against Liverpool.

Ice cool Robbo from the spot against Everton.

Archie Gemmill in action against Swindon Town.

Woodcock shoots, Clemence saves.

FOREST ENTER THE NEW YEAR STILL ON TOP...

Forest third goal against Swindon.

glancing header to earn a replay, Forest had survived but now faced an extra game. Wembley for the League Cup Final was within touching distance, but all those fans that thought the second leg against Leeds United was a formality, were in for a rude awakening. Leeds had by far the better of the opening exchanges against a subdued Forest team, surely they weren't going to succumb to nerves at the worst possible time. The workload on the players was so heavy at this time, that the management were concerned about tiredness. The schedule for the players during the week of the second leg makes interesting reading: Sunday, off. Monday, a stroll down the banks of the river, followed by half an hour's five a side. Tuesday, off. Wednesday, a ten minute jog, followed by the afternoon in bed, then the game. Thursday, off. Friday, another ten minute jog, followed by a team talk. What other manager would give his players licence to do nothing? Particularly in an era when it was still fashionable to flog footballers into the ground.

Larry Lloyd returned for his first appearance since before Christmas, but it was Frank Gray who was to make an early impact as he fired a twenty five yard thunderbolt past Chris Woods to give the visitors the fillip of an early lead, before Peter Withe, who now only seemed to score cup goals responded with an equaliser. However, within a minute Arthur Graham had put Leeds back in contention and shortly before half-time Tony Currie rattled the Reds' crossbar. Forest were on the ropes, the break couldn't come quick enough. Clough rallied the troops and it was a different team that emerged for the second half, goals from Bowyer, O'Neill and Woodcock destroyed Leeds 7-3 on aggregate and in scenes perhaps never before seen at the City Ground, vast areas around the terracing were filled by fans holding scarves above their heads in a joyous display of colour. Liverpool manager Bob Paisley, whose team had already qualified for the final, popped into the dressing room to congratulate the players, "It's not just about the final" he said, "but the hard work getting there". Whilst he was there he joined Brian Clough in his office for a coin toss to see who would wear their traditional red shirts at Wembley and it was left to young Nigel Clough to do the honours. Forest would be in Red. Ken Smales recalls the celebrations amongst the long serving (and suffering) back room staff who had endured such a barren time before the arrival of Brian Clough. Brian Clough's reponse, "I'm off on holiday", leaving Peter Taylor to look after the team.

This Forest team were always encouraged to play the 'right way' and that included no back chat to the referee. So as well as success on the pitch, it was always satisfying to receive praise for this almost unique sense of fair play that the management team encouraged. In the televised debate between Clough and Revie, on the evening of his sacking from the Leeds' job, Clough had always insisted he wanted to do things better than Revie and on meeting the Leeds' players for the first time he famously said, "Throw all your medals in the bin, because you won them by cheating".

Archie, Scott & Willie.

THREE GENERATIONS OF THE GEMMILL FAMILY.

So the praise from referee Clive Thomas, the official at the Leeds' game, was particularly welcome. "In the entire match, with tensions running high, there was not one whisper of dissent from one Forest player. Forest are a credit to the game, this is Clough's greatest achievement even if they do go on to win the treble".

English football has always been full of managers who talk a good game, their achievements never quite living up to the self promotion, larger than life characters, always good for a quote. John Bond at that time managing Norwich was one of those. He declared in the run up to the Forest game that he had devised a plan, a plan so cunning that it would stop Forest in their tracks. We can only imagine how he was feeling when only twenty four minutes into the game Norwich found themselves three goals down and the Forest fans taunting him with, 'What happened to your plan?'.

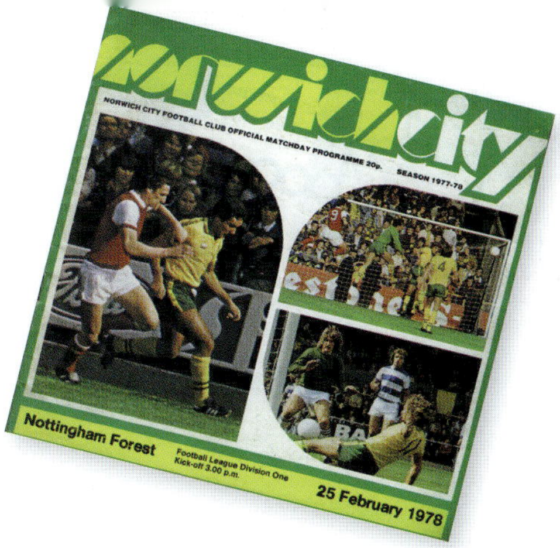

It turned out John Bond's plan was to play ex England hero Martin Peters in a sweeper's role, but let's give Bond some credit, after he switched Peters back into midfield Norwich fought back to draw 3-3. Surely Brian Clough, who missed this game wouldn't have allowed the team to slacken off so much, but they did, the last twenty minutes was a real backs to the wall performance. This was also the first time that Peter Shilton conceded more than one goal in a game since joining the club. John McGovern and Colin Barrett also picked up knocks, Barrett's was the more serious and he was out for the next ten games, that meant he would unluckily for the third time in his career miss out on the opportunity to play at Wembley.

Off the pitch there was sad news that club legend Wally Ardron had passed away. Although he hadn't signed for the club until he was into his thirties, he went on to play 191 times and score 124 goals for the Reds, helping the team to promotion from the old Division Three South along the way. The Commercial Department also announced that they had reached the amazing figure of 10,000 members of the official Supporter's Club, with thirty two branches across the country, from the Trent End to London and with numbers still growing. Ticket prices for Wembley had been announced,

Wally

ranging from £8 for the best £2.50 standing. Members and ticket holders were given the first whilst other supporters could qu tickets if they had enough vouch out from the match day program attached to the official sheet. The m who had missed the draw with N also missed the cup replay wit on the Monday, another disapp performance in front of over 40 the City Ground. Robertson gave the Reds a nineteenth minute lead from the penalty spot, but this was a more resilient Rangers team than earlier in the season and after getting a first half equaliser they held on for a draw despite playing extra time a man short after Clement was sent off. A coin toss in the dressing room was called correctly by McGovern, so the second replay was set to be played once more in Nottingham three days later Thursday. The press meanwhile ha having a field day with the absenc manager, they just couldn't und how he could leave the team at such stage of the season. But Clough wa ahead in his thinking, he knew th his influence on the players could it was overused, that is why he oft himself apart from the players al only appearing in the dressing room minutes before kick-off to elec effect. By the time of the second he was back, "Right you lot, I'v

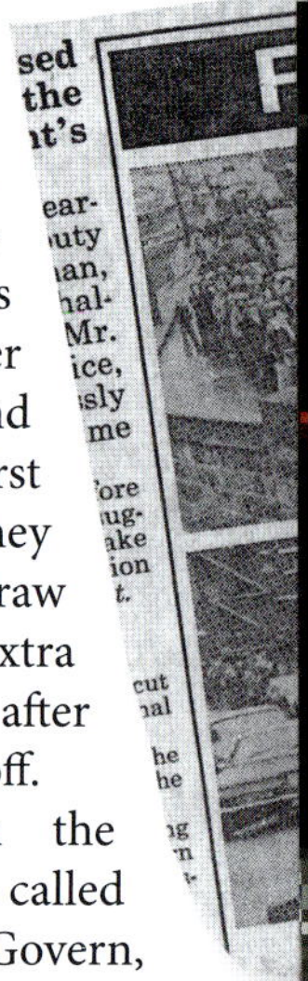

Woodcock scores against Notts County.

Ian Bowyer scores again.

THE REDS MARC

Leeds United 1
Nottingham Forest 3

Withe scores his first against Leeds.

Withe heads home his second.

many referees'
Reds' games at
any team mana
likely to be far
to the strict di
with. Could th
Reds? Pat Part
East like Cloug
him he did not
for Clough an
was effusive in
that they show
video evidence
probably wrong
he was still 'ri

Anyway, Forest
The replay was
following Wed
been due to pl
week and had
Scarborough aft
this game. Eve
now be postp
team thought
the bracing No
beneficial, so th
unaltered. Ove
for tickets, wi
the capacity of
was 55,000, the
Forest would b
change, asking
his groin strain
particularly with
of season to co

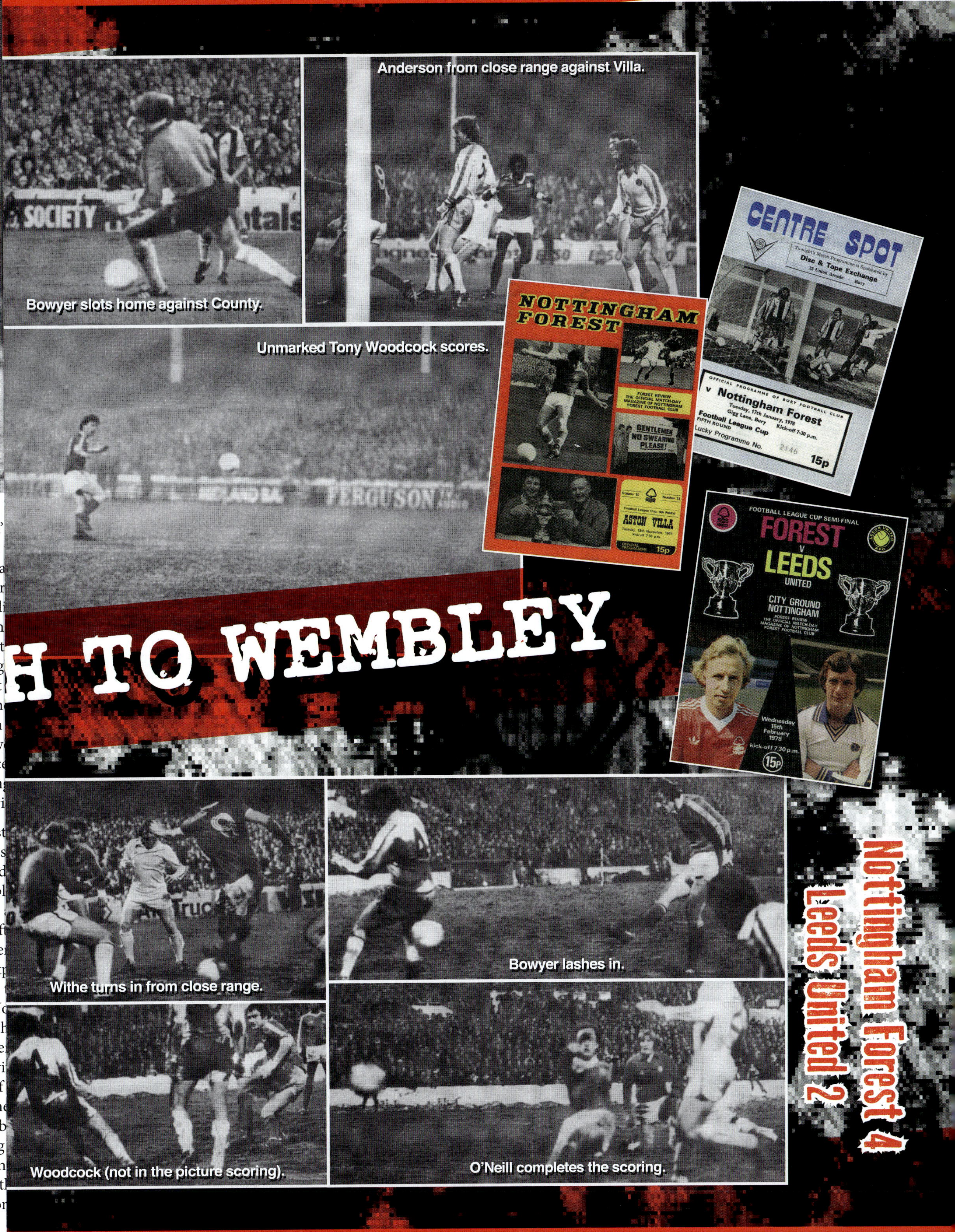

Bowyer slots home against County.

Anderson from close range against Villa.

Unmarked Tony Woodcock scores.

Withe turns in from close range.

Bowyer lashes in.

Woodcock (not in the picture scoring).

O'Neill completes the scoring.

against Leice
out on the W

This was a g
without, whi
the cup, both
closed the g
the Reds had
derby with a
potential ban
were a pitif
relegation. In
penalty was su
an uninspirin
preparations
earnest. The
final, althoug
about tickets
30,000 (14,0
there was no
As part of t
victorious 19
were invited t
along with o
Graham, Terr
Henry Newto
game with the

The team was
had been all
rooms at the
would occup
stadium. The
Committee

and an in
they were dow
Lloyd had m
returning from
McGovern wa
80%, whilst L
the cup tied
they were at fu
game for the p
had entered a
Clough descri
virgins', in co
team that had
the years. Alt
won this con
there would b

LEAGUE CUP FINAL MARCH 18TH ...WEMBLEY STADIUM

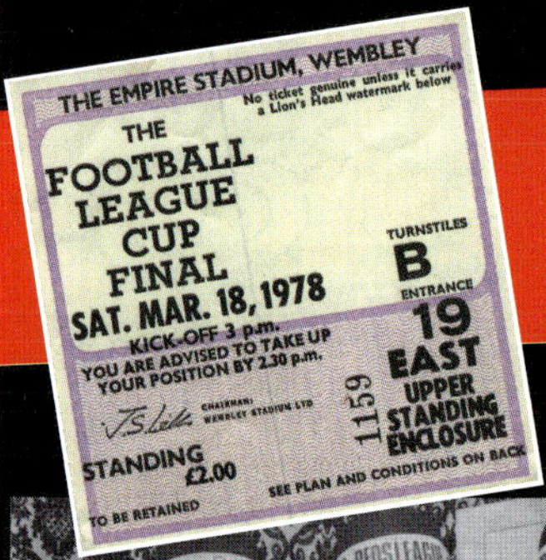

Henry Newton, Terry Hennessey, Ian Moore and to the front Derek Page.

Ian Bowyer bursts powerfully into the Liverpool penalty area.

Martin O'Neill shadows Ian Callaghan.

Steve Heighway tries a speculative shot at goal but, once again, the effort came to nothing.

Nottingham Forest 0 Liverpool 0

Man-of-the-Match, without any doubt, was Forest's teenage goalkeeper Chris Woods, who gave as good a performance as any keeper at Wembley. This time he's covered by sweeper Kenny Burns and England Under 21 full back Viv Anderson.

Chris Woods takes the applause from the Forest supporters as he leaves the Wembley pitch.

Robertson slots home the penalty.

O'Hare takes a tumble.

LEAGUE CUP FINAL REPLAY MARCH 22ND ...OLD TRAFFORD

Robertson fires in another effort.

Nottingham Forest 1 Liverpool 0

TWO NIL!

Dave Needham heads home against West Ham.

O'Hare forces home from close range against Newcastle.

Robertson clinches the game against the Hammers.

Woodcock with the last gasp winner at Villa Park.

REDS CLOSE IN ON THE TITLE!!

to be fouled by a combination of Nattrass and Kennedy as he burst into the area. A second goal from Viv Anderson steadied the nerves. It wasn't a wholly convincing performance, but the two points were gratefully accepted.

The annual PFA player awards dinner was held in London, and not surprisingly the players of Nottingham Forest figured prominently. Peter Shilton was given the senior award, with Archie Gemmill in second place and John Robertson also on the final list. Whilst Tony Woodcock was presented with the Young Player of the Season award. The Reds were quickly back in action, playing Middlesbrough in the fixture that had been cancelled a few weeks earlier. Forest twice went behind, but still summoned up the fighting spirit to secure a draw, although they were the team hanging on for the final whistle, especially after David Mills had headed wide, when even Shilton had given up. Amazingly in view of his reputation, Kenny Burns picked up his first booking of the season. Larry Lloyd and Dave Needham had alternated at times for the centre half position. Needham's unavailability for the League Cup and Lloyd's niggling injuries had forced the issue on several occasions. However, whereas the manager swung towards Needham for his goals and better passing, when it came down to it, he preferred the hardness of Lloyd, sometimes thinking that Needham was too nice for this position, but he was lucky to be served by two outstanding players.

By the time Forest took to the field for the home encounter with Chelsea, their lead at the top had been cut to only two points. Gordon Lee the Everton manager may have complained about his team having to play three times over Easter, but they had picked up a maximum six points to put themselves right back in contention. Chelsea and Wolves who had been promoted along with Forest were languishing in seventeenth and eighteenth place, emphasising the great strides that Forest had made in comparison.

The Chelsea team that visited the City Ground looked bland and boring compared to the vibrant team of the previous season. Somehow they took an early lead through Tommy Langley and then immediately set about defending that lead for the rest of the game. Continually riding their luck, they held on. Peter Bonetti who had enjoyed a fantastic career with the Blues looked a

Robertson completes the scoring with the third goal against Chelsea.

shadow of his former self, often flailing around and twice the referee came to his rescue, disallowing goals after he had been buffeted. In a rare tactical switch, the manager took off Archie Gemmill and moved Ian Bowyer from right back, into mid-field, putting substitute Colin Barrett in his place. This change worked almost immediately, Burns heading home the equaliser. Forest now laid siege to the Chelsea goal, only desperate defending kept the Reds at bay. Their resistance was finally broken in the 82nd minute, when a piledriver from O'Neill almost took the net off and then five minutes later an unstoppable shot from Robertson sealed the game. Meanwhile Everton continued their winning ways with a fifth successive victory to still remain only two points behind. Yet again, Brian Clough had committed the team for a testimonial game on the Monday, only two days before another vital game at Villa. This time the beneficiary was old Forest favourite Henry Newton and the opponents Derby. Forest took a full strength side to the Baseball Ground, as Clough told the players, "It says Nottingham Forest on the programme, not Nottingham Forest reserves".

Forest were coming under increasing pressure every time they took to the pitch. Every team was raising their game, hoping to be the first team to defeat them in a league game since November. Aston Villa were no different and they dominated the game, which was played in tornado like conditions. The Reds were lucky when referee Eric Hughes came to Forest's rescue when he missed Kenny Burns blatant handball, that kept out a Gordan Cowan's effort. The 'smash and grab' raid was completed with a move of sublime simplicity. A Robertson dart and cross, followed by a Woodcock header that won the points in front of the Holte End. Even better news for the players as they entered the dressing room, Everton had lost 1-0 to arch rivals Liverpool, leaving Forest with a four point lead and three games in hand on their closest rivals.

Surprisingly in light of the fixtures Forest still had left to play, they had no game on the Saturday. They had been due to play West Brom, but they were involved in an FA Cup semi final against Ipswich.

So it was not until the following Tuesday that they went to Maine Road to take on Manchester City. Forest supporters were on the receiving end of rough treatment this evening, as those fans that took the train to Manchester were made to walk to the ground through the Moss Side with little police presence. On the pitch there was a welcome return to form. The game might have finished 0-0 but the Reds had by far the better of the exchanges. Tony Woodcock was causing the City defence all sorts of problems and Mike Doyle resorted to his usual tactic of rough play, the referee finally losing patience with him and booking him after his third foul on the same player in only ten minutes. This harsh treatment continued and the referee must have been the only person in the ground that didn't see the foul on Woodcock that should have resulted in a penalty. Another clean sheet and an impressive return for Colin Barrett, how had City let him go for only £30,000?

It is scarcely believable that Forest sent out another full strength side the following evening for the Les Bradd testimonial game at Meadow Lane, over 10,000 turned up to ensure a bumper payout for the popular player. With two successive home games against Leeds and QPR coming up, Forest had the chance to wrap up the title on home soil. Injuries again were taking their toll, Woodcock was forced to miss the Leeds game and the versatile Bowyer was now asked to partner Withe up front.

In a nondescript game, Leeds took the lead late in the first half with a Frank Gray penalty, before Withe equalised, netting only his second league goal since October. For a team with a reputation for free flowing football, the lack of goals from the centre forward position would surely need addressing. By now Forest and QPR must have been sick of the sight of each other. The Tuesday game would be the fifth time they had faced off, and in this game it showed. Rangers stuck to their plan of attempting to cut off the supply to Robertson, whilst packing mid-field. It took yet another first half penalty from

Furious Forest launch a blitz

By STEVE McGILL Forest 3 Chelsea 1

YOU'VE got to hand it to Forest Brian Clough's champions (surely they won't let it slip now) hammered three goals in 22 minutes.

And the pressure had really been on too — with Chelsea scenting their second win of the season over them.

If brave Bonetti had not let a simple Burns header slip from his grasp, Forest could well have fallen ... forward like angry bees after

Robertson to claim the points, but it all felt a slightly anti-climactic way to clinch the title (two teams could match the Reds on points, but they were twenty goals behind on goal difference). To make it mathematically certain, another point was needed from the trip to Highfield Road to play Coventry. This would give Forest the title with four games to spare. The Sky Blues played their part, giving the Reds 12,000 tickets for the game. Viv Anderson returned to the line-up, but McGovern, Woodcock and Lloyd were missing. Lloyd was particularly upset, as the chance to clinch the title at the club that had written him off would have been extra satisfying, still the player had the last laugh with Jimmy Hill. This game's other major talking points, were the two magnificent Peter Shilton saves from Mick Ferguson, that won Forest the vital league clinching point. In particular, the close range header Shilton turned over the bar had echoes of Gordon Banks' save from Pele in the Mexico World Cup of 1970. It was yet another robust back to the walls display. Kenny Burns was the stand out player, as Forest, without Woodcock's pace, looked one dimensional in attack. Peter Taylor talking immediately after the game said, "We need two players to win the title again, we have identified them, now we need to go and get them".

As the match finished, the Forest fans had been asked to remain in place on the terraces so that the players could return to salute them. However, as the home team, Coventry fans were in no mood to stick to the script, they invaded the pitch and taunted the Reds' supporters. Initially they were ignored, but gradually a trickle and then a deluge got onto the pitch to confront them. The police then moved into action to keep fans apart. Too late, the disorder meant that under police instructions the players weren't allowed back out. In the dressing John McGovern remembers the atmosphere being slightly muted, it was the satisfaction of a job well done, but none of the excessive, over the top champagne celebrations that are common place today, seemingly for any kind of success. Peter Taylor recalls how the management dealt with things, "Brian and I used to switch roles after a game, before he would be bullish, but the games used to drain him, whereas for me, it was a release from the tension". The club had announced that Clough and Taylor had been granted a testimonial game against Derby, it couldn't have been easy for them to accept, seeing their closest rivals celebrating Championship success. The game was scheduled for the first of May, this meant that the team would play four games in only six days to end the season.

The away game at Ipswich was to be especially memorable for one player in particular, Frank Clark, who was to score the first and only league goal of his career spanning over 500 appearances. The evening had not started well for many Forest fans, hundreds missed the start of the game, after the Forestrail train was held up en route. In truth this encounter had an end of season feel to it, the Forest management definitely wanted to avoid defeat, but Ipswich who had reached the FA Cup final, looked as if they were set on avoiding any injuries. The game also turned out to have repercussions for another player, when, as Peter Taylor described it later, during the first half he turned to Clough and said let's pull him off and sell him for the best offer. He was talking about Peter Withe, as Taylor thought that they might have seen the best of him. At half-time they subbed him and sent on Frank Clark. As Clark recalls, "When they took Peter off, I thought that they would shuffle the pack so I could play in defence, but then Brian says, "Go and play centre forward, you can't do any worse than that big bugger over there". So the front two ended up being me and Archie Gemmill. I remember we had a corner and the ball dropped to me in the six yard box and bang, I hammered home, the celebrations were something else, nobody could quite believe I had scored".

The League Championship Trophy was presented before the game against Birmingham City. John McGovern finally getting his hands on a trophy before anyone else. There were great scenes as the players began their lap of honour, Brian Clough leading the applause as the club celebrated for the first and only time in their history, the accolade of being League Champions. In retrospect they should have saved the presentation for after the game, although the match itself was a good one, there was a feeling of, 'after the Lord Mayor's show', about the occasion. Despite a strong showing by the Blues, relieved of any relegation worries, it was another clean sheet for Shilton in a 0-0 draw.

Brian Clough was once more in the spotlight on the day of his and Taylor's testimonial game. He gathered together a group of Nottingham Constabulary, gave them the trophies and they joined with the players for various photo opportunities. Once more, Clough was placing himself on the right side of the law. Just two games left of a season that consisted of fifty six competitive fixtures, plus a whole host of friendly and testimonial games. All this achieved with a squad of only sixteen players to choose from. The aim now was to finish the season unbeaten. This would

WE ASK, VIV ANDERSON ANSWERS

FULL NAME: Vivian Anderson
BIRTHPLACE: Nottingham
BIRTHDATE: 29th July, 1956
HEIGHT: 6ft 1in
WEIGHT: 11st 7lb
PREVIOUS CLUBS: None
MARRIED: No
CAR: No
FAVOURITE PLAYER: I have many
FAVOURITE OTHER TEAM: Manchester United
MOST DIFFICULT OPPONENT: They're all difficult
MOST MEMORABLE MATCH: Beating United 4-0 at Old Trafford this season
BIGGEST THRILL: Winning promotion
BIGGEST DISAPPOINTMENT: Being injured — and losing
BEST COUNTRY VISITED: Switzerland
FAVOURITE FOOD: Steak and gammon
MISCELLANEOUS LIKES: Tennis, squash, snooker
MISCELLANEOUS DISLIKES: Bad manners, 12-1 o'clock on Saturdays
FAVOURITE T.V. SHOWS: When The Boat Comes In, all sports programmes
FAVOURITE SINGERS: I have lots
FAVOURITE ACTOR/ACTRESS: Clint Eastwood, Hilda Ogden from Coronation Street
BEST FRIEND: I hope I have many
BIGGEST INFLUENCE ON CAREER: The Forest staff, in particular Bert Johnson (now with Derby)
BIGGEST DRAG IN SOCCER: Travelling, losing
INTERNATIONAL HONOURS: None
PERSONAL AMBITION: To be happy and successful
PROFESSIONAL AMBITION: One day, to play for England
IF YOU WEREN'T A FOOTBALLER WHAT DO YOU THINK YOU'D BE? No idea
WHICH PERSON IN THE WORLD WOULD YOU MOST LIKE TO MEET? Clint Eastwood

CHAMPIONS AT LAST...

Shilton produces a world clas save to defy Mick Ferguson of Coventry.

O'Neill goes close against West Ham.

Peter Withe turns the ball in to the Leeds United net.

not be easy, first up West Brom who had beaten the Reds in the FA Cup and were having a good league campaign as well, lying in sixth place. This time the Reds managed to score twice in a 2-2 draw.

The final game fittingly, was away at Liverpool, the previous season's champions, who had by now leapfrogged Everton into second place after picking up sixteen points from their last nine games. Their players were also extra determined to get a positive result against Forest, the perceived injustice of the League Cup Final still rankled.

The Friday night encounter came just two days after the Albion game and also clashed with the Sportswriter's Awards Dinner held in London, where Kenny Burns was expected to pick up the main award. The manager tried to get the fixture changed, but with Liverpool once more contesting the European Cup Final, this was not possible. So the manager made the brave decision to allow Kenny Burns to miss the fixture so that he could pick up his trophy in person. Kenny had travelled so far in such a short space of time. The journey from so called 'wildman' of football, to award winning sweeper, is worthy of its own book, a real life story of redemption. In all honesty Kenny was never as bad as he was painted out to be, but he certainly had his demons at times on the pitch. When Brian Clough had told Sammy Chapman how he wished he had managed the player when he was younger, you can only imagine how that player's career might have turned out. Kenny, accompanied by Forest Chairman Brian Appleby travelled down to the Cafe Royal and with some irony was presented with his trophy by Glaswegian comedian Billy Connolly.

If the management team had any qualms about playing Liverpool without their stopper, it didn't show. The expected recall of Needham to replace Burns didn't happen, instead Colin Barrett slipped in with Clark going to left back. Even though they were also without Woodcock, Forest gave a good account of themselves and although they weren't to know it at the time, this match was not only a rehearsal for next season's European Cup, but also a blueprint of how to stifle Liverpool. Liverpool might have started the game strongly, but by the end they seemed to have run out of ideas as the fixture ended 0-0, thus completing an extraordinary run of 26 unbeaten league games for Nottingham Forest. How do you sum up such a season? Although there had been the usual optimism from Peter Taylor, the bookies had Forest down as one of the favourites for relegation, after all they had only just scraped promotion. No-one had thought to insert bonuses for winning the title or reaching Wembley into contracts, why should they. But once again almost everyone had underestimated the 'Clough effect'. We know that many of the players suffered from self doubts going into the season, but they all rose magnificently to the challenges. In particular Anderson, Woodcock, O'Neill and Robertson, who all blossomed in a higher grade of football. To call them misfits was insulting at the time and more so now when you realise that it has taken almost forty years for them to receive their true recognition.

It was a great team, well constructed and brilliantly managed and perhaps unlucky not to win an unprecedented 'treble'. It would seem strange to modern day Reds' supporters, but at the time, it didn't feel that unusual that Forest were on top of the football world. There was an expectation that with Brian Clough and Peter Taylor, anything was possible, just enjoy the ride. New signings were expected, there were plans for redeveloping the ground and of course European football to look forward to. Time to get the maps out, where would our first port of call be, Madrid, perhaps Turin, not long to wait now.

POST
6
NOTTINGHAM, MONDAY, APRIL 24, 1978
PRICE 8p
Pools
Your Distributor for "STANLEY" HAND TOOLS
POOLS TOOL CO. LTD., Carlton Street, Nottingham

We've won the League . . . happy Forest fans salute their heroes from the terraces at Coventry after the Reds had got that all-important point.

28 Evening Post, Wednesday, April 26, 1978

CLARK ON THE MARK AT LAST!

IPSWICH . . . 0 FOREST . . . 2

MAKESHIFT striker Frank Clark gleefully ended his career-long search for a League goal as Nottingham Forest's championship joy continued at Portman Road last night.

By John Lawson

Clark, a second half substitute for Peter Withe, sealed a Forest victory after an own goal by Paul Mariner had given them the lead.

Both goals came in a four minute period in the second half. The first can be written off as the most uneventful I have seen this season.

But Clark's goal brought the game to life, and even if the full significance of it was lost on most of the crowd, there was no disguising the delight in the Forest camp.

Players rushed from all angles to congratulate him and manager Brian Clough left from his seat in the dug-out to add his applause.

For 45 minutes a mixture of newly-crowned champions and FA Cup finalists did not lend itself to entertainment and there were long periods of dull, aimless football.

Happier

Ipswich's initial fire was soon dampened when Kenny Burns and a much happier David Needham established aerial control over Paul Mariner and Trevor Whymark, fighting for his place at Wembley.

It was Forest who provided the first real goal attempt in the 15th minute when Ian Bowyer found Peter White, who chested down for Martin O'Neill to shoot into Paul Cooper's arms.

Then John Robertson

and George Burley in quick succession.

Following a typical piece of O'Hare control outside the box, Barrett found space for another effort on the turn that went wide with Cooper diving anxiously across his goal.

Then Ipswich were in trouble when Bowyer broke up an attack to send Archie Gemmill sprinting clear from the halfway line for an angled drive that Cooper turned aside.

Over

Clark then responded quickly to O'Neill's intentions and played a one-two that opened up a gap until Ipswich defenders closed in just in time.

But in the 73rd and 77th minutes Forest scored the goals that their second half improvement promised.

The first was a tragedy for Mariner, back in his own box for a Barrett corner. It cleared both Needham and Russell Osman and when Mariner attempted to lob the ball back for Cooper he only succeeded in lifting it over the keeper and into the net via a post.

Then Clark grabbed his moment of individual glory. Following a probing run by Gemmill, O'Hare had a fierce shot blocked and when the ball dropped invitingly for Clark he lashed it home.

POOR LIONS CRASH

LEICESTER Lions were soundly trounced 46-32 by the aces of Manchester's Belle Vue side in their Gulf British League match at Blackbird Road last night.

Lions riders managed to win just two of the 13 races. Tom Godal, riding at number six, picked up three points in the second heat and Lions skipper John Bulger did the same in a nail-biting finish with Belle Vue's Alan Wilkinson in the tenth.

To complete a dismal night for the Lions they had two riders injured in a spectacular crash on the last lap of the eighth race.

KENNY BURNS

Forest into
Europe
FOREST
Celebrating The Reds'
Triumphant Season

NOTTINGHAM Forest had their most memorable season in 1977/78 by becoming the first side to win the double of League Championship and League Cup. That hardly tells the story of Fabulous Forest, who, as their manager Brian Clough would say, have done it with style. Clough and right-hand man Peter Taylor had a testimonial on May Day, where the trophies were proudly paraded. Our photographer was at the City Ground...

Captain John McGover

FOREST MAKE HISTORY

CRAZY

FACTS and FIGURES

Aug 15th 1977, CC, H, v. Notts County, Draw 1-1, Scorer Bowyer, AT 11,569, Middleton, Anderson, Clark, McGovern, Lloyd, Burns, O'Neill, Bowyer, Withe, Woodcock, Robertson.

Aug 20th 1977, A, v. Everton, Win 3-1, Scorers O'Neill, Withe, Robertson, AT 38,001, Middleton, Anderson, Clark, McGovern, Lloyd, Burns, O'Neill, Bowyer, Withe, Woodcock, Robertson.

Aug 23rd 1977, H, v. Bristol City, Win 1-0, Scorer Withe, AT 21,743, Middleton, Anderson, Clark, McGovern, Lloyd, Burns, O'Neill, Bowyer, Withe, Woodcock, Robertson.

Aug 27th 1977, H, v. Derby County, Win 3-0, Scorers Withe (2), Robertson, AT 28,807, Middleton, Anderson, Clark, McGovern, Lloyd, Burns, O'Neill, Bowyer, Withe, Woodcock, Robertson.

Aug 30th 1977, LC, H, v. West Ham United, Win 5-0, Scorers O'Neill, Bowyer (2), Withe, Woodcock, AT 18,224, Middleton, Anderson, Clark, McGovern, Lloyd, Burns, O'Neill, Bowyer, Withe, Woodcock, Robertson.

Sept 3rd 1977, A, v. Arsenal, Loss 0-3, AT 40,810, Middleton, Anderson, Clark, McGovern, Lloyd, Burns, O'Neill, Bowyer, Withe, Woodcock, Robertson, SUB Barrett.

Sept 10th, 1977, A, v. Wolverhampton Wanderers, Win 3-2, Scorers: Bowyer, Withe, Woodcock, AT 24,622, Middleton, Anderson, Barrett, McGovern, Lloyd, Burns, O'Neill, Bowyer, Withe, Woodcock, Robertson.

Sept 17th 1977, H, v. Aston Villa, Win 2-0, Scorers Woodcock, Robertson, AT 31,016, Shilton, Anderson, Barrett, McGovern, Lloyd, Burns, O'Neill, Bowyer, Withe, Woodcock, Robertson.

Sept 24th 1977, A, v. Leicester City, Win 3-0, Scorers O'Neill, Woodcock, Robertson, AT 21,447, Shilton, Anderson, Barrett, McGovern, Lloyd, Burns, O'Neill, Bowyer, O'Hare, Woodcock, Robertson.

Oct 1st 1977, H, v. Norwich City, Draw 1-1, Scorer Burns, AT 23,741, Shilton, Anderson, Barrett, Bowyer, Lloyd, Burns, O'Neill, Gemmill, Withe, Woodcock, Robertson.

Oct 4th 1977, H, v. Ipswich Town, Win 4-0, Scorer Withe (4), AT 26,845, Shilton, Anderson, Barrett, McGovern, Lloyd, Burns, O'Neill, Bowyer, Withe, Woodcock, Robertson.

Oct 8th 1977, A, v. West Ham United, Draw 0-0, AT 26,126, Shilton, Anderson, Barrett, McGovern, Lloyd, Burns, O'Neill, Bowyer, Withe, Woodcock, Robertson, SUB Gemmill

Oct 15th 1977, H, v. Man City, Win 2-1, Scorers Withe, Woodcock, AT 35,572, Shilton, Anderson, Barrett, McGovern, Lloyd, Burns, O'Neill, Bowyer, Withe, Woodcock, Robertson, SUB Gemmill.

Oct 22nd 1977, A, v. QPR, Win 2-0, Scorers Burns, Bowyer, AT 24,449, Shilton, Anderson, Barrett, Gemmill, Lloyd, Burns, O'Neill, Bowyer, Withe, Woodcock, Robertson.

Oct 25th 1977, LC, H, v. Notts County, Win 4-0, Scorers Bowyer (2), Woodcock, Robertson (Pen), AT 26,931, Woods, Anderson, Barrett, McGovern, Lloyd, Burns, O'Neill, Bowyer, Withe, Woodcock, Robertson.

Oct 29th 1977, H, v. Middlesbrough, Win 4-0, Scorers Anderson (2), McGovern, Bowyer, AT 27,373, Shilton, Anderson, Barrett, McGovern, Lloyd, Burns, Gemmill, Bowyer, Withe, Woodcock, Robertson, SUB O'Neill.

Nov 5th 1977, A, v. Chelsea, Loss 0-1, AT 36,116, Shilton, Anderson, Barrett, McGovern, Lloyd, Burns, Gemmill, Bowyer, Withe, Woodcock, Robertson, SUB O'Neill.

Nov 12th 1977, H, v. Man United, Win 2-1, Scorers Burns, Gemmill, AT 30,183, Shilton, Anderson, Barrett, McGovern, Lloyd, Burns, Gemmill, Bowyer, Withe, Woodcock, Robertson.

Nov 19th 1977, A, v. Leeds United, Loss 0-1, AT 42,925, Shilton, Anderson, Barrett, McGovern, Lloyd, Burns, Gemmill, Bowyer, Withe, Woodcock, Robertson.

Nov 26th 1977, H, v. West Bromwich Albion, Draw 0-0, AT 31,908, Shilton, Anderson, Barrett, McGovern, Lloyd, Burns, O'Neill, Gemmill, Withe, Woodcock, Robertson.

Nov 29th 1977, LC, H, v. Aston villa, Win 4-2, Scorers Anderson, Lloyd, Withe, Woodcock, AT 29,333, Woods, Anderson, Barrett, McGovern, Lloyd, Burns, O'Neill, Bowyer, Withe, Woodcock, Robertson.

Dec 3rd 1977, A, v. Birmingham City, Win 2-0, Scorers O'Neill, Woodcock, AT 29,925, Shilton, Anderson, Barrett, McGovern, Lloyd, Burns, O'Neill, Gemmill, Withe, Woodcock, Robertson.

Dec 10th 1977, H, v. Coventry City, Win 2-1, Scorers McGovern, O'Neill, AT 29,823, Shilton, Anderson, Barrett, McGovern, Lloyd, Burns, O'Neill, Gemmill, Withe, Woodcock, Robertson.

Dec 17th 1977, A, v. Man United, Win 4-0, Scorers Woodcock (2), Robertson, Greenhoff (OG), AT 54,374, Shilton, Anderson, Barrett, McGovern, Needham, Burns, O'Neill, Gemmill, Withe, Woodcock, Robertson.

Dec 26th 1977, H, v. Liverpool, Draw 1-1, Scorer Gemmill, AT 47,218, Shilton, Anderson, Barrett, McGovern, Needham, Burns, O'Neill, Gemmill, Withe, Woodcock, Robertson.

Dec 28th 1977, A, v. Newcastle United, Win 2-0, Scorers McGovern, Needham, AT 41,612, Shilton, Anderson, Barrett, McGovern, Needham, Burns, O'Neill, Gemmill, Withe, Woodcock, Robertson, SUB Bowyer.

Dec 31st 1977, A, v. Bristol City, Win 3-1, Scorers Needham, Woodcock, O'Neill, AT 31,990, Shilton, Anderson, Barrett, McGovern, Needham, Burns, O'Neill, Gemmill, Withe, Woodcock, Robertson.

Jan 2nd 1978, H, v. Everton, Draw 1-1, Scorer Robertson (Pen), AT 44,030, Shilton, Anderson, Barrett, McGovern, Needham, Burns, O'Neill, Gemmill, Withe, Woodcock, Robertson.

Jan 7th 1978, FAC, H, v. Swindon Town, Win 4-1, Scorers Withe, Woodcock (2), Robertson, AT 28,953, Shilton, Anderson, Barrett, McGovern, Needham, Burns, O'Neill, Gemmill, Withe, Woodcock, Robertson, SUB O'Hare.

Jan 14th 1978, A, v. Derby County, Draw 0-0, AT 33,384, Shilton, Anderson, Barrett, McGovern, Needham, Burns, O'Neill, Gemmill, Withe, Woodcock, Robertson.

Jan 17th 1978, LC, A, v. Bury, Win 3-0, Scorers O'Neill, Bowyer, Robertson, AT 21,268, Woods, Anderson, Clark, McGovern, Barrett, Burns, O'Neill, Bowyer, Withe, Woodcock, Robertson.

Jan 21st 1978, H, v. Arsenal, Win 2-0, Scorers Needham, Gemmill, AT 35,743, Shilton,

First Division 1977-78

		Pld	W	D	L	F	A	Pts
1	FOREST	42	25	14	3	69	24	64
2	Liverpool	42	24	9	9	65	34	57
3	Everton	42	22	11	9	76	45	55
4	Manchester City	42	20	12	10	74	51	52
5	Arsenal	42	21	10	11	60	37	52
6	West Bromwich Albion	42	18	14	10	62	53	50
7	Coventry City	42	18	12	12	75	62	48
8	Aston Villa	42	18	10	14	57	42	46
9	Leeds United	42	18	10	14	63	53	46
10	Manchester United	42	16	10	16	67	63	42
11	Birmingham City	42	16	9	17	55	60	41
12	Derby County	42	14	13	15	54	59	41
13	Norwich City	42	11	18	13	52	66	40
14	Middlesbrough	42	12	15	15	42	54	39
15	Wolverhampton Wand.	42	12	12	18	51	64	36
16	Chelsea	42	11	14	17	46	69	36
17	Bristol City	42	11	13	18	49	53	35
18	Ipswich Town	42	11	13	18	47	61	35
19	Queens Park Rangers	42	9	15	18	47	64	33
20	West Ham United	42	12	8	22	52	69	32
21	Newcastle United	42	6	10	26	42	78	22
22	Leicester City	42	5	12	25	26	70	22

Anderson, Barrett, McGovern, Needham, Burns, O'Neill, Gemmill, Withe, Woodcock, Robertson.

Jan 24th 1978, FAC, H, v. Man City, Win 2-1, Scorers Withe, Robertson, AT 38,509, Shilton, Anderson, Barrett, McGovern, Needham, Burns, O'Neill, Gemmill, Withe, Woodcock, Robertson.

Feb 4th 1978, H, v. Wolverhampton Wanderers, Win 2-0, Scorers McGovern, Woodcock, AT 28,803, Shilton, Anderson, Barrett, McGovern, Needham, Burns, O'Neill, Gemmill, Withe, Woodcock, Robertson.

Feb 8th 1978, LC, A, v. Leeds United, Win 3-1, Scorers O'Hare, Withe (2), AT 43,222, Woods, Anderson, Barrett, McGovern, Burns, O'Hare, O'Neill, Bowyer, Withe, Woodcock, Robertson.

Feb 18th 1978, FAC, A, v. QPR, Draw 1-1, Scorer O'Neill, AT 26,803, Shilton, Anderson, Barrett, McGovern, Needham, Burns, O'Neill, Gemmill, Withe, Woodcock, Robertson, SUB O'Hare.

Feb 22nd 1978, LC, H, v. Leeds United, Win 4-2, Scorers O'Neill, Bowyer, Withe, Woodcock, AT 38,313, Woods, Anderson, Barrett, McGovern, Lloyd, Burns, O'Neill, Bowyer, Withe, Woodcock, Robertson.

Feb 25th 1978, A, v. Norwich City, Draw 3-3, Scorers Barrett, O'Neill, Withe, AT 26,004, Shilton, Anderson, Barrett, McGovern, Needham, Burns, O'Neill, Gemmill, Withe, Woodcock, Robertson.

Feb 27th 1978, FAC, H, v. QPR, Draw 1-1, Scorer Robertson (Pen), AT 40,097, Shilton, Anderson, Clark, Needham, Lloyd, Burns, O'Neill, Bowyer, Withe, Woodcock, Robertson.

Mar 2nd 1978, FAC, H, v. QPR, Win 3-1, Scorers O'Neill, Woodcock (2), AT 33,950, Shilton, Anderson, Clark, Needham, Lloyd, Burns, O'Neill, Bowyer, Withe, Woodcock, Robertson.

Mar 4th 1978, H, v. West Ham United, Win 2-0, Scorers Needham, Robertson (Pen), AT 33,924, Shilton, Bowyer, Clark, O'Hare, Needham, Burns, O'Neill, Gemmill, Withe, Woodcock, Robertson.

Mar 11th 1978, FAC, A, v. West Bromwich Albion, Loss 0-2, AT 36,506, Shilton, Bowyer, Clark, McGovern, Needham, Burns, O'Neill, Gemmill, Withe, Woodcock, Robertson.

Mar 14th 1978, H, v. Leicester City, Win 1-0, Scorer Robertson (Pen), AT 32,355, Shilton, Anderson, Clark, O'Hare, Needham, Burns, O'Neill, Gemmill, Bowyer, Woodcock, Robertson.

Mar 18th 1978, LC, N, Wembley, v. Liverpool, Draw 0-0, AT 100,000, Woods, Anderson, Clark, McGovern, Lloyd, Burns, O'Neill, Bowyer, Withe, Woodcock, Robertson, SUB O'Hare.

Mar 22nd 1978, LC, N, Old Trafford, v. Liverpool, Win 1-0, Scorer Robertson (Pen), AT 54,375, Woods, Anderson, Clark, O'Hare, Lloyd, Burns, O'Neill, Bowyer, Withe, Woodcock, Robertson.

Mar 25th 1978, H, v. Newcastle United, Win 2-0, Scorers: Anderson, Robertson (Pen), AT 35,552, Shilton, Anderson, Clark, O'Hare, Needham, Burns, O'Neill, Gemmill, Withe, Woodcock, Robertson, SUB Bowyer.

Mar 29th 1978, A, v. Middlesbrough, Draw 2-2, Scorers O'Neill, Woodcock, AT 25,445, Shilton, Bowyer, Clark, O'Hare, Needham, Burns, O'Neill, Gemmill, Withe, Woodcock, Robertson.

Apr 1st 1978, H, v. Chelsea, Win 3-1, Scorers Burns, O'Neill, Robertson, AT 31,262, Shilton, Bowyer, Clark, O'Hare, Lloyd, Burns, O'Neill, Gemmill, Withe, Woodcock, Robertson, SUB Barrett.

Apr 5th 1978, A, v. Aston Villa, Win 1-0, Scorer Woodcock, AT 44,215, Shilton, Anderson, Barrett, O'Hare, Lloyd, Burns, O'Neill, Gemmill, Withe, Woodcock, Robertson.

Apr 11th 1978, A, v. Man City, Draw 0-0, AT 43,428, Shilton, Anderson, Barrett, O'Hare, Lloyd, Burns, O'Neill, Gemmill, Withe, Woodcock, Robertson.

Apr 15th 1978, H, v. Leeds United, Draw 1-1, Scorer: Withe, AT 38,662, Shilton, Barrett, Clark, McGovern, Lloyd, Burns, O'Neill, Gemmill, Withe, Bowyer, Robertson.

Apr 18th 1978, H, v. QPR, Win 1-0, Scorer: Robertson (Pen), AT 30,339, Shilton, Barrett, Clark, McGovern, Lloyd, Burns, O'Neill, Gemmill, Withe, Bowyer, Robertson.

Apr 22nd 1978, A, v. Coventry City, Draw 0-0, AT 36,881, Shilton, Anderson, Barrett, O'Hare, Needham, Burns, O'Neill, Bowyer, Withe, Gemmill, Robertson.

Apr 25th 1978, A, v. Ipswich Town, Win 2-0, Scorers: Clark, Mariner (OG), AT 30,062, Shilton, Anderson, Barrett, O'Hare, Needham, Burns, O'Neill, Bowyer, Withe, Gemmill, Robertson, SUB Clark.

Apr 29th 1978, H, v. Birmingham City, Draw 0-0, AT 37,625, Shilton, Anderson, Barrett, McGovern, Needham, Burns, O'Neill, Gemmill, Withe, Woodcock, Robertson, SUB Bowyer.

May 1st 1978, Test, H, v. Derby County, Win 2-1, Scorers McGovern, Withe, AT 18,272, Shilton, Anderson, Barrett, McGovern, Lloyd, Burns, O'Neill, Birtles, Withe, Needham, Robertson.

May 2nd 1978, A, v. West Bromwich Albion, Draw 2-2, Scorers Bowyer, Robertson (Pen), AT 23,523, Shilton, Anderson, Barrett, McGovern, Lloyd, Burns, O'Neill, Gemmill, Withe, Bowyer, Robertson.

May 4th 1978, A, v. Liverpool, Draw 0-0, AT 50,021, Shilton, Anderson, Barrett, McGovern, Lloyd, Clark, O'Neill, Gemmill, Withe, Bowyer, Robertson.

Back Row: I.Bowyer, V.Anderson, T.Woodcock, K.Burns,
Middle Row: J.Gordon, F.Clark, L.LLoyd, C.Woods, P.Shilton, C.Barrett, B.Clough
Front Row: P.Withe, D.Needham, J.McGovern, M.O'Neill, J.Robertson

"Liverpool.... bloody Liverpool", that was the first reaction of the management, players and fans to the draw for the European Cup first round. "Seems like a fix to me", was the second. Would Nottingham Forest's first foray into this competition be over before it had begun. After the initial shock, Peter Taylor pointed out the reaction in the Liverpool dressing room would have been exactly the same. After all it looked as if Forest had already shown that they had the style and tactics to defeat them.

The draw had been made in Zurich and the Forest party flew from Manchester airport along with officials from Liverpool. The Liverpool group had invited Ken Smales and co., to join them as they were obviously old hands at this. No need for a taxi, they travelled by tram to the official venue, a hotel in the centre of the city. That evening both groups went for dinner together at a restaurant recommended by Liverpool secretary Peter Robinson, oblivious to what would unfold the next day.

The draw was to be made at 12.00 mid-day in the banquet hall of the hotel where the delegates were staying. Officials from all thirty three clubs were represented, Albania who had been excluded for several years had now been re-admitted, the glamour was supplied by Ferenc Puskas, manager of AEK Athens who the Reds had already played in a pre-season friendly. Those clubs with a history of recent European success were seeded, so Forest obviously weren't. First out, Monaco versus Steaua Bucharest, then a variety of matches, Malmoe, Madrid came and went, the main concern was, please not behind the 'Iron Curtain'.

Excitement continued to mount, eventually the ninth tie was drawn, Nottingham Forest will play.....Liverpool, cue gasps from the audience, relief all round from those that had feared playing either team. Ken Smales was dumbfounded, even Albania might have been preferable now, all those thoughts of exotic travel pushed to the back of everyone's mind. Merseyside!!

As was traditional, Brian Appleby's fixed term tenure as chairman was over and the baton passed to Stuart Dryden with Geoffrey Macpherson elected as his vice chairman. The turnaround in the fortunes of the club will always be associated with Brian Appleby, but the incoming pair had contributed greatly to the more modern

78-79

NOTTINGHAM FOREST FOOTBALL CLUB

DIVISION ONE 1978 - 79

Back row, left to right: LARRY LLOYD PETER WITHE VIV ANDERSON DAVE NEEDHAM IAN BOWYER KENNY BURNS FRANK CLARK

Middle row, left to right: MARTIN O'NEILL ARCHIE GEMMILL JOHN ROBERTSON PETER SHILTON CHRIS WOODS TONY WOODCOCK STEVE ELLIOTT COLIN BARRETT

Front row, left to right: PETER TAYLOR (Asst. Manager) JOHN McGOVERN BRAIN CLOUGH (Manager) (Inset: GARRY BIRTLES)

Martin O'Neill (partially hidden) scores the opening goal in the defeat of Ipswich.

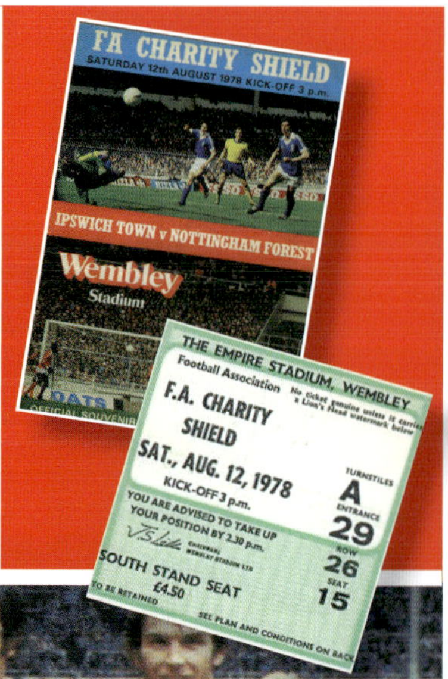

REDS SHOW NO CHARITY TO IPSWICH TOWN!

Action in the Ipswich goalmouth

approach pervading the club. Although the photograph taken to capture the presentation to the outgoing chairman looks little different to any picture taken of the committee taken over the past thirty years.

As alluded to previously, half a million pounds that could have been spent on players had to be diverted into ground improvements so the club could participate in the European Cup. Ken Smales had been here before. Indeed, after finishing second in 1967, having been fortunate with injuries, no players were added during the close season, this had resulted in the following campaign being anti-climatic, and an opportunity missed. History was to show that this had inexorably led to the club's subsequent decline and relegation. In fact that squad had been weakened when quality reserves such as Alan Hinton were allowed to leave. So with this in mind, plus Peter Taylor's claim that he knew the players he wanted, fans awaited news of the big names that would be needed to maintain momentum as the club were facing challenges on four fronts this season.

So what did the club get for the £500,000 spent on ground improvements? There was a complete reconstruction of the terracing along the East Stand and Bridgford End areas of the ground, along with new crush barriers, exit stairs and extra toilets, plus the installation of extra seating in front of the Main Stand. This led to the official capacity being reduced to 42,000. In line with EUFA regulations, a fence was installed in front of the terracing to deter fan encroachment, a sign of things to come. The club also installed an electronic scoreboard, the most advanced in the country at that time and extended the Jubilee Club, which had been such a resounding success, that it had paid for itself in only twelve months.

Season ticket sales were the highest ever and for the first time in the club's history all seats were sold out before the season began. As the management team would admit later, pre season preparations were not ideal. Instead of the usual routine of setting up camp in Germany, they exploited the commercial opportunities now open to the Champion's of England and played a series of stiff matches, including a tournament in Spain the week before the

season started. Many of the players had been on international duty that summer; Burns, Gemmill and Robertson had been in Argentina with Scotland for the World Cup, whilst Needham and Anderson had gone to New Zealand with England 'B'.

Pre-season was where Clough and Taylor traditionally worked the players hard, getting the fitness right before moving on to a more energy saving routine throughout the season. Games were

The Forest committee present Brian Appleby with an award to commorate his term as a Chairman.

usually against a mixture of good and not so good opposition, being ready for the new season was the only thing that mattered, but now it was different.

Their first game was against crack Yugoslavian outfit Red Star Belgrade.

Frank Clark recalls the occasion, "I was sitting on the bench when one of the Red Star players was shaping to shoot from thirty yards, you'll be lucky I thought, next minute it was in the top corner". A 3-2 defeat in front of a 30,000 crowd that resembled a cup tie rather than a pre-season work out, was not what was needed. Two days later another tough game against Dynamo Zagreb, this time a draw, with Needham netting. Then another draw against slightly weaker opposition in SK Osijek. It wasn't getting any easier, just two days later they stepped out to face Greek champions AEK Athens in super hot conditions, and another hard fought draw. This game would turn out to be an invaluable experience after they were drawn to play the same team in the second round of the European Cup. That these games gave the players an early glimpse of European opposition, has to be weighed against the disruption they caused to pre season preeration.

So what was learnt from this trip? The players could acquit themselves against decent European opposition in strange conditions, but the fact that the same eleven players started every game clearly indicated that extra numbers of the right quality needed to be added to the squad.

There was now a twelve days break until the next game, at Wembley against Ipswich Town in the season's traditional curtain raiser, the Charity Shield. Meanwhile, the Peter Withe saga rumbled on. The management had indicated that they were prepared to let him go, the player had asked for a move, but he continued to be picked for every game. What was happening? There was also paper talk of Forest making new signings, but no action.

A crowd of 64,000 were at Wembley for the showpiece game against Ipswich, where Forest fans heavily outnumbered the opposition. The game itself was a walkover for the Reds, a 5-0 hammering including two for Martin O'Neill who was perhaps spitefully substituted, thereby denying him the chance of a Wembley hat-trick. Ipswich Town manager Bobby Robson commented to Brian Clough that perhaps the score line wasn't a fair reflection on the game. Clough agreed, "It should have been ten", he replied. Brian Clough had again led the team out, as

Martin O'Neill fires home from close range against Spurs.

Archie Gemmill in action.

Tony Woodcock lets fly against Spurs.

Peter Withe shoots, but the keeper saves.

TOTTENHAM O'NEILL ARSENAL ROBERTSON

John Robertson scores from the penalty spot against Arsenal.

Ian Bowyer lashes home the winner against the Gunners.

once more the FA had refused the request that Peter Taylor be allowed to join him. Taylor himself was so upset at this, that he refused to attend the game, choosing to watch Bolton versus Oldham instead. It was also a special occasion for Colin Barrett as he finally got to play at Wembley after missing out three times previously.

Just seven days before the start of the new season, Forest jetted off to play in the 'City of Vigo' Trophy. How much money the club received for playing is not known, but it made no sense then or now and must have contributed to the slow start Forest subsequently made to the start of the campaign. At one point the club's participation was in doubt due to a strike by French Air Traffic Control (nothing changes), but Forest's obligations meant that they would have to get there by whatever means possible. It was two planes and a bus journey before the players arrived at their hotel at 11.45 pm on the Sunday evening, weary and stiff after the previous day's game. With delays it meant that they had been on the road for almost twelve hours, terrible preparation.

Celta Vigo the hosts, were joined by the Reds, Porto and Brazilian side Cruzeiros. Vigo versus Forest was the first game and again the Reds had difficulty scoring, only a late effort from Needham saving their blushes, although they lost the penalty shoot out. Worse still Larry Lloyd picked up an injury that meant he missed the first seven games of the new season. Forest also drew a blank in the third and fourth play-off match against Porto, finishing bottom of the tournament.

After resting on the Thursday, the party did not set off on the return journey until 5.00 am the next morning, and didn't arrive back in Nottingham until late that afternoon. They were due to begin the defence of the Championship trophy less than twenty four hours later.

Tottenham Hotspur provided the first opposition at the revamped City Ground. Spurs had been promoted the previous season on goal difference, after at one stage, looking as if they would run away with the title. They had amazed the football world when they made a couple of real glamour signings in Osvaldo Ardilles and Ricky Villa, who had just won the World Cup with Argentina.

There was a larger than usual Tottenham following in a capacity crowd, that proved too much for the regular away supporter's pen. Supporters of both sides spilled onto the pitch and scuffles ensued before order was restored. Police reported trouble before and after the game.

The game played in the usual first day sweltering conditions was a good one. Martin O'Neill gave Forest a first half lead before Villa gave the visiting news reporters the story they were looking for, when he equalised.

The crowds spills on to the pitch against Tottenham Hotspur

After the game, the gap between the management and Peter Withe was revealed to be wider than thought. Despite the player having requested a transfer, no-one really thought that he would leave, so when Forest accepted a bid of £250,000 from Newcastle, there was surprise all round. The player himself then withdrew his request and said that he wanted to stay, but Brian Clough was not for turning and despite no plans in place for a replacement the deal was completed. Withe now faced trips to Preston, Cambridge and Wrexham, rather than Athens, Zurich and Munich. Why did Clough and Taylor let Withe go? His league goals might have dried up, but his team mates appreciated his work rate and commitment. There were no rumours

of a replacement, even though the first round of the European Cup was only weeks away. Did the management team really think that they were infallible? Taylor was famed for his talent spotting and the philosophy of replace with better was well established, after all, if you believe what the management had said, they had long thought that Withe had passed his sell by date.

Had the ground improvements drained the club of cash? Clough, who had never been one for holding back if he thought that he wasn't being backed, never used this as an excuse, anyway supporters were nonplussed, there must be a backup plan. The immediate problem was who would step in to fill the centre forward spot. Clough wanted Steve Elliott, a nineteen year old who had scored regularly for the reserves, but never played for the first team in a competitive fixture and was also a completely different style of player. Peter Taylor pushed for Garry Birtles, who had not even been taken on the pre-season tour of Yugoslavia.

The pair then turned to Jimmy Gordon for a casting vote, but he plumped for John O'Hare. Clough made

Birtles, 1 - 0 to Nottingham Forest

Tony Woodcock's cushioned header to Colin Barrett.

FIRST LEG...
Wednesday 13th Sept. 1978

Forest	2
Liverpool	0

Colin Barrett has just lashed home the Reds' second against Liverpool.

SELL YOUR SCRAP METAL TO McINTYRES NOTTINGHAM'S LARGEST BUYERS

EVENING POST

No. 31,169

NOTTINGHAM, THURSDAY, SEPTEMBER 28, 1978

PRICE

It's that Euro-magic momen

Woodcock and Kennedy leave the Anfield pitch.

SECOND LEG...
Wednesday 27th Sept. 1978
Liverpool 0
Forest 0

Larry Lloyd clears from Dalglish.

Liverpool are beaten at their own s

Super Reds silence Kop and stride on into Europe

LIVERPOOL . . 0 NOTTM FOREST . . 0
(Forest won 2-0 on aggregate)

LIVERPOOL, past masters of containment, were comprehensively beaten at their own game last night as Nottingham Forest took a gigantic stride into Europe.

The double European Cup champions simply had no answer to the tactical ploy and deep commitment of a side that never looked like relinquishing the two-goal advantage they established at the City Ground a fortnight ago.

At the end of a deafening, tension-riddled evening at Anfield, Forest manager Brian Clough could not hold back his emotions as he jumped from the dugout to acclaim his team's achievement.

And everyone in the Forest side deserves a huge slice of glory for the way they out-fought out-manoeuvred

THE HERO

CUP

their best chance of the night when Woodcock forced a rare opening and Ray Clemence, sensing the danger, had to sprint from his goal to block Birtles' shot.

Burns picked up a booking for bringing down Heighway but it was kindergarten stuff compared with the tackles that Case and Co. had been dishing out.

Dalglish threatened early in the second half when he collected a

THE NEAREST defence. With Pete range header, Viv

Lat am

Woodcock takes on Phil Thompson.

LIVERPOOL FOOTBALL CLUB
LIVERPOOL
versus
NOTTINGHAM FOREST
27th SEPTEMBER, 1978
GROUND TICKET
ANFIELD ROAD
№ 2196
This portion to be retained

Issued subject to the Rules and Regs. of the Football Association.

LIVERPOOL FOOTBALL CLUB
European Champion Clubs' Cup Competition
1st Round—2nd Leg
LIVERPOOL v. NOTTINGHAM FOREST
AT ANFIELD
WEDNESDAY, 27th SEPTEMBER, 1978
Kick-off 7-30 p.m.
Admit to ANFIELD ROAD SOUTH
(VISITORS' SECTION)
VIA TURNSTILES 63 & 64 ONLY
ADMISSION £1.50 (Including VAT)
№ 2196
P. B. Robinson
General Secretary.
This Portion to be given up at turnstiles

On the night Forest recapture their style . . .

REDS WALK A EURO TIGHTROPE

by Michael Charters

MATCH FACTS

Paisley adamant despite Reds' sad Cup exit . . .

WE'RE STILL BEST IN EUROPE'

BY MICHAEL CHARTERS

ALTHOUGH their European Cup hat-trick dream was shattered last night by Nottingham Forest, Liverpool manager Bob Paisley still showed that familiar Liverpool brand of positive thinking by saying to-day: "We are still the best team in Europe . . . yet we're out of it."

the decision, Steve Elliott would get his chance. This was now a real 'Sliding Doors' moment, what would history have looked like if Steve Elliott had come in, played well and scored? His first opportunity came at Highfield Road against Coventry. His chances were made all the harder by the fact that at this time, Forest as a team were under performing and his cause wasn't helped when he hit the post rather than tucking away what would have been the winning goal.

Three more games followed, three more 0-0 draws, first at QPR where the fans gave the team a ticker tape welcome, (Argentinian fans had welcomed their players onto the pitch by throwing scraps of papers and streamers into the air) and away at Oldham in the League Cup. This was a particularly disappointing result as the opposition were down to their last eleven players and even hit the bar. Then finally West Brom, that also marked the seventh consecutive drawn game carried over from the previous season.

Things were getting desperate, the media were quick to point out the folly of selling your top scorer and fans couldn't understand why they didn't seem to be pursuing a quality replacement. The dam finally burst when Forest visited Mansfield Town for a testimonial game for Sandy Pate, a full strength side hit six goals. This was immediately followed up two days later with a 4-2 victory over Oldham in the League Cup replay. It also marked the end of Elliott's chance to claim his spot, he had neither scored nor really impressed, so Peter Taylor was to get his way and Garry Birtles would come in for the next game against Arsenal, the last fixture before the Liverpool European Cup game.

Birtles was joined in the team by Gary Mills, making his debut at only sixteen, Gary was considered a great prospect, he had represented England schoolboys, not only at football but also rugby. Gemmill and O'Neill were missing with knocks, but there was a welcome return for Larry Lloyd. Birtles immediately seemed at home and the team looked as if they had found their form just in time as they secured a confidence boosting 2-1 victory over the Gunners.

Liverpool at home in the European Cup with the scousers looking to emulate Ajax, by winning the trophy for a third successive year and also gaining revenge on a team that they condescendingly really thought weren't fit to lace their boots.
Liverpool in direct contrast to Forest had begun the season like an express train, even knocking seven goals past Tottenham. The press almost unanimously predicted victory for the Merseysiders, whilst Reg Drury from the News of the World even went as far as to say he hoped Liverpool would win, because they were the country's best hope for retaining the trophy due to Forest's lack of European experience. This game has been picked over so many times in the ensuing years. With a full strength team to choose from, Forest gave a good account of themselves, applying pressure constantly through the first half, Birtles giving Forest the lead with his first senior goal, although there could have been more.

Instead of the expected naivety from Forest, it was the supposedly more experienced Liverpool team that got suckered into chasing an equaliser and they got caught on the counter attack when full back Colin Barrett, ignored the expletive driven exhortations from the bench that he should return to his defensive duties, and instead found himself on the end of a cushioned header from Woodcock in the Liverpool box, and volleyed home an unstoppable second goal. The celebrations by the player were perhaps the most moving and exhilarating by a player from Nottingham Forest in their whole history. It has to be seen in the context of the opposition, who displayed a crass arrogance along with their supporters that it was their divine right to win. Constant goading by players that should have known better, that 1-0 was not enough, overly physical challenges, Souness thinking that he could kick John McGovern out of the game. Well they were firmly put in their place, they couldn't breach the Reds' defence for the fourth successive game.

Michael Charles writing for the Liverpool Echo, gave Forest due credit for their performance though, when he wrote, 'I have not seen Liverpool pushed back on the defensive like last night for many years, although Liverpool were looking as likely to score as the hosts during the closing stages, they had been outplayed and outrun for much of last night's game by a Forest team that had recaptured the style and glitter that had brought them the title last season. Key to the match was that Forest had McGovern and Bowyer breathing down the necks of Souness and McDermott so that the usual Liverpool control was non-existent. Souness booked in the eleventh minute for his first foul, made little impact as he struggled for space and time'.

Forest returned to the scene of their greatest performance of the previous season when they went to Old Trafford on the following Saturday. This was another fine performance that might well have emulated that result, but in the end they had to settle for a point in a 1-1 draw.
Forest now had to pull in an unwanted fixture, the County Cup final held over from the previous season against Mansfield. For one of the few times in his

Gary Birtles torments the Derby defence.

Woodcock heads home the Forest goal against the Rams.

Kenny Burns in an aerial duel with the Middlesbrough defenders.

DERBY WOLVES IPSWICH MIDDLESBORO BIRMINGHAM

Birtles nods home against Wolves.

Gemmill with the winner against Birmingham City.

Martin O'Neill fires a scorcher past Cooper the Ipswich keeper.

Birtles calmly lifts the ball over the diving Middlesbrough keeper and in to the net.

managerial career, Brian Clough put out a weakened team, making seven changes from the United game, with Chris Woods and Steve Burke given a chance, but they still won 4-0.

Garry Birtles notched the first league goals of his career as Forest took a two goal lead at home to Middlesbrough. Worryingly though, they conceded two second half goals to only draw 2-2, their sixth draw from seven league fixtures. If conceding two goals wasn't bad enough, Colin Barrett suffered bad knee ligament damage when John Mahoney caught him on the side of his leg. In ten days he had experienced the highs and lows of professional sport and he was to miss the next five months of the season.

The path was now clear for what was to be the defining game of the season, the return leg at Anfield. In a poll of the remaining twenty First Division managers, only three, despite Forest having a two goal advantage, thought that they would go through. The astute ones were John Neal of Middlesbrough, Alan Dicks of Bristol City and Ken Shilleto of Chelsea. Brian Clough often gave the impression of not bothering about the opposition, of only being concerned with how his team performed. In truth, he often made subtle alterations to minimise areas where the other team might prosper. For this game Frank Clark returned for his first appearance in four months whilst John Robertson knew that he was unlikely to get his usual freedom and had to help out the full back. Meanwhile Archie Gemmill was also instructed to tuck in on the right hand side to protect Viv Anderson from the attacking Alan Kennedy. Most of all, what was needed was character, a trait Nottingham Forest possessed in spades.

Clough had his way of pricking the opposition's supposed superiority, on this evening he led the players out onto the pitch after they had arrived at the ground and they all stood laughing and joking in front of the Kop. Immediately presenting the impression that they weren't intimidated and then as recounted by Viv Anderson, Clough's final words in the dressing room were, "You know that sign, the one you see when you run onto the pitch saying, 'This is Anfield', well so fucking what". Despite almost continuous pressure, the Forest players felt reasonably in control. Shilton might have had to make a couple of outstanding saves, but for a team with so much possession, the number of clear cut chances created by the home team were minimal. Once more Liverpool didn't cover themselves in glory with the manner in which they took defeat, Frank Clark bearing the brunt of a crude challenge from Jimmy Case that required seven stitches in a shin wound. Frank, who had felt left out of things after not even making the bench for the first leg, had now returned to the fold and would end his playing career in the finest possible way. Special mention too for Larry Lloyd who had perfected a way of handling Kenny Dalglish, realising that the player liked to back into a defender, then turn and spin when the ball was played into his feet. Larry would regale fellow players with his comedy routine of looking in his breast pocket and calling, "Kenny, you can come out now".

Bob Paisley gave the appearance of being gracious in defeat, claiming that he knew Forest would be difficult opposition and that he had gone to the bookies and put a bet on Forest to win the European Cup after the game. But in truth, along with many of his players, he thought Forest had been overly defensive and had not really deserved to go through. In an article in the Liverpool Echo published the following evening he claimed that Liverpool were still the best team in Europe and Forest would get a shock when they played European opposition. Whilst Liverpool skipper Emlyn Hughes added astonishingly that, "Forest will have to watch their tackling in future, they won't get away with what they got away with last night, otherwise they run the risk of having a player sent off".

Ken Smales, who often took members of the press pack to task in his match day programme column, had been particularly incensed by Reg Drury's article in the News of the World, in which he claimed it would be best for English football if Liverpool went through. Ken took great delight in visiting the press box afterwards to commiserate with the journalist who would have to 'endure' Forest in the next round.

The secretary and Peter Taylor once again went off to Zurich for the next round draw, which paired them with the familiar opposition of AEK Athens, whom they had played just two months previously in a friendly. They were a useful enough outfit, but only overconfidence could surely prevent Forest progressing.

Meanwhile the club had chartered an aircraft and were offering fans the chance to follow the team with a variety of options, one being a three day all inclusive trip including match ticket, which was available for only £177!!

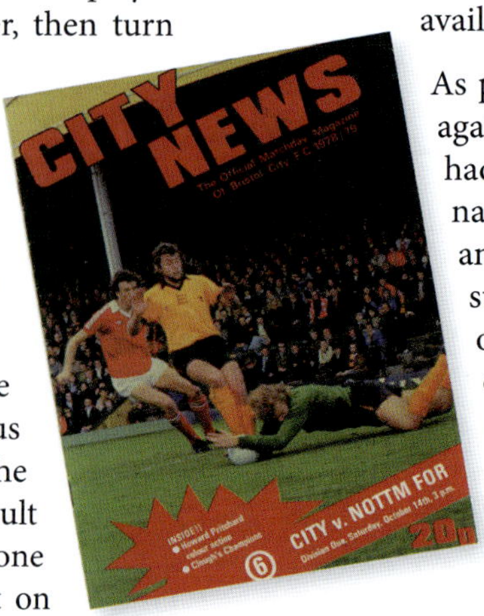

As part of the club's stance against hooliganism, they had taken to printing the name, address, crime and fine of any Forest supporter found guilty of a football related offence on page three of the programme. In addition to this, those fans were also banned from the City Ground for life.

Brian Clough claimed that his priority was retaining the League title, so three successive wins, away at Villa and Bristol City and at home to Wolves pleased him, eight goals were scored, plus another five in a sparkling win at Oxford United in the League Cup. Birtles contributed four goals in this run and it seemed as if Peter Withe was now just a distant memory. The stuttering start to the season looked over and Forest had crept almost unnoticed up to third place during their unbeaten start to the season.

Athens in October was still hot, but Forest would luckily not have to endure the 100 degrees temperature that they had been forced to endure in August. Brian Clough upset the waiting Greek newspaper reporters when he didn't stop at the airport for a press conference. They got their own back by attempting to whip the crowd up further, with a series of inflammatory articles. 'Boys of AEK, boys of Greece, attack. Break the snobbish British 3-0 or more and give the pleasure of victory to our little country'.

The team stayed in the same accommodation as before, a small complex of chalets close to a sandy beach. The atmosphere was relaxed, no formal training as such, just a little tag rugby on the sand that resulted in a group of players tripping Lloyd up, followed by everyone diving on top of him, before running away to escape revenge.

A delay in setting off for the stadium meant that the team bus was caught up in rush hour traffic and faced an extra-ordinary journey to get there on time. This evening the players were faced with a more frenzied and intimidating atmosphere than they had received pre-season. Bowyer came in to replace O'Neill, but otherwise it was an unchanged team. As at Liverpool, Clough made a point of holding his team talk out on the pitch in front of the most passionate Greek fans to show them that they would not be intimidated.

Forest had the boost of an early goal, McGovern poking home in the eleventh minute. Things got even worse for the home team ten minutes later, when Uruguayan international Milton Vierra punched Kenny Burns, who although he went down, claimed it was just to ensure the referee sent him off. Forest extended their lead just before half-time when Clark exploited the AEK offside trap to set up Birtles for number two.

Forest sat back in the second half and although AEK pulled one back after a disputed penalty, the Reds finished comfortable 2-1 winners.

Next day as the players gathered in the hotel foyer ready for the bus to take them to the airport, all the players bar one, Larry Lloyd , were dressed in slacks and club blazer, Larry was in jeans, shirt and leather jacket. He confirmed with captain John McGovern that he had not missed out on instructions regarding dress code and decided not to change. When the manager came down in his tracksuit he was even more convinced, but the manager, whatever his motivation, returned to his room and changed into the same outfit as the rest of the players. He then returned and told Lloyd to go and get changed, the player refused and there was a stand-off that wasn't resolved as the player stood his ground. The matter was then brought up at Friday's team meeting back in Nottingham. At which point the player was not only fined, but removed from the team that was due to play Ipswich the following day. The manager then disappeared off for a week's break in Spain leaving Peter Taylor to deal with the aftermath. This break allowed the situation to cool down, Lloyd paid his fine and Clough put him back in the team, but why did an incident that should have easily been resolved escalate. The manager felt that he could never allow his authority to be undermined, but in Lloyd as we have seen already, was an ego that felt able to stand up to the manager, perhaps he should have applied the creed, 'The manager might not always be right, but he is the manager'.

Two clean sheets followed, the first came in a 1-0 win over Ipswich. This game was followed by the final of that year's Forest Bowl competition, with a young Chris Fairclough playing for Top Valley Comprehensive School and then the following week, a 0-0 draw at Southampton, before AEK came to Nottingham. Unlike the unpleasant atmosphere that had surrounded the Liverpool game, Nottingham welcomed several hundred Greek fans who spent match day around the Market Square. Scarves and other memorabilia were swapped as fans mingled without any hint of trouble.

The manager was again forced to make changes, McGovern had taken a knock down at the Dell, whilst Burns was suspended. O'Hare and Needham came in to replace them. Gary Mills was named amongst the substitutes, no reflection on that player's ability, but Forest really should have been able to call on a more experienced player. Three months in to the new season and there was still no sign of new recruits.

Thomas Mavros had the first chance

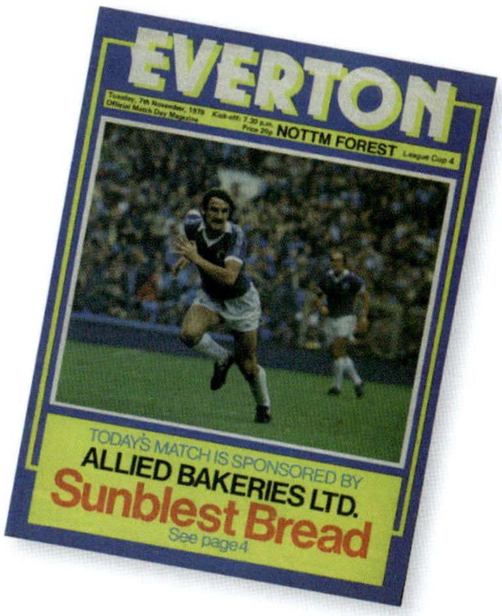

of the game in the third minute, but screwed his shot horribly wide. Then on the tenth minute, Needham powered in a header from a Woodcock corner to settle any nerves. It was then one way traffic throughout the first half as the Reds laid siege to the Athens goal. Woodcock headed home a pinpoint cross for 2-0 before Viv Anderson intercepted a clearance, took the ball past one defender before thumping the ball high into the net to make the aggregate score 5-1. With Forest surely through, there was no need to risk any more injuries, so Frank Clark who was carrying a slight knock was withdrawn, enabling Mills to make his European debut.

Inevitably the second half was not going to be as intense as the first and it was AEK who scored next when Bajevic prodded home, but normal service was quickly restored when Birtles added two more to his growing goals tally. The final aggregate score was 7-2, Forest had clinically dispatched their opponents. News got even better after the game, not only had Real Madrid been knocked out, but also Italian champions Juventus, the cup was up for grabs now.

The draw for the next round pitted them against Zurich Grasshoppers, who had beaten Real Madrid. The first leg was to be at home, although the game wouldn't take place until the following March, leaving Forest to continue their pursuit of Liverpool in the league and attempt to retain the League Cup.

Forest returned to league action in a 0-0 draw with Everton at the City Ground before playing the same opposition at Goodison Park in the League Cup on the Tuesday. After the home game Brian Clough said, "Our failure to strengthen the squad is a nightmare for Peter Taylor and me with every day that passes". David Millar writing in the Daily Express

ROUND TWO FIRST LEG...
Wednesday 18th Oct. 1978
AEK Athens 1
Forest 2

Glory in Greece
CLASSY FORE
STAY COOL F
FABULOUS W

John McGovern exchanges pre-match pennants.

The Reds' defence stands firm.

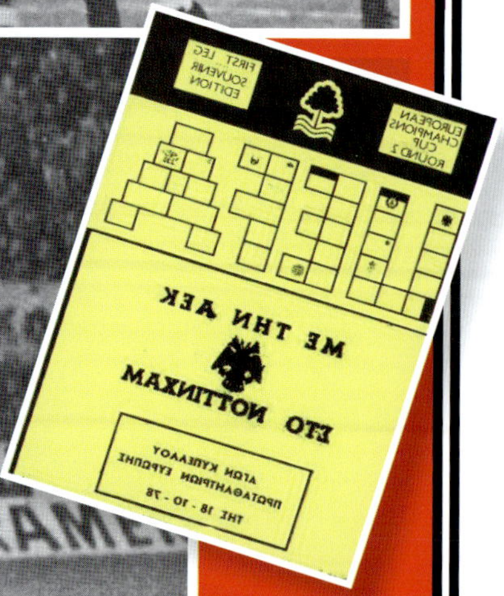

Garry Birtles nets Forest's second goal.

Tony Woodcock.

Dave Needham with another fine header opens the scoring for Forest.

ROUND TWO SECOND LEG...
Wednesday 1st Nov. 1978
Forest 5
AEK Athens 1

Tony Woodcock eyes closed heads in.

Viv Anderson curls in a beauty.

A foggy evening against Dynamo Zagreb

commented, 'Clough and Taylor must question whether they can hold out for the right players, or simply go out and buy a couple who are available, to get them through the winter'.

Forest were down to the bare bones for the cup game, Needham was forced to play in mid-field and Bowyer had to play left back because Clark had now joined Barrett on the injury list. It was a bad night for Kenny Burns, after falling awkwardly he injured his knee, (X-rays later showed it was cartilage damage and he was to miss the next twelve games) and he also put Everton ahead with an own goal. After a cortisone injection he limped on, as amazingly Forest hit three second half goals to lead 3-1 before a late consolation from Latchford. How the players continued to drag out performance after performance was unbelievable, as Brian Clough said, "Do we have to go unbeaten for another twelve months before anyone will admit we're a good side". Forest followed this up with probably their best league performance of the season, with what was on paper their weakest line up, at White Hart Lane, running out convincing 3-1 winners. Needham dropped in alongside Lloyd as they shared the roll usually taken by Burns in covering each other. Robertson fired in an effort that would surely be a contender for goal of the season.

Two more unbeaten games, although the first was a boring 0-0 with QPR, the second was a more impressive 1-0 win at Bolton Wanderers. This game even got a mention in the pages of the New Musical Express, as the entire Forest contingent pogoed at half-time in an attempt to keep warm. In spite of the lack of players available, the management had arranged a home friendly against Dynamo Zagreb Thanks to the vagaries of the British weather, the game was played out in dense fog before a small crowd of 5,000. The game would neither have started or finished if it had been a competitive fixture. Fans standing at one end of the ground could only guess what was happening at the other. Apparently the Reds won 2-0. The number of internationals on the Reds' books had now increased to ten, after Viv Anderson made history by being the first black player to represent England as he joined teammates Peter Shilton and Tony Woodcock for the fixture against Czechoslovakia.

England expects...

Three of a kind . . . that's Forest's England trio Tony Woodcock, Peter Shilton and Viv Anderson.

The search for players continued, it was revealed later when the player joined on loan the next season, that a fee had been agreed at that time with Derby for the transfer of Charlie George, however, those in charge at the Baseball Ground perhaps thought that Tommy Docherty might be making another mistake, so they vetoed the deal and refused to sell the player to Forest in a deal that had echoes of the Ian Moore saga six years earlier. In the space of only four years, the pendulum had swung and it was now Forest threatening to take the last of Derby's stars. Taylor was also casting his eye over Continental players, watching Dutchman Rudi Geels and the German Rainer Bonhoff. Bonhoff although great with the ball, was not considered 'hungry' enough to win the ball, so any interest was not pursued. The unbeaten League run of forty two games was to end at Anfield with a 2-0 defeat by Liverpool. Their players and fans celebrated as if they had won the World Cup, they had broken what they thought was a hoodoo, they didn't care that Forest were missing six players, they just wanted the win.

Brian Clough meanwhile applauded and hugged every Reds player as they left the pitch. Over subsequent years, Brian Clough and the players to a man, expressed how disappointed they were, that they didn't get the full recognition that their unbeaten run should have received. Not only was it achieved by a newly promoted team, but with a squad of only sixteen players that were competing for all three major trophies on pitches that would be considered laughable by today's superstars. They played a brand of attacking football that was refreshing for that era and they didn't resort to underhand tactics and foul play to wreck games in order to continue the run. It was an absolute disgrace that it took almost forty years for this feat to be acknowledged properly when they were inducted into the 'Hall of Fame'. The lack of respect for this team has never been helped by the churlish and downright arrogance of certain Liverpool players such as Graeme Souness, this and the disproportionate amount of ex Liverpool players in the media for many years, ensured that Forest were held to be inferior to Liverpool. They have just never been able to accept that for this period, Forest were the better team and this doesn't diminish their own legacy. As the manager reflected afterwards, "It's

John McGovern nets a rare goal against York City.

A snowbound and icy City Ground doesn't stop Martin O'Neill scoring against York City.

Needham turns away after scoring against Bristol City.

Needham scores against Bristol City.

YORK CITY BRISTOL CITY ASTON VILLA

David Needham celebrates his goal against Aston Villa.

Trevor Francis pokes in the Reds' second in the FA Cup victory against Aston Villa.

only two points, let's start another run". In fact it is overlooked that they played another forty games that season and lost only three more times. It is also worth pointing out, that the entire Forest team that lost at Anfield that day, cost less than the two Liverpool full backs.

Brighton just four days later at home in the fifth round of the League Cup presented an immediate opportunity to put this result behind them. A couple of players such as McGovern and Woodcock were to return as Forest cruised through to the semi-finals with a 3-1 victory with goals from McGovern, Robertson and Birtles. Pre match, Brian Clough was presented with a record breaking ninth, 'Manager of the Month' award.

Three further games took Forest up to the New Year, undefeated maybe, but points dropped as well. Archie Gemmill scored his first goal of the season in the 1-0 defeat of Birmingham City, followed by a 0-0 draw at Manchester City, finishing with a 1-1 Boxing Day draw at home with Derby. This match was not only 'all ticket' but kicked off at 11.00am under police instructions. Despite this, over 34,000 attended. A spell of snow and icy weather was to lead to the postponement of the next three games, at home to Norwich, away at Leeds and the FA Cup against Aston Villa. Five games now had to be shoehorned into an already congested season and if the club made further progress in any of the three cup competitions, there would be even more. The problem was exacerbated by the fact that all home, fixtures had to be completed by 30th April, as that was the day that demolition of the East Stand was due to begin, with the contractors on a very tight schedule to erect the new stand.

The year finished with the Reds in fifth place, six points behind Liverpool, with a game in hand. With the run of injuries that had been sustained, this was quite handy and if re-enforcements were brought in, retaining the Championship wasn't out of the question. The country meanwhile was spiralling out of control. The agreement Labour had with the Liberals to form a minority government, had ended and the country entered a period that was to later be called, 'The winter of discontent' as first the car workers, followed by postal and power workers went on strike. Unemployment reached a post war high of 1.500,000, inflation had not been below 10% per year since 1973, but still football went on as if nothing was happening. Brian Cloughs demand for higher crowds should be measured against this anxiety and the low crowds at other clubs such as Newcastle where 20,000 was now the norm. Forest were now to add their own story to this crazy situation. Unknown to

supporters, Clough and Taylor had settled on the player they most wanted to bring in, Trevor Francis from Birmingham City. This would be a real marquee signing, but wouldn't come cheap. The initial offer of £750,000 was dismissed out of hand, 'We want a million' announced Birmingham. Bearing in mind the record transfer fee in England at this time was half of that, this was a big leap. Forest returned with several higher offers, but Birmingham wouldn't budge. By now other clubs were alerted to the player's availability, Coventry also put a high bid in, that was also rejected. Forest had the allure of playing in Europe and the charisma of Brian Clough, but it might come down to just hard cash. The timing of this move was not the best for Forest either. The player was cup tied in both the FA and League Cups and according to EUFA rules he would be ineligible for the European Cup unless Forest reached the final. Nottingham Forest, the club where the committee wouldn't sanction spending any money and ummed and ahhed about buying Bert Bowery, was now on the verge of completing the most spectacular signing, ever, in British football.

The Aston Villa cup tie was immediately re-arranged for the following Wednesday and Forest had little trouble brushing them aside 2-0, although playing conditions were not ideal. They followed this up with a defeat at Arsenal, again under icy conditions, surprising, because the Gunners had been pioneers of under soil heating, but the weather was so extreme that as soon as the power was switched off, the pitch began freezing again. It didn't make the job of Lloyd and Needham any easier. Due to the postponement of the Manchester United fixture, the next three games would be in cup competitions.
Watford were the surprising opponents in the League Cup semi-final, having disposed of Stoke City in the previous round and Manchester United and Newcastle earlier in the competition. Under Graham Taylor they were forging their way up the League ladder and although presently in the Third Division, only a few years hence, they themselves would be in the top flight.

The cold spell had momentarily eased, but in its place was a quagmire of a pitch, even the Watford players said it was the worst pitch they had played on. Watford immediately showed why they were enjoying success when they took a ninth minute lead through Luther Blisset. Forest hit back almost immediately through Birtles. The match then swung to and fro before Forest took the lead as another Birtles shot was deflected past his own keeper by a Watford defender. Against the run of play Forest added a third to win 3-1.

The away leg two weeks later was a non event, as the Reds strangled the life out of the home team with a 0-0 draw. Back to Wembley again, but because the semi-finals had been brought forward, there was to be a wait of six weeks for the final. Southampton would be the opponents. After the Watford game, snow had fallen once more and in an effort to get the FA Cup tie at home to York City played, it had been decided to roll the snow flat, rather than clear it. It

Peter Taylor and Geoffrey McPherson await the quarter final draw in Zurich

worked, the old orange style football had to be used, and it found its way into the York net three times in a 3-1 win.

The club managed to pull in another game, a 3-1 win at Middlesbrough, before the weather worsened and three more games were postponed. There was now a backlog of fixtures to pull in, the hoped for progress in Europe and the FA Cup, would mean playing three matches a week regularly.

The big news finally came when it was announced that Forest had completed the signing of Trevor Francis for what was labelled the first £1,000,000 transfer, (Although Brian Clough insisted that the fee had been one pound less). Forest had gone up to £950,000, but Birmingham wouldn't budge, Peter Taylor thought this was getting ridiculous so phoned Jim Smith the City manager and agreed the fee. Then he phoned Clough and told him what he had done. "Good", said the manager.

There were still agreements to be made with the player, not about wages, but the concerns that Francis had committed himself to playing during the close season with Detroit Express, therefore would be playing non-stop for a year. The player couldn't get out of his contractual obligations so Forest were left with no choice. Francis famously made his debut for the third team down on the banks of the Trent, but with a slightly typical disregard for the technicalities Clough hadn't ensured the paperwork had been completed and the club were later hit with a small fine for this misdemeanour.

To get some game time, Forest sent a full team down to Exeter where the weather was milder, to play in the Nicky Jennings testimonial match. Almost 10,000 fans turned up to watch the champions win 5-0, including Trevor Francis who started on the bench, and then another testimonial game played at Witney in Oxfordshire against West Brom, just two days later.

Francis made his league debut against Bristol City after coming on as substitute. Clough again sent out the signal that everyone was equal when Francis in his role as sub had to collect tracksuit tops from the players before the game and then serve tea at half-time. Francis recalls the nerves he felt when coming on, "I thought that I was OK, but after I went on, I realised that every move I made would be scrutinized in relation to the fee, with every miss the pressure would increase, plus there was always away supporters who couldn't wait to chant, 'What a waste of money'".

Forest had been due to play Arsenal at home in the FA Cup, but the game like the others fell victim to the weather and eventually was played nine days after it had been scheduled in mid-week. Forest went down 1-0 despite playing well. This game halted a run of forty nine unbeaten home league and cup matches stretching back to Cardiff City during the last weeks of the promotion season. Frank Stapleton who had scored four goals in five appearances against the Reds knocked in the winner. Although the manager of course wanted to win every game, this defeat might turn out to be a blessing in disguise.

Trevor Francis eventually made his full debut in the away draw at Ipswich. There was a growing influx of foreign players at this time after the Football Association had relaxed the rules. Ipswich had snapped up two fine Dutchmen in Arnold Muhren and Franz Thijssen, with the latter making his debut in this game.

Inflation of transfer fees was a monthly occurrence, those that thought that Forest had overpaid for Peter Shilton, surely couldn't comprehend West Ham paying £550,000 for QPR keeper Phil Parkes, he was able enough but nowhere near the quality of Shilton.

Europe again now took centre stage with the home tie against Zurich Grasshoppers. The club announced an increase in ticket prices and this allied to the limited appeal of Zurich contributed to a poor attendance of less than 32,000. Surely Forest deserved an attendance far greater than that for this game, after all, some regular league fixtures had attracted far higher. The days when supporters didn't mind being crammed on terracing were passing though. Some fans wrote to the club with reasons why they weren't attending and after the usual excuses about hooliganism, the main concern was actually the ability to see the game. One supporter said that they had attended every game standing in the Trent End, but only seen three goals. The shallowness of the terracing and regular surges meant that larger crowds could be an unpleasant experience, particularly for older and female spectators.

Zurich were considered to be the weakest of the teams left in, most pundits had seemed to forget that they had knocked out Real Madrid in the previous round and that should not be dismissed as a fluke. Peter Taylor had been to see them play and wasn't overly impressed, although the management would always ensure that there was no complacency. However after the game many players admitted that they had perhaps not given the

64,000 dollar question—who goes?

Evening Post, Monday, February 26, 1979

Francis shadow looms over four Reds stars

NOTTINGHAM Forest's Two Million Dollar Man Trevor Francis had plenty of time — while Bristol City went from the negative, to the unadventurous, to the inept in Saturday's Division One match at the City Ground — to reflect on the 64,000-dollar question: Who eventually makes room for him?

By IAN MANNING

A ONE MILLION pounds cross! Forest's £1m. signing Trevor Francis, slides in the mud to get in his first touch of the match with a cross into Bristol City's goalmouth.

So frustrating for

opposition full respect. Martin O'Neill came into the side for his first taste of European action, otherwise the team virtually picked itself due to injuries.

If Forest thought they were in for an easy ride, Claudio Sulser's tenth minute

Three minute burst earns Reds a just win

FORREST ... 4 GRASSHOPPERS ... 1

WHAT A NIGHT! And what a fright Nottingham Forest gave their fans before building a 4-1 lead in the first leg of their European Cup quarter-final against the mixture of skill and strength — mostly strength — offered by Grasshoppers of Zurich at the City Ground last night.

A goal down in 11 minutes — the Super Reds scored twice in the last three minutes to give themselves a scoreline that was ... for Forest and yet harsh on Grasshoppers.

That's a contradiction, yet so was the match. Forest had 33 ... corners; Grasshoppers had three. Forest had 30 ... Grasshoppers had five.

Yet until Archie Gemmill's left foot and Larry Lloyd's head doubled Forest's ... in those last three minutes, it look... Grasshoppers had virtually ... the City Ground ...

Trevor Frecknall

REFUSED

ROUND THREE FIRST LEG...
Wednesday 7th March. 1978

Forest	4
Grasshoppers	1

Birtles nets the Reds' opener.

Forest in search of more goals.

Martin O'Neill cannot find a way through the packed Zurich defence.

Sulser strikes after ...

O'Neill hits back for Super Reds

Euro Cup special

MARTIN O' NEILL, cast into the shadows by the £1m. appearance at the C... of Trevor Francis, grabbed his ... European Cup limelight in Zu... O'Neill was the scorer of the all-im... equalised a harsh penalty given ... carried the "Super Reds" through ... on a comfortable 5-2 aggregate.

POACHED GOA...

His far post poaching came in the ... four minutes after Grasshoppers ... in this match.

The Grasshopper's goal came in a mann... which could have shattered teams le... composed than Forest.

Viv Anderson and midfield man Egli col-lided as they leapt for a high ball on the edge of the penalty area.

The home team seemed as surprised as Forest when Ital-ian referee Gian-franco Menegalli awarded the penalty, but star striker ... Sulser coolly ... Shilton

on their 4-1 first-leg lead.

Anderson raced up to get behind the Swiss defence but his cen-tre drifted out for a goal kick.

Central defenders David Needham and ... Lloyd were ... than

midfield, frequently created danger down the left with John Robertson having a field day.

One of his penetrating crosses almost gave ... the lead after ... But the

ROUND THREE SECOND LEG...
Wednesday 21st March.1978

Grasshoppers	1
Forest	1

O'Neill settles the Reds' nerves with an equaliser.

Lloyd with number four.

Robbo from the spot.

Gemmill scores.

Peter Shilton and Angela Rippon

opening goal disabused them of that. Forest stepped up the pressure immediately and after a couple of close efforts Birtles fastened on to a through ball and equalised. Birtles was also instrumental in the build up to the second, when a Swiss defender handled as he tricked his way into the penalty area, Robertson coolly slotted home the spot kick. Zurich might have snatched an equaliser, but they wilted towards the end of the game. The Swiss League had had a winter break and this was one of their first games back. After eighty eight minutes Lloyd implausibly found himself wide on the right and his cross found Gemmill unmarked, and he stabbed in. During injury time O'Neill hit the bar, followed by three corners, before Lloyd met the last of these to head home.

What could have been a close result had dramatically swung the Reds' way in little over two minutes. If the players thought that they had done enough to satisfy the manager, they were wrong. Entering the dressing room they were on the wrong side of a right rollicking, "You're just a bunch of bigheads, you think that you can just go out there and do this, you think you can do that and you think you can make mugs out of a side we told you could play, idiots". (Swear words removed!)

A couple of injuries meant the team was changed for the next fixture away at Everton. Barrett, Francis and O'Hare came in, Barrett scoring the Reds' goal, a stunning effort, "The best of the season", according to Clough. Because of fixture congestion, Forest were then forced to play a re-arranged home fixture with Norwich only three days before the League Cup Final, a 2-1 win, but more importantly no new injuries to report. Tony Woodcock showed a welcome return to goal scoring form with two goals, his first since Boxing Day. Important off field news came when Peter Shilton and newsreader Angela Rippon were named, 'Head of the Year' by the British Hairdresser's Association. This was an award for those celebrities whose high standard of personal hair grooming brought credit to the hairdressing profession!! The youth team meanwhile were showing great promise under the tutelage of Liam O'Kane. They progressed through to the fifth round of the FA Youth Cup after smashing six unanswered goals past Portsmouth. Gary Mills who had already made his first team debut, starred alongside Steve Burke and future first teamers Steve Sutton and Colin Walsh.

The evening before the Southampton final has gone down in Clough folklore. On many occasions the management had been known to use alcohol to reduce the tension, but on this night they pushed the limit. Archie Gemmill had gone to bed and was ordered to come down as twelve bottles of champagne, beer and sandwiches appeared in the games room that Brian Clough had commandeered. Dominoes, cards and bar billiards were the order of the day, before the players retired to their rooms about one in the morning. A light breakfast and a morning walk before the bus to Wembley Stadium.
The weather had been cold and snowy, the journey to London was not without its difficulties but Forest fans were there in great numbers, this time they occupied the opposite end of the stadium compared to the previous year.

Someone in the League's marketing department, who had clearly never played football before, thought it might be a good idea to introduce a brand new style of match ball. An awful looking thing with a circular red panel that gave the impression that it wasn't rolling properly. The players hated it, but this shouldn't be used as an excuse for the terrible performance from Forest during the first half, as the Reds went in 1-0 down.

The first shock came pre match, when the two teams had emerged from the tunnel, Peter Taylor resplendent in club blazer proudly led the team out. The week before the game Brian Clough had asked Peter Taylor, "Do you want to do it ?". Taylor as a Forest fan had dreamed of a moment like this. The pair decided to keep this to themselves in case League Secretary Alan Hardaker got wind of the idea and tried to stop it.
Half-time saw another innovation as Peter Taylor was interviewed by Radio Nottingham about his thoughts on the first half, "We've weathered it and will take them in the second half", he said. Meanwhile in the dressing room, a more traditional approach was taken by the manager, "How dare you underperform with your wives, girlfriends, relations and supporters in the stands", he told the players. The quality of the pitch helped neither team, it would have been wet and muddy anyway, but the 'Horse of the Year Show', that had been held there recently, ensured that it was not fit for the National Stadium or an important cup final.

Anyway, a different Forest emerged for the second half and blew the Saints away, two for Garry Birtles and one for Tony Woodcock doesn't tell the full story. Birtles had two further goals disallowed, a good penalty shout turned down and a whole host of other chances, even a late Southampton consolation goal couldn't take the gloss of another fantastic win. Garry Birtles, much as Kenny Burns had done the previous season had emerged from the shadows to make a huge impression. No time for over the top celebrations though, the second leg of the Zurich game was to be played on the following Wednesday.

Despite once more going behind in Zurich, Martin O'Neill scored his first European goal with the equaliser. The atmosphere in the ground was not as febrile as Anfield or Athens, in fact the game was played out to a cacophony of cow-horns and bells, which when listened to on the radio or television, along with

A Viv special at Goodison Park.

It's celebration time as Woodcock scores the winner against Everton.

HIGHLIGHTS OF THE REDS' RUN TO THE LEAGUE CUP SEMI FINAL!...

Robertson coolly scores from the spot against Oldham.

Garry Birtles hurdles the Brighton keeper before knocking in the Reds' third against Brighton.

SECOND FOR FOREST

England defender Viv Anderson in action against Watford at the City Ground.

WATCHED by £1 million Trevor Francis, Nottingham Forest hope to retain the League Cup they won so bravely last year. If Liverpool were difficult opponents in '78, Saints will be no easier, but Brian Clough's team have produced their best football in Cup games this season. This time stars such as Peter Shilton and Archie Gemmill — Cup-tied a year ago — will be available and extra keen to make up for missing last season's Wembley run.

ABOVE . . . It's that Wembley feeling! Forest show their joy after a goal against Watford. BELOW . . . Martin O'Neill rounds Watford 'keeper Steve Sherwood.

LEAGUE CUP FINAL MARCH 17TH ....WEMBLEY STADIUM

Nottingham Forest 3 Southampton 2

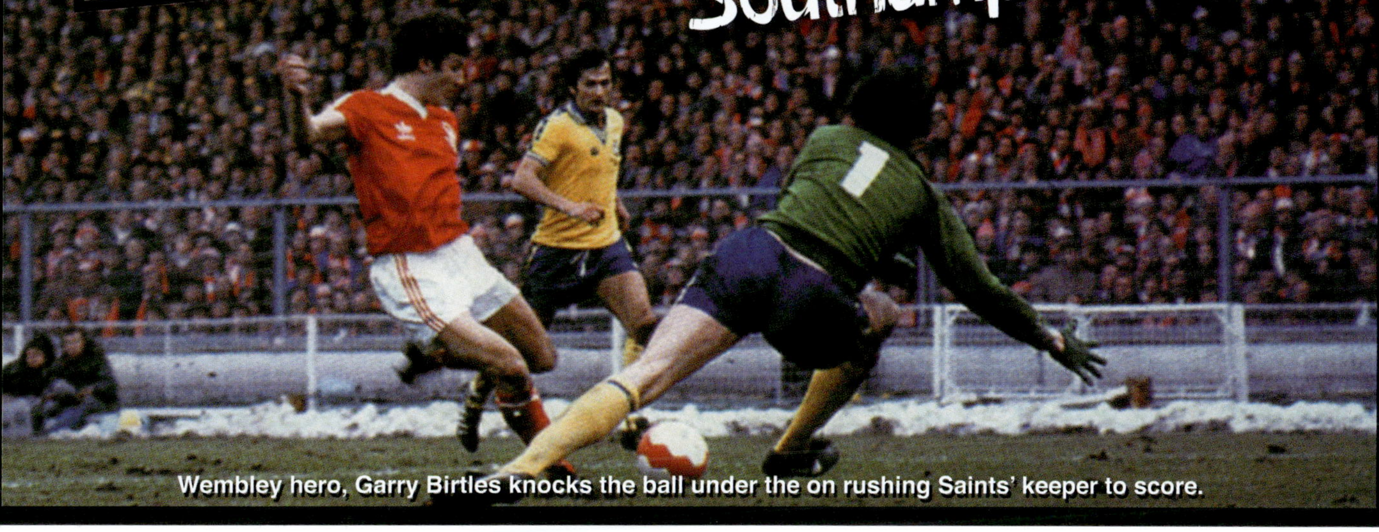

Wembley hero, Garry Birtles knocks the ball under the on rushing Saints' keeper to score.

An artists drawing of the proposed East Stand development

a commentary that sounded like it was coming from Mars, gave a typically European soundtrack for matches of that era.

Although Garry Birtles led the way with five goals in this competition, nine other players had also chipped in with a goal apiece.

Once more Ken Smales and Peter Taylor would return to Zurich for the draw and as they were both lovers of their food, the secretary would often give more details in the match day programme about what restaurants they had visited than the football. The other three teams who joined Forest in the draw were Cologne, the German champions who had knocked out Rangers, Malmo and Austria Vienna. Cologne were clearly the strongest of the teams that Forest could be drawn against, but when the two were pitted together, there was no fear from Forest that they couldn't get a result.

Forest amazingly had sixteen league fixtures to pull in before the end of season. Plans for the new East Stand had now undergone a full consultation period and the artist's sketches of how it would look were released. Nottingham City Council had agreed to act as guarantors for the one and a half million pound overdraft from Nat West that would fund the build. The Council were fully aware of the kudos that came with the success of Nottingham Forest in Europe, after all, they had been sending out business teams under Colin Slater (Information Officer for the Council), to coincide with away fixtures. These would be used to promote the area not only as a good place to conduct business but also for tourism.

The new stand, excitingly was to be called 'The Executive Stand', (as it had executive boxes). It would mean another drop in the ground capacity to a little over 35,000, but the number of seats would double, thereby maximising revenue. The design of the stand was very much in keeping with others built at the same time. A huge cantilevered roof with no obstructive pillars, executive boxes in between upper and lower tiers and more corporative facilities contained within. There had been protests at first about seating the lower tier as well as the upper, after all this meant a break with the past as there would be no standing along either side of the pitch. On a separate note, concerns were also raised about the view from the Bridgford End and whether money should be spent on a roof to keep these patrons dry. But for now the Stadium was being developed in the style of a modern and progressive organisation, paid for out of the profits of a successful football team. The builders Norwest Holst who had been fixed to a tight schedule with punitive penalties if they were late completing, were desperate to make an early start on demolition. Even though, only the lower tier with 2,800 seats and no roof, would be ready for the start of the new season, full completion would not be until December.

Five fixtures, including four at home before the European semi-final. An attack that had looked a little short earlier in the season, now boasted Francis, Birtles and Woodcock. They responded with nine goals in two games, firstly 3-0 against Norwich and 6-0 against Chelsea, three goals for a rejuvenated Woodcock and a hat-trick for Martin O'Neill in the second game.
Trevor Francis notched his first goal against Bolton, a last minute equaliser, but it was a point dropped. Normal service continued with a 4-0 win against Villa, who Forest particularly seemed to enjoy playing against, followed by a 3-1 victory at Chelsea, who were once more sliding towards relegation. Francis scoring in three successive matches. With the Cologne game in mind, the manager switched his team around. The left back position was filled by Bryn Gunn, saving Colin Barrett who would have to stand in for the suspended Viv Anderson.

Cologne had a strong looking team, Harald Schumaker in goal was the new national team keeper and an immense presence. Bernd Schuster, Herbert Neumann, Herbert Zimmerman, Heinz Flohe and Dieter Mueller were all German internationals, along with the Belgian Roger van Gool and the Japanese Yasuhiko Okudera. They also had one of the most respected coach/managers in world football, Hennes Weisweiler. In a sign of changing times, it was reported that Cologne received the equivalent of £25,000 to have a sponsor's name on the front of their shirts, this was not allowed in England at this time, and EUFA rules also prohibited them for wearing these shirts in their competition as well.

The game played on another City Ground mud heap, was a classic and the favourite for many Forest players of that time, including Martin O'Neill, who rated the atmosphere that night as the best he ever encountered in the game. The match itself had everything. In their usual manner, Forest were quick out of the blocks in an attempt to put the opposition on the back foot, but this was a quality team with a wily manager who got his tactics spot on. Cologne were ready for them and raced into an early two goal lead. Van Gool skipped forward, before hitting a shot that nestled in the net after hitting both posts. Worse was to come when Van Gool again fastened onto a through ball, cleverly drew Shilton, before slipping the ball to Mueller who slid the ball into an empty net. This was not going according to the plan. There was plenty of time left and the

Garry Birtles celebrates Dave Needham's goal against Coventry.

Tony Woodcock turns away after netting against the Canaries.

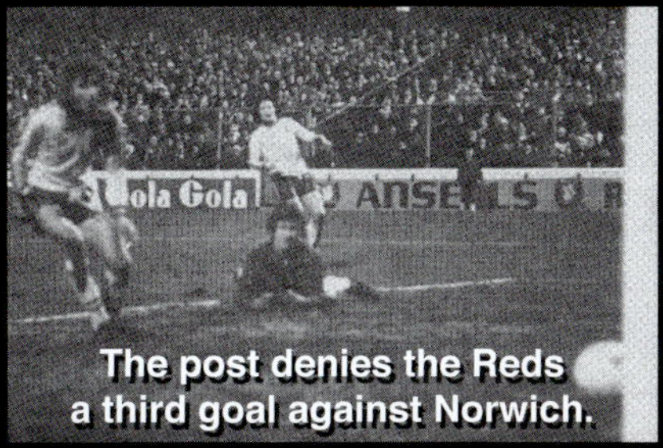

The post denies the Reds a third goal against Norwich.

Tony Woodcock with his second against Norwich City.

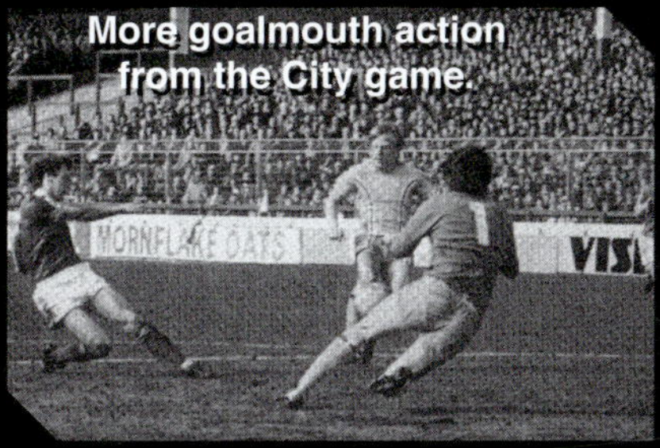

More goalmouth action from the City game.

CHELSEA NORWICH COVENTRY

Birtles nets his second.

Martin O'Neill, arm raised after he scored his hat-trick goal against Chelsea.

O'Neill once more against Chelsea.

Tony Woodcock's turn this time as the Reds hit Chelsea for six.

Great Forest fightback in six-goal thriller

GOALS, goals, goals at the City Ground last night. Above: Roger Van Gool drives Cologne into the lead. Above right: Winger John Robertson flies in to head Forest into a 3-2 lead after they had trailed 0-2.

Okudera's goal sets Reds herculean task

NOTTM FOREST . . 3 F.C. COLOGNE . . 3

PETER SHILTON, perpetrating the worst mistake of his brilliant 19 months with Nottingham Forest, summed up a night of defensive mayhem at the City Ground last night that now leaves the Reds with a herculean task to lift the European Cup.

The side must win outright in Cologne's palatial stadium in 13 day's time to reach the final against Wien of Austria or Malmoe at Munich on May 30. The ... realistic 4-4 draw — or higher

Ian Bowyer rifles Forest's second g...

SEMI FINAL...
Wednesday 11th April.1979
Forest 3
1.FC Cologne 3

Birtles starts the fight back.

David Needham goes for glory.

Bowyer blasts home the equaliser.

Ian Bowyer again goes close.

hands off". The Germans c
prepared for the unusual
approached the game. T
recalls talking to the hote
stayed in the same hotel fo
after he joined Cologne,
believe how low key we w
drinks, no training, they
home side to win". They
ones suffering from ove
local travel agent leafleted
the stadium with details c
to the final in Munich.

The Mungersdorf Stadiur
German arena of that tim
World Cup of 1974 and de
municipal sports, not only
had a running track ar
which didn't help with t
The club didn't own the s
10% of gate receipts to pla
included all upkeep. It als
deep moat to prevent any
6,000 Forest fans made th
been waiting for the fina
first trip abroad, but with t
edge, they couldn't afford

Cloughie kept his team
precise, "They will come
have to absorb a bit of pres
at half-time and in the sec
out and after about twenty
score and we'll hang on to
Peter Taylor took the pl
pitch to deliver his thoug
by Ken Smales, "Let us w
with a bit of arrogance.
to attack us down the
overawed, be prepared to
flair....Viv and Frank, do
of overlapping, right fr
necessary....be patient, w
the 89th minute if we hav

There was no special prov
and Taylor to sit close eno
to be heard, so the mana
himself to grab a coupl
chairs and position them
track closer to the action.
The Forest defence wa
strength, Burns and And
to the line-up with Ll
Ian Bowyer started in m
essential that Forest did
goal and they were pr
Cologne all the posse
wanted in their own half.
it was considered an awk
the home team, play for t
goal. If Cologne had los
one goal, they would ha

POST 6
No. 31,345 NOTTINGHAM, THURSDAY APRIL 26, 1979
THE MAGNIFICENT ELEVEN...
WE'RE on our way to Munich!
Forest clinch their place in the final
FOREST'S European Cup heroes returned home early today — to a rapturous welcome at the East Midlands Airport, Castle Donington.
They flew back after clinching their place in the May 30 final against Swedish champions Malmo in Munich's Olympic stadium with a stunning 1-0 win over West German champions FC Cologne...

SEMI FINAL...
Wednesday 25th April.1979
1.FC Cologne 0
Forest 1

Ian Bowyer stoops to conquer.

David Needham and Ian Bowyer acknowledge the supporters.

Celebrations, the Reds are Munich bound.

Larry Lloyd and Kenny Burns.

Reds weren't a team to
they gained the ascenda
first Bowyer hit the bar
nodded home after Nee
back across the box. C
for European competi
sitting back and the g
end to end. First Shilt
Knopka shot over the ba
went close when Schur
into a sprawling save
block brilliantly with hi
the wrong way from a
The last chance of the h
dangerous Van Gool wh
after beating Shilton. C
endured a torrid first h
whilst trying to stop the
that was to rule him ou
virtually end his Forest c

In the dressing room a
Clough was decisive. H
one for the thoughtle
often cajoled players t
if injured. However, c
Gemmill was withdrawn
was introduced at left ba
was pushed forward into
The changes had an a
effect, Birtles nodded dc
the path of 'Bomber' a
brought the scores leve
Forest had come from
crowd were in great voi
it looked as if Cologne
heavy pitch.
After further pressure,
Birtles wide on the right
the defender he clipped
box. It looked optimist
John Robertson ap
full length to head ho
particularly poignant m
whose brother had died
days before and who had
of playing.
When Neumann drove c

and then promptly dropped him. When Forest lost to Wolves in a game crammed into the schedule on the Monday evening, it was the third and last league defeat the team suffered, the same number as the previous season. The main problem was that nineteen games had been drawn and eight less goals had been scored, this inevitably affected the points total.

The crowd for the Southampton game was down to only 20,000, but by now the club had sold more tickets than this for Munich and money was being saved. Trevor Francis scored the only goal of the game and was now pressing hard to be included for the final. After drawing at Norwich, the curtain came down on the season at the City Ground against Manchester City. An emphatic 3-1 meant that they could still overhaul West Brom for second place, especially as they still had the Baggies to play.

Pulling in an extra game, this time a testimonial for Lawrie McMenemy at Southampton, a professional 4-0 win, they then went up to Leeds and came away with another win, 2-1 and a first senior goal for Gary Mills, the Elland Road fans earning the scorn of the country by chanting, 'Ripper ten, Police nil' in reference to the Yorkshire Police's inability to stop the killing spree. Now the stage was set for a last game showdown at the Hawthorns. A tight game settled in the Reds' favour by a Trevor Francis effort, now wearing the number seven shirt.

After overcoming so many hurdles, not least a seemingly never ending injury list, they finished the season in second place, losing only three games compared to Liverpool who lost four.

All eyes and preparation were now fixed on Munich, they had even managed to persuade Mansfield Town to stay in training so that they could play the County Cup Final the week before the European Final. Archie Gemmill was the main beneficiary as he came on for the final twenty minutes to try and persuade the manager that he was fit for selection.

Getting to the final was a case of planes, trains and automobiles for Forest supporters, all local bus companies ran trips as well as the official buses organised by the club. Many supporter's groups set off early, making a week of it. The club chartered eight trains, the first part of the journey taking fans to the port, then a channel crossing, before picking up a French train on the other side, after a wait

of a couple of hours. All those that sing the praises of European rail travel, would not have been impressed by the trains provided on this occasion. They seemed to be the oldest and worst carriages that they could find, indeed, with the reputation of English football fans, they weren't going to risk the decent ones. There were no refreshment facilities and toilets were rudimentary, worse still was the overcrowding. This was manageable on the way out, when the excitement was building, but the journey back after the game was terrible.

25,000 tickets had been sold for the game, even more than Liverpool when they played in Rome for the 1977 final, meaning that this was the largest English following for a European game. Malmo on the other hand would be backed by only 8,000 followers.

As far as the players were concerned, all they wanted to know was, were they playing? In truth there were only two places up for grabs, to be fought over by Trevor Francis and three players returning from injury. Nobody wants to miss out on what could be the pinnacle of their career, but clearly there were going to be two very disappointed players. Brian Clough always maintained that if all the players had been fit, there was no way that Francis would have played, but he clearly couldn't afford to risk two players, so he was in. Frank Clark recalls the manager asking the three of them, "Are you fit?", "Yes gaffer", was the reply from all of them, of course it would be. Frank Clark thinks that Clough trusted his reply just a little bit more than the others.

Brian Clough had arrived two days after the players, having taken his family on a quick holiday to Crete. The team hotel was outside Munich and the preparation was basically the same as for the semi-final, a little bit of training for the injured players, plus plenty of walks and an occasional alcoholic beverage. After ascertaining the fitness of the squad, he announced the team line up to the players whilst they sat on the grass at the side of the pitch in the Olympic Stadium, on the morning of the game. To say that Gemmill didn't take his exclusion well, would have been the understatement of the year, he let the manager know exactly what he thought of the decision. He has always maintained that the manager had told him that he would definitely play if he was fit. Gemmill's reaction was so severe that it probably led to the player leaving the club during the close season and missing his chance of playing in the final the following year. Gemmill's response soured the build up, every player in the team at one time or another had been in the same predicament, now they just wanted to prepare for the game. After abusing Brian Clough, the player then turned his attention to Peter Taylor as he tried to explain what a difficult decision it had been. Martin O'Neill who had had his share of disappointments in the past, this time to his credit, kept his thoughts to himself. O'Neill's hamstring was in fact to fail him several weeks later whilst on international duty, perhaps justifying that decision. Meanwhile thousands of supporters descended on Munich, filling the beer kellers and squares with a display of drunken good behaviour. Dennis McCarthy presented his Radio Nottingham afternoon show, live from the centre of Munich.

Peter Taylor thought that there was only one thing that could prevent Forest from lifting the trophy....over confidence. He had been to Sweden to watch Malmo in action and couldn't believe how bad they were. He told Clough, "We can't let the players find out". Malmo would also be without their first choice strikers, they were already considered a dour outfit under English coach Bob Houghton, this was unlikely to be a classic.

A wall of noise greeted the players as they were led out by the Austrian referee Erich Linemayr, Malmo were so badly hit by injuries that they were only able to name four substitutes, although they did have several quality players such as Robert Prytz, Steffan Tapper and the giant keeper Jan Moller. Forest did have one player that had already played in a European Final, Ian Bowyer, who had featured in the Cup Winner's Cup back in 1970, for Manchester City. Malmo had won the

NOTTINGHAM FOREST
V
MALMÖ FF

OLYMPIC STADIUM MUNICH

Dave Wrench, Rob Pack and the Author outside Munich's Olympic Stadium

It's there!

THE GOAL that won Forest the European Cup hits the Malmo net in Munich — putting the treasured trophy in captain John McGovern's hands (right), a smile on the face of manager Brian Clough as he leaves the Olympic Stadium with assistant manager Peter Taylor, and the ultimate crown on the head of the £1m scorer, Trevor Francis, whose first-ever goal in the competition will never be forgotten in Nottingham.

Trevor Francis dives to head John Robertson's left wing cross into the net for what proved Nottingham Forest's European Cup winning goal. (Left) Forest — Champions of Europe.

NOTTINGHAM NEWS
Inside your European Cup News today . . .
FRANTASTIC
Heroes' welcome
Thanks a million Trevor
for a golden goal

EVENING POST
NOTTINGHAM, FRIDAY, JUNE 1, 1979
NIGHT THEY PAINTED THE CITY RED!
Glory ride for Forest
CAPTURED IN ONE PICTURE . . . THE ECSTASY OF A CITY WITH A EURO-BEATING TEAM

toss and decided to play towards their own fans in the first half, whilst the Reds had the kick-off. Brian Clough always thought that it was important to get a good positive early touch and he must have been surprised when Kenny Burns, who never seemed fazed by anything, made an early hash of a clearance. As Kenny remembers, "I had nerves, who'd have thought it, me playing in a European final". Malmo, even more than expected dropped back into a defensive line, making good use of the offside trap.

The first half was a virtual non event until the last five minutes. Firstly Woodcock made one of his trademark bursts through the middle, but he never looked like positioning himself to get a shot away and then ran into the outsized frame of Jan Moller. Malmo then responded with an attack of their own before Anderson charged into the Swedes' penalty area and slashed the ball across the face of the goal. It looked as if the teams would go in goalless, but one moment of supreme quality changed that. Robertson had been pushed deeper and deeper to get in the game, but on this occasion he was further up the field. Collecting the ball from Bowyer, he ambled his way down the left touchline whilst Prytz as usual went over to support the full back. As Robbo had done so many times in his career, he shimmied as if he was cutting inside before hitting the after burner for a ten yard burst that took him past both players, opening the space for a cross. Every player in the Forest team knew to get up quickly in support when they saw this happening and Trevor Francis on the opposite flank began his fifty yard streak. The cross that Robbo produced could not have been bettered, struck with enough pace and accuracy to by pass four Malmo defenders and a keeper standing at 6ft 7". By the time it reached the head of Francis, it was barely a couple of feet from goal. Francis arriving at pace and with one eye on the circular patch of concrete by the goal, used as a base for shot putters, headed powerfully home, "That's just what I wanted to see". Exclaimed the BBC commentator, Barry Davies.

Brian Clough used to tell a story about a photograph that he had hanging in his study, that encapsulated his managerial career. The cross from a player who cost nothing, whose career he had helped turn around, headed in by the first million pound player in the country, paid for by all the success he had brought to the club. Sir Bobby Charlton who was co-commentating was sure that this goal would lead to more, but he wasn't convinced that this would persuade Malmo to alter their defensive, stifling tactics.

The second half indeed continued in the same vein, if Forest had managed to get a second, the floodgates would surely have opened, but they couldn't afford to go gung-ho and allow the Swedes back into the game, after all a win is a win and they would only be invited to participate in the competition next season if they were defending champions.

There were still chances however, Garry Birtles blazed over when he had time to bring the ball down, then Robertson hit the post after a great run by Francis and finally Woodcock's chip after he had battled hard for possession. All Malmo had to offer was a string of terrible free kicks that went high wide and handsome. Even as the minutes ticked down they never threw caution to the wind and Forest saw the game out comfortably.

Archie Gemmill sitting on the bench was beside himself with frustration, he begged the manager to get him on, arguing persuasively that even on one leg, he would bring more energy to the performance. The manager however, had shown throughout his career, that once he had his mind set, he would never want to look as if he was open to persuasion, even if common opinion was that he might be wrong.

As the whistle went, there was not a frenzied celebration amongst the players, as most of them realised it had been a poor game and they had wanted to put on a show. It wasn't until they were in the dressing room that Peter Taylor tried to whip things up, "Come on, you've won the European Cup". In truth this was almost one game to far, the sixty fifth of a long hard season, in the most competitive league in the world, with a small injury ravaged squad and with a backlog of fixtures caused by terrible weather in England that would have defeated any other team in the world. In truth they had already played two finals earlier in the tournament, against Liverpool and Cologne, the final just needed to be won. The story should not have been how poor the game was, but only how a provincial team had risen from the depths of the English Second Division and within two years won the European Cup, instead the poor quality final was once more used as a stick to beat the 'upstarts', as if one game was a true indication of their quality. After all, Liverpool against Bruges the previous year was an equally bad game, dual standards applied once more by the media.

The largest ever turn out by the people of Nottingham greeted the players on the open top bus tour of the city, that finished traditionally at the Council House in the Market Square. Brian Clough was absent, he had returned to Crete to continue his holiday, also absent was Peter Taylor.

The Nottinghamshire area had embraced and benefitted from the club's success in Europe, as we have seen previously, the City had been looking for a new identity with the decline of some of its traditional industries. The Council had jumped on board to use the European campaign to promote the area during away European fixtures and by going all the way, they were able to maximise this. The economic benefits to the area should never be underestimated, even now, almost forty years later, the mention of Nottingham on the continent gets either the response of Robin Hood or Brian Clough and Nottingham Forest.

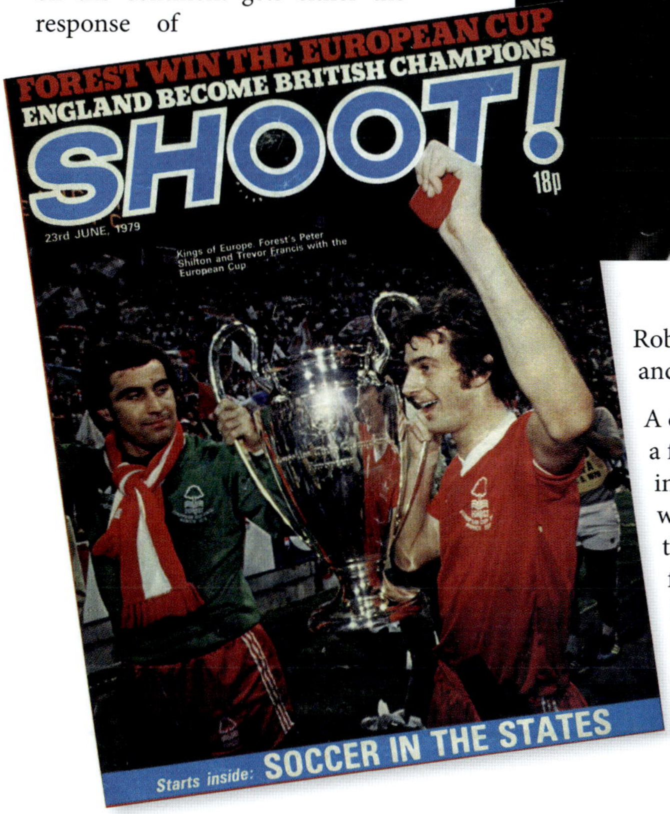

A decade that had started with a football club on a seemingly inexorable decline, ended with Nottingham Forest at the pinnacle of European football. In a decade of two halves, only five words are needed to explain how this happened...Brian Clough and Peter Taylor.

This is in no way meant to minimise the part played by any players or characters that were part of the fabric and history of the club during this period, but just an honest acknowledgement of the unique environment that they created that in turn allowed the players to express and fulfil their full potential.

To be a Nottingham Forest fan during this period was just fantastic, so many highlights, great trips alongside great friends.

They really were the **'Best of Times'**!

FACTS and FIGURES

Aug 12th 1978, Charity Shield, N, Wembley, v. Ipswich Town, Win 5-0, Scorers Lloyd, O'Neill (2), Withe, Robertson, AT 64,438, Shilton, Anderson, Barrett, McGovern, Lloyd, Burns, O'Neill, Gemmill, Withe, Woodcock, Robertson, SUB Needham.

Aug 19th 1978, H, v. Tottenham Hotspur, Draw 1-1, Scorer O'Neill, AT 41,223, Shilton, Anderson, Barrett, McGovern, Needham, Burns, O'Neill, Gemmill, Withe, Woodcock, Robertson.

Aug 22nd 1978, A, v. Coventry City, Draw 0-0, AT 28,585, Shilton, Anderson, Barrett, McGovern, Needham, Burns, O'Neill, Gemmill, Elliot, Woodcock, Robertson.

Aug 26th 1978, A, v. Queens Park Rangers, Draw 0-0, AT 17,971, Shilton, Anderson, Barrett, McGovern, Needham, Burns, O'Neill, Gemmill, Elliot, Woodcock, Robertson.

Aug 29th 1978, LC, A, v. Oldham Athletic, Draw 0-0, AT 13,793, Shilton, Anderson, Barrett, McGovern, Needham, Burns, O'Neill, Gemmill, Elliot, Woodcock, Robertson.

Sept 2nd 1978, H, v. West Bromwich Albion, Draw 0-0, AT 28,239, Shilton, Anderson, Barrett, McGovern, Needham, Burns, O'Neill, Gemmill, Elliot, Woodcock, Robertson.

Sept 6th 1978, H, v. Oldham Athletic, Win 4-2, Scorers Needham, Burns, Woodcock, Robertson (Pen), AT 18,669, Shilton, Anderson, Barrett, McGovern, Needham, Burns, O'Neill, Gemmill, Elliot, Woodcock, Robertson.

Sept 9th 1978, H, v. Arsenal, Win 2-1, Scorers Bowyer, Robertson (Pen), AT 28,124, Shilton, Anderson, Barrett, McGovern, Lloyd, Burns, Mills, Bowyer, Birtles, Woodcock, Robertson, SUB Needham.

Sept 13th 1978, EC, H, v. Liverpool, Win 2-0, Scorers Barrett, Birtles, AT 38,318, Shilton, Anderson, Barrett, McGovern, Lloyd, Burns, Gemmill, Bowyer, Birtles, Woodcock, Robertson.

Sept 16th 1978, A, v. Man United, Draw 1-1, Scorer Bowyer, AT 55,039, Shilton, Anderson, Barrett, McGovern, Lloyd, Burns, Gemmill, Bowyer, Birtles, Woodcock, Robertson.

Sept 23rd 1978, H, v. Middlesbrough, Draw 2-2, Scorers O'Neill, Birtles, AT 26,287, Shilton, Anderson, Barrett, McGovern, Lloyd, Burns, O'Neill, Bowyer, Birtles, Woodcock, Robertson, SUB O'Hare.

Sept 27th 1978, EC, A, v. Liverpool, Draw 0-0, AT 51,679, Shilton, Anderson, Clark, McGovern, Lloyd, Burns, Gemmill, Bowyer, Birtles, Woodcock, Robertson.

Sept 30th 1978, A, v. Aston Villa, Win 2-1, Scorers Woodcock, Robertson (Pen), AT 36,735, Shilton, Anderson, Bowyer, McGovern, Lloyd, Burns, O'Neill, Gemmill, Birtles, Woodcock, Robertson.

Oct 4th 1978, LC, A, v. Oxford United, Win 5-0, Scorers Anderson, McGovern, O'Neill, Birtles, Robertson, AT 14,287, Shilton, Anderson, Bowyer, McGovern, Lloyd, Burns, O'Neill, Gemmill, Birtles, Woodcock, Robertson, SUB O'Hare.

Oct 7th 1978, H, v. Wolverhampton Wanderers, Win 3-1, Scorers O'Neill, Birtles (2), AT 29,313, Shilton, Anderson, Clark, McGovern, Lloyd, Burns, O'Neill, Gemmill, Birtles, Woodcock, Robertson, SUB Bowyer.

Oct 14th 1978, A, v. Bristol City, Win 3-1, Scorers Birtles, Robertson (2), AT 26,947, Shilton, Anderson, Clark, McGovern, Lloyd, Burns, O'Neill, Gemmill, Birtles, O'Hare, Robertson.

Oct 18th 1978, EC, A, v. AEK Athens, Win 2-1, Scorers McGovern, Birtles, AT 36,000, Shilton, Anderson, Clark, McGovern, Lloyd, Burns, Gemmill, Bowyer, Birtles, Woodcock, Robertson.

Oct 21st 1978, H, v. Ipswich Town, Win 1-0, Scorer O'Neill, AT 28,911, Shilton, Anderson, Clark, McGovern, Needham, Burns, O'Neill, Bowyer, Birtles, Woodcock, Robertson.

Oct 28th 1978, A, v. Southampton, Draw 0-0, AT 22,429, Shilton, Anderson, Bowyer, McGovern, Lloyd, Burns, Gemmill, O'Hare, Birtles, Woodcock, Robertson, SUB Needham.

Nov 1st 1978, EC, H, v. AEK Athens, Win 5-1, Scorers Anderson, Needham, Birtles (2), Woodcock, AT 38,069, Shilton, Anderson, Clark, O'Hare, Lloyd, Needham, Gemmill, Bowyer, Birtles, Woodcock, Robertson, SUB Mills.

Nov 4th 1978, H, v. Everton, Draw 0-0, AT 35,515, Shilton, Anderson, Bowyer, O'Hare, Lloyd, Burns, O'Neill, Gemmill, Birtles, Woodcock, Robertson.

Nov 7th 1978, LC, A, v. Everton, Win 3-2, Scorers Anderson, Lloyd, Woodcock, AT 48,503, Shilton, Anderson, Bowyer, O'Hare, Lloyd, Burns, Gemmill, Needham, Birtles, Woodcock, Robertson, SUB Mills.

Nov 11th 1978, A, v. Tottenham Hotspur, Win 3-1, Scorers Anderson, Birtles, Robertson, AT 50,541, Shilton, Anderson, Bowyer, O'Hare, Lloyd, Needham, Gemmill, Mills, Birtles, Woodcock, Robertson.

Nov 18th 1978, H, v. Queens Park Rangers, Draw 0-0, AT 28,032, Shilton, Anderson, Bowyer, Needham, Lloyd, O'Hare, Mills, Gemmill, Birtles, Woodcock, Robertson.

Nov 25th 1978, A, v. Bolton Wanderers, Win 1-0, Scorer Robertson, AT 25,692, Shilton, Anderson, Clark, Needham, Lloyd, Bowyer, O'Neill, Gemmill, Birtles, Woodcock, Robertson, SUB O'Hare.

Dec 9th 1978, A, v. Liverpool, Loss 0-2, AT 51,469, Shilton, Anderson, Clark, Needham, Lloyd, Bowyer, Gemmill, McGovern, Elliot, Birtles, Robertson.

Dec 13th 1978, LC, H, v. Brighton & Hove Albion, Win 3-1, Scorers McGovern, Birtles, Robertson , AT 30,672, Shilton, Anderson, Clark, McGovern, Lloyd, Needham, Bowyer, Gemmill, Birtles, Woodcock, Robertson.

Dec 16th 1978, H, Birmingham City, Win 1-0, Scorer Gemmill, AT 25,224, Shilton, Anderson, Clark, McGovern, Lloyd, Needham, Bowyer, Gemmill, Birtles, Woodcock, Robertson.

Dec 23rd 1978, A, v. Man City, Draw 0-0, AT 37,012, Shilton, Anderson, Clark, McGovern, Lloyd, Needham, O'Neill, Gemmill, Birtles, Woodcock, Robertson, SUB Bowyer.

Dec 26th 1978, H, v. Derby County, Draw 1-1, Scorer Woodcock, AT 34,256, Shilton, Anderson, Clark, McGovern, Lloyd, Needham, O'Neill, Gemmill, Birtles, Woodcock, Robertson.

First Division 1978-79

		Pld	W	D	L	F	A	Pts
1	Liverpool	42	30	8	4	85	16	68
2	FOREST	42	21	18	3	61	26	60
3	West Bromwich Albion	42	24	11	7	72	35	59
4	Everton	42	17	17	8	52	40	51
5	Leeds United	42	18	14	10	70	52	50
6	Ipswich Town	42	20	9	13	63	49	49
7	Arsenal	42	17	14	11	61	48	48
8	Aston Villa	42	15	16	11	59	49	46
9	Manchester United	42	15	15	12	60	63	45
10	Coventry City	42	14	16	12	58	68	44
11	Tottenham Hotspur	42	13	15	14	48	61	41
12	Middlesbrough	42	15	10	17	57	50	40
13	Bristol City	42	15	10	17	47	51	40
14	Southampton	42	12	16	14	47	53	40
15	Manchester City	42	13	13	16	58	56	39
16	Norwich City	42	7	23	12	51	57	37
17	Bolton Wanderers	42	12	11	19	54	75	35
18	Wolverhampton Wand.	42	13	8	21	44	68	34
19	Derby County	42	10	11	21	44	68	34
20	Queens Park Rangers	42	6	13	23	45	73	25
21	Birmingham City	42	6	10	26	37	64	22
22	Chelsea	42	5	10	27	44	92	20

Jan 10th 1979, FAC, A, v. Aston Villa, Win 2-0, Scorers Needham, Woodcock, AT 29,550, Shilton, Anderson, Clark, McGovern, Lloyd, Needham, O'Neill, Gemmill, Birtles, Woodcock, Robertson.

Jan 13th 1979, A, v. Arsenal, Loss 1-2, Scorer Robertson, AT 52,189, Shilton, Anderson, Clark, McGovern, Lloyd, Needham, O'Neill, Gemmill, Birtles, Woodcock, Robertson.

Jan 17th 1979, LC, H, v. Watford, Win 3-1, Scorers Birtles (2), Robertson, AT 32,438, Shilton, Anderson, Clark, McGovern, Lloyd, Needham, O'Neill, Bowyer, Birtles, Woodcock, Robertson.

Jan 27th 1979, FAC, H, v. York City, Win 3-1, Scorers McGovern, Lloyd, O'Neill, AT 25,228, Shilton, Anderson, Bowyer, McGovern, Lloyd, Burns, O'Neill, Gemmill, Birtles, Woodcock, Robertson.

Jan 30th 1979, LC, A, v. Watford, Draw 0-0, AT 27,656, Shilton, Anderson, Bowyer, McGovern, Lloyd, Burns, O'Neill, Gemmill, Birtles, Woodcock, Robertson.

Feb 3rd 1979, A, v, Middlesbrough, Win 3-1, Scorers Birtles (2), Robertson (Pen), AT 21,330, Shilton, Anderson, Bowyer, McGovern, Lloyd, Burns, O'Neill, Gemmill, Birtles, Woodcock, Robertson.

Feb 24th 1979, H, v. Bristol C, Win 2-0, Scorers Needham, Birtles, AT 28,008, Shilton, Anderson, Clark, McGovern, Lloyd, Needham, O'Neill, Gemmill, Birtles, Woodcock, Robertson, SUB Francis.

Feb 26th 1979, FAC, H, v. Arsenal, Loss 0-1, AT 35,908, Shilton, Anderson, Clark, McGovern, Lloyd, Needham, O'Neill, Gemmill, Birtles, Woodcock, Robertson.

Mar 3rd 1979, A, v. Ipswich Town, Draw 1-1, Scorer Birtles, AT 27,188, Shilton, Anderson, Clark, McGovern, Lloyd, Needham, O'Neill, Gemmill, Birtles, Francis, Robertson.

Mar 7th 1979, EC, H, v. Grasshopper Zurich, Win 4-1, Scorers Lloyd, Gemmill, Birtles, Robertson (Pen), AT 31,949, Shilton, Anderson, Clark, McGovern, Lloyd, Needham, O'Neill, Gemmill, Birtles, Woodcock, Robertson.

Mar 10th 1979, A, v. Everton, Draw 1-1, Scorer Barrett, AT 37,745, Shilton, Barrett, Bowyer, McGovern, Lloyd, Needham, Francis, O'Hare, Birtles, Woodcock, Robertson,

Mar 14th 1979, H, v. Norwich City, Win 2-1, Scorer Woodcock (2), AT 24,046, Shilton, Barrett, Clark, McGovern, Lloyd, Needham, Francis, Gemmill, Birtles, Woodcock, Robertson.

Mar 17th 1979, LC, N,Wembley, v. Southampton, Win 3-2, Scorers Birtles (2), Woodcock, AT 100,000, Shilton, Barrett, Clark, McGovern, Lloyd, Needham, O'Neill, Gemmill, Birtles, Woodcock, Robertson.

Mar 21st 1979, EC, A, v. Grasshopper Zurich, Draw 1-1, Scorer O'Neill, AT 17,800, Shilton, Anderson, Barrett, McGovern, Lloyd, Needham, O'Neill, Gemmill, Birtles, Woodcock, Robertson.

Mar 24th 1979, H, v. Coventry City, Win 3-0, Scorers Needham, Birtles, Woodcock, AT 29,706, Shilton, Anderson, Barrett, McGovern, Lloyd, Needham, O'Neill, Francis, Birtles, Woodcock, Robertson.

Mar 28th 1979, H, v. Chelsea, Win 6-0, Scorers O'Neill (3), Birtles, Woodcock (2), AT 24,514, Shilton, Anderson, Bowyer, McGovern, Lloyd, Needham, O'Neill, Francis, Birtles, Woodcock, Robertson.

Mar 31st 1979, H, v. Bolton W, Draw 1-1, Scorer Francis, AT 29,015, Shilton, Anderson, Bowyer, McGovern, Lloyd, Needham, O'Neill, Francis, Birtles, Woodcock, Robertson.

Apr 4th 1979, H, v. Aston Villa, Win 4-0, Scorers O'Neill, Francis, Woodcock, Evans (OG), AT 27,056, Shilton, Anderson, Bowyer, McGovern, Lloyd, Needham, O'Neill, Gemmill, Francis, Woodcock, Robertson.

Apr 7th 1979, A, v. Chelsea, Win 3-1, Scorers O'Neill, Francis, Bowyer, AT 30,083, Shilton, Anderson, Gunn, McGovern, Lloyd, Needham, O'Neill, Gemmill, Francis, Bowyer, Robertson, SUB O'Hare.

Apr 11th 1979, EC, H, v. Cologne, Draw 3-3, Scorers Bowyer, Birtles, Robertson, AT 40,804, Shilton, Barrett, Bowyer, McGovern, Lloyd, Needham, O'Neill, Gemmill, Birtles, Woodcock, Robertson, SUB Clark.

Apr 14th 1979, A, v. Derby County, Win 2-1, Scorers O'Neill, Birtles, AT 30,156, Shilton, Anderson, Clark, Bowyer, Needham, Burns, O'Neill, Francis, Birtles, Woodcock, Robertson.

Apr 16th 1979, H, v. Leeds United, Draw 0-0, AT 37,397, Shilton, Anderson, Clark, McGovern, Lloyd, Burns, O'Neill, Bowyer, Birtles, Francis, Robertson.

Apr 18th 1979, H, v, Man United, Draw 1-1, Scorer: Francis, AT 33,074, Shilton, Anderson, Barrett, McGovern, Lloyd, Burns, O'Neill, Bowyer, Francis, Woodcock, Robertson.

Apr 21st 1979, A, v. Birmingham City, Win 2-0, Scorers Birtles, Robertson, AT 22,189, Shilton, Anderson, Clark, McGovern, Lloyd, Burns, O'Neill, Francis, Birtles, Woodcock, Robertson.

Apr 25th 1979, EC, A, v. Cologne, Win 1-0, Scorer Bowyer, AT 60,000, Shilton, Anderson, Clark, McGovern, Lloyd, Burns, O'Neill, Bowyer, Birtles, Woodcock, Robertson.

Apr 18th 1979, H, v. Liverpool, Draw 0-0, AT 41,898, Shilton, Anderson, Clark, McGovern, Lloyd, Burns, O'Neill, Francis, Birtles, Woodcock, Robertson.

Apr 30th 1979, A, v. Wolverhampton Wanderers , Loss 0-1, AT 23,613, Shilton, Anderson, Bowyer, McGovern, Lloyd, Burns, O'Hare, Francis, Birtles, Woodcock, Robertson.

May 2nd 1979, H, v. Southampton, Win 1-0, Scorer Francis, AT 20,388, Shilton, Anderson, Clark, McGovern, Lloyd, Burns, Francis, Bowyer, Birtles, Woodcock, Robertson.

May 5th 1979, A, v, Norwich City, Draw 1-1, Scorer Woodcock, AT 16,616, Shilton, Anderson, Clark, McGovern, Lloyd, Burns, Francis, Bowyer, Birtles, Woodcock, Robertson.

May 9th 1979, H, v, Man City, Win 3-1, Scorers Birtles, Woodcock, Bowyer, AT 21,104, Shilton, Anderson, Clark, McGovern, Lloyd, Burns, O'Neill, Francis, Birtles, Woodcock, Robertson, SUB Bowyer.

May 15th 1979, A, v, Leeds United, Win 2-1, Scorers Mills, Hawley (OG), AT 33,594, Shilton, Anderson, Clark, O'Hare, Lloyd, Burns, Mills, Francis, Birtles, Bowyer, Robertson, SUB Needham.

May 18th 1979, A, v. West Bromwich Albion, Win 1-0, Scorer Francis, AT 28,210, Shilton, Anderson, Bowyer, McGovern, Lloyd, Burns, O'Hare, Francis, Birtles, Woodcock, Robertson.

May 30th 1979, EC,N, Munich, v. Malmo, Win 1-0, Scorer Francis, AT 57,500, Shilton, Anderson, Clark, McGovern, Lloyd, Burns, Francis, Bowyer, Birtles, Woodcock, Robertson.

Back Row: Gary Mills, John Robertson, Ian Bowyer, Colin Barrett, Dave Needham, Viv Anderson, Kenny Burns
Middle Row: Martin O'Neill, John O'Hare, Jim Montgomery, Peter Shilton, Larry Lloyd, Jimmy Gordon
Front Row: Garry Birtels, Tony Woodcock, John McGovern, Peter Taylor, Brian Clough, Trevor Francis, Frank Gray

Thanks and Credits

As with any book of this detail, there have been a great many people involved in all aspects of its creation. We would like to start by thanking the many organisations who have allowed us to painstakingly work our way through their archives, collecting images and topics of interest. Many thanks to those ex players and supporters who have allowed us use of images from their private collections. Special thanks particularly to the Evening Post (Trinity Mirror).

The list is endless, but if we have left anyone out, it was totally accidental, we would like to thank (in no particular order): Ian Storey-Moore, John Barnwell, Henry Newton, Barry Lyons, Peter Grummitt, John Winfield, George Lyall, Ian Bowyer, Liam O'Kane, Frank Clark, John Robertson, Trevor Francis, Colin Barrett, Duncan McKenzie, John Lawson, Andy Smart, Peter Gibson, Mike West and Aidan Hallett
Simon Meakin, Design Associate
Adele Dolloway, Assisting Editor

Picture Credits

PA Images, Getty Images, Evening Post (Trinity Mirror), Football Post, The Pedigree Group Ltd, Haymarket Media Group, Color Sport. Supporters archive collection and the authors own collection. We have also made use of various players own collections.

Book Quote References and Research

Nottingham Forest, The Official Statistical History, Smales K. (1991)
The Forest Who's Who, Matthews T. (2004)
Forest 1865-1978, Lawson J. (1978)
Kicking with both feet, Clark F. (1999)
Clough, A Biography, Francis T. (1987)
Clough, The Autobiography, Sadler J. (1994)
His Way, The Brian Clough Story, Murphy P. (1993)
With Clough, By Taylor, Taylor P. (1980)
Archie Gemmill, Both sides of the Border, Gemmill A. (2005)
I Believe in Miracles, Taylor D. (2015)
From Bo'ness to the Bernabeu, McGovern J. (2012)
First Among Equals, Anderson V. (2010)
Only a Game, Dunphy E. (1975)
Inside Soccer, Woodcock T. (1985)
Regrets of a Football Maverick, Curran T. (2012)
Nottingham Forest programmes (1970-1980)
Nottingham Forest handbooks (1970- 1977)
Football Post Guides (1970-1974)
Various newspapers

Answers from pages 62 and 63:

A. Tommy Jackson B. Dave Serella C. John Cottam D. Jim Barron E. Doug Fraser F. Tommy Gemmell G. Peter Cormack H. Paul Richardson I. John Robertson J. Duncan McKenzie K. Barry Lyons & Martin O'Neill L. Jimmy McIntosh